European Union and its Neighbours in a Globalized World

Volume 20

The series publishes monographs and edited volumes in the field of European and international law and policy. A special focus is put on the European neighbourhood policy, current problems in European and international law and policy as well as the role of the European Union as a global actor. The series supports the publishing and distribution of research results of cross-border research consortia. Besides renowned scientists the series is also open for publication projects of young academics. The series emphasizes the interplay of the European Union and its neighbouring countries as well as the important role of the European Union as a key player in the international context of law, economics and politics.

Marc Bungenberg · Goran Koevski ·
Bianca Böhme · Ljuben Kocev · Mareike Fröhlich ·
Neda Zdraveva
Editors

Alternative Dispute Resolution in the Western Balkans

Trends and Challenges

SPONSORED BY THE

Federal Ministry
of Education
and Research

Springer

Editors
Marc Bungenberg
Europa-Institut
Saarland University
Saarbrücken, Germany

Bianca Böhme
Busse Disputes
Frankfurt am Main, Germany

Mareike Fröhlich
Europa-Institut
Saarland University
Saarbrücken, Germany

Goran Koevski
Saints Cyril and Methodius University
Skopje, North Macedonia

Ljuben Kocev
Saints Cyril and Methodius University
Skopje, North Macedonia

Neda Zdraveva
Saints Cyril and Methodius University
Skopje, North Macedonia

ISSN 2524-8928 ISSN 2524-8936 (electronic)
European Union and its Neighbours in a Globalized World
ISBN 978-3-031-76347-2 ISBN 978-3-031-76345-8 (eBook)
https://doi.org/10.1007/978-3-031-76345-8

This publication in the framework of the project "INVESTinADR - Promoting Mechanism for Alternative Dispute Resolution and Mediation in North Macedonia" is financed by the German Ministry for Education and Research.

This Springer imprint is published by the registered company Springer Nature Switzerland AG
The registered company address is: Gewerbestrasse 11, 6330 Cham, Switzerland

Preface

Alternative Dispute Resolution (ADR) is increasingly recognized as an attractive alternative to national court proceedings, especially in international trade and investment relations. Different ADR mechanisms, such as arbitration and mediation, allow internationally operating companies to solve their disputes in tailor-made procedures characterized by a high degree of flexibility, efficiency, and specialization. Given these advantages, ADR mechanisms are highly popular in the international business community.

This book focuses on ADR mechanisms in one specific geographical region: the Western Balkans. This region comprises Albania, Bosnia and Herzegovina, Croatia, North Macedonia, Montenegro, Kosovo, and Serbia. Although these countries generally have legal frameworks for ADR mechanisms in place, they remain largely underutilized in practice. Promoting ADR mechanisms in the countries of the Western Balkans could make them more attractive to foreign investors, thereby fostering economic growth. Additionally, the effective implementation of ADR mechanisms could have spill-over effects on national judiciaries, serving as exemplars of efficient dispute resolution. Furthermore, all Western Balkan countries, except for Croatia, aspire to become Member States of the European Union (EU). To achieve this, they are inter alia required to promote the use of ADR mechanisms and align their legal frameworks with EU standards.

Against this background, this book aims to explore the trends and challenges of ADR in the Western Balkans. The different chapters primarily focus on international commercial arbitration, investment treaty arbitration, and mediation. Some chapters address systemic challenges, such as capacity building and dispute prevention, which extend to the entire region. Others offer country-specific analyses of particular national framework. While some chapters adopt the perspective of international or EU law, others remain at the national level. Collectively, we hope that the wide diversity in topics and perspectives provides a comprehensive overview of the trends and challenges of ADR mechanisms in the Western Balkan.

The idea for this book arose within the research project "Promoting Mechanisms for Alternative Dispute Resolution and Mediation in North Macedonia" conducted by the Europa-Institut in Saarbrücken and the Ss. Cyril and Methodius University in

Skopje, Iustinianus Primus Faculty of Law. We are grateful to the German Federal Ministry of Education and Research, which sponsored this project, and to the various stakeholders who provided us with valuable feedback on the practical implementation of ADR mechanisms in the region. We also extend our gratitude to our diverse authorship, without whom this book could not have been brought to life. Finally, we thank Springer for publishing this book open access.

Saarbrücken, Germany — Marc Bungenberg
Skopje, North Macedonia — Goran Koevski
Frankfurt am Main, Germany — Bianca Böhme
Skopje, North Macedonia — Ljuben Kocev
Saarbrücken, Germany — Mareike Fröhlich
Skopje, North Macedonia — Neda Zdraveva

Contents

Challenges of Arbitration in the Western Balkans

Zlatan Meskic

Abstract The Western Balkan States have enormous potential to further develop arbitration as the most attractive method of alternative dispute resolution. The courts in this region are overburdened. The litigation in commercial cases takes too long. Arbitration should benefit from the lack of efficiency in litigation, but it does not. This paper aims to determine the challenges for arbitration in the Western Balkans to reach its full potential. Besides some legislative restrictions, the paper identifies gaps in legal education as one of the important reasons behind the small number of cases before local arbitration institutions. While it is true that arbitration institutions should do more to keep their arbitration rules attractive, this is usually not the reason for parties not to choose arbitration. The stakeholders simply lack awareness of all the benefits of arbitration. The expertise is present only in small circles of professionals, making it difficult to promote the use of arbitration for a broader audience.

1 Introduction

Arbitration institutions have been operative in the Western Balkans since the 19th century.[1] Arbitration in the Western Balkans today is more of a popular topic for legal discussion than it has been previously. This may be due to big investment arbitration cases against some of the Western Balkan States that made the topic popular for a broad audience. But in more narrow lawyer circles it is seen as a great opportunity to practice international and comparative law, to build international reputation, to cooperate with law offices from abroad, and of course, to be involved in important commercial cases of large size. Eventually, only very few practitioners get involved in arbitration cases repeatedly. Arbitration is commonly reserved for a

[1] Permanent Arbitration Court at the Croatian Chamber of Commerce, https://www.hgk.hr/english/the-organization-of-the-permanent-arbitration-court.

Z. Meskic (✉)
Chair of the Law Department, College of Law, Prince Sultan University, Riyadh, Saudi Arabia
e-mail: zmeskic@psu.edu.sa

M. Bungenberg et al. (eds.), *Alternative Dispute Resolution in the Western Balkans*,
European Union and its Neighbours in a Globalized World 20,
https://doi.org/10.1007/978-3-031-76345-8_1

somewhat closed circle of practitioners even in comparative legal practice, not just in the Western Balkans. While it is easier to build quality with a smaller group of practitioners, it is certainly not favorable for the popularization of arbitration as a true alternative to litigation. Despite all the efforts that the Western Balkan States have made to make arbitration more popular and effective, there could and should certainly be a higher caseload before domestic arbitral institutions. Although the available reports on caseload are not recent, the numbers in Croatia hardly exceed 50 cases annually and most of them are domestic.[2] In Serbia the number of cases before the PA between 2011-and 2015 was only 71.[3] It is worth remembering that the Foreign Trade Arbitration as the Federal Republic of Yugoslavia in the 1980s of the past century has a caseload of 70–141 cases annually, which was at that time not far behind well established institutions such as the ICC in Paris.[4] After the dissolution of Yugoslavia Croatia and Serbia have the highest numbers in the Western Balkans, simply due to their size and economy. But the number is quite low if we consider that the courts are overburdened with caseload and take several years to resolve commercial cases. In this paper, an attempt is made to discover some challenges that hinder further development of arbitration in the Western Balkans.

The development of arbitration in the Western Balkans has its common features but is not coordinated or even harmonized. This paper does not aim to present a comprehensive analysis of the challenges of arbitration in the Western Balkans, nor can it follow the promise to devote equal space and depth to each State of the Western Balkans. The aim is to follow an objective approach based on measurable parameters to give an overview of basic features of arbitration in the Western Balkans and then go into a specific analysis of an individual State when its particular features so require.

2 Level of Development of International Arbitration in the Western Balkans

There are no definite or universally agreed parameters regarding the level of development of arbitration in one State. It is undisputed that there should be a certain legal framework in place, quality and quantity of the stakeholders involved, some general awareness and continuous development. The approach chosen for this paper is to analyze the level of development of international arbitration in Western Balkans States based on 6 criteria, as it had been already done for other parts of the world[5]:

1. Acceding to the 1958 New York Convention on the Recognition and Enforcement of Foreign Arbitral Awards.

---

[2] Uzelac (2010), p. 9.

[3] Pavic and Djordjevic (2016), p. 308.

[4] Jovanovic (2022), p. 160; the ICC had 268 cases per year between 1981 and 1983; Derains (1985), p. 591.

[5] Reyes and Gu (2018), p. 3.

2. Adopting the UNCITRAL Model Law on International Arbitration in its original 1985 version or, preferably, in its current 2006 version (or as much of the latter as a jurisdiction feels it can adopt).
3. Establishing national institution(s) and international center(s) to administer arbitrations and provide venues for arbitrations within the jurisdiction, as well as to ensure that the arbitration rules of the institution(s) and center(s) keep pace (and comply) with ever evolving international best practices.
4. Establishing a corps of judges familiar with arbitration practice to ensure that courts enforce arbitration agreements, do not unduly interfere with the conduct of arbitrations, and enforce arbitral awards in accordance with best practices under the Model Law and the New York Convention.
5. Engaging in capacity-building activities (workshops, seminars, conferences, etc.) to ensure that all stakeholders (judges, in-house and external counsel, businesspersons) are familiar with and supportive of arbitration as a means of dispute resolution.
6. Constantly reviewing legislation relating to arbitration and to institutions administering arbitrations, so that the jurisdiction remains competitive with developments in the dispute resolution industry.

We may observe that the first three criteria are formal in nature as they only look at the legal framework in place, without assessing its implementation. The last three, on the other hand, are of a qualitative nature and more difficult to assess. They will be reviewed based on the available data.

Obviously, there could be several other criteria for assessment and some of them will be observed in this paper. Some criteria are overlooked that cause problems in the region as they are not addressed by the UNCITRAL Model Law, and the national legislators failed to address them properly. Foremost the problem of local jurisdiction for setting aside/annulment claims and the number of instances available for the setting aside procedures are not regulated properly in all Western Balkans States.

3 The Formal Criteria for the Development of Arbitration in the Western Balkans

The first three standards listed are formal and easier to assess. When we apply them to the development of international arbitration to the Westen Balkans States we see the following as in Table 1.

In the following, each criterion for development of international arbitration in the Western Balkans shall be considered separately.

Table 1 The formal criteria for the development of arbitration in the Western Balkans

	Albania	Bosnia and Herzegovina	Croatia	Montenegro	North Macedonia	Kosovo*	Serbia
NY Convention[6]	Yes	Yes	Yes	Yes	Yes	No*	Yes
UNCITRAL Model Law[7]	Yes	No	Yes	Yes	Yes	Yes	Yes
Arbitration Institution	No[8]	Yes	Yes	Yes	Yes	Yes	Yes

3.1 New York Convention in the Western Balkans

As we can see, all of the States are party to the New York Convention except for Kosovo. Kosovo is formally not listed as a State party.[9] However, the Arbitration Law of Kosovo corresponds fully to the New York Convention with regards to the reasons for non-enforcement in its Article 39(4).[10] The foreign arbitral award shall be submitted to the Commercial Court of Kosovo for recognition, and the party seeking recognition shall, in line with Article 39 of the Arbitration Law of Kosovo accompany its request with: (a) the authenticated original award or a duly certified copy thereof; (b) thc original arbitration agreement or a duly certified copy thereof; and (c) a duly certified translation of the arbitration agreement and the arbitral award into an official language of Kosovo if the award or agreement is not made in an official language of Kosovo. Apart from that, the majority opinion in the legal science in Kosovo states that Kosovo considers itself bound by the New York Convention, although it did not deposit the ratification in the UN, and therefore it does apply in Kosovo.[11] This may be important as Kosovo would benefit from the rich experience of other States on the interpretation of the New York Convention, but in any case, the arbitral awards from Kosovo will not enjoy the same benefits of enforceability abroad until Kosovo formally becomes a party to the New York Convention.

---

[6] Assessment made based on the New York Convention website: https://www.newyorkconvention.org/countries. (1/5/2024).

[7] Assessment made based on the UNCITRAL website: https://uncitral.un.org/en/texts/arbitration/modellaw/commercial_arbitration/status (1/5/2024); Kosovo is not listed at the UNCITRAL website probably due do its status, however, it adopted an Arbitration Law based on the UNCITRAL Model Law in 2007, Law No. 02/L-75.

[8] According to the available information, the arbitral institution in place could not operate without the new law, so it is expected that with the new law, the arbitral institution will start operating, see: https://practiceguides.chambers.com/practice-guides/international-arbitration-2023/albania#:~:text=There%20are%20no%20specialised%20courts,jurisdiction%20in%20handling%20such%20proceedings (1/5/2024).

[9] https://uncitral.un.org/en/texts/arbitration/conventions/foreign_arbitral_awards/status2.

[10] Halili and Kutllovci (2014).

[11] See with further references to the majority and minority opinion Morina (2018), p. 35.

Under Article 16(4) of the Law on Foreign Investment[12] of Kosovo, if an arbitral award is issued by a foreign or international arbitration body under a procedure authorized by Article 16 of the Law on Foreign Investment of Kosovo, such award shall be enforceable in accordance with the New York Convention, regardless as to whether that convention is otherwise binding on Kosovo. In accordance with Article 16 of the Law on Foreign Investment of Kosovo, such "authorized procedure" of dispute settlement may be in accordance with a Bilateral Investment Treaty (BIT) ratified by Kosovo (Article 16 (1) of the Law on Foreign Investment of Kosovo), or by arbitration under the ICSID, the UNCITRAL Rules or the ICC Rules.

Under Article VIII of the New York Convention, Kosovo could become a member of the New York Convention although it is not a member of the UN, as it is a member of two UN specialized agencies: the International Monetary Fund[13] and the World Bank.[14] The State of Palestine acceded to the New York Convention in 2015, although it is not a UN Member State, and its sovereignty is questioned by some influential Members of the UN.[15]

The rest of the Western Balkan States are all members of the New York Convention. Thus, this first and purely formal criteria for development of arbitration is fully satisfied with regards to all other Western Balkan States except for Kosovo.

3.2 UNCITRAL Model Law in the Western Balkans

When it comes to the UNCITRAL Model Law, Bosnia and Herzegovina and Kosovo are not listed at the UNCITRAL website as Model Law States. Albania is the newest member of this ever-growing group of arbitration-friendly States as the Albanian Parliament adopted the Arbitration law only on 6 July 2023. The legislative process took over six years.[16] The new Arbitration Law of Albania clearly falls under the UNCITRAL Model Law family and is listed as such at the UNCITRAL website.

The website does not reveal the criteria that a State needs to fulfill to be listed. The States who are on the list are considered "arbitration-friendly". In the words of the UNCITRAL Model Law digest, by adopting the UNCITRAL Model Law, States are "enhancing the confidence of foreign parties, as the primary users of international arbitration, in the reliability of arbitration law in the enacting State".[17] Simply, the States adopted the UNCITRAL Model Law in an effort to increase foreign investment

---

[12] Law No. 02/L-33, 2005.

[13] https://www.imf.org/external/np/sec/memdir/memdate.htm.

[14] https://www.worldbank.org/en/about/leadership/members.

[15] Kölbl (2019), p. 523.

[16] UNCITRAL Model Law, Law No 52/2023 on Arbitration in the Republic of Albania, see https://arbitrationblog.kluwerarbitration.com/2023/08/19/new-era-begins-in-albania-parliament-passes-arbitration-law/.

[17] UNCITRAL (2012) Digest of Case Law on UNCITRAL Model Law on International Commercial Arbitration, p. 1, para. 3, available at: https://uncitral.un.org/sites/uncitral.un.org/files/media-documents/uncitral/en/mal-digest-2012-e.pdf.

and provide assurance that in case of any dispute, investors feel confident that their investment may be protected in arbitration as a neutral and efficient dispute resolution method. It is undisputed that the high quality of solutions in the UNCITRAL Model Law is a valid reason for its adoption. Still, individual States often disagree on some particular details in the UNCITRAL Model Law and wish to include some additions to the solutions, a variation of the formulations, or not to adopt specific provisions. The whole concept of harmonization is endangered if the States get too creative when incorporating the UNCITRAL Model Law into their legislation. UNCITRAL is trying to convince the States to adopt as few changes as possible.[18] In fact, when many scholars dispute the quality of a specific solution, UNCITRAL reacts by providing two different options of wording as it did with regard to the form of the arbitration agreement in Article 7 of the Model Law.[19]

The Arbitration Law of Kosovo was adopted in 2007 and is largely based on the UNCITRAL Model Law before its amendments in 2006.[20] It is assumed that Kosovo is not listed as a UNICTRAL Model Law State on the UNCITRAL website due to its lack of membership to the UN and lack of official status as a State. It is, however, not questionable that the Arbitration Law of Kosovo is based on the UNCITRAL Model Law.

On the other hand, it is undisputed that Bosnia and Herzegovina is not a UNCITRAL Model Law State. Bosnia and Herzegovina does not have one single arbitration statute. Although it shares its legislative history with former Yugoslav republics like Serbia,[21] Croatia,[22] Montenegro, and Macedonia,[23] who adopted separate arbitration acts, Bosnia and Herzegovina did not follow this path. We cannot state that there have not been any initiatives to do so. On the contrary—the U.S. Commercial Law Development Program, the German Gesellschaft für Internationale Zusammenarbeit (GIZ), the Arbitration Court in Sarajevo, and NGOs like the Association Arbitri have tried to raise attention to the importance of a new arbitration law. Still, the complex structure of the State of Bosnia and Herzegovina together with the need for reforms in other areas have never made the arbitration legislation a priority. There are some new initiatives to pass an independent arbitration statute by the Regional Attorney Chamber of Sarajevo, but it is premature to discuss this initiative. In any case, all proposals have always been entirely based on UNCITRAL Law.

---

[18] Ibid.

[19] Ibid., p. 25, para. 2 (23 October 2023), https://uncitral.un.org/sites/uncitral.un.org/files/media-documents/uncitral/en/mal-digest-2012-e.pdf.

[20] Law No. 02/L-75; Konrad (2010).

[21] Official Gazette of Serbia, no. 46/2006.

[22] Official Gazette of Croatia, no. 88/01.

[23] Official Gazette of Macedonia, 39/2006.

The current arbitration regulation is divided into two sets of laws. The Litigation Procedure Acts (LPA of FBiH,[24] LPA of R. Srpska,[25] and LPA of D. Brčko[26] of FB&H[27]) and The Private International Law (PIL) Act.[28]

The reason for Bosnia and Herzegovina to have three Litigation Procedure Acts may be found in its Constitution which is part of the Dayton Peace Agreement. Bosnia and Herzegovina consists of two entities: the Federation of Bosnia and Herzegovina and The Republic of Srpska and District Brcko,[29] all of which have legislative competencies in commercial law.

The LPA, in its Art 434–453,[30] contains a Chapter on the "Arbitration Procedure". However, the LPA dates from 2003 and was part of a significant legal reform supported by foreign governmental organizations. Nevertheless, the arbitration procedure was not in focus, and the chapter is in most part taken word by word from the Yugoslav Civil Procedure Act.[31] There is a whole set of provisions that are in line with the UNCITRAL Model Law, although they are not as detailed as the solutions of the UNCITRAL Model Law. To list a few, the form of the arbitration agreement is satisfied under Art, 435 of the LPA if there exists "telecommunication means that may provide the written evidence of a concluded agreement"; There is a freedom to choose arbitrators and the method of choice of arbitrators, it is mandatory to choose an uneven number of arbitrators, and the two chosen arbitrators will nominate the presiding, the nomination by the court is the last resort (Arts 437–440 of the LPA); Parties are free to agree on proceedings (Art. 443), and the decision shall be made ex aequo et bono only if empowered by the parties to do so (Art. 445). Although the provision of Art. 445 LPA leaves room for interpretation that the empowerment to decide ex aequo et bono may be done explicitly or even impliedly, the leading commentary confirms that such empowerment should be conducted explicitly in line

---

[24] Official Gazette of Federation of Bosnia and Herzegovina nos. 53/2003, 73/2005, 19/2006 and 98/2015.

[25] Official Gazette R. Srpska nos. 58/2003, 85/2003, 74/2005, 63/2007, 105/2008 – decision of the Constitutional Court, 45/2009 – Constitutional Court, 49/2009, 61/2013 and 109/2021.

[26] Official Gazette of District Brcko, nos. 28/18 and 6/21.

[27] Civil Procedure Act of the Federation of BiH, Bosnia and Herzegovina/Federation of BiH, Official Gazette of Federation of Bosnia and Herzegovina, nos. 53/03, 73/05, 19/06, and 98/15.

[28] Act Concerning the Resolution of Conflicts of Laws with Provisions of Other States in Certain Matters of 1982, Official Journal of the Socialist Federal Republic of Yugoslavia, nos. 43/82 and 72/82, Official Journal of the Republic of Bosnia and Herzegovina, no. 2/1992, no. 13/1994; Official Journal of the Republic of Srpska, no. 21/1992.

[29] In addition, because of the geographical and strategic importance of Brčko, the political parties were unable during the Dayton negotiations to reach an agreement on the area surrounding the city Brčko. However, the parties agreed to binding arbitration on the disputed territory (Art. 5 of the Annex II of the Dayton Peace Agreement) and the Arbitral Tribunal issued a Final Award on 5 March 1999, establishing the Brčko District as a unit of self-government under the sovereignty of Bosnia and Herzegovina. The District Brčko is considered to be a de facto third entity, which cannot be regarded as a federal unit since it is not afforded the right to participate at the State central level.

[30] In District Brcko it is regulated in the Arts. 427–446.

[31] Official Gazette of SFRJ, nos. 4/77, 36/77, 6/80, 36/80, 43/82, 69/82, 72/82,58/84, 74/87, 57/89 and 20/90.

with Art 28 (3) UNCITRAL Model Law.[32] However, a simple comparison of the LPA with the UNCITRAL Model Law reveals several questions that are entirely left unregulated or are not regulated appropriately[33]:

- There is no regulation on the commencement of the arbitration proceedings, which creates problems for the interruption of statute of limitations and various other questions;
- There is no regulation on the means of communication between the parties themselves and with the arbitral tribunal;
- There is no regulation on the waiver of the right of the party to object; in case the party proceeds with the arbitration without objecting to some procedural mistakes, no rule discourages the parties from submitting such objection late in the proceedings or even keeping it for the annulment;
- There is no adequate regulation of courts' support to conduct certain procedural acts and take measures for the arbitration, except for the court's assistance in obtaining evidence that cannot be acquired by the tribunal (Art. 444 (2) LPA);
- There is no regulation of interim measures arising from arbitration proceedings, nor of their recognition and enforcement. In practice, courts reject to grant interim measures for claims that are subject to an arbitration agreement with the reasoning that they have no jurisdiction[34];
- The grounds and procedure for challenging the arbitrators are not regulated properly;
- There is no regulation for arbitrators who cannot or do not perform under the arbitration proceedings or how to appoint substitute arbitrators;
- There is no regulation of the competence-competence or the separability doctrine;
- Basic principles of arbitration are left out: (i) equal treatment of the parties, (ii) efficiency;
- There is no regulation on the power of the arbitral tribunal to assess the admissibility, relevance, materiality, and weight of any evidence;
- There is no regulation on the place of arbitration;
- The language of arbitration is not regulated;
- There is no regulation on the basic procedural steps, the basic elements of the statement of claim and defense, nor the hearing;
- There is no regulation of expert witnesses, neither for the party-appointed nor for the tribunal-appointed expert witnesses;
- There is no regulation of the applicable law except for the regulation on deciding ex aequo et bono; it is possible to draw some conclusions from the PIL act, but the PIL act regulated the applicable law before courts with no explicit regulation of the arbitration proceedings;
- There is no regulation of settlement in arbitration;
- The grounds for annulment are not in line with the UNCITRAL Model Law.

---

32 Čizmić (2009), p. 906.

33 See also Jevremovic (2015).

34 Kasumagić (2019), pp. 91–108.

It is without doubt that a new arbitration regulation is needed in Bosnia and Herzegovina, whether within the Civil Procedure Act or not. It is highly recommended to make a reform based on the UNCITRAL Model Law solutions to benefit from the legal security that the uniformity of arbitration regulation brings to investors.

3.3 *Arbitration Institutions in the Western Balkans*

Each of the Western Balkan States has at least one arbitration institution except for Albania. While the first arbitration institution in Sarajevo dates back to 1909,[35] there are currently two permanent arbitration institutions: the Arbitration Court at the Foreign Trade Chamber of Bosnia and Herzegovina in Sarajevo[36] and the Foreign Trade Court of Arbitration in the Republic of Srpska in Banja Luka.[37] In Croatia, there is one main arbitration institution, which is the Permanent Arbitration Court at the Croatian Chamber of Commerce in Zagreb with a long history of institutional arbitration dating back to 1853.[38] In Kosovo, there is an Alternative Dispute Resolution Center within the American Chamber of Commerce in Kosovo.[39] In North Macedonia, there is the Permanent Court of Arbitration attached to the Economic Chamber of North Macedonia,[40] same as in Montenegro with an Arbitration Court at the Chamber of Commerce of Montenegro.[41] In Serbia, there are two permanent arbitral institutions: Permanent Arbitration at the Chamber of Commerce and Industry of Serbia (Permanent Arbitration)[42] and the Belgrade Arbitration Center (BAC).[43]

Albania is currently the only State in the Western Balkans without an arbitral institution. The arbitral institution could not be established, due to a lack of an arbitration legislative framework. However, it is expected that an arbitration institution will be established soon, as Albania finally adopted the Arbitration Act in 2023. Under Art 4 (3) of the new Arbitration Law of Albania, there is now a legal possibility to establish a "Permanent Institution of Arbitration" as a legal entity, established by natural or legal persons, domestic or foreign, according to Albanian law, whose purpose of activity is the administration of arbitral proceedings.[44]

---

[35] Morait (2022).

[36] Arbitration Court in Sarajevo, https://komorabih.ba/pravilnik-o-arbitrazi-2/.

[37] Foreign Trade Court of Arbitration in Banja Luka, https://komorars.ba/arbitraza/.

[38] Permanent Arbitration Court at the Croatian Chamber of Commerce, https://www.hgk.hr/english/the-organization-of-the-permanent-arbitration-court.

[39] ADR Center in Kosovo, https://www.amchamksv.org/charter-of-arbitration-center/.

[40] Permanent Court of Arbitration at the Economic Chamber of North Macedonia, https://arbitraza.mchamber.mk/index.aspx?lng=2.

[41] Arbitration Court at the Chamber of Commerce in Montenegro, https://komora.me/pkcg/arbitrazni-sud.

[42] Permanent Arbitration in Serbia, https://www.stalnaarbitraza.rs/en/permanent-arbitration/.

[43] Belgrade Arbitration Center, https://www.arbitrationassociation.org/en/belgrade-arbitration-center/.

[44] Elmazaj (2023), p. 1.

In conclusion, all Western Balkan States except for Albania have an arbitration institution. Further, all of the institutions listed also have their rules of procedure. The Arbitration Court at the Chamber of Commerce in Montenegro adopted the newest arbitration rules in December 2023,[45] the Skopje Rules by the Permanent Court of Arbitration attached to the Economic Chamber of North Macedonia were updated in 2021.[46] The Rules of Permanent Arbitration in Serbia date back to 2016,[47] the Belgrade Arbitration Center Rules are from 2014,[48] the Kosovo Arbitration Rules are from 2011,[49] the Sarajevo Rules from 2003[50] and the Banja Luka Rules are from 2018.[51] In this section, this is observed as a formal criterion. A substantive analysis would require a qualitative assessment of the institutional rules of each arbitration institution, the number and size of cases resolved before the institution, the selection and quality of arbitrators, and further elements that will be considered within the further analysis of this paper. A constant review of the institutional rules to keep them up-to-date is a separate criteria to estimate the development of arbitration in each state, and therefore it will be dealt with in the last chapter of the paper.

4 Is There a Corps of Judges Familiar with Arbitration in the Western Balkans?

A State cannot be considered arbitration-friendly if the courts and judges do not support arbitration. The main criterion of assessment of the court's support is the percentage of awards that are set aside or denied enforcement in that particular State. Unfortunately, for the purpose of this paper it was not possible to find studies with numbers on set-aside arbitral awards, or foreign arbitral awards that are denied recognition and enforcement in the Western Balkan States nor is it known if such studies exist. It would be particularly interesting to see the percentage of awards set aside or denied recognition and enforcement in each State as well as the grounds for it. It is always alarming if the State courts are excessively using the ground of public policy for setting aside foreign arbitral awards or refusing recognition and enforcement of foreign arbitral awards with the aim to protect domestic companies. Setting aside awards for public policy reasons is more dangerous, as it is in most cases set aside awards in the state of the seat of arbitration will not be recognized and

[45] https://komora.me/pkcg/arbitrazni-sud.

[46] See https://arbitraza.mchamber.mk/upload/Skopje%20Arbitration%20Rules.pdf.

[47] https://www.stalnaarbitraza.rs/uploads/regulations/2017Rules%20of%20the%20Permanent%20Arbitration%20in%20%20English_%20Pravilnik%20o%20Stalnoj%20arbitraz%CC%8Ci-ENG.pdf.

[48] https://www.arbitrationassociation.org/en/belgrade-arbitration-center/rules/.

[49] https://www.amchamksv.org/procedural-rules-2/.

[50] https://komorabih.ba/wp-content/uploads/2019/05/Pravilnik-o-arbitrazi-engleski-jezik.pdf.

[51] https://komorars.ba/arbitraza/.

enforced elsewhere due to Article V (1)(e) of the NYC.[52] The arbitration-friendly legislation in the Western Balkans surely limits the possibility of negative interference by the courts. There is no prominent example of an annulled award in the Western Balkans that could be linked to any political reasons or other non-legal reasons.

While we argue with high degree of certainty that there is no negative attitude of the courts towards arbitration currently, it is still far away from concluding that there is a corps of judges familiar with arbitration and supportive of arbitration in the enforcement or annulment proceedings, or enforcement of arbitration agreements. It may be assumed that for a "corps of judges" to be formed, there needs to be a centralized local jurisdiction of the courts for all matters related to arbitration. Montenegro may serve as a positive example, as Article 6 of the Arbitration Law of Montenegro states that the Commercial Court of Montenegro shall have jurisdiction, "when this law provides for a court jurisdiction for a decision on the nomination of arbitrators, on the objection to the jurisdiction of the arbitral tribunal, service of the award, decision on the request for setting aside of the arbitral award, as well as on the request for recognition of a foreign arbitral award or a preliminary measure".[53] The same is true for Croatia, where either the Commercial Court in Zagreb or the County Court in Zagreb decides all issues on arbitration.[54]

Obviously, having one or two courts in the relatively small-sized Western Balkan States deciding all issues regarding arbitration would make it much easier to develop a body of judges familiar with arbitration and supportive of it. However, in several Western Balkans States the arbitration legislation failed to regulate this matter properly. There is a rather urgent need for reform in Bosnia and Herzegovina on this matter. The Laws of Civil Procedure of the Federation of Bosnia and Herzegovina and the Republic of Srpska in their relevant chapters on Arbitration declare "that the court that would have been competent for the first instance proceedings if the arbitration contract had not been made shall be competent for the appointment of an arbitrator or the president of the arbitration board".[55] The same is true for annulment of arbitral awards.[56] This means that any municipal court in Bosnia and Herzegovina may decide on issues like annulment of the arbitral awards. It is very difficult to build knowledge for a specific group of judges, and if almost any judge may have to decide on arbitration issues, it becomes even more difficult.

The situation is not much better in some Western Balkans States, even if they followed the UNCITRAL Model Law. For example, in Serbia the arbitration law did

---

[52] The Russian courts are in particular (but not the only ones) famous for the extensive use of public policy to set aside arbitral awards issued against Russian public companies, and that is why courts in France, Netherlands and other states have enforced such arbitral awards despite the fact that they have been set aside in the state of the seat. Under the Article V (1)(e) of the NYC courts "may", but do not have to refuse enforcement of arbitral awards set aside in the state of the seat. A party may rely on a national law providing for a more favourable enforcement regime by invoking Article VII(1) of the NYC; Lazic-Smoljanic (2018), p. 218, Rana (2017), p. 815.

[53] Art. 6 of the Arbitration Law of Montenegro.

[54] Art. 43 of the Croatian Arbitration law.

[55] Art. 440 (3) of the Law of Civil Procedure of FBiH; Law of Civil Procedure of R. Srpska.

[56] Art. 450 of the Civil Procedure Act of FBIH, Law of Civil Procedure of R. Srpska.

not regulate either the subject matter jurisdiction or the territorial jurisdiction for the court support for the nomination of arbitrators, and it also does not indicate if this should be done in a litigious or non-litigious procedure.[57] Depending if the procedure would be litigious or not, different courts would have jurisdiction. The literature in Serbia suggests that the Commercial Appellate Court should have jurisdiction,[58] but such a solution is not yet adopted.

It is assumed that in States with centralized jurisdiction for arbitration matters the judges are familiar with arbitration cases, while in other States this assumption cannot be made. Courts in such States might face only one arbitration case during their whole career and their handling of the case will depend on other capacity-building activities, education, or in general cooperation with other courts.

5 Capacity-Building Activities to Make Sure that Stakeholders Are Familiar with and Supportive of Arbitration

The quality of the judiciary in the Western Balkan States that have not joined the European Union (EU) is one of the main obstacles on their way towards the EU Membership. Chapter 23 on the judiciary is an evergreen when negotiating EU membership, foremost on its independence, impartiality, professionalism, competence and efficiency. The EU invests a lot of time and effort into developing well-functioning Alternative Dispute Resolution (ADR) mechanisms in the Western Balkan States. It is well known that sustainable dispute resolution is also a part of the UN sustainable development goals (SDG 16).[59] ADR including arbitration is a real alternative and the general framework is already set in all Western Balkan States. However, while the courts are one of the slowest in Europe, the number of arbitration cases remains relatively low. Why is that?

In the author's personal view, most lawyers are simply not sufficiently familiar with arbitration. There is a long tradition of having arbitral institutions in former Yugoslavia, but it has always been considered a special field of law for a small number of experts. One part of the problem that is often overlooked is legal education. It is understood that legal education should not be solely decisive for the later expertise of the practitioners, but students graduate mostly without knowing the basic terminology of arbitration. How do we expect to have appropriate arbitration agreements or increase of the current number of arbitration practice if students did not even see a model arbitration clause during legal studies? The legal studies in the Western Balkans are usually heavy with many courses and high load of teaching material for the students. The legal curriculum in the Western Balkans is not reduced to what is a bare minimum required to earn an LL.B, but the students are rather overburdened

[57] Stanivuković (2013), p. 137.

[58] Ibid.

[59] Shhadah Alhussein et al. (2023), p. 3.

with numerous legal and interdisciplinary topics. In such a heavy curriculum it is rather unusual and worrisome that some topics on arbitration did not find their place either in existing courses or in a separate course. The easiest way to make sure that lawyers, judges, and counsels are familiar with arbitration is to include it in their legal education. Most practitioners get familiar with arbitration after their legal education, but it is truly questionable if it should be this way.

The Bachelor of Law studies in Zagreb, Belgrade and Zenica offer an arbitration course, but only as a track course. This means that it is chosen by a small group of students and is not obligatory for all. At the Law College in Sarajevo, there is an elective clinic for International Sale of Goods and Arbitration, while in Skopje it is part of the master's studies. Is there not some part of arbitration proceedings that all law students should be familiar with? Arbitration clauses and an overview of the New York Convention would already be a great start. If we can somehow get the selection of arbitrators, competence-competence, and separability in some of the courses, we would already have new generations of students who would not be terrified if they get an arbitration case in practice.

On the other hand, litigation procedures are studied extensively. I do not think that the argument can be made that criminal procedural law, litigation and administrative procedures are something that students must know while arbitration is not. If we look at it from the perspective of teaching students purely what they will do in their professional lives, many of them might not represent parties in courts at all. Education should be about enabling students to practice, rather than teaching them what used to be the standard years ago.

The most important step towards more attention on arbitration law would be to include it in the bar exam. The laws listed as mandatory literature for bar exams in Bosnia, Croatia, Serbia, Macedonia and Montenegro[60] do not require the candidates to take a look at the arbitration legislation, although the list of laws that have to be studied for the bar exam is very long. For example, the list usually includes insolvency proceedings and arbitration proceedings should at least be equally relevant. Insolvency is also a specialized area that most students will never get the chance to practice later in their professional life. Naturally, a larger number of arbitrations would automatically create more jobs in arbitration in law offices and thus the need for education would become more obvious. However, most law offices in the Western Balkans are not aware of the benefits of including more arbitration clauses in the contracts.

Until the curricula of legal studies are reformed, the realistic goal needs to be to educate attorneys and judges once they have entered their professional lives. This goal is already followed in all the Western Balkan States. The judicial centers as well as the arbitration institutions are doing many events to educate and promote

---

[60] Bar exam program in Bosnia and Herzegovina available at: http://www.mpr.gov.ba/biblioteka/podzakonski_akti/11_19.pdf; For Montenegro, Official Gazette of Montenegro no. 75/2004; Bar exam program in Croatia, available at: https://www.mpravde.gov.rs/sekcija/58/pravosudni-ispit.php; Bar exam program in Serbia, available at: https://www.mpravde.gov.rs/tekst/16772/polaganje-pravosudnog-ispita.php; Bar exam program in North Macedonia, available at: https://www.pravda.gov.mk/ispit-documenti/1/potrebno.

current arbitration matters. In addition, there are NGOs, such as the Association *Arbitri* in Sarajevo,[61] that are organizing events and taking initiatives to promote arbitration. One should not underestimate the importance of the Willem C. Vis International Commercial Arbitration Moot in the Western Balkan region as a pool for developing capacities in arbitration. Many law faculties from the region such as Belgrade, Zagreb, Skopje, Zenica and Prishtina have repeatedly been successful at the Vis Moot competition in Vienna, and many students participating in the Vis Moot later started a career in arbitration. It should be mentioned that the U.S. Commercial Law Development Program (CLDP) actively sponsors teams from the Western Balkans to participate in the Vis Moot, and also organizes events and educations for practitioners. The same is true for German governmental organizations such as the German Foundation for International Legal Cooperation (IRZ) and the German Agency for International Cooperation (GIZ).

In any case, it is the author's strong belief that a firm place for arbitration in mandatory legal education would make this alternative dispute resolution mechanism a true option for more attorneys. How to convince attorneys to include more arbitration clauses in the contracts of their clients if they do not feel prepared to represent their clients in arbitration once a dispute arises. However, higher education reforms in the region are happening slowly and are not coordinated. The inclusion of arbitration in the bar exam would force law faculties to take arbitration legislation into consideration when doing their next curriculum review.

6 Constant Review of the Legislation Relating to Arbitration and to Arbitral Institutions

The constant review of legislation is important as both national practice and comparative experience showcase deficiencies that need to be removed. Also with new challenges, such as COVID-19 or current political challenges, answers need to be found for the parties who chose arbitration believing in efficient dispute resolution.

The need for review certainly exists. Despite adopting the UNCITRAL Model Law, some Western Balkan States have adopted restrictive legislation regarding unexpected issues. In Croatia and North Macedonia, one of the most controversial limitations lies in the differentiation between international and domestic arbitration. Pursuant to the Croatian Arbitration Act, in disputes between legal persons established under Croatian law or natural persons whose domicile or habitual residence is in Croatia, as well as in disputes for which the exclusive jurisdiction of courts in the Republic of Croatia is prescribed by separate law, arbitration is permitted only if the place of arbitration is in Croatia (Article 3, paragraph 2 of the Arbitration Act, in connection with Article 2, paragraph 1, items 6 and 7 of the Arbitration Act).[62] Pursuant to Article 1 of the Arbitration Act of North Macedonia, the resolving of the

---

[61] https://arbitri.ba/.

[62] Babić (2011).

disputes may be submitted to an arbitration that has place outside the territory of the Republic Macedonia, only if, at least one of the parties, at the time of the conclusion of the arbitral agreement, is a natural person with domicile or habitual residence abroad, or a legal person whose place of business is abroad. These provisions are quite limiting, because even in disputes in which the subject matter lies outside of the territory of Croatia or North Macedonia respectively, parties are only able to agree on a seat of arbitration in Croatia/North Macedonia, unless one of the companies is established under foreign law. The question is if the foreign arbitral award issued in a situation, where none of the parties was established abroad, would be enforceable in Croatia and North Macedonia.

The only provision that could be applied to object against the enforcement of such foreign arbitral award would be the subject-matter arbitrability under Art. 40 (2)(a) of the Croatia Arbitration Act, Art. 35 (2)(b)(1) of the Arbitration Act of North Macedonia or Art V(2)(a) of the New York Convention. As rightly pointed out in Croatian literature, a foreign arbitral award should not be considered non-enforceable in such situation, as it is not about a subject matter not being capable of being settled in arbitration but a territorial restriction under the Croatian Arbitration Law.[63] It may be a matter of subject-matter arbitrability when parties choose foreign arbitration for a dispute that falls under the exclusive jurisdiction of Croatian courts, but not when two Croatian companies opt for foreign arbitration. In such a case, it is a restriction regarding the persons involved (*ratione personae*) rather than regarding the subject matter (*ratione materiae*).[64]

Even if the limitation set by the Croatian Arbitration Act or the Arbitration Act of North Macedonia for domestic companies to opt solely for an arbitration seat in Croatia/North Macedonia may be overcome in the enforcement stage, it creates a risk that many parties will not be willing to take. Opting for an arbitration clause with a foreign seat, although knowing that it is explicitly prohibited by the Croatian/North Macedonian Arbitration Act, will certainly not be advised by the law offices who do not want to explain to their clients later why they spent hundreds of thousands of dollars on an arbitration award that may eventually not be enforceable in Croatia/North Macedonia.

The differentiation between domestic and international arbitration in Croatia and North Macedonia is in stark contrast to Montenegro where the law does not make any such differentiation.[65] In Serbia, the difference is that in international arbitration parties may agree that the procedural arbitration rules are foreign. However, the international character of arbitration should be understood widely, and it should not be necessary related solely to the seat or the domicile of the parties. Under Art. 3 (2) of the Serbian Arbitration Act, it is sufficient that (a) the place of arbitration, if determined in, or pursuant to, the arbitration agreement, or (b) the place where a substantial part of the obligations of the business relationship is to be performed

63 Ibid, p. 13.

64 Ibid.

65 Article 2 of the Montenegrin Arbitration Act defines the differentiation between domestic and international arbitration, but it has no further implications.

or the place with which the subject matter of the dispute is most closely connected; Art. 3 (3) the parties have expressly agreed that the subject matter of the arbitration agreement relates to more than one country.

Further, mostly unreported problems exist with regard to ad hoc arbitration. Arbitration agreements are often unprecise with regards to arbitration proceedings and while the consent to arbitrate might be clear, where and how to arbitrate may be an enigma. In case unsophisticated parties draft an arbitration clause in which they just express the intent to arbitrate, but do not choose neither an institution nor ad hoc arbitration or specific arbitration rules, there is no established theory or practice that would resolve the dilemma if the clause if pathological, or it shall be upheld in favor of ad hoc or institutional arbitration. Companies without proper legal advice that enter into arbitration agreements wishing for a speedy dispute resolution and wishing to stay away from courts, might end up in a contrary situation. By signing an arbitration clause without details on the number of arbitrators or the mechanism for their nomination, the parties might end up with the local court doing both. The court may not have any experience either in determining the number of arbitrators nor nominating them in case the defendant obstructs the nomination process, and parties might end up without the proper expertise of arbitrators. In a recent case that was decided before the courts in Sarajevo as well as the Arbitration Court in Sarajevo, the parties agreed on the following arbitration clause: "Any disputes shall be resolved amicably and in arbitration, and in case it is not successful, the courts in Bosnia and Herzegovina shall have jurisdiction".[66] With no clear distinction between pre-arbitral proceedings and arbitration, no institution or ad hoc arbitration chosen, choice of jurisdiction of courts after amicable dispute resolution and arbitration, the clause poses more problems than it resolves and there are many examples like this. In a recent interview with *Dr. Stefan Kröll*, Chairman of the Board of Directors of the German Arbitration Institute (DIS) and Ms. Dara Sahab, Deputy Chief of ADR in the Saudi Center for Commercial Arbitration, both named ad hoc arbitration clauses to pose the most challenges in arbitration in their respective countries.[67] Business persons often feel that avoiding any institution, including any arbitral institution, would save them time and give them the flexibility to resolve disputes in a more amicable manner. But once the parties are in a dispute and cannot agree on anything anymore, such clauses do not offer sufficient precision to build the dispute resolution process properly and the help from the court's side depends on their experience and expertise on such issues.

When it comes to arbitration rules, it has become a trend that the major arbitration centers update their rules quite frequently to stay ahead of their competing institutions. This is only partly true for arbitral institutions in the Western Balkans. Montenegro has adopted the newest arbitration rules in December 2023, whereas the

[66] Municipal Court in Sarajevo (2017) 65 0 Ps 682348 17 Ps,; the arbitration clause was upheld in favor of institutional arbitration in Sarajevo in arbitration and before the courts in Sarajevo.

[67] Discussion in Riyadh, Saudi Arabia, organized by Prince Sultan University and the Saudi Centre for Commercial Arbitration titled "Dispute Resolution Methods—There are Appropriate Approaches for Every Situation, but the Human Factor Remains Constant", 7 November 2023.

previous version was from 2015.[68] The Skopje Rules by the Permanent Court of Arbitration attached to the Economic Chamber of North Macedonia were quite recently updated in 2021, after their updates in 2016 and 2011.[69] The Rules of Permanent Arbitration in Serbia date back to 2016,[70] while the Belgrade Rules are of 2014.[71] The Kosovo Arbitration Rules are from 2011,[72] the Sarajevo Rules from 2003[73] and the Banja Luka Rules are from 2018.[74] Obviously, the quality of the rules cannot be judged simply by the year of its adoption, but it is fair to say that the rules could not have anticipated the new developments that even the major arbitral institutions included only recently and the regular update is very important. It is clear that a good arbitrator can make the arbitration proceedings work very well with any of the listed arbitration rules. But some institutes may simply not be available as they are not foreseen in the rules or are very limited, such as joinder, consolidation, use of electronic means and other developments that simply arose only recently as important factors in the arbitration process.

7 Conclusion

The Western Balkans is not a coherent region with regard to the development of international commercial arbitration. While some States belonged to the same legal system within the former Yugoslavia, the current legislation in all States was adopted several years after the dissolution of Yugoslavia. Nevertheless, the Western Balkan States do share some common challenges. Foremost, the number of cases referred to arbitration in all the Western Balkans States does not justify the enormous effort put into legislative reforms and the establishment of arbitral institutions. The number of cases stays low even though the courts in this region are overburdened, and commercial cases often take several years to be decided. One proposed solution would be to introduce arbitration in legal education at least partly within existing courses or as a separate course, and to include it in the bar examination. Most practitioners become familiar with arbitration only after they have already started practicing law. Choosing a completely unknown dispute resolution method is quite difficult to promote. Many arbitration institutions in the region do not update their arbitration rules frequently and should do more to provide answers to modern challenges. While from the perspective

---

68 https://komora.me/pkcg/arbitrazni-sud.

69 See https://arbitraza.mchamber.mk/upload/Skopje%20Arbitration%20Rules.pdf.

70 https://www.stalnaarbitraza.rs/uploads/regulations/2017Rules%20of%20the%20Permanent%20Arbitration%20in%20%20English_%20Pravilnik%20o%20Stalnoj%20arbitraz%CC%8Ci-ENG.pdf.

71 https://www.arbitrationassociation.org/en/belgrade-arbitration-center/rules/.

72 https://www.amchamksv.org/procedural-rules-2/.

73 https://komorabih.ba/wp-content/uploads/2019/05/Pravilnik-o-arbitrazi-engleski-jezik.pdf.

74 https://komorars.ba/arbitraza/.

of the arbitral institutions, it may not seem necessary to continue reforming the institutional rules because of a smaller number of cases, the arbitral institutions should do everything in their power to become a more attractive choice for dispute resolution. Finally, a centralized court with jurisdiction for all matters related to arbitration should be introduced in all States to facilitate building a corps of judges familiar with arbitration. This will provide legal certainty with regard to the judicial support for arbitration, in particular with enforcement and annulment proceedings.

References

Babić D (2011) Limits on arbitration outside Croatia according to the Croatian arbitration act. SSRN: https://ssrn.com/abstract=1974413
Čizmić J (2009) Komentar Zakona o parnicnom postupku. Privredna Stampa, Sarajevo
Derains Y (1985) International chamber of commerce arbitration. Pace l Rev 5(3):591–605
Elmazaj S (2023) Albania: reinstating the law on arbitration. ICC Disput Resolut Bull 3. https://jusmundi.com/en/document/publication/en-albania-reinstating-the-law-on-arbitration
Halili F, Kutllovci Sh (2014) Award of international commercial arbitration. SSRN. https://ssrn.com/abstract=2488133
Jevremovic N (2015) The peculiar case of arbitration in Bosnia and Herzegovina. Kluwer arbitration blog. https://arbitrationblog.kluwerarbitration.com/2015/10/28/the-peculiar-case-of-arbitration-in-bosnia-and-herzegovina/.
Jovanovic M (2022) Doprinos Mihaila Konstantinovića Modernizaciji Jugoslovenske Privrede – Stvaranje Spoljnotrgovinske Arbitraže. Anali Pravnog Fakulteta u Beogradu - Poseban Broj u Čast Profesora Mihaila Konstantinovića 70(5):159–182
Kasumagić I (2019) Granting and enforcing interim measures in international commercial arbitration in Bosnia and Herzegovina. In: Meskic Z, Kunda I, Popović D V, Omerović E (eds) Balkan yearbook of European and International Law, Springer, Cham, pp 91–108
Kölbl A (2019) In: Wolff R (ed) New York convention – commentary, 2nd edn. C. H. Beck, Munich
Lazic-Smoljanic V (2018) Enforcing annulled arbitral awards: comparison of approaches in the United States and in The Netherlands. Zbornik Pravnog Fakulteta Sveucilišta u Rijeci 39(1):215–240
Morait B (2022) Arbitražno rješavanje sporova u Bosni i Hercegovini. https://bmoraitobligacije.com/arbitrazno-rjesavanje-sporova-u-bosni-i-hercegovini/
Morina I (2018) Durchsetzung von Schiedsprüchen in Kosovo. ZfRV 29–37
Pavic V, Djordjevic M (2016) Resolution of international commercial disputes before Serbian arbitral institutions – certain salient features of the new institutional rules. In: Varady T et al (ed) Liber Amicorum Gaso Knezevic. Pravni fakultet Univerziteta u Beogradu, Beograd, pp 304–346
Rana R (2017) The enforceability of awards set aside at the seat: an Asian and European perspective. Fordham Int Law J 40(3):813–838
Reyes A, Gu W (2018) Introduction: towards a model of arbitration reform in the Asia Pacific. In: Reyes A, Gu W (eds) The developing world of arbitration – a comparative study of arbitration reform in the Asia Pacific. Hart Publishing, Oxford, pp 1–17

Shhadah Alhussein H, Meskic, Z, Al-Rushoud A (2023) Sustainability and challenges of arbitration in administrative contracts: the concept and approach in Saudi and comparative law. Special issue access to justice in Eastern Europe, pp 10–22
Stanivuković M (2013) Ad Hok arbitraža na teritoriji Srbije: Pokretanje postupka i konstituisanje arbitražnog suda. Zbornik Radova Pravnog Fakulteta u Novom Sadu 47(3):123–144
Uzelac A (2010) Croatia. In: Mistelis L, Shore L, Smit H (eds) World arbitration reporter, vol I, 2nd edn. Juris Publishing, New York

The Nexus of the Rule of Law and Alternative Dispute Resolution: Who Boosts or Sets Back Whom?

Mareike Fröhlich

Abstract This chapter examines the complex relationship between alternative dispute resolution (ADR) and the rule of law, and how each influences the other. Essential to democratic governance, the rule of law ensures legal certainty, judicial independence and the protection of fundamental rights, while promoting fairness and accountability. ADR has become popular, particularly in regions with underdeveloped legal systems, as a means of attracting foreign investment and resolving disputes more efficiently. This chapter highlights the work of the INVESTinADR project in North Macedonia, which has explored the impact of ADR on investment promotion. ADR offers a flexible and less adversarial alternative to traditional litigation, particularly in commercial and international disputes. However, it faces challenges such as rising costs, delays and power imbalances, which can undermine its effectiveness and alignment with the rule of law. The quality of ADR depends on the impartiality of mediators and arbitrators, and issues such as limited remedies and lack of appellate review are of concern. In addition, ADR decisions often lack precedential value, which affects continuity and legal certainty, and there are increasing calls for transparency, particularly in cases of public interest. The relationship between ADR and the rule of law is complex and varies by context, with no clear consensus on whether one strengthens or weakens the other. In developing countries, ADR can improve access to justice where formal systems are distrusted, but success depends on balancing local and external needs. Concerns about the privatisation of justice through ADR and the need for transparency are significant, although ADR could also drive improvements in traditional justice systems. Ultimately, ADR and the rule of law are interdependent and can be mutually reinforcing if effectively integrated.

M. Fröhlich (✉)
Europa-Institut of Saarland University, Saarbrücken, Germany
e-mail: froehlich@europainstitut.de

M. Bungenberg et al. (eds.), *Alternative Dispute Resolution in the Western Balkans*, European Union and its Neighbours in a Globalized World 20,
https://doi.org/10.1007/978-3-031-76345-8_2

1 Introduction

The relationship between alternative dispute resolution (ADR) and the rule of law is complex, with a degree of interdependency between the two. This chapter attempts to answer the question of whether the rule of law is boosted or set back through ADR, or if ADR is boosted or set back through the rule of law. The rule of law is seen and understood as one of the most important principles for the functioning of a democratic state and is used by the EU, World Bank, and others as an indicator of a country's development. It is considered in each development strategy for countries in the Global South and is part of many development projects. Interestingly, especially in these countries, ADR has become very popular and is supported in projects aimed at increasing foreign investments. The mechanism of ADR is intended to minimise the risks of investors in countries that do not offer a comparable, functioning legal system.

This is also the underlying presumption for the project INVESTinADR, through which this publication was developed.[1] The project of the Europa-Institut of Saarland University and the Iustinianus Primus Faculty of Law of the Ss. Cyril and Methodius University in Skopje analysed the legal framework for ADR in North Macedonia to boost investment in projects and companies. Based on this analysis and additional feedback from practitioners and other stakeholders, recommendations for action were published. One key issue in supporting the development of ADR is the education of lawyers and raising awareness of ADR as an option to settle a conflict. To address this, an executive training course was designed and is now offered to graduates and practitioners in Skopje. The course aims to prepare them for upcoming challenges in the field of ADR practice.

In this context, the chapter explores the interconnected link between the rule of law and ADR. This complementary approach to justice can enhance the efficiency, accessibility and flexibility of dispute resolution. For a common understanding, the different definitions of the rule of law will first be explained (2.), followed by a description of the different components of ADR (3.). The chapter will then analyse which principles must be considered in ADR to truly support the rule of law (4.). The following section will discuss the inherent risks of ADR and how they impact the rule of law (5.). The final section will use these discussions to answer the introductory question of whether one boosts or sets back the other (6.).

---

[1] The project INVESTinADR is funded by the German Federal Ministry for Education and Research for the timeframe of 2021–2024. The purpose of the project was to analyse the legal situation of ADR in North Macedonia and give advice for improval of the legal framework.

2 A Definition or Key Elements of the Rule of Law

Conceptualising the rule of law is challenging because there is no universally accepted definition, making its content and scope complex. However, the importance of the principle has never been questioned. Its roots can be traced back to ancient times, when Plato and Aristotle discussed the equality of all citizens. The concept of the rule of law dates back to the Magna Charta of 1215, which limited the king's power in regard to the liberties of freemen and declared the king subject to the law. This led to the development of the English legal system, which supported an independent judiciary, the principle of parliamentary sovereignty, and the separation of powers. These ideas were especially promoted by *Locke* and *Montesquieu*, who saw them as protections against unfair governments and as safeguards for the liberty of men.[2] Since then, the rule of law has found its way into the constitutions of democratic countries and international organisations. The preamble of the Universal Declaration of Human Rights states: "[...]. Whereas it is essential, if man is not to be compelled to have recourse, as a last resort, to rebellion against tyranny and oppression, that human rights should be protected by the rule of law, [...]".[3]

In attempting to define the rule of law in general, it can be said that it is a principle ensuring that all members of a society, including the government itself, are equally subject to publicly disclosed legal codes and processes. According to *Dicey*, three key fields of action must be addressed: Regulating the power of the government ("absence of arbitrary power on part of the government"), ensuring equality before the law ("every man is subject to ordinary law administered by ordinary tribunals"), and privileging the judicial process (constitutional rights "are not the source but the consequence of the rights of individuals").[4] In continental Europe, especially in Germany and France, the principle of the rule of law developed differently, focussing more on the nature of the state rather than the judicial process. This distinction is reflected in the terms "Rechtsstaat" and "État de droit".[5] These different views are often categorised into a formal and a substantive/material theory, depending on the legal environment in which it developed. The formal theory deals with instrumental limitations and follows a minimalist approach, whereas the substantive understanding includes notions of justice and ideals within the definition.[6]

Even though there are different theories explaining the rule of law, most identify common key elements, such as legal certainty and clarity, equality before the law, a fair and impartial judiciary, proportionality, legal accountability, the protection of human/fundamental rights, access to justice, the limitation of government power, and respect for legal processes and institutions. In summary, laws must be publicly promulgated, which means that they are accessible and transparent. They should be equally enforced so that everyone is treated equally under the law. In cases of

---

[2] Chesterman (2007), margin number 3 et seq.

[3] https://www.un.org/en/about-us/universal-declaration-of-human-rights.

[4] Dicey.

[5] Chesterman (2007), margin number 7 et seq.

[6] Chesterman (2007), margin number 12, El-Khoury and Wolfrum (2021), margin number 5 et seq.

violations, laws much be independently adjudicated, which requires an independent judiciary to interpret and apply the laws. Additionally, the rules must be consistent with international human rights norms and align with fundamental human rights standards.[7]

The UN General Assembly' 2012 Resolution on the rule of law at the national and international levels calls to promote access to justice for all. Based on this, the following conditions need to be addressed:

1. Due process and fair trial by "[...] committ[ing] to an effective, just, non-discriminatory and equitable delivery of public services pertaining to the rule of law, including criminal, civil and administrative justice, commercial disputes settlement and legal aid."[8]
2. Access to dispute settlement by recalling "[...] to take all necessary steps to provide fair, transparent, effective, non-discriminatory and accountable services that promote access to justice for all [...]."[9]
3. Judicial independence by upholding the "[...] independence of the judicial system, together with its impartiality and integrity, and ensuring that there is no discrimination in the administration of justice."[10]
4. Consistency, predictability, and transparency by "[...] recogniz[ing] the importance of fair, stable and predictable legal frameworks "[...]."[11]

The rule of law is fundamental for ensuring fairness, preventing abuse of power, and providing a framework within which social, economic, and political interactions occur. Therefore, its role in post-conflict societies cannot be underestimated. The legislative framework in these countries is often characterized by non-functioning institutions, an unfair and discriminatory legal framework, exhausted resources, a neglect of fundamental rights, and the misuse of political or other powers. This leads to societal instability, mistrust, and insecurities that affect all areas of governance, including the judiciary, making ADR an appropriate or even preferable alternative for settling disputes.[12]

3 Components and Advantages of Alternative Dispute Resolution

Often, ADR is described as a new form of settling disputes, but the opposite is true. Negotiation is the first form of exchanging different views and attempting to balance them, and this is as old as humanity. From this, different forms of settling disputes

[7] El-Khoury and Wolfrum (2021), margin number 16 et seq.

[8] UN Declaration (2012), recital 12.

[9] UN Declaration (2012), recital 14.

[10] UN Declaration (2012), recital 13.

[11] UN Declaration (2012), recital 8.

[12] UN Security Council (2004), p. 10.

have evolved over time.[13] ADR refers to methods used to resolve disputes without resorting to traditional court litigation. It encompasses different methods, each with unique procedures and benefits, but all aim to provide a more flexible, efficient, and less adversarial means of resolving conflicts. This is especially common in business, commercial and investment disputes, a practice that dates back to the New York Chamber of Commerce in the late 18th century.[14]

As mentioned above, ADR mechanisms take different forms. Negotiations are the basis for all forms of ADR and are recognised by direct discussions between parties to reach a voluntary settlement. This process can be formal or informal. A more facilitated process is mediation, where a neutral third party (mediator) helps the disputants reach a mutually acceptable resolution without imposing a decision. Similar to mediation is conciliation, but the conciliator may take a more active role in suggesting solutions and terms of settlement. The most formal approach is arbitration, a private dispute resolution process where an impartial third party (arbitrator) makes a decision. Decisions in ADR procedures can be binding or non-binding, depending on the agreement between parties. ADR is used in various fields of legal disputes, but mainly in commercial and investment disputes, both at the national and international level. Prominent areas for negotiations and mediation are matters of labour law and family law.

While ADR operates outside the formal judicial system, it offers various benefits and supports the rule of law in several ways. These will be examined in the following section by using arbitration as an example. There are important differences among the different modes of ADR but some of the benefits apply across all ADR processes. For example, arbitration "gives the parties the opportunity of resolving their dispute: (i) in a neutral place of arbitration; (ii) by a tribunal of experienced, independent, and impartial arbitrators; (iii) selected by or on behalf of the parties themselves for their suitability for the task; (iv) working in the language of the contract and of the frequently voluminous documents that form part of that contract; and (v) in a manner which will result in a binding decision that is internationally enforceable."[15]

---

[13] Barrett and Barrett (2004), pp. 1 et seq., Born (2009), pp. 8 et seq.

[14] Barrett and Barrett (2004), p. 72.

[15] Blackaby et al. (2023), margin number 1.122. A wider definition by Sternlight (2007), p. 575 says that ADR "(1) may increase access to justice by making it easier for people who are poor; illiterate, or geographically dispersed to bring or respond to a claim; (2) it may reduce the amount of money and time needed to resolve disputes; (3) it may provide an alternative or biased court systems; (4) it may promote foreign investment opportunities; (5) it may provide justice to groups, such as women and minorities, whose interests are not well served by the formal legal system; (6) it may bring community members together and establish greater social harmony; and (8) it may help community members work together to better protect their individuals rights."

3.1 Efficiency

ADR processes are typically faster and less costly than traditional litigation, helping to alleviate court congestion and reduce legal expenses. This is achieved by avoiding time-consuming procedural aspects like evidence, immunity, discovery or other matters which typically evolve in national court litigation.[16] Moreover, some arbitral institutions allow fast-track procedures with a single arbitrator and a fixed timeframe. Nevertheless, the objective of efficiency in terms of time and costs has become less tenable. With a 30-fold increase in cases in the last 50 years, counting only the requests made to the ICC International Court of Arbitration,[17] delays have become more common. These delays are often due to the time needed to establish an arbitral tribunal and issue an award, exacerbated by the workload of arbitrators, who often have additional professional commitments.[18]

Furthermore, the costs of ADR proceedings can be high, as arbitrators and/or arbitral institutions must be paid. In addition, parties bear the costs for supporting staff (such as translators or IT experts), witnesses and legal advisors.[19] Although this is often not mentioned when compared with national court litigation, parties in court cases also participate in these costs. However, in court litigation, the salaries, fees and reimbursements for actual expenses have not increased to the same extent as in ADR proceedings. Governments often cap or cover these costs, rather than passing them on to the parties. Even though both national court litigation and ADR involve similar costs and timeframes, these expenses must be accepted to ensure a correct and fair decision.[20]

One aspect which is often underestimated is the function ADR could fulfil in supporting the formal justice system. It could step in to minimize the workload of courts, acting as a supplement to the formal justice system. This would be particularly effective in handling small cases or in situations where a consistent line of decision-making already exists.[21]

3.2 Accessibility

ADR can provide more accessible justice, particularly in communities where formal legal systems are inadequate or overloaded. Accessibility is usually linked to the need for "equal protection of the law for all citizens and others in the national territory", as well as equal opportunity to seek and receive remedies for alleged violations of one's legal rights by public or private actors before courts and other conflict

[16] Born (2021), p. 85.
[17] Born (2021), p. 92.
[18] Blackaby et al. (2023), margin number 1.147.
[19] Blackaby et al. (2023), margin number 1.144 et seq.
[20] Blackaby et al. (2023), margin number 1.148.
[21] Reuben (2010), p. 6.

resolution mechanisms".[22] This ensures that those who break the law do so with the understanding that they may be sanctioned by the courts. However, this system may not function effectively when courts are understaffed, underfunded, or when access is too complicated due to foreign or unfamiliar procedural rules, costs, language barriers, distance, weak legal frameworks, or inexperienced judges.[23] In these cases, ADR steps in where the formal justice system fails to fulfil its social role and where the conditions for proper decision-making are lacking.[24]

Moreover, national courts are often not equipped and competent enough to understand the consequences of their decision for both parties in international commercial or investment disputes.[25] In this context, the benefit of ADR lies in the possibility for the parties to participate in or decide on the selection of appropriate arbitrators and the composition of arbitral tribunals. Since both parties can substantially influence the selection of arbitrators, they ensure that there is no bias, prejudice or partiality. Additionally, they can request that the arbitrators be skilled and experienced in the subject matter. This increases the parties' confidence in the outcome of the arbitration process and is a prerequisite for a "fair and effective arbitration".[26]

3.3 Flexibility

ADR offers flexible solutions tailored to the specific needs and interests of the parties involved, which may not always be achievable through court judgments. Except for a few basic principles, there is no fixed procedural code, allowing the arbitration process to be adapted to the circumstances of each case.[27] This reflects party autonomy, which exists in formal justice but is maximized in ADR, along with procedural flexibility. It enables the parties to respond to the specific circumstances of the case. In general, parties have the freedom to agree on the existence and extent of discovery or disclosure, the methods for presenting facts and expert evidence, the duration of the hearing, the format for site inspections, the arbitration schedule, and other related matters. This flexibility allows them to shape the length and outcome of the proceedings, contributing to a more efficient resolution for the parties.[28]

Another significant benefit of ADR is the lack of an appellate review mechanism in most cases. Decisions are final, and a review is typically only possible on grounds of procedural fairness, jurisdiction, or public policy. This reduces the costs and duration of litigation, a factor that is particularly important to most companies. Some legal

---

[22] World Bank (2007), pp. 66 et seq.

[23] Butler (2023), p. 159.

[24] World Bank (2007), pp. 66 et seq.; Michel (2011), p. 17.

[25] Born (2021), pp. 77 et seq.

[26] Blackaby et al. (2023), margin number 1.31, 1.32 et seq. (for more details on the person of an arbitrator).

[27] Blackaby et al. (2023), margin number 1.127.

[28] Born (2021), pp. 81 et seq.

jurisdictions now offer an opt-in/opt-out option for appellate review, allowing parties to contractually define the grounds for review in ADR.[29]

3.4 *Preservation of Relationships*

ADR often focuses on collaborative solutions, which can preserve or even improve the relationships between parties, unlike the adversarial nature of court proceedings. ADR is constructed to facilitate an amicable settlement of the dispute which can only be achieved if both parties are in favour of a cooperative approach to arbitration.[30] Sometimes, ADR is the only way how parties can avoid bringing the dispute to one of the home courts, which may be biased, or prevent multiple litigations in different national courts.[31]

For the same reason, ADR procedures are usually subject to the principles of privacy and confidentiality, which is only in a few exceptional cases available in courts. However, a distinction must be made between privacy and confidentiality. In principle, all ADR proceedings are private and conducted to the exclusion of the press and other interested parties. The principle of confidentiality with regard to the award and its underlying reasons is no longer as strictly applied. On the one hand, parties may have a vested interest in making a decision public if it involves a standard case constellation. On the other hand, the principle of transparency increasingly requires ADR proceedings to be opened up, at least in the area of arbitration.[32]

4 Challenges of ADR and its Implications for the Rule of Law

While ADR may offer many benefits, such as efficiency, cost-effectiveness, and flexibility, it is not without risks. Issues such as power imbalances, lack of formal legal protections, enforcement challenges, and potential biases need to be carefully considered.

To mitigate these risks and to support the rule of law, certain conditions must be fulfilled. Parties should thoroughly assess the suitability of ADR for their specific dispute, seek experienced and impartial neutrals, and consider obtaining legal advice to ensure their interests are adequately protected throughout the process. Participation in ADR should be voluntary, ensuring that parties are not coerced into a process that may not suit their needs. States should provide a supportive legal framework that recognizes and enforces ADR outcomes, providing legal certainty and upholding

---

[29] Born (2021), pp. 80 et seq.

[30] Born (2021), p. 89.

[31] Born (2021), pp. 72, 74.

[32] Blackaby et al. (2023), margin number 1.125; Born (2021), p. 88.

the integrity of the process. Nevertheless, some of the advantages can also have drawbacks, which may impact the rule of law and raise questions about the legitimacy and efficiency of ADR.

In the following subsections the different concerns will be elaborated.

4.1 *Imbalance of Power*

One main concern is the power imbalance between the parties. Without the structure of a formal court setting, there is a risk that parties feel coerced into accepting unfavorable terms. Different power dynamics can disadvantage weaker parties, who may be pressured into settlements due to power imbalances or lack of legal representation. There is no formal protection against the manipulation by the other party.

Moreover, ADR does not know formal discovery. ADR processes, especially mediation, often lack the formal discovery procedures found in court litigation, which can lead to unequal access to evidence and information. It is up to the parties to define the procedure, the length, as well as the limits for seeking evidence. In formal justice, this is not possible, as the organisation of the evidence procedure is essential for a fair trial. Nevertheless, it can also be seen as an expression of party autonomy, allowing them to decide not to include a lengthy discovery procedure.

The question is whether both parties fully understand the consequences of this decision, especially given the limited procedural safeguards. The informal nature of ADR can sometimes result in inadequate procedural protections, especially for parties who may be less knowledgeable or less powerful. However, portraying ADR as depriving parties of all procedural rights available in formal proceedings is also inaccurate. Parties may benefit from regional human rights protections. The ECtHR has ruled that, although it is permissible to waive the formal legal processes and exclude the public in the case of ADR proceedings,[33] it is not possible to waive all judicial rights to a fair trial.[34] This includes ensuring the impartiality of the tribunal and a fair trial,[35] principles which must also be observed in ADR proceedings.

Another problem is the equal access to investment arbitration. Due to the contractual construction of investor-state arbitration where host states offer in bilateral investment treaties (BIT) or other agreements the possibility to initiate arbitration proceedings but investors usually do not or rather cannot offer this in advance.[36]

In case where there is an imbalance of power between the parties, legal support should be provided. But in contrast to most formal justice systems, ADR does not require mandatory legal representation. Parties may choose to represent themselves, which can be risky if they lack sufficient understanding of the law or the process, potentially leading to unfavourable outcomes. However, mandatory representation

[33] ECtHR, *Tabbane v. Switzerland*, App no. 41069/12, para. 25.

[34] ECtHR, Souvaniemi and others v. Finland, App no 41069/12.

[35] ECtHR, Souvaniemi and others v. Finland, App no 41069/12.

[36] Reinisch (2023), pp. 229 et seq.

would undermine the principle of party autonomy. This would leave the responsibility for safeguarding the parties' interest to the members of the tribunal.

4.2 *Quality of ADR*

In this case, the quality of ADR needs to be high, which largely depends on the quality of the members of the tribunal. The effectiveness of ADR heavily relies on the skills and experience of the mediator or arbitrator, as inadequate expertise can lead to poor decision-making. One major concern is the potential for bias among the selected individuals. Questions about the impartiality and neutrality of the arbitrator or mediator may arise, especially if they are selected by one of the parties. To avoid this, there are different possibilities: the selection could be made by a neutral third party with no vested interest in the case, as in the *Lake Lanoux*[37] and the *Rann of Kutch* case.[38] Another option is the development of a permanent tribunal, like the proposed multilateral investment court (MIC),[39] or the establishment of permanent and institutionalised dispute settlement tribunals, as included in some new investment agreements.[40] It is also argued that the possibility of acting as arbitrator and counsel at the same time (so-called double hatting) should be avoided and prohibited. This should be included in future agreements and become a standard so that rejections of arbitrators on such grounds will be eliminated.[41]

In addition, ADR offers only limited scope for legal remedies. It may not provide the full range of remedies available in court, such as injunctive relief or punitive damages, which are generally only available in formal justice systems. In addition, some complex disputes require significant intervention or comprehensive remedies that only a court can provide. Another issue arises with multiparty arbitrations, which can only proceed when all parties agree.[42] This might not always be possible due to conflicting interests, but an affect the quality of the proceedings. Moreover, most

[37] Lake Lanoux Arbitration (France v. Spain) (1957), 24 ILR 101.

[38] Indo-Pakistan Western Boundary (Rann of Kutch) (India v. Pakistan) (1968) 50 ILR 2.

[39] Bungenberg and Reinisch (2021a), pp. 1 et seq.

[40] E.g. Section F (Resolution of investment disputes between investors and states) of Chapter 8 of the Comprehensive Economic and Trade Agreement (CETA) between Canada, of the one part, and the European Union and its Member States, of the other part, OJ L 11, pp. 23 et seq. The agreement entered into provisional application in 2017. Most of the agreement is in force, but not all parts. The provisions related to investment protection and the Investment Court System (ICS) are excluded from provisional application. For more details, see Bungenberg and Reinisch (2021b), pp. 470 et seq.

[41] Reinisch (2023), pp. 224 et seq.

[42] Blackaby et al. (2023), margin number 1.131 et seq.

ADR processes do not include an appellate mechanism. While this can be an advantage in saving money and time, it also means that an incorrect award cannot be properly reviewed or corrected. Therefore, modern solutions like the mentioned multilateral investment court and the tribunals in some agreements include an appellate tribunal.

4.3 Lack of Continuity and Legal Certainty

Binding further development of the law is also advantageous for high-quality and consistent decision-making within the framework of ADR procedures. However, this is one of the disadvantages of ADR. Decisions in ADR, especially in arbitration, do not set a precedent for future cases. This is even more important, as ADR proceedings rarely have an appeal instance. Awards are generally final and binding. As a result, two tribunals with the same facts could come to a different decision—"Each award stands on its own". Even if an older award is available, it has no effect on subsequent cases.[43]

Legal precedents play an important role in the development of the law. They lead to consistency and uniformity in case law and thus promote legal certainty and trust in the legal system. Precedents supplement and interpret written law, closing regulatory gaps efficiently. The role of case law is particularly important in the dynamic development of law in rapidly changing areas, ensuring legal certainty. ADR procedures do not inherently support such a role, but in recent years, concerns about transparency have been raised, leading to more public disclosure of awards, partly for this reason. Another development is de facto case law by some international courts and tribunals or better a notion of persuasive authority in the field of investment arbitration. Here, earlier investment awards and their reasoning are taken into account using it as persuasive evidence of interpretation and specification of law.[44] Different is the possibility of authoritative interpretations by the parties of an agreement, where joint bodies of the agreement interpret the different provisions.[45]

The limited role of legal development in ADR is concerning, because the rising use of ADR might hinder the formal justice system from using its opportunity to decide crucial cases, develop and interpret the law, and uphold the rule of law.[46] Therefore, already in the phase of drafting an arbitration treaty, like in investment arbitration the international investment agreements, a more precise language is used and various definitions are offered.[47] The idea of an appellate mechanism would not

[43] Blackaby et al. (2023), margin number 1.137 et seq.

[44] Reinisch (2023), pp. 232 et seq.

[45] Reinisch (2023), pp. 235 et seq.

[46] Moffitt (2010) p. 8.

[47] Reinisch (2023), pp. 234 et seq.

only include a review instrument and improve the impartiality of the arbitrators but would lead to a more coherent decision-making.[48]

4.4 Transparency and Accountability

All these reservations merge into the big discussion about whether ADR procedures should not be more transparent. In principle, one of the major advantages of ADR is that the procedure and the decision are confidential. However, this is criticised, as illegal business practices can be hidden without the public scrutiny inherent in court proceedings.

This is particularly the case if there is a public interest in the legal dispute. This is less likely the case in commercial disputes, but awards rendered against host states in investment arbitration usually concern taxpayers' money.[49] Moreover, due to the regulatory nature of the measures involved in these kind of disputes, important public interests require special procedural adaptations. Hence, these inherent public interests justify more transparent proceedings in investor-state-disputes or other cases where the state/government is involved.[50] The question was raised if this could have some spill-over effects for commercial arbitration.[51]

Therefore, there should be a distinction between the type of ADR procedure. While ADR can be confidential, there should be mechanisms to ensure that the process is transparent when a public interest is concerned. Moreover, transparency and publicity ensure that arbitrators and mediators are held accountable for their conduct which will raise the overall quality of ADR.

4.5 Potential for Inefficiency and Enforceability Restraints

ADR attracts many parties, but they should be aware about the enforceability of decisions. There are some processes, like mediation, that may result in non-binding agreements, which can lead to further disputes if one party does not adhere to the settlement. The enforcement depends on the type of ADR, since arbitration awards are generally enforceable, but the enforcement of ADR outcomes can vary based on the seat and the specific terms of the agreement. At least arbitration produces in most of the cases enforceable and final awards. Without such high degree of enforceability, the outcome of the arbitration itself would not be useful.[52]

[48] Reinisch (2023), pp. 237 et seq.

[49] Blackaby et al. (2023), margin number 1.125.

[50] Reinisch (2023), pp. 238 et seq.

[51] Blackaby et al. (2023), margin number 1.126.

[52] For more details Born (2021), pp. 75 et seq.

Finally, there is a major risk of duplicative processes. If ADR does not result in a settlement, parties might end up going to court anyway, resulting in additional time and expenses. This may lead to prolonged negotiations. Mediation and negotiation processes can sometimes drag on without resolution, delaying the final settlement of the dispute. This would undermine the efficiency of ADR.

5 Conclusion

Returning to the initial question of whether the rule of law is boosted or set back through ADR, or whether ADR is boosted or set back through the rule of law, the answer is simple: there is no definitive conclusion, and instead, more questions need to be raised. The common understanding that ADR and court litigation are exclusive need to be overcome and an inclusive system should be set up.[53] The relationship between ADR and the rule of law varies, depending on the different perspectives one may take.

First of all, in the developing context, ADR plays a crucial role in implementing and enhancing the rule of law and access to justice for citizens in these countries. Often, their trust in the formal justice system is lacking. The idea is that, as a side effect, such a system can also help develop and eventually take over the role of formal justice. However, a balance in support from countries and development cooperation has to be found. It is questionable whether this transition is really needed or if it reflects a Global North perspective. More research is needed to determine if primarily ADR-based justice system can fully meet the right to access to justice.

Second, the question arises whether ADR allows or supports the privatization of justice, which is characterized by confidentiality and lack of transparency. This leads to less public accountability and loss of the educational function of dispute settlement.[54] While this argument can be made, it is generally agreed that the rule of law should limit the excessive use of ADR, making the process more transparent—though this risks ADR no longer being an alternative to the traditional judiciary. But this could also be seen as an opportunity, especially in developed countries, to reform and improve the traditional judiciary. In this scenario, ADR would serve as an alternative where the standards of decision making in courts are not guaranteed. By using ADR mechanisms, the rule of law could actually be strengthened, raising decision-making standards in respective countries, potentially attracting more foreign investments and improving trade. This, in turn, could boost economic welfare and allow countries to invest more in their traditional judiciary.

Third, a lack of rule of law standards is less problematic in commercial disputes where parties exercise their autonomy, but it is more dangerous when public interests are involved. The possibility of biased or impartial tribunal members could cause greater or different harm, namely jeopardizing public opinion, compared to most

[53] Sternlight (2007), p. 581 et seq.

[54] Sternlight (2007), p. 570.

commercial disputes. Such disputes are driven by private parties and their autonomy, which cannot and should not exist unconditionally for public actors, for democratic reasons.

Finally, the original question might have been the wrong one. Instead, the question should be whether either can exist independently. *Moffitt* calls this the "symbiotic mutualism", like the relationship between clownfish and anemones, where each protects the other from different enemies.[55] This is an ideal picture to explain the relationship between the rule of law and ADR. Both need each other: developing the rule of law globally requires the implementation of ADR in countries where formal justice systems are not trusted or effective. On the other hand, for an ADR system to effectively complement the formal justice system, rule of law principles must be respected.

References

Barrett JT, Barrett J (2004) A history of alternative dispute resolution. Wiley, San Francisco

Blackaby N, Partasides C, Redfern A (2023) Redfern and hunter on international arbitration. Wolters Kluwer, Oxford

Born G (2021) International commercial arbitration, vol I, 3rd edn. International Arbitration Agreements. Wolters Kluwer, The Hague

Bungenberg M, Reinisch A (2021a) Draft statute for the mulitlateral investment court. Nomos, Baden-Baden

Bungenberg M, Reinisch A (2021b) A paradigm change: the CETA investment chapter. Z Für Europarechtliche Studien (ZEuS) 24(3):437–484

Butler P (2023) Human rights in international commerical and investment arbitration. In: Kröll S, Bjorklund AK, Ferrari F (eds) Cambridge compendium of international commercial and investment arbitration. Cambridge University Press, Cambridge, pp 139–185

Chesterman S (2007) Rule of law. In: Peters A (ed) Max planck encyclopedias of international law. Oxford University Press, Oxford

El-Khoury N, Wolfrum R (2021) Rule of Law. In: Grote R, Lachemann F, Wolfrum R (eds) Max Planck Encyclopedia of Comparative Constitutional Law. Oxford University Press, Oxford

Michel J (2011) Alternative dispute resolution and the rule of law in international development cooperation. Justice & development working paper series 12/2011

Moffitt M (2010) Which is better, food or water? The rule of law or ADR? Disput Resolut Mag 2010:8–14

Reinisch A (2023) Investment arbitration and the rule of law. In: Kröll S, Bjorklund AK, Ferrari F (eds) Cambridge compendium of international commercial and investment arbitration. Cambridge University Press, Cambridge, pp 211–243

Reuben RC (2010) ADR and the rule of law: making the connection. Disput Resolut Mag 2010:4–7

Sternlight JR (2007) Is alternative dispute resolution consistent with the rule of law? lessons from abroad. DePaul Law Rev 56(2):569–592

UN General Assembly (2012) The rule of law at the national and international levels, resolution, A/RES/67/1

UN Security Council (2004) The rule of law and transitional justice in conflict and post-conflict societies, report of the Secretary General, S/2004/616

[55] Moffitt (2010), p. 9.

World Bank (2007) Justice sector assessments – a handbook, http://documents.worldbank.org/curated/en/803711468338346161/Justice-sector-assessments-a-handbook

The Case for Judicial Capacity Building Through International Arbitration

Greg Lourie

Abstract Judicial capacity building is recognized as a vital element of development policy. However, with resources for (judicial) capacity building being limited, this paper seeks to address first the question of why states should dedicate the limited resources available to invest in capacity building through international arbitration. Second, if such investment is to be made, what should be the focus of capacity building efforts in order to achieve the best long-term success? In answering these questions, this paper posits that international arbitration should be considered by states as a pivotal element of judicial capacity building because it contributes to an effective judiciary and political stability, in turn enabling the state to better attract foreign direct investment (FDI). A well-functioning legal framework for international arbitration may act as a catalyst for FDI by boosting investor confidence and economic development. Countries with robust arbitration frameworks may be able to attract significant FDI despite inefficiencies in their domestic judicial systems. The availability of effective dispute resolution mechanisms also fosters political stability and economic development by strengthening the rule of law and contributes to maintaining public confidence and social stability. For successful capacity building, all stakeholders—including government officials, legislators, the judiciary, lawyers, and arbitrators—must be involved. Training government officials ensures informed policy-making, while judicial training ensures that the established arbitration framework properly functions in practice. Training local practitioners and arbitrators fosters acceptance and trust in arbitration. Lastly, robust arbitral institutions are crucial in capacity building. They fulfill this role not only through knowledge-sharing and training initiatives but also by acting as intermediaries between the parties and

The author extends his sincere thanks to Oguzhan Samanci, Research Fellow and Ph.D. Candidate at Humbold University Berlin, for his valuable assistance in the preparation of this chapter.

G. Lourie (✉)
Counsel, Schellenberg Wittmer, Zurich, Switzerland
e-mail: greg.lourie@swlegal.com

Present Address:
Former Counsel and Head of ICA 3 Case Management Team, ICC International Court of Arbitration, Paris, France

M. Bungenberg et al. (eds.), *Alternative Dispute Resolution in the Western Balkans*, European Union and its Neighbours in a Globalized World 20,
https://doi.org/10.1007/978-3-031-76345-8_3

the arbitral tribunal. In this capacity, strong arbitral institutions foster trust in the arbitral process by ensuring the quality of selected arbitrators and maintaining a high standard of arbitral awards.

1 Introduction

Capacity building, "*as the process of developing and strengthening the skills, instincts, abilities, processes and resources that organizations and communities need to survive, adapt, and thrive in a fast-changing world*",[1] is widely regarded as a crucial element of development policy.[2] The reason for this is that policy recommendations and even legislative reforms cannot make a difference on their own. Unless the surrounding factors are designed in such a way that allows the proper implementation of and support for the reforms, they will most probably not lead to the desired outcome. Hence, building capacity by way of informing and training individuals on the ground is nowadays considered to be an essential component of development strategies worldwide. While there are numerous areas deserving capacity building measures, this chapter argues that international arbitration, as a means of resolving domestic and international disputes, can make a significant contribution to judicial capacity building and strengthening the rule of law.

Arbitration has many advantages compared to litigation in state courts. It allows the parties to adapt the procedure to their needs, to choose specialised decision makers as arbitrators, and to obtain a final and binding decision that can only be challenged on very limited grounds and usually only within a short time after it was rendered, thus greatly contributing to an efficient resolution of commercial disputes.[3] However, what stands out particularly for commercial actors entering into cross-border transactions is the neutrality of the forum where the dispute is resolved.[4] By definition, arbitration involves three neutrals resolving the dispute which are bound to be independent and impartial and have no ties to either of the parties, and in particular no financial ties.[5]

Against this background, it is not surprising that empirical studies have confirmed that businesses prefer to resolve their international disputes through arbitration rather

---

[1] United Nations Academic Impact, Capacity Building, available at: https://www.un.org/en/academic-impact/capacity-building.

[2] Joubin-Bret et al. (2011), p. 16.

[3] Blackaby et al. (2023), paras. 1.122, 1.123, 1.127, 1.128.

[4] Cf. Blackaby et al. (2023), para. 1.122.

[5] Cf. Blackaby et al. (2023), para. 1.122.

than cross-border litigation.[6] It is estimated that approximately 80% of all international contracts contain arbitration clauses,[7] and 90% of respondents preferred arbitration over cross-border litigation before domestic courts.[8]

However, judicial capacity building is a resource-intensive process, and capacity building in arbitration has to compete against a number of other areas of capacity building. This chapter therefore seeks to answer two questions stakeholders may face when deciding on projects in capacity building: first, why should judicial capacity building efforts be directed specifically to international arbitration? And, second, if the decision is made in favour of arbitration capacity building, how should capacity building efforts for international arbitration be implemented in order to achieve the best long-term success?

In answering these questions, this chapter makes two propositions:

First, considering that resolving international disputes through arbitration is, based on the above, consistent with parties' preferences, the conclusion is that states that intend to strengthen their participation in international trade should engage domestically in capacity building for international arbitration. Even though correlation may not be equated with causation and is thus supportive rather than conclusive proof, it is notable that countries where arbitration is well-established among and accepted by lawmakers, practitioners and the judiciary are able to procure significant FDI flows in their economy.

Second, capacity building for international arbitration should, apart from the need to introduce modern arbitration laws and adopt international treaties, in particular build capacity among government officials, a state's judiciary and its domestic practitioners.[9]

2 The Case for Capacity Building for International Arbitration

Over the last three decades, arbitration has become the preferred dispute resolution mechanism in commercial transactions, particularly, but not exclusively, in the context of cross-border transactions.[10] There is a strong argument to be made that the provision of the legislative and judiciary framework that enables international arbitration leads to economic growth and political stability.

The case for capacity building in arbitration rests on two principal propositions: First, the availability of efficient, effective and reliable means of dispute resolution

---

[6] Vogenauer and Hodges (2008), p. 45; White & Case and Queen Mary University of London (2021), p 5.

[7] Myburgh and Paniagua (2016), p. 599.

[8] White & Case and Queen Mary University of London (2021), p. 5.

[9] Cf. Greer (2022), p. 170; Markert (2019), p. 243; Meltz (2022); Mills and Shanker (2021), p. 9.

[10] Born (2021), p. 1.

may contribute to an increase in FDI, which in turn is "a major catalyst to development"[11] and an integral part of an open economic system. Second, the same holds true for the political stability of a state.

2.1 International Arbitration as a Catalyst for FDI

Empirical studies have repeatedly shown that an influx of FDI contributes to income growth in the receiving country and more generally, creates a macroeconomic stimulus for the receiving economy as a whole.[12] FDI flows allow to create employment opportunities, raise productivity, improve education, training and the country's infrastructure, foster exports and transfer technology.[13] It is noteworthy that studies have shown that emerging economies benefit the most from FDI, likely because the incoming capital is met with a sufficient level of education, technology and infrastructure to enable it to fully reap the full benefits of the foreign investment, such as technology transfer and increase in international trade integration.[14]

Against this background, it has been suggested that the availability of international arbitration increases FDI flows.[15] This is because the absence of effective mechanisms to resolve commercial disputes has an adverse effect on investor confidence and can lead to them deciding against investing in a particular country.[16] Arbitral procedure is also comparable, irrespective of where the dispute may arise, which gives foreign investors the confidence of familiarity with the dispute resolution process as opposed to having to deal with the intricacies and/or deficiencies of a given judicial system.[17] Establishing an effective commercial dispute resolution regime, in particular for international arbitration, is therefore essential for creating a better investment climate.[18] The need to implement a well-functioning arbitration regime is particularly pressing in countries where the domestic court system is inefficient or unreliable. Lengthy proceedings and doubts as to the independence of the judges can severely hamper a country's investment climate.[19]

Looking into the macroeconomic figures, there are indicators that the availability of efficient means of dispute resolution contributes to the flow of FDI into a country. The prime example here are International Investment Agreements (IIAs), specifically in the form of bilateral and multilateral investment treaties.[20] These treaties afford

[11] OECD (2002), p. 3.

[12] Ibid, p 9.

[13] Joubin-Bret et al. (2011), p. 15; Meltz (2022).

[14] OECD (2002), pp. 10–11.

[15] Myburgh and Paniagua (2016), p. 597; cf. Meltz (2022).

[16] Mills and Shanker (2021), p. 8.

[17] Myburgh and Paniagua (2016), p. 599.

[18] Mills and Shanker (2021), p. 8.

[19] Cf. Myburgh and Paniagua (2016), p. 598; OECD (2021), p. 112.

[20] Mills and Shanker (2021), p. 8.

certain substantive protections to foreign investors, which must fulfill certain requirements to qualify for protection under the treaty, and have made a protected type of investment in accordance with the IIA.[21] If all of these requirements are fulfilled, and the host state breaches a substantive standard of protection, for example, by unlawfully expropriating the investor's investment, the investor can typically claim compensation from the host state. More important than the substantive standards of protection, however, is the fact that investment treaties offer international arbitration as a means of enforcing compliance with said obligations of substantive protection.[22] This is because international arbitration offers a neutral forum where disputes for a state's breach of its substantive obligations can be heard by an independent tribunal, as opposed to domestic courts.[23] And although empirical evidence is scarce, the perception that domestic judges may favour their own national remains strong, irrespective of the jurisdiction concerned.[24]

The past three decades have seen a substantial proliferation of investment treaties around the world, having created sufficient data points to draw first conclusions.[25] While the question of whether there is a direct link between concluding investment treaties and increased FDI flows remains controversially debated, it seems hard to deny at least some degree of correlation between the two, as studies have confirmed that the availability of investment treaty protections has an impact on a company's investment decisions.[26] A 2009 UNCTAD report has concluded that "*IIAs add a number of important components to the policy and institutional determinants for FDI, and thereby contribute to enhancing the attractiveness of countries to foreign investors. In particular, they improve investment protection and add to the security, transparency, stability and predictability of the investment framework*".[27]

The experience from the International Court of Arbitration at the International Chamber of Commerce (ICC) confirms, at least to some extent, the conclusion that international arbitration, rather than the substantive protections, may be the relevant factor for FDI flow. As the leading international arbitration institution globally, the ICC administered 890 cases in 2023, and 1800 pending cases each year, across a variety of sectors.[28] In 2022, parties in ICC arbitrations came from 134 countries, with four emerging economies, including Brazil, China, India, and Mexico among the top 10 of the most frequent parties.[29]

---

[21] McLachlan et al. (2017), paras. 2.14, 5.01 ff., 6.01 ff., 7.01 ff.

[22] International arbitration in investment treaties is based on the concept of "arbitration without privity" whereby a state extends an offer to arbitrate all disputes arising out or in connection to any qualified investor, having made a qualifying investment under the IIA, see Paulsson (1995).

[23] Dugan et al. (2008), p. 15. It is further worth noting that while most investment treaties provide an investor with the option of referring a dispute for the breach of a substantive standard to domestic courts or international arbitration, it is extremely rare for an investor to choose the former option.

[24] Polanco (2019), p. 45.

[25] Joubin-Bret et al. (2011), p. 15.

[26] Ibid, pp. 15, 22, 23.

[27] UNCTAD (2009), p. 111.

[28] Cf. ICC (2023c).

[29] ICC (2022a), p. 5.

Comparing the development of FDI flows worldwide with the development of the number of ICC arbitration cases in the same period therefore provides an insight into the correlation between higher levels of FDI flows and a higher number of arbitrations.[30]

A good example here is Brazil: while Brazilian courts are perceived to have certain shortcomings, Brazil is nonetheless successfully attracting significant foreign investment. Brazil's judiciary is notoriously slow and there is a significant backlog in court proceedings.[31] As of 2019, Brazil is estimated to have 80 million pending cases, while the judiciary consists of only 18,000 judges to resolve them. This has resulted in a backlog of 72 million cases.[32] At the same time, according to the UNCTAD World Investment Report 2023, the FDI inflow in Brazil amounted to USD 86 billion, placing Brazil 6th in the ranking of the top FDI host economies in 2022.[33]

Apart from many other relevant economic factors, there are good grounds to attribute at least some part of this success to Brazil's robust arbitration framework. Brazil is known for having an arbitration-friendly legal regime and national courts that are equally supportive with respect to arbitration proceedings.[34] ICC's statistics on Brazil corroborate this conclusion: in 2020–2022, Brazilian parties were consistently placed second among all nationalities in ICC arbitrations, which is attributed in particular to a high number of domestic arbitrations.[35] Looking at the broader South and Central America regions, the ICC statistics of 2022 show that the numbers increased to 17.3% of parties from these regions.[36]

A similar correlation can be seen when looking at the impact of joining the New York Convention on FDI inflows. One can observe a significant increase in FDI inflows after the respective countries joined the New York Convention.[37]

2.2 *Political and Economic Development Through Strengthening the Rule of Law*

Another factor that warrants capacity building for international arbitration is that the latter forms part of a country's (private) judicial architecture. Its proper implementation and support are crucial to strengthening the rule of law. The ability to enforce one's rights through public or private dispute resolution mechanisms is closely linked

[30] Cf. ICC (2021), p. 9; UNCTAD (2023a).

[31] Cf. U.S. Department of State (2023).

[32] Columbia University, School of International and Public Affairs (2020), p. 4.

[33] UNCTAD (2023b), p. 5.

[34] Cf. U.S. Department of State (2023); U.S. Department of State (2023).

[35] ICC(2021), p. 10; cf. ICC (2011), p. 9.

[36] ICC (2022a), p. 5.

[37] Myburgh and Paniagua (2016), p. 603.

with the political stability and economic development of a country.[38] If communities do not have any confidence in their ability to resolve disputes in a timely, peaceful and effective manner through such channels, this has the potential to be a catalyst for instability.[39] Establishing reliable institutions and dispute resolution mechanisms is therefore essential for countries that intend to foster economic and political development by strengthening the rule of law.[40] While arbitration and other forms of ADR are only a piece of the puzzle, especially in countries where the judicial system may be inefficient, international arbitration can be a contributing factor in creating trust in the functioning of the society.

2.3 The Adverse Effects of a Lack of Capacity Building

The backlash against investor-state arbitration witnessed over the last decade is a good example of the ramifications if key stakeholders lack knowledge of international arbitration. Despite the fact that there are certainly aspects of the system that deserve criticism, such as the sometimes very broad interpretation of the standards of protection by investment arbitration tribunals, nationality planning through corporate special purpose vehicles and the lack of consistency in decisions of investor-state tribunals, the public debate has focused on ill-founded and straight out polemic positions.

The Transatlantic Trade and Investment Partnership (TTIP), a comprehensive free trade and investment agreement between the European Union and the United States that was negotiated between 2013 and 2019, may serve as a case study. Once negotiations were announced, and long before its text was published, the backlash overwhelmed the public discussion. Op-eds in reputable media outlets declared investor-state settlement "*a full-frontal assault on democracy* [...] *that would let rapacious companies subvert* [the British] *laws, rights and national sovereignty*".[41] Although the European Commission projected that TTIP would have bolstered the European economy by €120 billion, the US economy by €90 billion and the rest of the world by €100 billion,[42] the treaty eventually fell prey to public criticism, not least because policymakers from a number of countries reverted their stance on TTIP in the wake of the backlash, and was finally buried by then U.S. President Donald Trump as part of the Government's "America first" policy.

It is difficult to second-guess whether early capacity building would have prevented this effect. But there are reasons to believe that if government officials had been well-trained in drafting investment treaties, they could have pre-empted some of the justified criticism, and opposed the ill-founded criticism so that the

[38] See the references in McConnaughay (2017), p. 100.

[39] See e.g. Africa Center for Strategic Studies (2011).

[40] Cf. Rawls (2017), pp. 85, 89.

[41] Monbiot (2013).

[42] European Commission (2014).

debate would have been at least conducted with more reason. Noticeably, countries that engaged in capacity building through knowledge sharing and early education, such as Sweden, where the Stockholm Chamber of Commerce has actively conducted educational seminars and issued publications setting out the facts of TTIP,[43] had a lower degree of backlash against investor-state dispute settlement.[44] In this respect, it should be noted that Sweden has also not signed the agreement on the termination of intra-EU BITs in the aftermath of the Court of Justice of the European Union (CJEU) decision in the case of *Slovak Republic v Achmea BV*, which effectively dismantled investor-state arbitration within the EU.[45]

3 How to Build Capacity in International Arbitration

The definition of capacity building as the act of "*strengthening skills, instincts, abilities, processes and resources*" as a whole evinces that all stakeholders should be involved in the process for it to succeed.[46] In the case of international arbitration, this involves four main categories of actors:

(1) Government officials and legislators, as those responsible for the arbitration policy and legislative framework of a country;
(2) the state's judiciary, responsible for ensuring the effectiveness of this legal framework;
(3) lawyers, ensuring that arbitration is offered to and accepted by their clients as a means of dispute resolution;
(4) arbitrators, responsible for the quality of the arbitral proceedings and arbitral decisions.

3.1 Government Officials and Legislators

Capacity building starts with the branches of the government responsible for setting the policy towards arbitration. Primarily, these will be the members of the state's legislative branch as the ones responsible for the enactment of an arbitration-friendly legal framework. However, the role of the executive branch, as the one setting the general judicial policies should not be underestimated. The consequences of a lack of capacity building among government officials have already been discussed above.[47]

[43] See e.g. SCC (2015).

[44] Notably, even the Trade Union Confederation, the umbrella organization of the Swedish trade unions, has declared public support for TTIP, see Swedish Trade Union Confederation (2016).

[45] *Slovak Republic v Achmea BV* (CJEU, Judgment of 6 March 2018); Agreement for the termination of Bilateral Investment Treaties between the Member States of the European Union, SN/4656/2019/INIT.

[46] OECD (2006).

[47] See above, Sect. 2.3.

Stakeholders need to have a sufficient level of understanding of the concepts of arbitration in order to enable them to convey this information to their constituencies. Government officials must be supported in making educated decisions by providing guidance on how to implement domestic legal instruments in practice.[48]

For government officials, there is another good reason to engage in capacity building, particularly for those from emerging economies: international arbitration, in an increasingly interwoven legal order whose value goes beyond the individual dispute, contributes to shaping how international law and transnational principles are interpreted and applied by both domestic and international courts and tribunals.[49] International tribunals today frequently rely on case law from other jurisdictions and have therefore contributed to a body of "transnational law". For states, the ability to engage with the international dispute resolution system has therefore become an important element to advance strategic long-term interests, rather than being merely a reactive observer.[50]

3.2 *Training the Judiciary*

Safe for proceedings under the ICSID Convention, arbitration is not a self-contained regime. Arbitral proceedings are anchored in a jurisdiction, commonly referred to as the "seat" or "place" of arbitration.[51] The arbitral seat will determine the procedural legal framework applicable to the arbitration and which courts are competent to hear requests for interim measures and challenges to the award.[52] Therefore, the judiciary at the place of arbitration must have the requisite knowledge of arbitral proceedings in order to ensure the functioning of the arbitration process. Together with the legislative framework, this is generally referred to as "arbitration friendliness" of a legal system.[53]

As indicated above, a judiciary that is not aware of its obligations regarding international commercial arbitration will discourage foreign direct investment and the use of arbitration by the country's businesses.[54] Arbitration has significant differences to court proceedings, which is why the judiciary must be trained in understanding the benefits and disadvantages and its own supporting role in relation to arbitration proceedings.[55] It is notable that the leading arbitral seats have not only a well-functioning judicial system, but have also created additional incentives, such

---

[48] Cf. Meltz (2022), Papa (2013), p. 92.

[49] Papa (2013), p. 88.

[50] Ibid.

[51] Blackaby et al. (2023), paras. 1.25, 1.76.

[52] Blackaby et al. (2023), paras. 1.25, 1.76, 3.47; cf. Articles 1 (2), 17J, 34 UNCITRAL Model Law.

[53] Cf. Blackaby et al. (2023), paras. 1.12, 1.25.

[54] See above, 2.1.

[55] Cf. Meltz (2022); Mills and Shanker (2021), p. 9.

as specialized courts, concentrating the arbitration expertise of their judiciary in one place, and even providing a dedicated foreigner-friendly system for the judicial process in connection with arbitration. The Singapore International Commercial Court, for example, includes not only Singaporean judges but also judges from jurisdictions such as England, Australia and France who are experts in arbitration and/or commercial law,[56] and in the International Chamber of the Commercial Court of Paris, cases can be conducted in both French and English.[57]

For the same reason, the judiciary must also be trained in the foundations and conduct of setting aside proceedings. Finally, trainings on the recognition and enforcement of foreign arbitral awards will help create trust in the country's judicial system and thus make it more attractive as a destination for FDI, too.[58] To do so, capacity building efforts for the judicial branch must convey that arbitration does not stand in competition with domestic court proceedings but is a means to supplement it in certain contexts, where it may be the preferable means of dispute resolution. In this respect, especially jurisdictions with overburdened courts profit from the fact that cases that would otherwise land on the judge's docket can be resolved through arbitration.[59] At the same time, it is important to clarify that in matters that touch upon important public policy considerations of a state, courts will maintain the final say to ensure that disputes that belong to this sphere do not escape court supervision.[60] Judges that are so trained are in a position to strike the delicate balance between the interest of (foreign) commercial actors, even if they are directed against their own state, and the interest of the state in upholding certain paramount principles of the domestic legal system.

3.3 Training Practitioners

Creating an effective legal framework to facilitate arbitration and the recognition and enforcement of arbitral awards alone does not suffice for the purpose of creating trust; the efforts must be supported by capacity building measures to ensure that there is a well-trained body of local practitioners who understand and support the arbitral process.[61] There are two principal reasons why without domestic legal practitioners who are experienced in the conduct of arbitrations, arbitration cannot become an accepted option for domestic commercial actors.

---

[56] Singapore International Commercial Cour, Judges, available at: https://www.judiciary.gov.sg/singapore-international-commercial-court/about-the-sicc/judges.

[57] Commercial Court of Paris, The International Chamber, available at: https://www.tribunal-de-commerce-de-paris.fr/fr/the-international-chamber.

[58] See above, 2.1.

[59] Cf. Münch (2022) para. 11.

[60] Article 34 (2) (b) (ii) UNCITRAL Model Law; see also Lourie (2021).

[61] Mills and Shanker (2021), p. 9.

First, as a consequence of the differences between arbitration and court litigation, practitioners need to have a certain degree of expertise in order to be able to advise and represent clients. Especially small and medium sized companies which have little to no experience with arbitration may be reluctant to hire international law firms which provide high-quality service but at a high cost. Training local practitioners who can advise such companies on various dispute resolution mechanisms and represent them before arbitral tribunals is therefore crucial to promoting the use of arbitration.[62]

Second, by default, transactional and contract lawyers, who are often those advising companies on the means of dispute resolution to be included in the contract may not be familiar with arbitration and thus may favour domestic courts over international arbitration. In order to allow them to comprehensively advise their clients on the most suited means of dispute resolution, capacity building in arbitration should not be limited to dispute resolution practitioners but must expand to the domestic legal profession as a whole.

3.4 Training Arbitrators

The trust in the arbitral system will furthermore depend on the quality of the decision makers, i.e. the arbitrators. Arbitrators must be trained in how to conduct arbitral proceedings and in the drafting of arbitral awards. Training of arbitrators contributes to the proliferation of arbitration on two levels: First, in order for arbitration to be accepted, the quality of the decisions rendered by arbitrators must be at least on par, and preferably superior to that of domestic courts. Second, while the international community is not short of capable arbitration practitioners, it is equally crucial for the acceptance of arbitration that domestic practitioners sit as arbitrators.

In that respect, the experience from Africa gives helpful examples, where the acceptance of arbitration has significantly increased over the last 10 years, and so has the number of qualified arbitrators sitting in high profile disputes.[63]

Hence, many of the ICC's trainings and events are directed at future arbitrators. The Advanced Arbitration Academies, covering Asia, Eastern Europe, Latin America, North America, Africa and the Middle East, are intended to equip rising arbitration practitioners with the necessary skills for a career as an arbitrator and to teach them how to conduct proceedings, how to write awards and how to make sure that they are enforceable.[64]

---

[62] Mills and Shanker (2021), p. 9; cf. Papa (2013), p. 83; United Nations, Guidance Note on Strengthening United Nations Support to States, Upon Their Request, to Implement Sound Commercial Law Reforms, available at: https://uncitral.un.org/sites/uncitral.un.org/files/englishguidance_note.pdf, paras. 14–15.

[63] Anjomshoaa (2024); cf. ICC Bulletin Vol 22/No 1, pp. 7, 12; ICC (2021), pp. 10, 14.

[64] ICC (2023b).

3.5 Strong Arbitral Institutions as Capacity Building Drivers

Arbitral institutions are a key driver for capacity in international arbitration. Arbitration institutions operate on the intersection between the parties and their representatives as the users of international arbitration, and arbitral tribunals which deliver the service of resolving the parties' dispute. In this capacity, arbitral institutions can play a crucial role in ensuring the quality of the arbitral process and the development of arbitration.

In the case of the ICC, this follows from a number of functions performed by the Secretariat and the Court, including:

- Offering inexperienced parties explanation and advice about the arbitral process and clarifications on questions in connection with the ICC Rules;
- Advising arbitrators on the very same issues;
- Ensuring the quality of arbitral awards through the ICC's unique scrutiny process whereby an award is reviewed by the ICC Court not only in respect of compliance with formal prerequisites, but also allows the Court to draw the arbitral tribunal's attention to points of substance, in order to ensure the enforceability of the award;
- Ensuring diversity in the broader sense, i.e. including gender and generational diversity when called upon to appoint arbitrators.

The latter point is crucial from a capacity building perspective. Statistics show that when parties appoint arbitrators, they tend to appoint male candidates with a certain seniority.[65] In many jurisdictions, parties may be under the impression that only an arbitrator of a certain seniority is capable of providing a high quality, irrespective of the amount in dispute, even though the dispute may be well-apt for a more junior arbitrator. This creates an entry barrier for new arbitration practitioners to sit as arbitrators and thereby hampers the proliferation of arbitration in a given country.

Arbitral institutions, on the other hand, tend to appoint more junior and more diverse practitioners.[66] Strong arbitral institutions therefore play an important role in creating and maintaining the parties' trust in more junior arbitration practitioners by ensuring that the quality of their decision corresponds to the expectations of the parties. In the case of the ICC, this is in particular created through the scrutiny process, which ensures the quality of the award.

In more general terms, arbitral institutions can take an active role in knowledge-sharing, training and the establishment of the domestic arbitration community. The ICC Advanced Arbitration Academies observed above are only one example of the actions undertaken by the ICC for capacity building. The ICC has been conducting training for stakeholders in various jurisdictions, including, most recently, Moldova, Kazakhstan, Azerbaijan, Mongolia and several countries that intend to apply for EU membership.[67] The ICC global events and flagship conference taking place in

---

[65] See e.g. ICC (2022b); cf. ICCA (2022).

[66] ICC (2022b).

[67] Cf. ICC (2023a).

particular in emerging economies are often among the most visited domestic arbitration events. Other institutions have equally been active in the field. The Permanent Court of Arbitration, an institution primarily dedicated to the resolution of disputes under international law, including investor-state and state-state disputes, frequently conducts trainings for government officials.[68]

3.6 *Capacity Building Should Start Early*

An important takeaway from all capacity building measures is that they are the most efficient, the earlier they commence. Arbitration is no exception to this rule.

The inclusion of arbitration into the curriculum of universities has certainly contributed to the growth and acceptance of international arbitration. This is reflected not only in the growth of the arbitration field as a whole but also by the growth of specialized master programs in arbitration, such as the LL.M. programs of the Geneva Graduate Institute (MIDS), the Sciences Po, the University of Miami and many others, which continue to enjoy popularity. Another example is the Willem C. Vis Moot Court, which sees growth in participating universities globally every year.

The ICC Young Arbitration and ADR Forum (ICC YAAF) is intended to connect and train young lawyers with an interest in dispute resolution through numerous educational and social events every year during which they can learn more about best practices and current issues and network with one another.[69]

Such events convey critical skills for a successful career in international arbitration, which is why engaging with them is so important for capacity building purposes.

References

Africa Center for Strategic Studies (2011) Alternative dispute resolution in Africa: preventing conflict and enhancing stability. https://africacenter.org/publication/alternative-dispute-resolution-in-africa-preventing-conflict-and-enhancing-stability/

Anjomshoaa P (2024) LIDW 2024: the rise of African arbitration – is Africa leading the way? https://arbitrationblog.kluwerarbitration.com/2024/05/16/lidw-2024-the-rise-of-african-arbitration-is-africa-leading-the-way/

Blackaby N, Partasides C, Redfern A (2023) Redfern and hunter on international arbitration, 7th edn. Oxford University Press, Oxford

Born G (2021) International commercial arbitration, 3rd edn. Kluwer Law International, Alphen aan den Rijn

Columbia University School of International and Public Affairs (2020) The future of AI in the Brazilian judicial system. https://www.sipa.columbia.edu/sites/default/files/migrated/downlo

[68] PCA (2022), p. 40.

[69] ICC, ICC YAAF, available at: https://iccwbo.org/dispute-resolution/professional-development/yaaf-programme/.

ads/SIPA%2520Capstone%2520-%2520The%2520Future%2520of%2520AI%2520in%2520the%2520Brazilian%2520Judicial%2520System.pdf.
Dugan CF, Wallace D Jr, Rubins ND, Sabahi B (2008) Investor-state arbitration. Oxford University Press, Oxford
European Commission (2014) The expected impact of the TTIP on EU member states and selected third countries. https://www.europarl.europa.eu/RegData/etudes/IDAN/2014/536403/EXPO_IDA(2014)536403_EN.pdf
Greer S (2022) Seeing the wood from the trees: a holistic approach to arbitration legislative reform in the Caribbean (Chap. 9). In: Beaumont B et al (eds) international arbitration: Quo Vadis? Kluwer Law International, Alphen aan den Rijn, pp 163–182
ICC (2011) 2010 statistical report. In: ICC Bull 2011 22(1)
ICC (2021) Dispute resolution statistics 2020
ICC (2022a) Dispute resolution statistics 2022
ICC (2022b) ICC acts to encourage diversity in selection of arbitrators. https://iccwbo.org/news-publications/news/icc-acts-to-encourage-diversity-in-selection-of-arbitrators/
ICC (2023a) ICC advanced arbitration academy for Eastern Europe. https://2go.iccwbo.org/icc-advanced-arbitration-academy-for-eastern-europe.html#description
ICC (2023b) ICC launches Advanced Arbitration Academies. Available at: https://iccwbo.org/news-publications/news/icc-launches-advanced-arbitration-academies/.
ICC (2023c) Preliminary Statistics. https://iccwbo.org/news-publications/news/icc-releases-preliminary-2023-arbitration-and-adr-statistics/
ICCA (2022) Report of the cross-institutional task force on gender diversity in arbitral appointments and proceedings. https://www.arbitration-icca.org/icca-reports-no-8-report-cross-institutional-task-force-gender-diversity-arbitral-appointments-and
Joubin-Bret A, Rey ME, Weber J (2011) International investment law and development (Chap. 2). In: Gehring MW et al (eds) Sustainable development in world investment law. Kluwer Law International, Alphen aan den Rijn, pp 15–31
Lourie G (2021) Europarecht. In: Nueber M (ed) Handbuch Schiedsgerichtsbarkeit und ADR. LexisNexis, Vienna, pp 685–699
Markert L (2019) Die neuen Schiedsgerichtsordnungen der JCAA 2019 – Zugleich ein Update zum japanischen Schiedsmarkt. SchiedsVZ 242–251
McConnaughay PJ (2017) The potential of private commercial arbitration for facilitating economic growth in less developed countries. In: Menaker A (ed) International arbitration and the rule of law: contribution and conformity, ICCA congress series no. 19. Kluwer Law International, Alphen aan den Rijn, pp 100–114
McLachlan C, Shore L, Weiniger M (2017) International investment arbitration: substantive principles, 2nd edn. Oxford University Press, Oxford
Meltz D (2022) International arbitration as an instrument of economic development: the Indo-Pacific case study. https://arbitrationblog.kluwerarbitration.com/2022/04/29/international-arbitration-as-an-instrument-of-economic-development-the-indo-pacific-case-study/
Mills T, Shanker M (2021) Promoting investment through arbitration – Recent reforms in the South Pacific. In: Norton Rose Fulbright (ed) International arbitration report – Issue 17: 8–10
Monbiot G (2013) This transatlantic trade deal is a full-frontal assault on democracy. https://www.theguardian.com/commentisfree/2013/nov/04/us-trade-deal-full-frontal-assault-on-democracy
Münch J (2022) Vorbemerkung zu § 1025. In: Münchener Kommentar zur Zivilprozessordnung, 6th edn. C.H. Beck, Munich
Myburgh A, Paniagua J (2016) Does international commercial arbitration promote foreign direct investment? J Law Econ 59(3):597–627
OECD (2002) Foreign direct investment for development maximising benefits, minimising cost. https://www.oecd.org/investment/investmentfordevelopment/1959815.pdf
OECD (2006) The challenge of capacity development: working towards good practice. https://www.oecd-ilibrary.org/economics/the-challenge-of-capacity-development_oecd_papers-v6-art2-en

OECD (2021) Improving the legal environment for business and investment in Central Asia. https://www.oecd.org/eurasia/Improving-LEB-CA-ENG%2020%20April.pd
Papa M (2013) Emerging powers in international dispute settlement: from legal capacity building to a level playing field? J Int Disput Settl 4(1):83–109
Paulsson J (1995) Arbitration without privity. ICSID Rev 10(2):232–257
PCA (2022) Annual report 2022. https://docs.pca-cpa.org/2023/07/341817ff-pca-annual-report-2022.pdf
Polanco R (2019) The return of the home state to investor-state disputes: bringing back diplomatic protection? Cambridge University Press, Cambridge, pp 29–52
Rawls A (2017) Improving the impact of international arbitration on economic development. In: Menaker A (ed) International arbitration and the rule of law: contribution and conformity, ICCA congress series no 19. Kluwer Law International, Alphen aan den Rijn, pp 85–99
SCC (2015) DG trade concept paper investment in TTIP and beyond – the path for reform, observations by the arbitration institute of the Stockholm Chamber of Commerce (SCC). https://sccarbitrationinstitute.se/sites/default/files/2022-11/dg-trade-concept-paper-6-may-2015_scc-remarks.pdf
Swedish Trade Union Confederation (2016) Yes to TTIP, but with common sense. https://www.lo.se/english/news/yes_to_ttip_but_with_common_sense
UNCTAD (2009) The role of international investment agreements in attracting foreign direct investment to developing countries. https://unctad.org/system/files/official-document/diaeia20095_en.pdf
UNCTAD (2023a) Global foreign direct investment flows over the last 30 years. https://unctad.org/data-visualization/global-foreign-direct-investment-flows-over-last-30-years
UNCTAD (2023b) World investment report 2023. https://unctad.org/system/files/official-document/wir2023_en.pdf
U.S. Department of State (2023) 2023 investment climate statements: Brazil. https://www.state.gov/reports/2023-investment-climate-statements/brazil/
Vogenauer S, Hodges C (2008) Civil justice systems in Europe: implications for choice of forum and choice of contract law. https://www.fondation-droitcontinental.org/fr/wp-content/uploads/2013/12/oxford_civil_justice_survey_-_summary_of_results_final.pdf.
White & Case, Queen Mary University of London (2021) International arbitration survey: adapting arbitration to a changing world. https://arbitration.qmul.ac.uk/media/arbitration/docs/LON0320037-QMUL-International-Arbitration-Survey-2021_19_WEB.pdf.

Some Peculiarities of the Legal Framework on Commercial Arbitration in Bosnia and Herzegovina

Zinka Grbo and Sevleta Halilović

Abstract In Bosnia and Herzegovina, arbitration emerges as a promising mechanism for resolving disputes, especially those involving foreign parties. Nevertheless, an overview of the legal framework shows several obstacles that impede this from becoming a reality. Upon examination of the legal framework, a patchwork of laws governing arbitration, dispersed across B&H's territorial units, is revealed. However, even fragmented, this framework provides a solid ground for arbitration proceedings to be conducted. This is shown by analyzing certain aspects of arbitration, including arbitrability, arbitrator appointments, arbitration agreements, and awards, shedding light on both strengths and weaknesses. Although there is room for improvement in the legal framework, its current deficiencies cannot be the sole reason why arbitration proceedings rarely occur in B&H. The paper also explores the current state of play of institutional arbitration, through the analysis of the Court of Arbitration attached to the Foreign Trade Chamber of Bosnia and Herzegovina, identifying areas for improvement. Ultimately, the authors advocate for a human-centered approach to arbitration reforms, emphasizing clarity, efficiency, and accessibility. By addressing the system's challenges with empathy and pragmatism, B&H can unlock the full potential of arbitration as a cornerstone of dispute resolution.

1 Introduction

In Bosnia and Herzegovina (hereafter B&H), national courts are the primary instance of settling commercial disputes between domestic parties. While arbitration was introduced in the B&H's legal system decades ago, this alternative way of resolving disputes is not recognized as attractive enough by the parties to be chosen over more

Z. Grbo (✉) · S. Halilović
Department of Civil Law, Faculty of Law, University of Sarajevo, Sarajevo, Bosnia and Herzegovina
e-mail: z.grbo@pfsa.unsa.ba

S. Halilović
e-mail: s.halilovi@pfsa.unsa.ba

M. Bungenberg et al. (eds.), *Alternative Dispute Resolution in the Western Balkans*, European Union and its Neighbours in a Globalized World 20,
https://doi.org/10.1007/978-3-031-76345-8_4

traditional methods. However, the story differs regarding international disputes, most often involving a foreign party. In contracts where one party has its seat outside of B&H, arbitration clauses are commonly incorporated based on the *take-it-or-leave-it* principle. This indicates that in such business relationships, arbitration is favored over other dispute resolution methods, and domestic parties are willing to consent to arbitration in these circumstances. Notwithstanding the arbitration agreement's conclusion, B&H is rarely chosen as the seat of arbitration, as these clauses often refer to reputable and famous arbitral institutions and their rules, and on/or ad hoc arbitration with the application of the Arbitration Rules by the United Nations Commission on International Trade Law (UNCITRAL Arbitration Rules).

This may reflect a lack of trust in arbitration as a dispute resolution method or a lack of understanding of arbitration and its advantages. Another reason for this may be the fact that the vast majority of legal advisors, such as attorneys (counsels) in B&H refrain from recommending arbitration to their clients, since the whole concept of arbitration is unknown to them, compared to litigation where they can rely on familiar (and multi-instanced) practices.

In a situation where the national judicial system suffers from overload and undercapacity, and as a result, the average duration of pending commercial cases before first-instance courts is 464 days,[1] it is unclear why arbitration is avoided. With so many positive characteristics, arbitration can and should be beneficial for the commercial sphere of B&H, which naturally raises the question of its disproportionate usage compared to litigation.

The special provisions on arbitration exist in B&H but are rather located in several different acts. The assertion of *lex specialis* as an argument is presented as a significant deficiency within the normative framework of B&H, a characterization that the authors deem inaccurate. Consolidating the norms governing arbitration within a single act, rather than dispersing them among several, does not guarantee an improvement; in fact, it may even yield unintended consequences. The primary focus should be on enhancing the existing norms regardless of their form.

In this chapter, the authors are going to endeavor to override this argument focusing on argumentation that is *in favorem* arbitration in B&H but also critique of certain segments of the legal framework. The chapter should also serve as a substantial contribution to the existing literature on arbitration in B&H,[2] while affirmation of arbitration as a concurrent way of resolving disputes in B&H can only be partially addressed within these pages.

---

[1] See European Union (2019), p. 35.

[2] Trifković and Omanović (2001), p. 46, Trifković et al. (2009), Lasić (2013), Bikić (2019), pp. 299–322, Gagula (2020), pp. 13–22, Gagula (2019), Kasumagić (2020).

2 Overview of the Legal Framework

Provisions that regulate arbitration in B&H are dispersed into several different acts. Before we dive into the discussion on the legal framework, it is important to take a moment to understand the distinctive political system of B&H. B&H consists of the Federation of B&H (FB&H), Republika Srpska (RS), and Brčko District B&H (BD B&H). The Constitution of B&H delegates the majority of the State's powers to the entities/districts, thereby restricting the competencies of B&H to those explicitly outlined within. Upon the distribution of power, entities/districts created their regulatory frameworks to govern specific areas of law, with arbitration being one such field.

Arbitration legislation in B&H is integrated into the Civil Procedure Acts (hereafter CPA)[3] of every mentioned territorial unit. As each of these three acts contains 19 identical provisions on arbitration, we will henceforth only refer to the CPA of FB&H. While enforcement of domestic arbitration decisions is regulated by related enforcement laws of entities/district,[4] provisions that concern recognition and enforcement of foreign arbitral awards are placed in the State level act that regulates matters of private international law.[5] In this sense, B&H did not follow the trend of neighboring countries which, after the dissolution of the joint state Yugoslavia, adopted special laws on arbitration based on the UNCITRAL Model Law. Arbitration legislation in B&H is rather dispersed among the mentioned acts.

This, however, does not make B&H any less arbitration-friendly, since this relatively small number of provisions still represent a solid legal basis for conducting complete arbitration proceedings. Besides that, some of the most preferred seats of arbitration, such as Switzerland,[6] do not have a *lex specialis* on arbitration, which has been found comforting. The stance that B&H did not use all possibilities for the development of arbitration is justified,[7] while the stance that it is necessary to adopt a special act on arbitration is understandable, but not considered crucial.

The potential adoption of a *lex specialis* on arbitration would entail not only the extraction of rules from different acts and combining them into a single, cohesive act, but also the need for the adoption of such a law at the state level. However, the undertaking of passing a law at the state level may be difficult or even impossible due to the already mentioned division of competencies between the state and its constituent units by the Constitution.[8] It is a matter of fact that the State of B&H has no explicit power to adopt such an act.

---

[3] Civil Procedure Act of FBIH (Articles 434–453), Civil Procedure Act of RS (Articles 434–453) and Civil Procedure Act of BD (Article 427–446).

[4] For more details, see Cross-border Recognition and Enforcement of Foreign Judicial Decisions in South East Europe and Perspectives of HCCH 2019 Judgments Convention (2021).

[5] Act on the Resolution of Conflicts of Laws with the Regulations of Other Countries in Certain Relations (1982).

[6] International Arbitration Survey (2021).

[7] Čizmić (2016), p. 1219.

[8] Article IV of the Constitution of Bosnia and Herzegovina.

In terms of international sources, the New York Convention[9] and the European Convention on International Commercial Arbitration[10] are applicable on the territory of B&H.

3 A Closer Look at the CPA

Arbitration in B&H operates under a limited set of rules[11]—a characteristic that should not necessarily be viewed negatively. While the number of arbitration rules in the CPA may be limited, their adequacy alone determines how effectively they regulate the process. The existing provisions in the CPA lack clarity, particularly regarding their applicability to institutional or ad hoc arbitration. Additionally, it is unclear whether these rules apply solely to domestic, foreign, or both types of arbitration, and whether they exclusively govern commercial arbitrations or extend to other types. Put simply, the scarcity of rules equates to limited regulatory guidance.

Nevertheless, despite the deficient regulatory framework, arbitration implementation—be it domestic or foreign, institutionalized, or *ad hoc*, commercial or otherwise—remains unhindered, although one should not feed the misconception[12] that arbitration in B&H is regulated absolutely in accordance with contemporary comparative legal solutions.

Interestingly, the provisions on arbitration in the CPA are located in the fifth chapter, titled "Special Proceeding".[13] The rationale behind the legislature's decision to place the arbitration procedure among other specialized procedures is not quite clear.[14] However, this classification has significant implications for arbitration in B&H. For example, since the 19 provisions relating to arbitration do not contain general principles on arbitration,[15] all general principles established in the first chapter of the CPA, titled "Basic Principles" can be applied subsidiarily.[16]

---

[9] Convention on the Recognition and Enforcement of Foreign Arbitral Awards (1958).

[10] European Convention on International Commercial Arbitration (1961).

[11] It should be emphasized that these are positive regulations, whose texts are not only harmonized with each other, but rather identical (F B&H and RS), that is, to the greatest extent synchronized (BD B&H). Such similarity between these rules means that there is no fear of legal uncertainty.

[12] Trivun and Domazet (2011), p. 46.

[13] Special proceedings, according to the CPA, are Proceedings in Litigation Concerning Labour Relations, Proceedings in Litigation Concerning Trespassing and Small Claim Disputes Proceedings.

[14] Even more so, with the amendments of 2015, the *claim for the protection of collective interests* was found in the subsection of the chapter. This decision of the legislator is also subject to scrutiny, bearing in mind that it is not a question of related procedures, nor a usual nomotechnical solution.

[15] Some principles, such as party autonomy, can be abstracted from Articles like Article 434, which empowers parties to choose arbitration for dispute resolution mechanism and Article 453, which prohibits the waiver of rights from certain Articles by agreement. This, *argumentum a contrario*, means that all other rules that concern arbitration can be waived by the sole agreement of the parties.

[16] For more on the principles of the CPA, see Čalija and Omanović (2000), pp. 46–49.

Not to leave things unclarified, only provisions that expressly refer to matters of arbitration serve as a source of law for arbitration procedures in B&H. Other provisions of the CPA can be applied only if the parties expressly opt for their application, or in the absence of procedural rules. Therefore, the application of other provisions of the CPA to arbitration proceedings is limited and subsidiary in an appropriate manner, which leaves the parties with the opportunity to organize the proceedings in the way that suits them best. Typically, when parties seek a thoroughly regulated and predetermined procedure, they opt for an institution capable of providing such assurance.

To gain a closer look at these provisions, the ensuing subsections will correspond to the matter regulated within them—namely, arbitrability, the arbitration agreement, the appointment of arbitrators, and arbitration awards.

3.1 Arbitrability

The prerequisite for a dispute to be settled by arbitration is to be recognized as arbitrable. In this regard, the CPA defines arbitration as possible except in cases where the claim is against compulsory legal rules or if the disputes fall under the exclusive jurisdiction of the court. The broad definition constructs a challenge of determining which claims are suitable for arbitration, necessitating a case-by-case approach. This burden arises from poorly drafted regulations, which suggest that unless another regulation explicitly states that a particular dispute is arbitrable (which is never the case) or designates it as falling under the exclusive jurisdiction of the court, there remains ample room for conservative court interpretations to deem the dispute non-arbitrable.

In practice, most arbitration cases, if not all of them, deal with commercial contractual claims, while disputes related to the Articles on association, intellectual property, share purchase agreements, competition law, and similar matters, are generally considered unsuitable for arbitration.[17] This uncertainty regarding their arbitrability is not unique to B&H but is also present in other jurisdictions.

Yet, we find B&H to be arbitration-friendly[18] for at least some non-negligible number of claims. This is true for arbitrations with their seat in Bosnia and Herzegovina, whether the dispute involves foreign elements or not. However, there is no

[17] More on this in Zlatović (2016). pp. 42–64; more on arbitrability in general in Varady et al. (2012), pp. 253–257.

[18] "Arbitration-friendly" is a term that describe a jurisdiction that supports and facilitates the process of arbitration as a mechanism for resolving disputes. Counties that are considered not or less arbitration friendly are the ones with the courts that have greater authority to manage disputes within their jurisdiction and tend to intervene more, particularly in politically sensitive cases. Moreover, such countries might impose certain limitations on the arbitration process, like requiring the involvement of locally qualified lawyers and restricting the selection of arbitrators. More on topic in Latham and Watkins (2014). pp. 18.

evidence of an arbitration without a domestic party having its seat in B&H ever occurring.

3.2 Appointment of Arbitrators

The CPA uses a universally accepted formula regarding the appointment and number of arbitrators. Thus, it stipulates that the number of arbitrators must be odd, without limit on the total number of arbitrators. The choice is made by consensus between the parties, if there is one arbitrator, while in the absence of an agreement, each party chooses an arbitrator, which then jointly choose the presiding arbitrator.[19]

There is, however, a concerning Article, which regulates cases where the party does not appoint an arbitrator, or when the arbitrators cannot agree on the election of the presiding arbitrator of the arbitration tribunal. In that case, according to Article 440, the appointing authority would be "the court that would otherwise be competent for that dispute in the first instance if an arbitration agreement had not been concluded".[20] While this rule poses no challenge for disputes in which all parties are based in Bosnia and Herzegovina, in situations where a court in a foreign country would have jurisdiction, it seems that the whole procedure would be unreasonably complicated. Such a situation is not unthinkable, but it would certainly conflict with arbitration as an inherently efficient procedure. Therefore, business entities based in B&H are not faced with this potential problem. On the other hand, this provision provides an ideal solution in situations in which, for various reasons, the parties, or arbitrators, cannot independently complete the formation of the tribunal. This is an argument that goes in favor of arbitration as a private way of resolving disputes for domestic (business) entities.[21]

The wording *"the court that would have jurisdiction in a specific dispute if an arbitration agreement had not been concluded"* is used in several other Articles and consequently poses a challenge in those instances as well. For example, this court would be competent to deal with requests for the annulment of the arbitral award,[22] and when it comes to an obligation to keep the original arbitration award and confirmation of its delivery.[23] It seems that this provision was drafted for *ad hoc* procedures since most institutionalized arbitrations have mechanisms and apparatus to deal with cases after the completion of procedures.

---

[19] Article 437 paragraph 1 and 2 of the CPA.

[20] Such a practical solution, which was made possible by the court's assistance in cases where the parties are unable to appoint an arbitrator, although modified, exists in comparative law.

[21] On the contrary, very critically, in the context of international commercial arbitration in Bosnia and Herzegovina, see: Kasumagić (2020).

[22] Article 450 paragraph 2 of the CPA.

[23] Article 448, but according to Čizmić (2016), p. 1230, this provision is referred not only to the award and following documentation on delivery, but rather the whole file of a case. More on the assistance of state courts in arbitral proceedings in B&H in Jevremović (2017).

From this, it becomes evident that the CPA's provisions on arbitration are created and are more suitable for cases in which all parties are from B&H. The subjective scope of the provisions of the CPA is not expressly limited to entities from B&H, but it is obviously more favorable to them than to foreign parties.

3.3 Arbitration Agreement

The arbitration agreement is a formal contract, which means that the written form has *ad solemnitatem* effect for this type of agreement. This is a generally accepted standard in the world. This very approach is visible in the Convention on the Recognition and Enforcement of Foreign Arbitral Awards (hereafter NY Convention) where an "agreement in writing" includes an arbitral clause in a contract or an arbitration agreement, signed by the parties or contained in an exchange of letters or telegrams.[24] The CPA regulates this matter in accordance with the NY Convention but with a clear tendency towards an extensive interpretation of the written form, which matches the one of the UNICITRAL Model Law.

According to the CPA, an arbitration agreement is valid when it is concluded in writing and signed by all parties. However, the written form requirement is also fulfilled if this agreement is concluded through the exchange of letters, telegrams, telexes, or other means of telecommunications that provide written evidence of the concluded agreement.[25] The arbitration agreement fulfills the written form requirement even when it is referred to by one party in the claim, and the other party, through the counterclaim, does not contest the agreement.[26] Finally, this requirement is also fulfilled when there are references to the agreement contained in another act, such as arbitration clauses contained in the general conditions of business of a legal entity.[27]

It is visible that the traditional written form, known in theory, is expanded by including modern means of communication if a written record of the agreement is ensured. In terms of form, therefore, B&H does not lag the countries in the region or the world's set standards and practices. However, it is just to say that a certain level of familiarization of courts with the rules and concept of pro-arbitration could have a strong impact on the destiny of some arbitration agreements.

---

[24] Article 2 paragraph 2 of the CPA.

[25] Article 428 paragraph 2 and 3 of the CPA.

[26] Article 435 paragraph 3 of the CPA.

[27] The general business conditions of a legal entity must be directly communicated with the correlating parties because, according to court practice in B&H, "*referring to the consultation of the general business conditions on the website cannot be considered as publication of the general conditions in the usual way*". Therefore, clauses that contain arbitration provisions in online published general business conditions cannot be considered a legitimate source of power for arbitration proceedings. Such position was taken by the Cantonal Court in Odžak in Decision No. 25 0 Ps 031613 17 Pž 3 dated 7 March 2017. However, a strong opposing stance can be found in Matić (2016). pp. 7–31, Šabić Učanbarlić (2019), p. 535.

3.4 *Arbitral Award*

The arbitral award is final unless the parties' agreement specifies otherwise. However, if permitted by the agreement, the decision can be challenged in a higher-level arbitration. The award may be annulled upon a party's claim, with specific limited grounds on which annulment is permissible.[28] Given the absence of known issues or particularities concerning the handling of domestic and foreign arbitration awards, particularly in terms of their enforcement, we will not address this topic further.

4 Institutional Arbitration in B&H

As previously mentioned, the legislative framework does look more favorable for ad hoc arbitration, but it gives the same solid legal ground for the establishment and existence of both ad hoc and institutional arbitration proceedings. The key answer for this disbalance could lay in the drafting history of provisions that are regulating arbitration in B&H. In the same year (2003) when the CPA was adopted and entered into force,[29] the Rules on the Organization and Operation of the Court of Arbitration (hereafter Rules) were adopted. The Rules are the primary legal source for the operation of the Court of Arbitration that is attached to the Foreign Trade Chamber of Bosnia and Herzegovina (hereafter Court of Arbitration),[30] which is the only institutional arbitration at the level of the State.[31]

The parallel development of the rules of this institution eliminated the need for the legislator to include detailed provisions on institutional arbitration in the CPA. It is widely recognized that such institutions usually have their own set of procedural rules.[32]

[28] Article 451 of the CPA.

[29] The existing legal framework has been applied without changes for twenty years, following the continuity of normative solutions from earlier regulations dating back to 1998. It is significant to state that the Civil Litigator for Bosnia and Herzegovina from 1883 prescribed rules for the so-called "obraničku" (chosen) procedure which legally capable parties could contract in connection with a dispute whose subject matter they could freely dispose of, i.e. conclude a settlement on it. For more see Trifković and Omanović (2001).

[30] Arbitration Court at the Foreign Trade Chamber of Bosnia and Herzegovina is established in 2003 by the Law on the Foreign Trade Chamber of Bosnia and Herzegovina, with its headquarters in Sarajevo. In accordance with Article 20 of this law, the Chamber organizes the Arbitration Court, before which economic entities can resolve their disputes amicably, through mediation, or by arbitration, if the parties agree to the jurisdiction of this arbitration court.

[31] There is an arbitration institution established on level of Republika Srpska, created as a part of the Chamber of Commerce of Republika Srpska.

[32] Born (2021), p. 28.

4.1 Rules on the Organization and Operation of the Court of Arbitration

The procedure before the Court of Arbitration is conducted in accordance with the provisions of the Rules, unless the parties agree that the UNCITRAL Arbitration Rules are applied to the procedure.[33] In this situation, the Rules are still applied if there are no corresponding provisions in the UNCITRAL Arbitration Rules.

The Rules also prescribe that, if there are no necessary provisions in the Rules and the parties have not agreed otherwise, the provisions of the Civil Procedure Act shall be applied.[34] The specific Civil Procedure Act is not addressed, and since there are three such acts on the territory of B&H, the applicable would be the one which the arbitrator(s) deem to be the most acceptable in the given case.[35]

For a more comprehensive understanding of the Rules, the following subsections will delve into their specific aspects in greater detail, including some comparisons with the CPA.

4.2 Arbitrability

By Article 2 of the Rules, requirements for a claim to be arbitrable, are set. These requirements are no novelty since they have been incorporated in the Act since its original drafting. According to the Rules, a dispute is arbitrable if the following conditions are met cumulatively:

- it is a commercial dispute in which the parties can freely dispose of the subject of the dispute;
- the dispute does not fall under the scope of exclusive jurisdiction of the national court; and
- the parties have agreed on the jurisdiction of the institution in question.

These provisions align entirely with those of the CPA. However, their consolidation into a single location is a welcome change and should be a pattern to follow for future amendments in the arbitration legislation of B&H.

[33] Article 43 of the Rules.

[34] The original phrasing suggests that the term "zakon o parničnom postupku" (Civil Procedure Act) is written in lowercase, giving the impression that it refers to a generic term rather than a specific act. In this context, the questions arises whether any Civil Procedure Act could be applied in addition to the three in Bosnia and Herzegovina.

[35] Article 42, paragraph 2 of Rules. Unless a *lapsus calami* was committed, all the provisions of any of the three acts on civil procedure in B&H would be applicable to the arbitration procedure. Another version of the interpretation implies that the *ratio legis* was such as to allow the tribunal to decide which particular provisions of one of the laws on civil procedure would be the most acceptable. The solution to the dilemma about the way to interpret this provision would provide an argument for or against the claim that the CPA as such is (not) a source of arbitration law in B&H.

4.3 Appointment of Arbitrators

The appointment of arbitrators is an area where, without a doubt, the legislator made some omissions. The Rules prescribe the choice of one or three arbitrators (setting three as a maximum) that can be appointed from the official lists[36] created by the institution. These lists were designed in a way that one contains the names of potential arbitrators for domestic disputes, while the other is for international disputes. These lists are open, allowing for party appointment and selection outside of them, while according to the practice the presiding arbitrator is selected from the designated list.

This approach of suggesting or restricting the pool of potential arbitrators is generally abandoned because it is believed to limit the parties' ability to select a trusted individual based on their own preferences.[37] Another issue concerns the requirements for becoming an arbitrator on the list. According to the Rules, *when determining the list of arbitrators, it is necessary to take care that they are highly skilled persons who possess specialized knowledge in a certain area of law and business relations*[38]—this provision is contrary to the opinion of many authors,[39] and contrary to something that is already common knowledge in arbitration: arbitrators do not have to be lawyers, nor to have *specialized knowledge in a certain area of law.* As a matter of fact, they are considered "private" judges selected for particular qualities or experience, with parties' freedom to establish these unique conditions for arbitrators through mutual agreement.[40] An opposing argument that has been made by some authors is that arbitrators act as judges and thus require a certain level of legal expertise.[41] While they are not required to meet the same qualifications as appointed judges, they must possess specific qualifications.

To "save the day", the long-awaited changes in this area finally happened at the end of 2023. However, the new and refined provisions did not achieve the expected effect. The provisions missed setting essential criteria, such as professional experience and language proficiency, necessary for membership in such a body. The recent changes could have achieved the necessary modernization and enhancement of the Rules smoothly. However, this did not occur. Instead, the changes only superficially altered the provisions and failed to address the core issues.

---

[36] Lists accessible via: https://komorabih.ba/wp-content/uploads/2020/07/2020-07-17-Lista-arbitara-I.pdf and https://komorabih.ba/wp-content/uploads/2020/07/202-07-17-Lista-arbitara-II.pdf.

[37] Born (2014), pp. 1809–1810.

[38] Article 23 paragraph 3 of the Rules.

[39] Born (2021), pp. 166–169, Jakšić (2003), p. 305.

[40] Gaillard and Savage (1999), p. 576.

[41] Bikić (2019), p. 309.

4.4 Language of Arbitration

So far, the untouched matter of the language of arbitration[42] must be addressed when discussing *in favorem* of institutional arbitration in B&H. The chapter of the CPA that regulates arbitration is silent on the language of arbitration proceedings, which indicates that other provisions of the CPA are applicable. On the other hand, according to the Rules, parties are free to agree on the language of the arbitration,[43] and in the absence of agreement, the arbitrator(s) will decide on the language of the proceedings, with a special possibility that, until the language of the proceedings is determined, all submissions may be submitted in one of the languages of B&H or the language of the main contract or the language of the arbitration agreement. The extensive flexibility in selecting the language of arbitration should make the procedures under these Rules appealing to parties of various linguistic regions. At this stage, however, we will not delve into the matter of whether the Court of Arbitration can handle disputes in foreign languages other than English, nor will we examine the availability and capability of arbitrators to effectively manage such disputes.

4.5 Expenses

The financial aspect is very important in the world of arbitration. This is often the reason why the parties in a dispute opt for arbitration (quick and efficient resolution of the dispute)—to save themselves from losses on the market that may arise for them until the dispute is resolved. Although the parties are willing to pay much more for arbitration than for proceedings before a national court (due to the favorable characteristics of arbitration), it is still desirable that the service of arbitration be obtained at a lower price. This same reason makes the Court of Arbitration an attractive choice since it demands objectively low fees. According to Article 10 of the Tariff on Costs of Arbitration,[44] 800 BAM (~407.92 EUR) is the value of the administrative fee if the value of the dispute is up to 50.000 BAM (~25,495.01 EUR), and for the value of the dispute over 50,000 BAM, the administrative fee corresponds to 60% of the arbitrator's fee, which is calculated according to the table from the Tariff as well.[45]

---

[42] On this matter, see Perovic (2016), pp. 274–289, Bantekas (2020). pp. 127–152.

[43] Article 5 of the Rules.

[44] Decision on Determining the Tariff on Costs of Arbitration.

[45] The authors have translated the contents of this table. Costs have been converted into Euros in approximate value to facilitate easier comparison and comprehension.

The arbitrator's fees are determined as follows:

- For claims valued from 25,000 to 51,000 EUR, the arbitrator's fee is 2,000 EUR.
- For claims valued from 51,000 to 102,000 EUR, the arbitrator's fee is 2,000 EUR.
- For claims valued from 102,000 to 255,000 EUR, the arbitrator's fee is 3,500 EUR.
- For claims valued from 255,000 to 510,000 EUR, the arbitrator's fee is 5,500 EUR.
- For claims valued from 510,000 to 1,000,000 EUR, the arbitrator's fee is 7,000 EUR.

For example, for claims valued from 25,500 to 51,000 €, the arbitrator's fee is 1,000 €. In practice, this means that if there is a claim with a value of 51,000 EUR, the administrative fee amounts to approximately 600 EUR.[46] This shows how affordable the procedures before the Court of Arbitration can be, most likely because these numbers have remained unchanged since 2013.

5 Steps Forward—Conclusion

The landscape of arbitration in B&H presents both challenges and opportunities for improvement. Despite its long-standing presence, arbitration remains underutilized compared to traditional court proceedings. This discrepancy is particularly evident in domestic disputes, where arbitration clauses are less common, despite its potential to take away the burden from the national justice system.

The dispersed nature of arbitration regulation across different acts reflects the complex political structure of B&H. While this may complicate the efforts to consolidate and streamline arbitration laws, it also underscores the need for a more cohesive and comprehensive approach to arbitration regulation.

Efforts to promote arbitration through training programs and academic courses are promising steps toward fostering a greater understanding and appreciation of arbitration's benefits. Very good examples are the Public Institution Center for Judicial and Prosecutorial Training of FBiH and the Public Institution Center for Judicial and Prosecutorial Training of RS, which provide training in the field of arbitration and alternative dispute resolution. Also, by the end of the academic year 2023/2024, the Faculty of Law of the University of Sarajevo will welcome a second generation of master's students in law specializing in the field of Arbitration and Alternative Dispute Resolution. In addition to this, the Faculty of Law is slowly establishing the practice of forming teams for the Willem C. Vis International Commercial Arbitration Moot competition.

However, more concerted efforts are needed to modernize and update the arbitration framework to align with global standards and best practices, especially within courts and bar associations. Recent revisions to the Rules governing institutional arbitration are a step forward, but further reforms are necessary to address underlying issues and enhance the attractiveness of arbitration as a dispute resolution mechanism in B&H.

Overall, B&H enables the conduct of arbitration proceedings even with the existing legal framework. It is true that changes are necessary, but none of the deficiencies are so significant that they prevent arbitration proceedings from being used more often. On the other hand, by embracing reforms and promoting awareness of arbitration's advantages, B&H can unlock the full potential of arbitration as a preferred method for resolving commercial disputes, at least between domestic parties.

For claims valued over 1,000,000 EUR, the arbitrator's fee is 10,000 €.

[46] For example, the same dispute before ICC would cause administrative fees of 4,700 EUR.

References

Bantekas I (2020) Language selection in international commercial arbitration. Ohio State J Disput Resolut 36(1):127–152

Bikić A (2019) Arbitraža u Bosni i Hercegovini. Godišnjak Pravnog fakulteta u Sarajevu, vol LXII, pp 299–322

Born G (2014) International commercial arbitration, 3rd edn. Kluwer Law International, The Hague

Born G (2021) International arbitration: law and practice, 3rd edn. Kluwer Law International, The Hague

Čalija B, Omanović S (2000) Građansko procesno pravo. Pravni fakultet Univerziteta u Sarajevu, Sarajevo

Čizmić J (2016) Komentar Zakona o parničnom postupku Federacije Bosne i Hercegovine, Sarajevo

European Union (2019) Analytical report attached to the opinion on Bosnia and Herzegovina's application for membership in the European Union, SWD (2019) 222 final. https://neighbourhood-enlargement.ec.europa.eu/system/files/2019-05/20190529-bosnia-and-herzegovina-analytical-report.pdf

Gagula A (2019) Arbitrability of shareholders dispute in Bosnian law. In: Balkan yearbook of European and international law. Springer, Cham, pp 1–15

Gagula A (2020) Advokatski troškovi u arbitražnom postupku – bosanska perspektiva. Anali Pravnog Fakulteta Univerziteta u Zenici 24:12–22

Gaillard E, Savage J (1999) Fouchard Gaillard Goldman on international commercial arbitration. Kluwer Law International, The Hague

International Arbitration Survey (2021) Adapting arbitration to a changing world. https://arbitration.qmul.ac.uk/research/2021-international-arbitration-survey/

Jevremović N (2017) The role of the courts in supporting arbitration in Bosnia and Herzegovina – overview of the legal framework and legal practice. Young Arbitr Rev 6(27):66 et seqq

Jakšić A (2003) Međunarodna Trgovačka Arbitraža. Pravni Fakultet Univerziteta u Beogradu, Belgrade

Kasumagić I (2020) Granting and enforcing interim measures in international commercial arbitration in Bosnia and Herzegovina. In: Balkan yearbook of European and international law 2019. Springer, Cham, pp 91–107

Latham and Watkins LLP (2014) Guide to International Arbitration. Latham & Watkins LLP. https://www.lw.com. Accessed 28 May 2024

Lasić M (2013) Arbitražno pravo. Sveučilište u Mostaru-Pravni fakultet. Mostar

Matić T (2016) Elektronički oblik arbitražnog ugovora. Pravna Misao (Sarajevo) 1–2:7–31

Perovic J (2016) Jezik arbitražnog postupka u međunarodnoj trgovinskoj arbitraži. In: Liber amicorum Gašo Knežević, Beograd, pp 274–289

Šabić Učanbarlić A (2019) Potrošački sporovi pred arbitražom. Godišnjak Pravnog fakulteta u Sarajevu LXII:529–549

Trifković M, Omanović S (2001) International business law and arbitration. Faculty of Economics, University of Sarajevo

Trifković M et al (2009) Međunarodno poslovno pravo. Ekonomski fakultet Univerziteta u Sarajevu, Sarajevo

Trivun V, Domazet A (2011) Elaborat o osnivanju privredne-gospodarske arbitraže Udruženja poslodavaca Federacije Bosne i Hercegovine. In: The dictionary of substances and their effects. Sarajevo. http://www.upfbih.ba/uimages/dokumenti/ArbitraC5BEa.pdf. Accessed 5 Apr 2024

Varady T, Barchelo JJ, Merhem TA (2012) International commercial arbitration, 5th edn. Thomson Reuters, St. Paul

Zlatović D (2016) Arbitražno rješavanje sporova u svezi sa zaštitom prava industrijskog vlasništva. Pravna Misao (Sarajevo) 9–10:42–64

Challenges in the Process of Recognition and Enforcement of Foreign Arbitral Awards in the Republic of North Macedonia

Ljuben Kocev

Abstract Arbitration is increasingly becoming the preferred method for the resolving of international cross-border disputes among business persons. One of the main advantages of arbitration is that arbitral awards are more easily recognized and enforced than judicial awards, mainly due to the New York Convention. Consequently, the process of recognition and enforcement of foreign arbitral awards has a pivotal role in facilitating international trade and investment by providing a mechanism that enables the parties to easily enforce awards rendered in arbitration proceedings. In the Republic of North Macedonia, as in many countries of the Western Balkans, arbitration is still in its early stages, and arbitration practice remains relatively low. As a result, arbitration-related issues pose challenges to national courts and all relevant stakeholders. While national courts have a pro-arbitration attitude, there were some instances in the past where the courts, and the legal system at large, have failed to adhere to international standards to the detriment of the parties involved in the arbitration process. The chapter aims to provide an analysis of the challenges that have arisen in the past concerning the recognition and enforcement of arbitral awards, through the analysis of the laws and procedures related to the process, as well as an analysis of relevant case law.

L. Kocev (✉)
Department of International Trade, Faculty of Economics - Skopje, Ss. Cyril and Methodius University in Skopje, Skopje, North Macedonia
e-mail: ljuben.kocev@eccf.ukim.edu.mk

M. Bungenberg et al. (eds.), *Alternative Dispute Resolution in the Western Balkans*, European Union and its Neighbours in a Globalized World 20,
https://doi.org/10.1007/978-3-031-76345-8_5

1 Introduction

Today, commercial arbitration is widely considered to be the preferred method for dispute resolution between business persons. Its prominence is even more increased in cross-border disputes. When compared to traditional litigation in front of state courts, arbitration offers numerous advantages, including, among others, its neutrality, confidentiality, speed, and arbitrators' expertise.[1]

Annual surveys conducted by the Queen Mary University, School of International Arbitration, on various topics and areas of international arbitration, repeatedly confirm arbitration as the preferred method for dispute resolution (with more than 90% of the respondents choosing arbitration over litigation), either on a stand-alone basis or in conjunction with other ADR methods.[2] In the surveys from 2006 through 2018, which focused primarily on commercial arbitration, respondents continuously pointed to the enforceability of arbitral awards either as the most valuable, or one of the most valuable characteristics of arbitration.[3]

The primary reason why arbitral awards are more easily recognized and enforced than judicial awards is the United Nations Convention on the Recognition and Enforcement of Foreign Arbitral Awards from 1958 (hereafter, the New York Convention).[4] The Convention sets forth the conditions for recognition and enforcement of foreign arbitral awards in a manner that provides only limited grounds for refusal. To this date, it is the most widely accepted international instrument in the arbitrationk sphere, with a total of 172 parties.[5]

Recognition and enforcement of an arbitral award is in principle a process that commences only after the award has been rendered by an arbitral tribunal or a sole arbitrator. As such, it can be viewed as a process detached from the arbitration proceedings. Yet, at the same time, it is an integral and essential element of the arbitration, since without recognition and enforcement of the arbitral award (particularly where the debtor fails to comply with the award voluntarily), the arbitration proceedings, and by extension the entire method of resolving disputes by arbitration, becomes obsolete.

While arbitration is an antipode to litigation, the process of recognition and enforcement of arbitral awards places the parties back within the judicial system from which they opted out in the first place by deciding to submit their dispute(s) to arbitration. In other words, there is a high likelihood that the parties that agreed to avoid a specific legal system or national court would be later required to return to the same legal system to enforce the arbitral award. Granted, the process of recognition

---

[1] Moses (2008), pp. 3–4.

[2] Queen Mary University of London, School of International Arbitration, Research Projects, available at: https://arbitration.qmul.ac.uk/research/.

[3] Ibid.

[4] United Nations Convention on the Recognition and Enforcement of Foreign Arbitral Awards (New York, 10 June 1958).

[5] Status of parties to the New York Convention, available at: https://treaties.un.org/pages/ViewDetails.aspx?src=TREATY&mtdsg_no=XXII-1&chapter=22&clang=_en.

and enforcement of an award is significantly different from the process of resolving the dispute. The powers of the courts in these proceedings are much narrower and extend only to limited control over the arbitral award. However, there is a possibility that the same flaws and weaknesses within that jurisdiction would resurface in the process of recognition and enforcement.

While in many countries in the world international arbitration is the default method for the resolving of cross-border commercial disputes, in the Republic of North Macedonia, the arbitration practice is still in its infancy. Although there has been an increased number of arbitration cases in the past decade, arbitration and ADR methods in general, are yet to reach wider acceptance in the business community. Nevertheless, as Macedonian companies become more engaged in international arbitration with their foreign partners, the number of cases where recognition and enforcement of foreign arbitral awards is sought in front of national courts is increasing. The aim of this chapter is to analyze the process of recognition and enforcement of foreign arbitral awards in the Republic of North Macedonia, by taking a look at the legal framework within the country and the procedure for recognition and enforcement, before focusing on some of the challenges that exist.

2 Laws Governing the Recognition and Enforcement of Foreign Arbitral Awards

The recognition and enforcement of foreign arbitral awards is governed by several acts: the Law on International Commercial Arbitration (hereafter, LICA),[6] the New York Convention, the Private International Law Act (hereafter, PILA)[7] and the Law on Enforcement (hereafter, LE).[8]

The LICA is a verbatim adoption of the UNCITRAL Model Law on International Commercial Arbitration. However, unlike the UNCITRAL Model Law, the LICA does not contain provisions that explicitly pertain to the process of recognition and enforcement of foreign arbitral awards. Rather, the LICA contains only one Article stipulating that the recognition and enforcement of foreign arbitral awards shall be carried out according to the provisions of the Convention signed in New York on 10 June 1958 on the recognition and enforcement of foreign arbitral awards.[9] The LICA also defines what constitutes a foreign arbitral award. According to Article 37 of the LICA, a "*foreign arbitral award shall be the arbitral award that was not made in*

[6] The Law on International Commercial Arbitration (Official Gazette of RN Macedonia, No. 39/2006).

[7] The Private International Law Act (Official Gazette of RN Macedonia, No. 32/20).

[8] The Law on Enforcement (Official Gazette of RN Macedonia, No. 72/16, 142/16, 233/18, 14/20 and 154/23).

[9] LICA, Article 37(3).

the Republic of Macedonia" and "*it shall be treated as an award pertaining to the state in which it was made.*"[10]

The Republic of North Macedonia is a contracting state of the New York Convention. The New York Convention was signed and ratified in 1982[11] by the former Socialist Federation of Yugoslavia (SFRY), of which North Macedonia was then part. After the dissolution of the SFRY, the Republic of North Macedonia notified its succession to the Convention on 10 Mar 1994.[12] Initially, the Republic of North Macedonia, as part of the SFRY, adopted the New York Convention with both a reciprocal and a commercial reservation.[13] With the enactment of the LICA, the reciprocal reservation was withdrawn, but the commercial reservation remains.[14]

Consequently, in terms of the conditions for recognition and enforcement, the domestic legislation does not create its own rules but rather opts for the method of indirect regulation with referral to relevant international legal sources. As a result, the conditions for the recognition and enforcement of foreign arbitral awards in North Macedonia are the conditions that are set within the New York Convention. Also, the grounds on which recognition and enforcement of a foreign arbitral award can be refused are those listed in Article V of the New York Convention.

Unlike the conditions for recognition and enforcement, Article III of the New York Convention envisages that the rules of procedure for recognition and enforcement are laid out in the national legislation.[15] In the Republic of North Macedonia, the procedures for recognition of a foreign arbitral award are contained in the PILA. According to Article 174 of the PILA, the rules regulating the recognition of foreign judgments will also apply to the recognition and enforcement of foreign arbitral awards.[16] According to Article 173 of the PILA, a foreign judgment, (or a foreign arbitral award), that has been recognized by national courts, "*shall be enforced in accordance with the laws of the Republic of North Macedonia governing the enforcement*".[17]

In line with this, the conditions for the recognition and enforcement of foreign arbitral awards in North Macedonia are a verbatim adoption of the conditions contained in the New York Convention, and as such, there is no need for their further elaboration. Their application by national courts will be elaborated in Sect. 4 below. The procedure for the recognition and enforcement, which is laid out in the PILA and LE, will be briefly elaborated in the following section.

---

[10] Ibid., Article 37(1) and Ar(2).

[11] Official Gazette of SFRY, International Agreements, No. 11/81.

[12] Status of parties to the New York Convention, available at: https://treaties.un.org/pages/ViewDetails.aspx?src=TREATY&mtdsg_no=XXII-1&chapter=22&clang=_en.

[13] Declarations and reservations on parties to the New York Convention, available at: http://www.newyorkconvention.org/list+of+contracting+states.

[14] Ibid.

[15] Ibid., Article III.

[16] PILA, Article 174.

[17] Ibid., Article 173.

3 Procedure for the Recognition and Enforcement of a Foreign Arbitral Award

While, in principle, the recognition and enforcement of foreign arbitral awards are used as inextricably linked, they are two separate processes and consequently can be regulated by different rules and procedures. Namely, if a party against whom an award is made can comply with it voluntarily, there may be no need for either recognition or enforcement of the award. Furthermore, an award can be recognized without being enforced, simply because there is no need for its enforcement. This is part of a defensive process in which a party may seek only recognition to prevent the initiation of court proceedings by the counterparty for the same dispute. Finally, parties may not only seek recognition but also enforcement of an award. In this case, recognition of the award is a necessary precondition for seeking enforcement. According to *Redfern* and *Hunter*, "*where a court is asked to enforce an award, it is asked not merely to recognize the legal force and effect of the award, but also to ensure that it is carried out, by using such legal sanctions as are available.*"[18] In principle, the purpose of the recognition of an award is to act as a shield whereas the purpose of the enforcement of an award is to act as a sword for the parties.[19] Below, I provide a broad overview of both procedures in North Macedonia.

3.1 Procedure for the Recognition of a Foreign Arbitral Award

As already noted, the procedure for recognition of an arbitral award is regulated in the PILA. This is a non-contentious procedure.[20] The procedure is initiated with an application for recognition in front of a competent court.[21] In North Macedonia, no single court has jurisdiction related to the process of recognition of a foreign arbitral award. Rather, according to the PILA, any court having jurisdiction on the subject matter shall also have territorial jurisdiction for the recognition.[22]

Article 159 of the PILA contains the formal conditions for the recognition of a judgment or an arbitral award, which are in principle identical to the conditions in the New York Convention. Nevertheless, this provision, and in general, similar provisions in the national jurisdictions related to the formal conditions for recognition and enforcement of arbitral awards, are superseded by the New York Convention,[23]

---

[18] Blackaby et al. (2016), p. 611.

[19] Lew et al. (2003), pp. 689–690.

[20] PILA, Article 172.

[21] Ibid., Article 165(1).

[22] Ibid., Article 166(2).

[23] Deskoski (2017), pp. 335–336.

particularly Article IV. According to Article IV, the applicant should at the time of the application, supply:

- The duly authenticated original award or a duly certified copy;
- The original arbitration agreement or a duly certified copy; and
- A certified translation of the award and/ or arbitral agreement made by an official or sworn translator or by a diplomatic or consular agent, if they are not in the official language of the country where recognition and enforcement are sought.[24]

After a proposal is submitted, a sole judge of the basic court will decide on the recognition of the award.[25] In this instance, the court has the duty to examine ex officio if there is:

- A lack of a certificate of legal force (no original award or a duly certified copy has been submitted by the applicant);
- Exclusive jurisdiction of the courts of the Republic of North Macedonia (non-arbitrability);
- Excessive jurisdiction of the arbitral tribunal;
- A final decision on the same matter between the same parties (*res judicata*, or if a proceeding is pending before the court of the Republic of North Macedonia, initiated earlier, on the same matter and between the same parties);
- A violation of public policy.[26]

If none of these obstacles exist, the sole judge will issue a procedural decision for the recognition of the award.[27] The decision for recognition of the award is then served to the respondent. If unsatisfied, the respondent has 30 days from the receipt of the award to object to the procedural decision.[28] The objection can be only on limited grounds that are listed in Article V of the New York Convention:

- Incapacity of the parties to conclude an arbitral agreement or invalidity of the arbitration agreement;
- Violation of due process;
- Differences not falling within the terms of, or decisions on matters beyond the scope of, the submission to arbitration;
- Improper composition of the arbitral authority;
- Award which is not yet binding, or is set aside, or suspended;
- Non-arbitrable disputes; and
- Violation of public policy.[29]

---

[24] New York Convention, Article IV.

[25] PILA, Article 166(1).

[26] PILA, Article 165(2), in connection with Articles 159 through 163.

[27] Ibid., Article 168(1).

[28] Ibid., Article 168(2).

[29] New York Convention, Article V.

As evident, there is some overlap between the grounds listed in the PILA and those listed in the New York Convention. Even more, according to the New York Convention, only non-arbitrability and violation of public policy are examined ex officio. In contrast, the challenging party must prove the existence of the other grounds. In this regard, the PILA envisages a broader obligation for national courts to examine grounds on which an award may be refused recognition ex officio.

If an objection is made, the same court, with a panel of three judges and after holding a hearing, decides whether the objection is justified.[30] The unsatisfied party has the right to appeal to a court of appeal against the decision of the basic court, within 15 days after its receipt.[31] The PILA does not contain any further rules relating to the procedure for the recognition of foreign arbitral awards, but rather stipulates that the provisions on non-contentious procedure shall apply.[32] According to Article 23 of the Law on Non-Contentious Procedure (hereafter, LNCP), the appeal has a suspensive effect on the procedural decision, unless otherwise provided within the law.[33] The court, however, can decide that the appeal would not have a suspensive effect if the delay might cause irreparable harm.[34] In practical terms, the decision cannot be formally recognized nor subjected to enforcement until the appellate court issues a decision that would be final and binding for the parties.

The Law on Civil Procedure (hereafter, LCP) regulates the procedure in front of appellate courts.[35] In 2010, the Law was amended and a deadline in which the appellate court has to decide upon an appeal was introduced. According to Article 335-a of the LCP, the appellate court should issue a decision on an appeal within three months at the latest, and in more complex cases within six months from the day the case is accepted for work.[36] However, although the courts are bound to decide within a fixed deadline, in practice, very often the courts take much longer to decide, in many cases taking up to more than a year. The appellate court is the final instance that decides on the recognition of the award since no extraordinary appeal or revision in front of the Supreme Court is allowed. Once all legal remedies have been exhausted the decision becomes final.

---

30 PILA, Article 169.

31 Ibid., Article 170.

32 Ibid., Article 172.

33 The Law on Non-Contentious Procedure (Official Gazette of RN Macedonia, No. 9/2008 and 77/18), Article 23(1).

34 Ibid., Article 23(2).

35 Law on Civil Procedure (Official Gazette of the Republic of Macedonia no. 79/05, 110/08, 83/09, 116/10 and 124/15).

36 Ibid., Article 335-a.

3.2 Procedure for the Enforcement of a Foreign Arbitral Award

While the process of enforcement of arbitral awards does not generate much attention in the literature, which is primarily focused on the process of recognition, it is undisputed that in many instances, it is an essential part of the process that enables the prevailing party to receive what it is entitled under an arbitral award. In light of this, and in line with recent developments and case law in North Macedonia on this issue, this section will briefly outline the process of the enforcement of arbitral awards before analyzing potential challenges.

After the decision becomes final, again the party against which the award is made can comply voluntarily. In this case, the recognition of the award is the last necessary legal step. However, in some instances, the debtor might still be reluctant to comply, even though the award has been successfully recognized and has become final and binding. In this case, the party seeking enforcement would have to undertake further legal steps.

As already noted, according to Article 173 of the PILA, foreign arbitral awards that have been recognized would be enforced under the laws of the Republic of North Macedonia governing the enforcement. In North Macedonia, the enforcement procedure is regulated in the Law on enforcement. According to Article 8 of the LE, the decision of a foreign court (or arbitral tribunal) can be enforced in the Republic of North Macedonia if the decision has been recognized under the national law or an international agreement ratified in accordance with the Constitution of the Republic of Macedonia.[37]

In the past, the enforcement of arbitral awards was conducted solely by national courts and there was no private enforcement mechanism. However, this system created major backlogs that resulted in years of delays. In 2006, this system was abandoned, and enforcement through private entities—bailiffs—was introduced. Bailiffs are appointed by the Ministry of Justice for the area of a district court.[38] The Ministry of Justice is also the supervisory body exercising control over the work of the bailiffs.[39] The new system significantly accelerated the enforcement of decisions that were previously stuck in the judicial system for many years. Regardless, there are drawbacks to the new system for enforcement as well. A clear indication of this is the fact that since 2006, the Constitutional Court has struck down provisions of the law on 7 occasions—4 times related to the Law on Enforcement from 2006,[40] and 3 times related to the latest Law on Enforcement that was enacted in 2016.[41]

[37] Law on Enforcement, Article 8.

[38] Ibid., Article 32(1).

[39] Ibid, Article 54.

[40] Amendments to the Law on Enforcement from 2006 by the National Assembly and by the Constitutional Court, available at: https://praksis.mk/Document/Index/?Id=166588&type=1.

[41] Amendments to the Law on Enforcement from 2006 by the National Assembly and by the Constitutional Court, available at: https://praksis.mk/Document/Index/?Id=174114&type=1.

4 Challenges to the Process of Recognition and Enforcement of Foreign Arbitral Awards

As outlined in the previous section, the legislation in North Macedonia related to the recognition and enforcement of foreign arbitral awards is in line with the most widely adopted international standards. The LICA is based on the UNCITRAL Model Law, the New York Convention is directly applicable to the recognition and enforcement, the current version of the PILA was adopted in 2020, and the LE envisages enforcement through private entities—bailiffs, which significantly speeds up the process when compared with the judicial enforcement that was used in the past. However, the adoption of the most widely recognized international standards is only one element of the process of recognition and enforcement of foreign arbitral awards. Another element that is equally important, if not more important, is the application of these standards by courts and all relevant institutions involved in the process.

As already noted, arbitration is still in its infancy in the Republic of North Macedonia, which is reflected in the low level of arbitration practice in the country, as well as the low level of familiarity of all relevant actors with the concept and mechanisms of arbitration. Unfamiliarity very often leads to distrust, doubtfulness, and skepticism. However, in the past decade arbitration, and ADR in general, have gained more attention primarily as a result of increased cross-border dealings of Macedonian companies. Similarly, judges are becoming more aware and familiar with arbitration because they need to deal with issues related to commercial arbitration on a more regular basis.

As a result, there has been a slow but positive shift in the attitude of national courts towards commercial arbitration. From the available cases published on the Judicial Portal of the Republic of North Macedonia, all cases where questions related to arbitration were raised date from the past decade, the vast majority being from 2010 onwards. Albeit primarily related to parties invoking arbitration agreements to contest the jurisdiction of national courts, in the majority of cases with an international element, courts have accepted the objection of the parties, rejected their jurisdiction, and referred the parties to arbitration.[42] There are also cases where national courts have denied the jurisdiction of arbitral tribunals. However, in the cases where the national courts found that the tribunals lacked jurisdiction, it was not because there was some sort of pathology with the arbitration agreement, but rather because they considered that either the parties had failed to raise a timely objection to the jurisdiction of an arbitral institution, thereby accepting the court jurisdiction,[43] or that the

---

[42] For example, Decision of the Basic Civil Court in Skopje, Case Number 61TC-1/18, from 25.09.2018; Decision of the Basic Court Veles, Case Number TC—108/11, from 08.06.2011; Decision of Appellate Court in Skopje, Case Number TCЖ-1217/17, from 22.03.2018; Decision of Appellate Court in Skopje, Case Number TCЖ—2526/10, from 30.06.2011; Decision of Appellate Court in Skopje, Case Number TCЖ—1030/13, from 16.09.2013; and Decision of Appellate Court in Shtip, Case Number TCЖ—91/13, from 19.02.2013.

[43] Decision of the Supreme Court, Case Number Рев1- 781/2010, from 26.05.2011.

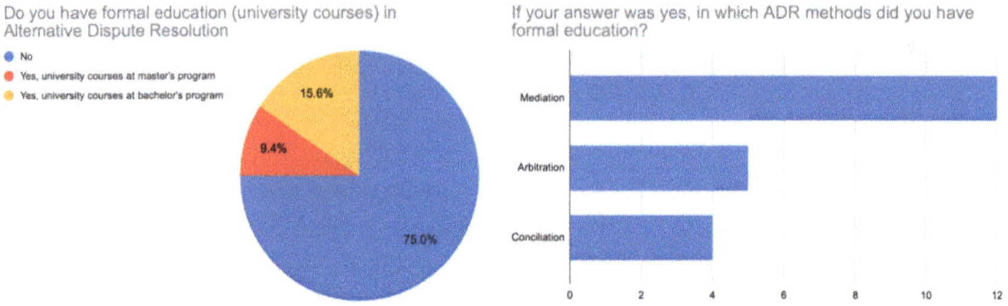

Fig. 1 Formal (University level) education of judges in ADR. *Source* Questionnaire distributed by the author

parties concluded an optional arbitration agreement, giving them the discretionary right to choose between arbitration or litigation.[44]

While, in general, courts and the legal system at large have had a positive attitude toward arbitration, there have been some controversial cases in the past years that gained public attention, which bring into question the efficiency of the entire process of recognition and enforcement of foreign arbitral awards in the country.

4.1 Challenges to the Process of Recognition of Foreign Arbitral Awards

Since the rules applicable to the procedure for the recognition of foreign arbitral awards are aligned with international standards, the challenges that arise in this step of the process pertain primarily to the way they are being applied by national courts. Some of these challenges can be attributed to the fact that arbitration has gained prominence in the country only recently, and as a result, many of the judges who have to deal with questions related to arbitration may not have sufficient experience, expertise, or specific knowledge in the area.

To obtain data related to various aspects of alternative dispute resolution (ADR) mechanisms, a questionnaire was distributed to relevant stakeholders which among others, included judges and courts. A total of 33 judges responded, and 3 of the largest basic courts (Skopje, Bitola, and Prilep) shared data related to cases that dealt with arbitration. While the sample of responses is not sufficient for a thorough and all-encompassing analysis, it can still provide insight into the current state of play.

In terms of formal education and informal training related to ADR, as evident in Fig. 1, 75% of the judges answered that they had no formal education in ADR, and from the ones that had formal education, the majority had education in mediation rather than arbitration.

[44] Decision of Appellate Court in Skopje, Case Number ТСЖ—982/16, from 14.10.2016; and Decision of Appellate Court in Skopje, Case Number ГЖ—6223/17 from 01.03.2018.

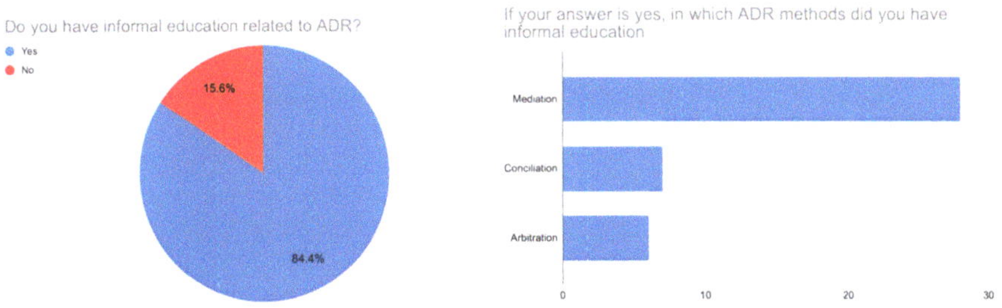

Fig. 2 Informal education of judges in ADR. *Source* Questionnaire distributed by the author

In terms of informal ADR education, as evident from Fig. 2, most judges answered positively, with only 15.6% responding that they never had informal education in ADR. However, here again, most judges answered that they had either courses or training in mediation, and only a few had informal education in arbitration.

Consequently, a potential challenge to the process for recognition and enforcement of arbitration, as well as for better cohesion between national courts and arbitral tribunals, is the fact that judges have very little education in ADR in general, and even less in arbitration.

In addition, judges have limited experience in deciding matters related to arbitration, regardless of whether it is related to challenges of arbitral agreements, arbitrators, arbitral awards, or granting interim measures. As already noted, while there are cases where courts had to decide on the validity of arbitration agreements, these were only a handful of publicly available cases. In terms of experience with cases where recognition of foreign arbitral awards was sought, from Table 1 it is evident that in the 5 years spanning from 2018 to 2022, the courts had a very limited number of cases.

It is noteworthy that in all cases there was an objection to the procedural decision for recognition. However, the objection was rejected by the court in all cases. While the questionnaire was only filled by 3 basic courts (Skopje, Bitola, and Prilep) out of the 14 courts that have jurisdiction for this subject matter, it must be noted that

Table 1 Statistics related to cases for recognition of foreign arbitral awards (2018–2022)

Year	Number of cases where recognition of foreign arbitral award was saught	Number of cases where there was an objection by the counterparty to the decision for recognition and enforcement	Number of cases where the objection was rejected	Number of cases where the objection was accepted
2022	4	4	4	0
2021	5	5	5	0
2020	6	6	6	0
2019	3	3	3	0
2018	3	3	3	0

Source Questionnaire distributed by the author

Table 2 Statistics related to the number of cases for recognition of foreign arbitral and judicial awards (2018–2022)

Year	Number of cases where recognition of a foreign arbitral award was sought	Number of cases where recognition of a foreign judicial award was sought
2022	4	~164
2021	5	~142
2020	6	~131
2019	3	~182
2018	3	~158
Total	21	~777

Source Questionnaire distributed by the author

these are some of the courts with the highest number of cases, particularly the Basic Civil Court in Skopje.

Another indicator that reflects the experience of national courts in matters related to arbitration is the comparison of the number of cases where recognition of foreign arbitral awards was sought and the number of cases where recognition of foreign judicial awards was sought. As evident from Table 2, the number of cases where recognition of judicial awards was sought in the last 5 years is almost 40 times higher than the number of cases for recognition of arbitral awards.

However, this difference should not have an impact in terms of the procedure for recognition, since, as already noted, the procedure for the recognition of foreign arbitral awards is identical to the procedure for the recognition of foreign judicial awards. Much more challenging is the application and interpretation of the conditions for the recognition and enforcement of foreign arbitral awards, particularly the conditions under which recognition of foreign arbitral awards can be rejected, which are laid out in Article V of the New York Convention.

Although a significant amount of scholarly guidance and commentary exist about each of the grounds listed in Article V,[45] their application still poses a challenge even in more developed jurisdictions. While the grounds listed in Article V(1) of the New York Convention have limited scope, the grounds listed in Article V(2)—non-arbitrability and especially the violation of public policy—have been problematic. The public policy objection is very often a "catch-all" objection that could be used by the unsatisfied parties to seek a review of the award on the merits.[46]

From the questionnaire that was distributed to basic courts, all of them pointed out that in cases where recognition of a foreign arbitral award was sought, the violation of public policy has been the most often used objection.[47] This is also in line with the practice in many other jurisdictions. A paper in which analysis was conducted

[45] See Kronke et al. (eds) (2010); Frischknecht et al. (2018), Born (2015).

[46] Sasson (2022a, b).

[47] Questionnaire for the analysis of the level of familiarity of the professional public in the Republic of North Macedonia with the methods for alternative dispute resolution, distributed to basic civil courts (2023).

on 1,000 cases from more than 30 jurisdictions, contained in the Kluwer Arbitration database, found that objections based on public policy have been raised in 44% of recognition and enforcement proceedings and in 38% of setting aside proceedings.[48]

However, while the public policy objection can be used by parties objecting recognition to seek broad protection, in principle there is consensus in the literature and practice that the public policy objection should be interpreted narrowly.[49] Most authors make a distinction between national, international, and transnational public policy.[50] There is also agreement that international public policy is much narrower in scope, and that at least in international arbitration, it should prevail over national public policy.[51] However, authors such as *Moses* argue that although there is a difference in their scope, both national and international policy are defined at the national level.[52] *Moses* argues that transnational policy is truly international since it is "*not the public policy of any one state, but rather involves public policy that transcends state boundaries.*" According to her, "*such public policy is defined as arising out of an international consensus regarding universal standards as to norms of conduct that are generally recognized and agreed upon as unacceptable in most civilized countries, such as slavery, bribery, piracy, murder, terrorism, and corruption*".[53]

In the analysis of the cases available in the Kluwer Arbitration database, *Sasson*, when analyzing national courts' decisions regarding the recognition and enforcement of foreign arbitral awards, makes a distinction between substantive and procedural public policy. Examples of the violation of the former encompass matters of national sovereignty, duress, protection of minors, statute of limitations, fraud, corruption, damages, penalty, violations of applicable law, the invalidity of the arbitration agreement, and *res judicata*.[54] Examples of the latter encompass lacking impartiality or due process, ineffective service of process, and lack of reasoning in the award.[55] It is noteworthy that some of these violations are listed as separate grounds in Article V of the New York Convention, although as evident, courts consider them to fall within the notion of public policy as well.

An important aspect of *Sasson*'s paper, aside from the number of cases where the public policy objection was raised, is the success that these objections had. According to the analysis of the cases where recognition of foreign arbitral awards was sought, and where the public policy objection was raised, the success rating was 19%. In comparison, if we compare this with the responses that were received from the questionnaires distributed to basic civil courts in North Macedonia, we can conclude that

---

48 Sasson (2022a, b), p. 411.

49 See UNCITRAL Secretariat (2016) pp. 240–241; Parsons & Whittemore Overseas v. Société Générale de L'Industrie du Papier (RAKTA), Court of Appeals, Second Circuit, United States of America, 508 F.2d 969, 974 (1974).

50 See Moses (2018); Lalive (1987), pp. 258–318; Renner (2009) pp. 533–555; Zekos (2016) p. 49.

51 Ibid.

52 Moses (2018).

53 Ibid.

54 Sasson (2022a, b), pp. 414–422.

55 Ibid, pp. 422–425.

the percentage of success of the public policy objection is lower, since as indicated in Table 1, in all cases where objections were raised, they were rejected by the court. However, one court indicated that on one occasion, it rejected the application for recognition and enforcement of foreign arbitral award ex officio. No clear information on whether the application was rejected due to non-arbitrability of the dispute or violation of public policy was provided.

Regardless of the statistics, there is one particular case, that attracted a lot of attention, that is seemingly not reflected in the courts' responses. A Macedonian and a Polish company entered into a consortia agreement to bid on a tender for the construction of a highway segment in Poland. The agreement contained an ICC arbitration clause. The consortium won the tender, however, due to violations of the terms of the tender, the investor (The General Directorate for National Roads and Motorways (GDDKiA)) sought to activate the bank guarantees that were provided by both companies as part of the tender requirements. Accordingly, GDDKiA initiated court proceedings seeking payment against the Macedonian company in Poland, but at the same time, the Macedonian company initiated court proceedings in front of a domestic court in North Macedonia, seeking declaratory relief, along with an interim measure that would freeze the bank guarantee. Both parties prevailed in front of their national courts, where they initiated proceedings, but GDDKiA was effectively prevented from collecting the bank guarantee since it was issued by a Macedonian bank. Unable to activate the bank guarantee for the Macedonian company, the investor collected the entire amount from the Polish company.[56]

As a result, the Polish company initiated arbitration proceedings under the consortia agreement seeking redress. The arbitral award was rendered in 2017, granting the claim of the Polish company.[57] In 2020, the company sought to recognize and enforce the arbitral award in front of the Macedonian courts.

After the request was submitted, a sole judge in the Basic Civil Court in Skopje first recognized the arbitral award.[58] Upon objection by the Macedonian company, the same court, in a panel of three judges, annulled the procedural decision that granted the request for recognition.[59] According to the court, the recognition of the arbitral award would violate the country's public policy. The court considered that the award dealt with a question that is *res judicata* and as such it could not be recognized as it would jeopardize the principle of legal certainty. While *res judicata* is undoubtedly a ground for refusal of recognition of an arbitral award, it is interesting how the court interpreted it. Namely, the Court deemed that, since the investor GDDKiA had already sought to activate the bank guarantee of the Macedonian company in the past, and since the court in Skopje already ruled that the Macedonian company is

[56] The judicial awards from both cases are unpublished and unavailable to the author.

[57] The arbitral award is unpublished and unavailable to the author.

[58] Decision of the Basic Civil Court in Skopje, Case Number 2ВПП 22/20, from 26.05.2020 (unpublished).

[59] Decision of the Basic Civil Court in Skopje, Case Number 3ПСО1 22/20, from 09.09.2020 (unpublished).

not liable towards the investor, the Macedonian company is shielded from further liability in all matters related to the tender agreement.

Several important aspects arise from the court's decision:

- Firstly, while *res judicata* would fall even under the narrowest definition of public policy, from an academic point of view, it is noteworthy that when interpreting and defining public policy, the court focused solely on national public policy without referencing international or transnational public policy.
- Secondly, although the court recognizes that under Article V it does not have the power to examine the arbitral award on the merits of the case, in its substantiation of the decision the court delves into the analysis of the legal relationship of the parties, de facto making a review on the merits of the case. Although a public policy defense would most likely require analysis of the merits of the arbitral award, here, the court pushed itself into analyzing the decision of the arbitral tribunal on the merits, primarily due to the way it defined *res judicata*.
- Thirdly, and most importantly, the court's interpretation of the notion of *res judicata* is problematic. According to the PILA, *res judicata* is defined as a final decision rendered *for the same matter* and *between the same parties*.[60] Regardless, the court adopts a very wide definition of *res judicata* by deciding that, firstly, a decision in which two different parties participated would also have a claim precluding effect on a non-participating party, and secondly, it considered that two different claims from different contract to be the same legal matter. Although two different contracts can be for the same legal matter, in the case at hand the dispute between the investor (GDDKiA) and the Macedonian company concerned a violation of the tender agreement, whereas the dispute between the Macedonian and the Polish company concerned the division of profits and losses from the consortia agreement.
- Finally, due to its approach, the court was also compelled in its rationale to heavily rely on the decision of the Macedonian court in the case between the Macedonian company and the Polish investor (GDDKiA). The fact that there were parallel court proceedings resulting in conflicting decisions favoring one decision over the other is also problematic. However, while the court acknowledged that a conflicting decision had been issued by a Polish court, it convincingly disregarded this decision on the basis that it was not yet final and binding upon the parties.

While there are several red flags throughout the decision, unfortunately, the Basic Civil Court in Skopje is the sole instance in which the request for recognition was decided due to certain omissions on the side of the Polish company and its legal representatives. While the decision was appealed, the appeal was rejected as untimely,[61] preventing further legal analysis and making it final and binding on the parties. Although the main function of the process of recognition of arbitral awards is for the courts to have some control over the arbitral process, it is certainly not for the courts to have the possibility to decide the case on the merits anew, either through very

[60] PILA, Article 162(1).

[61] Decision of the Appellate Court in Skopje, Case Number ТСЖ-1175/20, from 21.01.2021.

flexible interpretations or interpretations of transnational concepts primarily through the lenses of national law.

4.2 Challenges to the Process of Enforcement of Foreign Arbitral Awards

The enforcement of an arbitral award that has been recognized by a state court is generally not a topic that is much discussed in arbitration literature. Nevertheless, it becomes essential if the losing party fails to comply voluntarily. It is very often pointed out that if an arbitral award is not recognized in the country where the debtor has assets, it will be just a dead letter. However, in the absence of a functional system for enforcement, the recognized award would be just a dead letter as well.

An ongoing case in front of several national courts and institutions has sparked a lot of controversies and has brought into question the functioning of the process for the enforcement of arbitral awards. An Austrian company and a Macedonian company concluded a contract for cooperation and exclusive distribution of agricultural products. The contract contained an arbitration clause in favor of the Vienna International Arbitration Centre (VIAC). A dispute between the parties arose, and the parties submitted it to VIAC. The decision issued in January 2023 was then submitted by the Austrian company for recognition to Macedonian courts. The defendant objected arguing a violation of public policy, although the reasoning was that the contract violated national competition law, and these disputes fall within the exclusive jurisdiction of the national competition authority (which is a non-arbitrability objection).[62] Regardless, the decision was confirmed in the second instance by the Basic Civil Court in Skopje upon objection, and finally by the Appellate Court in Skopje upon Appeal.[63]

What seemed like an efficient procedure for the recognition and enforcement of a foreign arbitral award turned into a dispute that gained wide media attention, and a dispute that is yet to be finally resolved. Accordingly, during the arbitration proceedings and later during the process of recognition of the arbitral award, the Austrian company sought the freezing of the assets of the Macedonian company in fear of alienation of the property. Some of the requests for interim measures were rejected, while others were initially granted by the basic courts but later revoked by the Appellate Court in Skopje. Additionally, the Macedonian company became

[62] Decision of the Basic Civil Court in Skopje, Case Number IBПП 48/23, from 9.3.2023, and subsequently, Decision of the Basic Civil Court in Skopje, Case Number III ПСО1-1/23, from 12.7.2023 and Decision of the Appellate Court in Skopje, Case Number ТСЖ-1266/23, from 3.10.2023.

[63] Ibid.

insolvent,[64] which caused additional complications in terms of jurisdiction and available legal measures at disposal. From the available information, it seems very likely that the Macedonian company used the period leading to the issuance of the arbitral award, as well as the period in which recognition of the award was sought, to transfer most of its assets to another Macedonian company. What is even more problematic is that the company to which the assets were transferred is owned by the wife of the owner of the first company. On top of that, it was reported in the news that the wife was a close relative of the former prime minister of the country.[65]

The controversy surrounding the case stirred up the public and even resulted in an open letter by the Austrian ambassador in the country in which he accused the two Macedonian companies of capturing the judiciary and officers of the law, calling for the removal of all incompetent and biased judges and prosecutors in these cases.[66] This letter attracted even more attention, resulting in mixed responses from state officials, institutions, and involved politicians.[67] Shortly after, the Basic Public Prosecutor's Offices in Gevgelija and Skopje, as well as the Higher Public Prosecutor's Office in Skopje, took three separate proceedings, following criminal charges filed by the Austrian company, aimed against notaries, bailiffs, as well as employees of the Real Estate Cadastre Agency.[68] The cases are still ongoing, and to this date, no final decision has been made.

This case is an example of the fragile state in which the legal system of the country is. It shows that even where the process of recognition of foreign arbitral awards functions without interruptions, there are ways through which effective enforcement of the award can be denied. While the current case gained traction and publicity which seems to have put pressure on the institutions to prevent further abuses, it should not be necessary for the whole expert pubic and diplomatic pressure to be involved for a party to be able to exercise its legal rights. In expectations of the aftermath,

---

[64] Status of the company obtained from the Central Registry of the Republic of North Macedonia, available at: https://www.crm.com.mk/mk/otvoreni-podatotsi/osnoven-profil-na-registriran-subjekt?s=ДЕНА%25Продукт&embs=6238432.

[65] Article on SeeNews, 29/6/2023, available at: https://seenews.com/news/amma-seeking-45-mln-euro-in-damages-from-n-macedonias-dena-embassy-827155.

[66] Article on the letter from the Austrian Ambassador, Radio Free Europe/ Radio Liberty, 28/6/2023, available at: https://www.slobodnaevropa.mk/a/32478539.html.

[67] Article on the response from the President of the country, Media Information Agency, 28/6/2023, available at: https://mia.mk/en/story/pendarovski-legitimate-duty-of-ambassadors-to-protect-interests-of-their-countries-private-businesses; Article on the response from the president of the Notary Chamber of North Macedonia, Media Information Agency, 28/6/2023, available at: https://mia.mk/en/story/notary-chamber-dismisses-reactions-against-notaries-in-austrian-embassys-open-letter; Article on the Response from the former prime minister, 360 degrees, 27/6/2024, available at: https://360stepeni.mk/zaev-do-avstriskiot-ambasador-ushte-edno-spomenuvane-na-moeto-ime-vo-negativna-konotatsija-i-ke-se-vidime-na-sud/.

[68] Article on the actions taken by the Public Prosecutor's Office, Media Information Agency, 28/6/2023, available at: https://mia.mk/en/story/prosecutors-office-takes-proceedings-on-three-criminal-charges-filed-by-austrian-company-amma.

hope remains that the Austrian company will be able to enforce the arbitral award—otherwise it would prove to be just a dead letter, further eroding the already fragile arbitration practice in the country.

5 Conclusion

This chapter provided an analysis of the current challenges connected with the recognition and enforcement of foreign arbitral awards in the Republic of North Macedonia. On a global scale, commercial arbitration has already become a preferred method for dispute resolution, and even more in cross-border disputes. However, the arbitration practice in North Macedonia is still in its infancy and is yet to reach acceptance and recognition by all relevant stakeholders.

In terms of recognition and enforcement of foreign arbitral awards, the legislation in the country is on par with the most current international standards. The New York Convention has been ratified and is directly applicable to these proceedings. All other relevant acts applicable to the procedure for the recognition and enforcement of foreign arbitral awards, such as the LICA, the PILA, the LCP, the LNCP, and the LE do not contain limitations that would prevent parties seeking enforcement by imposing limitations of procedural or substantive character.

However, the low level of education and familiarity of judges, and other practitioners with arbitration and ADR in general is a limiting factor. This, coupled with the low level of arbitration practice in the country, leads to potential problems when judges are faced with arbitration-related issues. In these cases, judges tend to rely primarily on national legislation and concepts embedded in national law, which may differ from concepts that are well-established in the international arbitration practice. Consequently, an effort should be made to increase the awareness and knowledge of all relevant stakeholders of arbitration and ADR in general.

North Macedonia is not one of the countries that are considered to have a hostile attitude towards arbitration, where arbitral awards are often annulled or denied recognition and enforcement. National courts have generally a positive outlook on arbitration and have decided in favour of arbitration in cases where arbitration agreements have been challenged as well as in procedures for recognition and enforcement of foreign arbitral awards. However, several cases in the past have harmed the country's perception as an arbitration-friendly jurisdiction. Since arbitration is still in its infancy in the country, it is imperative that a pro-arbitration attitude is established from the outset.

References

Blackaby N, Partasides C, Redfern A, Hunter M (2016) Redfern and hunter on international arbitration, 6th edn. Oxford University Press, Oxford

Born GB (2015) International arbitration: cases and materials, 2nd edn. Kluwer Law International, Alphen aan den Rijn

Deskoski T (2017) International arbitration law. Megjunarodno Arbitrazno Pravo, Faculty of Law "Iustinianus Primus"

Frischknecht AA, Lahlou Y et al. (2018) Enforcement of foreign arbitral awards and judgments in New York. Kluwer Law International, Alphen aan den Rijn

Kronke H, Nacimiento P et al (eds) (2010) Recognition and enforcement of foreign arbitral awards: a global commentary on the New York convention. Kluwer Law International, Alphen aan den Rijn

Lalive P (1987) Transnational (or truly international) public policy and international arbitration. In: Sanders P (ed) Comparative arbitration practice and public policy in arbitration: 8th international arbitration congress, pp 258–318

Lew JDM, Mistelis LA, Kroll SM (2003) Comparative international commercial arbitration. Kluwer Law International, Alphen aan den Rijn

Moses M (2008) The principles and practice of international commercial arbitration. Cambridge University Press, Cambridge

Moses M (2018) Public policy: national, international and transnational. Kluwer arbitration blog. http://arbitrationblog.kluwerarbitration.com/2018/11/12/public-policy-national-international-and-transnational/.

Renner M (2009) Towards a hierarchy of norms in transnational law? J Int Arbitr 26(4):533–555

Sasson M (2022a) Public policy in international commercial arbitration. J Int Arbitr 39(3):411–432

Sasson M (2022b) Public policy: is this catch-all provision relevant to the legitimacy of international commercial arbitration? Kluwer Arbitration Blog. https://arbitrationblog.kluwerarbitration.com/2022/06/18/public-policy-is-this-catch-all-provision-relevant-to-the-legitimacy-of-international-commercial-arbitration/

UNCITRAL Secretariat (2016) Guide on the convention on the recognition and enforcement of foreign arbitral awards, New York, 1958

Zekos G (2016) Arbitrability and regulation (EU) 1215/2012. Disput Resolut J 70(4):47–63

Annulment of Arbitral Awards Rendered in Albania: Trends and Challenges

Flutura Kola Tafaj and Silvana Çinari

Abstract The law no. 52/2023 "On Arbitration in the Republic of Albania", which regulates domestic and international arbitration seated in Albania, entered into force in 2023, after decades of legal vacuum. The adoption of this law is a very welcome positive step. Firstly, it solves all the problems stemming from the lack of an arbitration law in Albania. Secondly, it comes at a time when the Albanian courts' backlog is huge, mainly due to judicial reforms. Hence, in these times, the use of alternative dispute resolution mechanisms, including arbitration, assumes particular importance for the business community. One of the main problems solved with the entry into force of the arbitration law is the possibility of challenging arbitral awards, which was previously impossible for domestic and international arbitration awards rendered in Albania, due to the lack of an arbitration law. This chapter aims to focus precisely on the novelties brought by the new arbitration law regarding the annulment of arbitral awards rendered in Albania, whether in domestic or international arbitration. Also, although drafted based on the UNCITRAL Model Law, the Albanian arbitration law is not a verbatim adoption. Several differences exist in the provisions regulating the annulment of arbitral awards. For this reason, this chapter will also focus on the challenges related to the implementation of the provisions on the annulment of arbitral awards in Albania. The aims of this chapter are achieved following an analytical and comparative approach.

F. K. Tafaj (✉) · S. Çinari
Civil Law Department, Faculty of Law, University of Tirana, Tirana, Albania
e-mail: flutura.tafaj@fdut.edu.al

S. Çinari
e-mail: silvana.cinari@fdut.edu.al

M. Bungenberg et al. (eds.), *Alternative Dispute Resolution in the Western Balkans*, European Union and its Neighbours in a Globalized World 20,
https://doi.org/10.1007/978-3-031-76345-8_6

1 Introduction

After the 1990s, changes in Albania's political system were also accompanied by legal changes. The first legal act that brought changes in the field of arbitration was Decree no. 682, dated 4/11/1993,[1] which dissolved State arbitration and determined that monetary disputes between enterprises and State institutions would be settled by the district court, while monetary disputes, in which one of the parties is a foreign legal or natural person, would be settled by the district court or by voluntary arbitration when in the contract or the parties themselves have accepted the settlement by arbitration, regulated respectively by the Albanian legislation or by the relevant international conventions. However, private (voluntary) arbitration would be unregulated until the adoption of Law no. 8116, dated 29/3/1996 "Civil Procedure Code" (CCP). The CCP contained a separate chapter on arbitration, which until 2001 regulated both domestic and international arbitration. In 2001, the provisions governing international arbitration were repealed and replaced by an article providing that international arbitration shall be governed by a special law. In 2013, with the Law no. 122/2013 and Law no. 160/2013, the provisions regulating domestic arbitration in Albania were also repealed. The intention was that arbitration would be regulated by a special law. However, only in 2023 was it possible to adopt a law on arbitration (hereinafter referred to as the Arbitration Law or Law no. 52/2023), which regulates domestic and international arbitration with the place of arbitration in Albania and was drafted based on the UNCITRAL Model Law on International Commercial Arbitration (Model Law).

The lack of national legislation governing arbitration was problematic, especially regarding the exercise of the right to ask for the annulment of domestic and international arbitral awards given in Albania. Although since 2000, Albania has ratified the European Convention on International Commercial Arbitration (hereinafter referred to as the Geneva Convention) with Law no. 8687, dated 9/11/2000, and the Convention on the Recognition and Enforcement of Foreign Arbitral Awards (hereinafter referred to as the New York Convention or NYC) with Law no. 8688, dated 9/11/2000, these legal instruments did not provide a solution to the problem of the impossibility of setting aside arbitral awards rendered in Albania.

Whether the losing party in an arbitration proceeding can challenge an arbitral award depends on several factors. Do the arbitration rules chosen by the parties provide for an internal challenge procedure? Does the law of the country where the arbitration took place provide for the possibility of challenging the arbitral award? If so, within what period and on which grounds can the arbitral award be challenged? Have the parties waived their right to challenge the award and if so, is this waiver valid? For most of the questions and to assess whether an arbitral award can be challenged, the existence of the law of the seat of arbitration is a necessity.

The purpose of this chapter is precisely the analysis of the provisions of the new Albanian Arbitration Law on the annulment of domestic and international arbitral

[1] More on the history of arbitration law in Albania see: Kola Tafaj (2022), pp. 1–23; Kola Tafaj and Çinari (2019), pp. 23–32.

awards given in Albania. The analysis aims to highlight the novelties of the new Arbitration Law no. 52/2023 provisions related to the annulment of arbitral awards, problems and challenges related to their application, as well as to provide suggestions on possible solutions, following analytical and comparative research methods. To achieve these goals, the chapter first deals with procedural aspects of the annulment of arbitral awards. The other sections are dedicated to the grounds for annulling arbitral awards in Albania and the consequences of annulment.

2 Annulment of Arbitral Awards Before the Albanian Courts: Procedural Aspects

The new Albanian Arbitration Law brought novelties regarding the possibility of applying for the annulment of arbitral awards rendered in Albania and the annulment procedure. The lack of legal provisions regulating international arbitration in Albania for over two decades made it impossible for the parties to request the annulment of arbitral awards. Although Albania has ratified the Geneva Convention, it does not regulate the annulment of arbitral awards, despite Article IX, which is entitled "Setting aside of the arbitral award". Article IX only limits the effects of the annulment of the award in one Contracting State to its enforcement in another Contracting State.[2] Consequently, in the absence of the internal legal framework that would determine the grounds and the procedure for the annulment of international arbitral awards in Albania, the latter could only proceed with the recognition and enforcement, denying the losing party the right to request its annulment.[3]

The situation before the entry into force of the new Arbitration Law in Albania was somehow different concerning the possibility of challenging a domestic arbitral award in Albania. In 2013, Article 30 of Law no. 122/2013 dated 19/4/2013 "On some additions and changes to the Law no. 8116, dated 29/3/1996 'On the Civil Procedure Code of the Republic of Albania'" provided in Article 30 that Title IV of the Second Part (Articles 400–44 regulating arbitration) was repealed. However, according to the transitional provision of this law, specifically Article 49 paragraph 2, it was provided that Article 30 (the repealing provision) enters into force with the approval of the new law on arbitration. Meanwhile, a few months later, Law no. 160/2013 amended Article 49 (the transitional provision) of Law no. 122/2013, which among others, did not provide anything more for paragraph 2, and consequently, Article 30 of Law 122/2013 entered into force, thus repealing the provisions on domestic arbitration. Experts in the field think that the amendment of Article 49 of Law no. 122/2013, by

[2] Hascher (2011), p. 535.

[3] VEGA LLC (Albania) v. The Ministry of Transport and Infrastructure of the Republic of Albania & Port of Durrës Authority (Albania)—ICC Rules (2015); Balkan Resources Inc (BRC) v. Albanian Sinomine Resource CO (ASM) & Sinomine Resource Group Company (SRC) (2012); Case no. 12016/ACS/FM "BE-HA-SE" v. General Directorate of Roads & The Ministry of Transport and Infrastructure of the Republic of Albania (ICC) (1996); Case no. 13205-FM "ITALSTRADE" SPA v. Republic of Albania (ICC).

not including paragraph 2, was a mere mistake and not a deliberate choice.[4] However, the jurisprudence of the High Court of Albania has maintained that the provisions of the Civil Procedure Code regulating domestic arbitration continued to be in force until a new arbitration law entered into force.[5]

With the entry into force of the new Arbitration Law in Albania in 2023, the intricate situation concerning the annulment of domestic arbitral awards and the impossibility of challenging international arbitration awards rendered in Albania were resolved. The new Arbitration Law applies to domestic and international arbitration seated in Albania. Hence, it provides unified rules of procedure and grounds for the annulment of arbitral awards rendered in domestic and international arbitration in Albania. The new Arbitration Law in Albania, including the provisions concerning the annulment of arbitral awards, was drafted based on the UNCITRAL Model Law.[6] Nevertheless, the Albanian Arbitration Law is not a verbatim adoption of the Model Law. The Albanian Arbitration Law enshrines the core principles of the Model Law, such as the presumptive validity of arbitral awards, providing for their finality and enforceability as of the moment they are made,[7] and being subject only to a request for annulment based on limited grounds,[8] which are almost identical to the grounds stipulated in the Model Law. However, some differences are also noticed, such as a lack of regulation on whether the grounds of annulment are discretionary[9] or on the burden of proof, which will be elaborated below.

2.1 *The Competent Court*

Law no. 52/2023 provides that the request for annulment of the arbitral award is presented to the court of appeal with general jurisdiction, in whose jurisdiction is the

[4] Kola Tafaj and Vokshi (2018), p. 326, note 723; Dano (2021).

[5] Albanian High Court Decision, no. 467, dated September 18, 2014, p. 4; Albanian High Court Decision, no. 00-2018-1229, dated 27 December 2018, paras. 10–11. In both decisions, the High Court does not analyze the amendment made to Art. 49 with the Law no. 160/2013. In the latter, however, the High Court made a note holding that "here [when providing that Article 30 (the repealing provision) enters into force with the approval of the new law on arbitration] the legislator has made a material error, as the law cannot be repealed without the subsequent law coming into force. This means that the proper constitutional term should be "upon entry into force" and not "upon approval", as from the point of view of the constitutional legislative process these two moments present different legal consequences" (p. 6, note 1).

[6] See: https://uncitral.un.org/en/texts/arbitration/modellaw/commercial_arbitration/status; See also: Explanatory report of the Law "On Arbitration in the Republic of Albania", available at: https://konsultimipublik.gov.al/Konsultime/Detaje/292.

[7] Law "On Arbitration in the Republic of Albania" no. 52/2023, Article 39(4) & Article 45(3).

[8] Ibid., Article 44.

[9] Article 34(2) of the Model Law provides that "an award may be set aside …", while in the Albanian Arbitration Law the word "may" is not used. Instead, it provides that "the request for annulment of an arbitral award is submitted with the appeal court of general jurisdiction in the seat of arbitration, based on the following grounds …".

place of arbitration.[10] The provisions of the Code of Civil Procedure, which regulated domestic arbitration, did not provide for the forum where the request for annulment of the award was submitted, bringing confusion in practice. In certain cases, the interested parties submitted the request to the arbitration institution, missing the legal time limit for exercising the right to challenge the award. The new law expressly provides that the request for annulment of the arbitral award is submitted to the appellate court of the place of arbitration. Given that with the new judicial map approved by the decision of the Council of Ministers in July 2022, there is only one court of appeal of general jurisdiction in Albania, which is located in Tirana, the place of arbitration within the Republic of Albania remains irrelevant concerning the determination of the competent appellate court that decides on the annulment of arbitral awards.

2.2 *Time Limit for Submission of a Request for Annulment of an Arbitral Award*

Similarly to the Model Law, which in Article 34(3) provides for a 3-month time limit for submitting a request for annulment of an arbitral award, according to Article 44(2) of Law no. 52/2023, the time limit for submitting such a request is 90 days from the day of notification of the arbitral award to the parties. If one of the parties requested the correction of errors, interpretation, or completion of the award, the term begins from the date of notification of the arbitral tribunal decision on such requests.

2.3 *Rules for Examining the Request for Annulment of Arbitral Awards*

According to Article 45 of the Albanian Arbitration Law, the appellate court examines the request for annulment of the award according to the rules of the Code of Civil Procedure for examining cases in appeal. The appeal must be considered within 30 days from its filing in the court of appeal. The court first verifies whether the request meets the formal criteria. If the request for annulment has formal defects, the court of appeals assigns the applicant a reasonable time for their rectification. If the applicant does not rectify the defects within the assigned time limit, the appellate court dismisses the request. If the request for annulment of the award meets the formal criteria for its submission or is rectified within the assigned time limit, the court of appeal schedules a hearing.

The submission of the request for annulment does not suspend the enforcement of the arbitral award. Exceptionally, the court, at the request of the party, may suspend

[10] Law "On Arbitration in the Republic of Albania" no. 52/2023, Article 44.

the enforcement when it assesses that there is a risk of irreparable damage caused to the party.

2.4 *Burden of Proof on the Grounds for Annulment of Arbitral Awards and the Court's Power to Assess the Grounds Ex Officio*

The Model Law (Article 34), the arbitration laws of various countries based on the Model Law[11] or the New York Convention (Article V, grounds for refusal of recognition), divide the grounds for the annulment of arbitral awards into grounds for which the party requesting the annulment must present evidence and grounds which the court finds ex officio. In contrast, the Albanian Arbitration Law does not make such a division, thus not determining the burden of proof on the grounds for annulment of arbitral awards and not determining whether the court has the power to assess any of the grounds ex officio.

Specifically, Article 44 of the Arbitration Law no. 52/2023 provides that: "… The request for annulment of an arbitral award is submitted with the appeal court of general jurisdiction in the seat of arbitration, based on the following grounds: (a) … (b) … (c) … (ç) … (d) … (dh) … (e) …". Paragraphs (dh) and (e) are equivalent to Article 34(2)(b) of the Model Law, while paragraphs (a), (b), (c), (ç), and (d) are equivalent to Article 34(1) of the Model Law.

Although Article 44 does not determine the burden of proof, referring to the general principle on the burden of proof, that the one who makes the claim should prove it, it can be concluded that the party who requests the annulment of the award should prove the grounds. What remains unclear is whether the court should consider the grounds provided for in Article 44 only if they are claimed by the party requesting annulment or ex officio. The literal interpretation of Article 44 implies that the court can verify the grounds for annulment of arbitral awards only if they are claimed by the parties. Such an interpretation would be unacceptable, given the protection by the judicial system of those legal norms and principles of due process that cannot be waived by agreement of the parties.

An award that conflicts with the norms of public policy, or with other mandatory norms of the law that cannot be waived by agreement of the parties, must also be reviewed ex officio by the court. Both the Model Law and other arbitration laws[12]

[11] German Arbitration Law (Section 1059 ZPO), available at: https://www.disarb.org/fileadmin/user_upload/Wissen/Deutsches_Schiedsverfahrensrecht_98_-_Englisch.pdf; Croatian Arbitration Law published in the Official Gazette no. 88/2001, Article 36, available at: https://www.vsrh.hr/CustomPages/Static/HRV/Files/Legislation__Law-Arbitration-RC.pdf; Kosovo Arbitration Law no. 02/L-75, Article 36, available at: https://gzk.rks-gov.net/ActDocumentDetail.aspx?ActID=2579; Arbitration Law of the Republic of North Macedonia published in the Official Gazette no. 39/2006, Article 35, available at: https://www.international-arbitration-attorney.com/wp-content/uploads/2013/07/Macedonia-Arbitration-Law.pdf.

[12] Ibid.

expressly provide that the court decides to annul the award ex officio if (a) the subject-matter of the dispute is not capable of settlement by arbitration (b) the award is in conflict with the public policy of this state. For other grounds, such as those provided in Article 44(1)(a), (b), (c), (ç), and (d) of the Albanian law, the court takes them into consideration only when they are raised at the request of the interested party. We are of the opinion that Article 44 of the Albanian Arbitration Law should be interpreted in the same way.

3 Grounds for Annulment of Arbitral Awards

The grounds on which a request for annulment of an arbitral award can be made are provided in Article 44(1) of Law no. 52/2023. These grounds reflect the grounds for refusing recognition of a foreign arbitral award provided for in the New York Convention (Article V) and the grounds for annulment of an arbitral award under the Geneva Convention (Article IX) and the Model Law (Article 34). Therefore, the analysis will follow a comparative approach. Albanian law, following the Model Law, does not grant the parties the right to challenge an arbitral award on a question of fact or law and therefore "closes the door" to the judicial jurisdiction to examine the merits of the case.

3.1 Lack of Capacity to Act

According to Article 44(1)(a) of Law no. 52/2023, a ground for annulment of the award can be "if one of the parties to the arbitration agreement did not have the capacity to act according to the special law that determines the acquisition of the capacity to act, as well as their organization and functioning". The lack of capacity of the parties to enter into an arbitration agreement means that the arbitration agreement would have no effect on the parties and therefore the award would be null and void. The capacity of the parties to act must be assessed at the time of signing the arbitration agreement. Although this is not expressly defined in Article 44(1)(a) of Law no. 52/2023, it is implied since the verb used in this article is in the past tense.[13]

Article 44(1)(a) of Law no. 52/2023 is similar to the Geneva Convention (Article IX(1)(a)) and the New York Convention (Article V(1)(a)), which provide as a grounds for annulment and refusal of recognition to the arbitral award, the incapacity of the parties according to the law applicable to them. In comparison, the Model Law (Article 34(1)(a)) makes no reference to the applicable law for the capacity of the parties.

The same provision as Article 44(1)(a) of Law no. 52/2023 regarding the applicable law for determining the capacity of the parties is also found in Article 8.

[13] For a similar interpretation of Art. V(1)(a) of the NYC see: Wolff (2012), p. 272, para. 101.

Specifically, according to the third paragraph of this article, the arbitration agreement can be concluded by any private natural or legal person and that their capacity is regulated by the special law that regulates gaining the capacity to act, as well as their organization and functioning. Thus, to determine the legal capacity of the parties to an (arbitration) agreement that has foreign elements, Albanian courts will refer to Law no. 10 428, dated 2/6/2011 "On Private International Law" (PIL). According to this law (Article 11), the capacity to act of a foreign natural person and the limitation or removal of the capacity to act are regulated by the law of the country of which they have citizenship. Whereas, in relation to legal entities, this law provides that their capacity to act is regulated by the law of the state in which they are registered (Article 15).

Regarding the capacity of public legal entities to conclude arbitration agreements, the Albanian Arbitration Law no. 52/2023 provides that the arbitration agreement can also be concluded by a ministry or local government unit. Subsidiary institutions, autonomous agencies, as well as State companies may enter into an arbitration agreement after obtaining the prior consent, as the case may be, of the responsible minister or the Prime Minister. Local government units may enter into an arbitration agreement after obtaining the prior consent, as the case may be, of the municipal council or the district council (Article 8(4)). So, unlike the previous provisions that regulated arbitration in Albania, with the new arbitration law, obtaining the consent of the minister or the Prime Minister and the municipal council for the conclusion of arbitration agreements by State agencies or companies and local government units is a limitation of the capacity of the latter to conclude arbitration agreements. Failure to comply with this requirement of the Albanian Arbitration Law may lead to the invalidity of the arbitration agreement. However, the effect of the lack of prior consent according to Article 8(4) of Law no. 52/2023 on the validity of the arbitration agreement must be seen in relation to the specific circumstances of the case and Article II of the Geneva Convention, which Albania has ratified. Article II of this Convention is interpreted as meaning that States and public entities cannot rely on their domestic legislation to claim a lack of capacity to enter into an arbitration agreement and the invalidity of the arbitration agreement on that ground.[14]

3.2 *Invalid Arbitration Agreement*

According to Article 44(1)(b) of Law no. 52/2023, a ground for annulment of the award can be "when the arbitration agreement is invalid according to the provisions of the legislation in force chosen by the parties or by the arbitral tribunal, or, in cases where the parties have not determined the applicable legislation, according to the provisions of the legislation of the Republic of Albania".

The above provision is similar to the Model Law (Article 34(2)(a)(i)) and Article (V)(1)(a) of the NYC (*analogous provision for recognition of awards*). Regarding

[14] Kröll (2013), pp. 10–11. Marzolini (2012), p. 33.

the law applicable to the validity of the arbitration agreement, the Albanian law, in contrast to the Model Law or the NYC, refers alternatively to the law chosen by the parties, as well as the law chosen by the arbitral tribunal. Hence, there is a difference in the wording of the Albanian law which implies or grants equal opportunities or rights to the parties, as well as the arbitral tribunal to decide on the applicable law for the validity of the arbitration agreement. The determination of the law applicable to the validity of the arbitration agreement is not a procedural issue that can be decided by the arbitral tribunal. Certainly, it is the arbitral tribunal's duty to determine the applicable law. However, it does not do it independently of the will of the parties. On the contrary, the arbitral tribunal determines the applicable law based on the will of the parties, expressed or implied, and if this is not possible then the arbitral tribunal shall apply the Albanian law.

In examining the request for annulment of the award due to the invalidity of the arbitration agreement, the court must take into consideration the principle of the autonomy of the arbitration agreement, according to which the grounds for the invalidity of the arbitration agreement must be assessed independently of the grounds for the invalidity of the main contract.[15]

The invalidity of the arbitration agreement based on Article 44(1)(b) of Law no. 52/2023 concerns the material invalidity, which is related to the way the arbitration agreement was formed and the will of the parties to arbitrate. Allegations of fraud, signature forgery, pathological, and asymmetric agreements, etc. relate to cases of material invalidity of the arbitration agreement. If one of the parties requests the annulment of the award because the arbitration agreement did not exist, the court must consider the fact whether the party interested in the annulment of the arbitral award has raised or not the claim for the inexistence of the arbitration agreement in its submission to arbitration. If the party has not raised such a claim, then, it cannot claim the non-existence of the arbitration agreement and thus the annulment of the arbitral award under Article 44(1)(b). Exceptionally, it may do so if that party has not been given the opportunity by the arbitral tribunal to make its submissions.[16]

3.3 *Lack of Proper Notice and Inability to Present the Case*

According to Article 44(1)(c) of Law no. 52/2023, a ground for annulment of the award can be "if the parties have not been given proper notice of the appointment of an arbitrator or the initiation of the arbitration procedure, as well as for any other reason, that did not allow the parties to present their case." This provision is drafted in full compliance with the Model Law (Article 34(2)(a)(ii)) and Article V(1)(b) of the New York Convention. It guarantees the respect of the basic principles in the arbitration procedure, which cannot be waived. If a party did not have the opportunity to present its case, it means that the party was not given the opportunity to be heard

[15] Born (2021), p. 3452.

[16] UNCITRAL (2012), p. 144.

in the process, to apply the adversarial principle, and to be treated impartially by the arbitral tribunal. The annulment of the award based on Article 44(1)(c) of Law no. 52/2023 should be allowed only when the procedural violation has significant effects on the arbitral procedure or the result of the tribunal's decision,[17] although Article 44(1)(c) of Law no. 52/2023, unlike the legislation of some countries,[18] and paragraph 44(1)(d), do not expressly provide for it.

Some of the procedural violations that may fall within the scope of this provision are the impossibility of the party's participation in the arbitration process if this was due to the arbitral tribunal or another cause beyond the control of the party, which requires the annulment of the award,[19] failure to provide information to the party about the constitution of the arbitral tribunal[20] not notifying the parties of the dates of the hearings or various submissions.[21] Refusal of the arbitral tribunal to admit evidence from one party is generally not considered a violation of the right to be heard.[22] Also, the arbitral tribunal cannot base its award on investigations conducted by it, and without giving the parties to the arbitration the opportunity to be heard on these investigations.[23]

3.4 Excess of Authority

According to Article 44(1)(c) of Law no. 52/2023, a ground for annulment of the award can be "when the award deals with a dispute that has not been examined by the arbitral tribunal or the award deals with a dispute that was not contemplated by the arbitration agreement as well as one or more disputes resolved by the arbitral tribunal were not within its jurisdiction. In this case, when it is possible for the decisions on

[17] Born (2021), p. 3541; Ortolani (2020), p. 878.

[18] English Arbitration Act of 1996, Article 68(1), Netherlands Code of Civil Procedure, Art. 1704(2)(g).

[19] Ontario Supreme Court, Corporation Transnacional de Inversiones, SA de CV v. STET International SpA, P. p. 18, 20, [65], [73], available at: http://arbitrationplace.com/digitallibrary/CLOUT%20Cases-Canada/UNCITRAL%20Model%20Laë%20Commercial%20Arbitration/391%20Re%20Corporacion%20Transnacional%20de%20Inversiones,%20S.A.%20de%20C.V.%20et%20al.%20and%20STET%20International,%20S.pA%20et%20al.%201999%20CanLII%2014819%20(ON%20SC.pdf.

[20] CLOUT case no. 562 [Hanseatisches Oberlandesgericht Hamburg, Germany, 6 Sch 04/01, 8 November 2001], p. (II)/1, 6, available at: http://www.dis-arb.de/de/47/datenbanken/rspr/hanseat-olg-hamburg-az-6-sch-04-01-datum-2001-11-08-id145.

[21] Superior Court Canada, Louis Dreyfus, sas (SA Louis Dreyfus & Cie) c. Holding Tusculum, bv, No. 500-05-015828-963, December 8, 2008, p. 104, http://www.canlii.org/en/qc/qccs/doc/2008/2008qccs5903/2008qccs5903.html.

[22] UNCITRAL (2012), p. 148. Available at: http://www.uncitral.org/pdf/english/clout/MAL-digest-2012-e.pdf.

[23] Apex Tech Investment Ltd V. Chuang's Development (China) Ltd [1996] HKCA 593; [1996] 2 HRC 155; [1996] 2 HKC 293; CACV 231/1995 (15 March 1996), p. 8, 22, 1995, No. 231, available at: http://www.hklii.hk/eng/hk/cases/hkca/1996/593.html.

matters, that were under the jurisdiction of the arbitral tribunal, to be separated from that part of the decision on matters that were not part of its jurisdiction, the court annuls only that part of the arbitral award that has resolved disputes that were not under its jurisdiction." This provision is also drafted under the Model Law (Article 34(2)(a)(iii)) and Article V(1)(c) of the New York Convention.

If the State court mandate is derived by law, the arbitral tribunal power derives from the parties' arbitration agreement. A valid arbitration agreement is a condition for the existence of the arbitral tribunal's jurisdiction. The arbitral tribunal cannot exceed the powers given to it by the arbitration agreement. The ground for annulment provided for in this Article does not relate to the invalidity of the arbitration agreement but includes cases when the dispute on which the arbitral tribunal decided does not fall within the scope of the arbitration agreement or the award of the arbitral tribunal concerns issues that were not claimed by the parties.[24]

Any decision of the arbitral tribunal made in relation to claims not submitted by the parties is considered to have been made in excess of authority. Any award taken in excess of authority, also known as *ultra petita*, must be considered null and void. In such a case, that part of the award that was made in excess of authority should be annulled by the court. As for the case when the arbitral tribunal does not express itself for all the requests submitted by the parties (*infra petita*), the new Arbitration Law no. 52/2023, unlike the provisions of the Civil Procedure Code that regulated domestic arbitration, does not expressly provide for it as a ground for the annulment of the award. Even the Model Law does not expressly provide for *infra petita* as a ground for the annulment of the award. Commentators of the Model Law hold the position that Article 34(2)(a)(iii) does not apply in *infra petita* cases.[25] However, there are authorities who state that *infra petita* should be a reason for the annulment of the award even when it is not expressly provided by law, and only in cases where substantial injustices are caused.[26]

For an arbitral award to be annulled on grounds of excess of authority, the violation must be very obvious. The nuances between submitted or not submitted claims must be interpreted in favor of the arbitral tribunal because the latter has the right to decide on its jurisdiction. A typical *ultra petita* case would exist when the arbitral tribunal grants a payment of interest that the party did not request. In such a case, the court should annul the award on the part concerning the interests and leave in force the rest of the arbitral award. Another ground for the annulment of the arbitral award (under Article 44(1)(c)) may be given when the arbitral tribunal decides the case *ex aeque et bono* without being authorized by the parties. Under Article 37 of Law no. 52/ 2023, the arbitral tribunal may decide the dispute according to the *ex aequo et bono* or *amiable compositeur* principle only if the parties have expressly agreed.

---

[24] Born (2021), p. 3575.

[25] Ortolani (2020), p. 879.

[26] Born (2021), p. 3583.

3.5 Violation of Procedural Rules

According to Article 44(1)(d) of Law no. 52/2023, a ground for annulment of the award may be given "when the composition of the arbitral tribunal or the arbitration procedure was not in accordance with the provisions of this law or with the arbitration agreement, provided that their violation has consequences on the way the dispute is resolved by the arbitral tribunal".

This paragraph of Article 44 of Law no. 52/2023 is not in full compliance with the Model Law. According to Article 34(2)(a)(iv) of the Model Law, the arbitral award may be annulled "when the composition of the arbitral tribunal or the arbitral procedure was not in accordance with the agreement of the parties unless such agreement was in conflict with the provision of this Law from which the parties cannot derogate, or, failing such agreement, was not in accordance with this Law". Albanian Law no. 52/2023, providing alternatively for (i) the procedural rules provided for in Albanian law or (ii) those determined by agreement of the parties, regarding the composition or arbitral procedure, does not provide a solution to the situation when these two groups of norms have conflicting provisions. Unlike the Model Law, Albanian law does not give priority to the agreement of the parties and successively foresees the implementation of Albanian procedural law. Also, Law no. 52/2023, unlike the Model Law, has expressly provided that violations of the rules of procedure will be grounds for annulment of the award, only if the violation has consequences on the way the dispute is resolved by the arbitral tribunal. However, although the Model Law does not expressly provide for such a condition, most courts annul arbitral awards for violation of the rules provided for in the agreement of the parties or in the absence of them, in the law, only in case of serious violations that cause material damage to the party requesting the relief.[27] Examples of possible violations according to this paragraph are, the lack of reasons for the arbitral award, when the arbitration law or the arbitration rules chosen by the parties require a reasoned award, the arbitral tribunal does not consist of the number of arbitrators that the parties have agreed, or the chairman of the arbitral tribunal was not chosen in accordance with the agreement of the parties, etc.

The procedural violations mentioned above must be challenged during the arbitration proceedings. A party that is aware of a violation of a provision of this law or of the other party's failure to fulfill an obligation arising from the arbitration agreement and, despite this, continues the arbitration procedure without objecting immediately and, in any case, not later than 5 days after becoming aware of the relevant violation, is considered to have waived the right to object (Art. 36 of Law 52/2023).

---

[27] Born (2021), pp. 3554–3555, 3561.

3.6 *Arbitrability*

According to Article 44(1)(dh) of Law no. 52/2023, a ground for annulment of the award may be given "if the award deals with a dispute that is not allowed by law to be resolved through arbitration". Arbitrability of the dispute is one of the basic criteria to have a valid arbitration procedure. Fulfillment of this criterion is a condition for the jurisdiction of the arbitral tribunal and is a violation that must be controlled ex officio by the court. Due to the importance of this criterion, the *lex arbitri* in most countries permits the control of arbitrability at several stages of the process. This criterion is also a ground for the refusal to recognize the arbitral award in accordance with Article V(2)(a) of the New York Convention. Unlike the Model Law, the Albanian Arbitration Law does not state which law regulates arbitrability at the annulment stage. In the spirit of the Model Law (Article 34(2)(b)(i)) and the New York Convention, we think that the law that governs the arbitrability of the dispute at the annulment stage should be the law of the country where the annulment of the award is requested.[28] In the case of domestic and international arbitral awards in Albania, the assessment of arbitrability as a ground for annulment of arbitral awards must be done on the basis of Albanian law.

In applying this provision, the court must take into account Article 7 of Law no. 52/2023, which provides for the scope of the arbitration agreement. The subject matter of an arbitration agreement can be any property claim or claim arising from a property relationship, except when special legislation prohibits the settlement of the dispute through arbitration or when it determines that the settlement of a dispute by arbitration can only be carried out in certain conditions. Article 8 of Law no. 52/2023 also provides that "[t]he parties may enter into an arbitration agreement even if the dispute between them is being examined by the court unless the resolution of the dispute is under the exclusive jurisdiction of the court". Thus, other legal provisions that provide for the exclusive jurisdiction of Albanian courts (such as Article 72 of the Albanian PIL) should also be taken into account. By providing for the exclusive jurisdiction of Albanian courts, the Albanian law has provided for the exclusion of these disputes from the jurisdiction of the arbitral tribunals and any contrary agreement leads to the annulment of the arbitral award.

3.7 *Public Policy*

According to Article 44(1)(e) of Law no. 52/2023, another ground for annulment of the award is given when "the enforcement of the award would be contrary to public policy". This provision without any reason refers to the "enforcement of the award" and not the "award" that violates public policy. In contrast to the Model Law, the Albanian Arbitration Law does not expressly address the violation of the public policy of which country is relevant for the purpose of annulment of the award. Article

[28] Ortolani (2020), p. 892.

34(2)(b)(ii) of the Model Law provides a ground for annulment when the arbitral award conflicts with the public policy of the place of arbitration. Despite the absence of this definition in the Albanian Arbitration Law, we think that Article 44(1)(e) of Law no. 52/2023 should be interpreted as referring to the public policy of the Republic of Albania. Also, although, unlike the Model Law, Albanian Arbitration Law does not expressly provide for it, this ground of annulment must be controlled ex officio by the court.

Public policy does not have an exhaustive definition. The basic material and procedural principles of justice and morality are considered part of public policy.[29] Some of the fundamental principles of public policy are *pacta sunt servanda*, prohibition of abuse of rights, *veniere contra factum proprium*, the principle of good faith (*bona fide*), prohibition of discrimination, corruption, due process, *res judicata*, etc. The principles of the protection of human rights may be included in the norms of public policy, but this does not mean that the court should check whether the arbitral tribunal has complied with all the principles of Article 6 of the European Convention on Human Rights (ECHR). In implementing this provision, those principles of the ECHR that cannot be waived in arbitration must be taken into consideration.[30] Also, not every mandatory rule of the *lex arbitri* is part of public policy. Such are only those mandatory rules that underlie the legal and moral order of a State, which cannot be waived,[31] for example rules for the protection of competition.

4 Agreements Limiting or Expanding Grounds for Annulling Arbitral Awards

4.1 Agreement to Waive or Limit the Annulment Grounds

Unlike the legislation of some European countries,[32] Law no. 52/2023 does not expressly provide for waiver of the right to request annulment of the award. However, considering that Article 44(2) of the law states that: "Unless the parties have agreed otherwise, the request for annulment of the arbitral award is made ...", it is understood that the Albanian law indirectly accepts the waiver by agreement of the right to request annulment of the arbitral award. What remains unclear is whether the parties can waive the right to the annulment of the award entirely or only on some grounds.

In a literal interpretation, Article 44(2) of Law no. 52/2023 seems to indirectly allow the complete waiver of the right to annulment of the award. However, within the framework of respecting the constitutional right to due process, we think that the

[29] International Law Association (2022), Recommendation 1(d).

[30] Kola Tafaj (2012).

[31] Born (2021), pp. 3605–3606.

[32] Article 192(1) Swiss Private International Law Act; Article 1718 of the Belgian Judicial Code; Article 1522(1) of the French Code of Civil Procedure; Sections 67, 68, 69 of the English Arbitration Act (1996).

parties cannot waive the right to the annulment of the arbitral award for any ground. They can waive annulment only on those grounds, which can be taken into account by the court only at the request of the party, but they cannot waive the grounds, which can also be raised ex officio by the court, such as public policy or arbitrability.[33]

4.2 Agreement on the Expansion of the Annulment Grounds

The parties may provide in the arbitration agreement that the arbitral award shall be challenged by other means or for other grounds beyond those provided for in Article 44 of Law no. 52/2023. However, the question arises whether such an agreement will be enforceable.

The doctrine has presented several arguments for and against the expansion of the judicial review mechanism of arbitral awards. Whereas the need to protect the parties from irresponsible arbitral awards, which would question the effectiveness of the arbitration process are mentioned as arguments in favor, the violation of efficiency and the principle of confidentiality are mentioned as arguments against.[34]

In most arbitration laws, the grounds for annulment of an arbitral award are exhaustive and cannot be expanded by agreement of the parties.[35] In the *Hall Street v. Mattel* case, the Supreme Court of the United States stated that the parties cannot provide by their agreement to expand the causes of judicial review (even for questions of fact or law) beyond the provisions of the arbitration law (FAA).[36] However, the same decision left room for courts in different states to reach different conclusions in the case of annulment of awards based on state rather than federal arbitration laws.[37] German courts, also, since 2007, based on the principle of the autonomy of the will of the parties, hold the position that the agreement of the parties on the expansion of the grounds for annulment of the arbitral award is enforceable.[38]

Albanian procedural law does not address this issue, and there is no judicial practice related to it. In our opinion, the parties' agreements on the expansion of the grounds for annulment of an arbitral award in courts are invalid, because the rules and functioning of the judicial jurisdiction are defined in Albanian procedural law (*forum regit processum*) and cannot be dictated by the agreement of the parties.

---

[33] Such an interpretation was made to Article 1059 of the German Arbitration Law, which was taken into consideration when the Albanian Arbitration Law was drafted. See: Kroll and Kraft (2015), para. 7; Born (2021), p. 3665. The German doctrine also holds that the waiver of the grounds that cannot be verified *ex officio* by the court can be done in advance only if the facts that constitute a ground for the annulment of the award were known by the parties before they waived such grounds. See: Kroll and Kraft (2015), para. 7.

[34] Further on this, see Wasco (2010), pp. 614–616. See also: Scherer (2016), pp. 447–456.

[35] See: Scherer (2016), p. 445.

[36] Hall Street Assocs., LLC v. Mattel Inc., 552 US 576 (USSCt. 2008).

[37] Klau (2012).

[38] Scherer (2016), pp. 445–446.

5 Consequences of the Annulment of Arbitral Awards

Although rare, annulment of arbitration awards occurs in practice. In cases where it does, the question is what are the consequences of a court decision setting aside an arbitral award, and what are the legal effects of the annulled arbitral award?

First, a final domestic or international arbitral award rendered in Albania can be annulled in whole or in part by the court of appeal (Article 44(1)(c)) of Law no. 52/2023), and the court's decision is non-appealable to the Supreme Court (Article 45(4) of Law no. 52/2023).

Secondly, Law no. 52/2023 (Article 44(3)) provides that, when the appellate court decides to annul the award, it may, if deemed reasonable, also decide to remit the case for retrial to the arbitral tribunal or order the undertaking of any other action that eliminates the grounds for annulment of the award. This new provision of Law no. 52/2023 completely changes the previous regulation of the CCP, according to which, when the appeal court overturned or changed the award of the arbitral tribunal, it decided on the merits of the case within the limits of the mission assigned to the arbitral tribunal. This provision also differs from the Model Law according to which "[t]he court, when asked to set aside an award, may, where appropriate and so requested by a party, suspend the setting aside proceedings for a period of time determined by it in order to give the arbitral tribunal an opportunity to resume the arbitral proceedings or to take such other action as in the arbitral tribunal's opinion will eliminate the grounds for setting aside" (Art. 34(4)). We consider that Article 44(3) of Law no. 52/2023 is a wrong adaptation of Article 34(4) of the Model Law.

According to the current Law no. 52/2023, it seems that the appellate court, when deciding on the request to annul the arbitral award, has three options: (i) to overturn the arbitral tribunal's award; (ii) when it deems it reasonable to send the case for retrial to the arbitral tribunal; or (iii) order the taking of any action that eliminates the grounds for annulment. Regarding the decision to send the case for retrial, we think that it refers to the cases where the annulment of the award did not come as a result of the invalidity of the arbitration agreement, the lack of arbitrability, or the incapacity of the parties to conclude an arbitration agreement. The arbitration agreement continues to exist, although the arbitral tribunal may have committed a procedural violation. In such a case the parties are free to restart a new arbitration procedure. In our assessment, the appellate court should not remand the case to the arbitral tribunal that issued the award, because it is *functus officio* at the time of the award (Art. 41(3)), but may refer the case to arbitration since the agreement in this second case remains valid. Regarding the order of the arbitral tribunal by the appellate court to take any other action that eliminates the grounds for the annulment of the award, we think that, interpreted literally, it contradicts the principle of the autonomy of arbitration from the judicial jurisdiction. The appellate court is mandated by procedural law to review the grounds for annulment of an arbitral award, but it cannot be mandated to direct or dictate the resolution of the case by ordering the manner of hearing the case. Most likely, this article of Law no. 52/2023 will remain inapplicable.

6 Conclusions

The entry into force of the new Arbitration Law in Albania in 2023 was a long-awaited event. The adoption of this law is a very positive step, which not only solved the intricate situation concerning the annulment of domestic arbitral awards and the impossibility of challenging international arbitration awards rendered in Albania but also comes at a time when the Albanian courts' backlog is huge, mainly due to the judicial reform process. Hence, the adoption of the new arbitration law might serve as a good incentive for the parties to resort to arbitration, as a faster and more effective mechanism to resolve their disputes.

The new Arbitration Law applies to domestic and international arbitration seated in Albania. Hence, it provides unified rules of procedure and grounds for the annulment of domestic and international arbitral awards rendered in Albania. The new Arbitration Law in Albania, including the provisions concerning the annulment of arbitral awards, was drafted based on the UNCITRAL Model Law. However, the above analysis of the provisions of the Albanian Arbitration Law concerning the annulment of arbitral awards showed that they are not a verbatim adoption of Article 34 of the Model Law. The most notable difference concerns the lack of division in the grounds for the annulment of arbitral awards into grounds that should be raised by the parties and those that can also be raised ex officio by the court. The authors' opinion is that Art. 44 of the Albanian Arbitration Law should be construed and applied as granting courts the right to raise ex officio the invalidity of an arbitral award on grounds of lack of arbitrability and violation of public policy. This difference, along with the other issues analyzed, such as the provision providing for the court's right to remit the case to the arbitral tribunal, or the issues of waiver or expansion of the grounds of annulment, remain a challenge to the Albanian courts.

References

Born GB (2021) International commercial arbitration, vol III, 3rd edn. Wolters Kluwer, Alphen aan den Rijn

Dano O (2021) Challenges and prospects of the Albanian domestic arbitration. https://www.mondaq.com/arbitration-dispute-resolution/1111008/challenges-and-prospects-of-the-albanian-domestic-arbitration

Hascher DT (2011) European convention on international commercial arbitration of 1961, commentary. Yearbook Commun Arb'n XXXVI 504–562

International Law Association (2022) Final report on public policy

Klau D (2012) Can parties contract for expanded judicial review of arbitration awards? http://appealinglybrief.com/2012/09/27/can-parties-contract-for-expanded-judicial-review-of-arbitration-awards

Kola Tafaj F (2012) Implementation of the European Convention on Human Rights in Arbitration Proceedings. German Arbitration Journal SchiedsVZ: 184–188

Kola Tafaj F (2022) Albania – national report, World Arbitration Reporter (WAR), 2nd edn, pp 1–23. https://arbitrationlaw.com/library/albania-national-report-world-arbitration-reporter-war-2nd-edition

Kola Tafaj F, Çinari S (2019) History of the development of arbitration in 100 years of the state. Albanian Socio Econ Rev 1(98):23–32
Kola Tafaj F, Vokshi A (2018) Civil procedure, first part, 2nd edn. Albas, Tirana
Kroll S, Kraft P (2015) Recourse against the award. In: Bockstiegel K, Kroll S, Nacimiento P (eds) Arbitration in Germany. Wolters Kluwer, Alphen aan den Rijn
Kröll S (2013) The European convention on international commercial arbitration. The tale of a sleeping beauty. Aust YB Int Arb 26:3–22
Marzolini P (2012) The involvement of states and state-owned entities in international arbitration-the international conventions and Swiss perspectives. Romanian Arb J 2:27–37
Ortolani P (2020) Article 34, application for setting aside as exclusive recourse against arbitral award. In: Bantekas I, Ortolani P, Ali S, Gomez M, Polkinghorne (ed) UNCITRAL model law on international commercial arbitration: a commentary. Cambridge University Press, Cambridge, pp 858–898
Scherer M (2016) The fate of parties' agreements on judicial review of awards: a comparative and normative analysis of party-autonomy at the post-award stage. Arb Int 32(3):437–457. https://doi.org/10.1093/arbint/aiw018
UNCITRAL (2012) Digest of case law on the model law on international commercial arbitration. http://www.uncitral.org/pdf/english/clout/MAL-digest-2012-e.pdf
Wasco MD (2010) When Less is more: the international split over expanded judicial review in arbitration. Rutgers LR 62(2):559–626. https://rutgerslawreview.com/wp-content/uploads/2011/08/When-Less-is-More-The-International-Split-Over-Expanded-Judicial-Review-in-Arbitration.pdf
Wolff R (ed) (2012) New York convention on recognition and enforcement of foreign arbitral awards of 10 June 1958, article-by-article commentary. C. H. Beck, Munich, Hart, Oxford, Nomos, Baden-Baden

Promotion of the Rule of Law in the Western Balkans: The Impact of Investment Arbitration

Vlatko Tokarev

Abstract The Western Balkans is a region comprising six Southeastern European countries that are still not European Union Member States but are currently pursuing reforms aimed at strengthening the rule of law—considered as a key prerequisite for EU accession, economic development and the building of a prosperous society. However, it has been noted that Western Balkan countries are facing difficulties and making slow progress towards this policy goal. Investment treaties are considered as mechanisms which may potentially have a positive influence on the promotion of the rule of law and good governance. Such treaties introduce high standards of treatment of foreign investors and governance as international law obligations of host states, which if not satisfied could provoke a foreign investor to seek legal protection through investment arbitration. To avoid liability arising out of investment arbitration, it is argued that host States encourage long-term reforms of administrative and judicial processes. In this chapter, this theory is examined in the context of Western Balkan countries. I conclude that investment arbitration has until recently had little to no impact on the rule of law in the relevant countries, due to various factors elaborated in the chapter. In the last few years, as the number of investment claims has been rising, so is the awareness of governments in the region of the threat of investment arbitration and the need to respond to such threats. I describe how policy makers are for this reason increasingly influenced by investment arbitration and are making efforts to strengthen domestic capacities and capabilities to prevent and effectively handle investment disputes. Whether such efforts will lead to long-term and structural reforms remains to be seen.

V. Tokarev (✉)
Faculty of Law "Iustinianus Primus", University of Ss. Cyril and Methodius, Skopje, North Macedonia
e-mail: vlatkotokarev@gmail.com

M. Bungenberg et al. (eds.), *Alternative Dispute Resolution in the Western Balkans*, European Union and its Neighbours in a Globalized World 20,
https://doi.org/10.1007/978-3-031-76345-8_7

1 Introduction

The dissolution of the Federal Yugoslav Republic and the period of transition from socialism to a liberal and capitalist economy was for the Balkan region a turbulent period plagued with political turmoil, tensions and economic and violent conflicts. Most Balkan countries were and are to this day affected by such troubled times in the 90s, experiencing difficulties in building stable democracies, well-functioning institutions, and efficient and independent judiciary systems. In the early and mid-2000s, the prospects of European Union (EU) accession and favourable global circumstances facilitated economic recovery and boosted economic and institutional reforms in the region, yet for six Balkan countries—EU integration and overall effective reforms are still a challenge. This has prompted the governing bodies of the EU to coin the geopolitical term 'the Western Balkans' referring to those countries in Southeastern Europe that are not EU member states but could aspire to join the bloc. Originally, the Western Balkan region consisted of seven countries—Albania, Bosnia and Herzegovina, Kosovo,[1] Macedonia, Montenegro, Serbia and Croatia—but Croatia has since joined the EU.[2]

As noted by the European Court of Auditors, corruption remains a cause of concern in all countries in the region, particularly as governments have passed many laws favouring cronyism, with impacts including the award of privileged contracts, industry monopolies and the employment of poorly qualified public officials who will enable corruption.[3] The European Commission has identified reforms in the area of the rule of law, fundamental rights and good governance as the most pressing issue for the Western Balkans. Deficiencies in these areas are considered a deterrent to investment and trade. The Commission has also accentuated that a precondition for economic development is the independence of the judiciary and individual judges, which are essential to ensuring fairness and to holding the executive and legislative branches of government to account.[4] To improve the lives of its citizens, encourage investment and achieve the goal of full EU membership, Western Balkan countries are thus prioritizing efforts of strengthening the rule of law and their administrative capacities to govern effectively and justly. The conclusion of investment treaties is in general thought to contribute to such efforts.[5]

Certain studies indicate that developing countries continuously lose around a quarter of the total investment that they have managed to attract. After starting to operate, investors subsequently opt to withdraw their investments because of undesirable conduct by public agencies.[6] Foreign investors invariably prefer that their

---

[1] Without prejudice to positions on status.

[2] See Dabrowski and Myachenkova (2018), p. 2.

[3] European Court of Auditors (2022), pp. 10–11. As observed by and shared in Transparency International (2020).

[4] European Commission (2018) 65 final. Available at: https://eur-lex.europa.eu/legal-content/EN/TXT/?uri=celex%3A52018DC0065.

[5] See Schill and Djanic (2018), p. 4.

[6] Echandi (2019) p. 61.

exposure to political risks, regulatory shortcomings and judicial inconsistency in developing countries and economies in transition, such as the ones mentioned above, are offset by legal protections offered in an investment treaty. Such treaties introduce high standards of investor treatment and governance as international law obligations of host States, which if not satisfied could be the subject of an arbitration claim by the investor before an independent international investment tribunal. Therefore, international investment law (IIL) and its enforcement through arbitration is seen as an important tool of ensuring basic rule of law demands from the legal system of host states and a stable investment climate for foreign investors.[7] Besides attracting investment, it is argued that investment treaties and arbitration could in theory also encourage reform of administrative and judicial processes in the host State, by making a host State liable to foreign investors if government decision-making fails to meet these procedural standards.[8] In this chapter I look into this hypothesis in relation to the Western Balkan region and examine how has investment arbitration, or the threat thereof, actually impacted these countries' adherence to the principles of the rule of law and stimulated domestic reforms. The impact of investment arbitration is comparable in all Western Balkans countries due to the similar legal and political circumstances under which these countries have and are developing, which will be addressed in this chapter. This topic is of relevance for the countries concerned, as it is a legal issue potentially affecting the countries' policies of entering into future investment treaties and their approach to handling investment arbitration cases.

In the following I first lay out in more detail how this perceived benefit of investment arbitration is considered to positively influence the rule of law in domestic legal systems. I then examine some factors which have contributed towards the insignificant impact investment arbitration has had thus far on administrative and judicial reforms in Western Balkan countries. Finally, I describe how certain Western Balkan countries have responded to an increased number of investment claims and their potential negative consequences on State budgets, prompting a conclusion that the threat of investment arbitration is increasingly influencing policy makers in promoting the rule of law by strengthening domestic capacities and capabilities to prevent and effectively handle investment disputes.

2 The Disciplining and Stimulating Effect of Investment Arbitration

The Council of Europe has defined the notion of rule of law as a requirement that everyone is treated by State decision-makers with dignity, equality and rationality and in accordance with the law, and to have the opportunity to challenge decisions before independent and impartial courts for their unlawfulness, where they are accorded fair

[7] Reinisch (2023), p. 211.

[8] See Bonnitcha (2017), p. 6.

procedures.[9] These rights and treatment guarantees are in the essence of the various investor protections offered by investment treaties, which are especially embodied through the fair and equitable treatment (FET) standard—incorporated as a staple in investment treaties. Scholarly analysis has identified seven non exhaustive elements of the rule of law which render the FET standard operable in practice, which are not discrete causes of action but indications that assist in arguing a breach of the FET standard. These are (a) the principle of legality; (b) administrative due process and the denial of justice; (c) the protection of legitimate expectations; (d) the requirement of stability, predictability and consistency regarding the legal framework; (e) non-discrimination; (f) transparency; and (g) the principles of reasonableness and proportionality.[10] As FET violations are considered the most common types of breaches claimed though investment arbitration,[11] the adherence to these substantive and procedural principles relevant to the rule of law is the most important obligation e that investment treaties impose on host States. Investment arbitration is this context is argued to act as a substitute of 'dysfunctional' courts in 'unreliable' countries.[12] *Schultz* and *Dupont* explain that 'dysfunctional' courts refer to courts that have limited respect for the rule of law and, allow or support arbitrary and unpredictable interference of their government with an investment.[13] In substituting foul play in domestic litigation with hypothetically non-dysfunctional international adjudication, investment arbitration seeks to improve the regulatory quality of investment protection in the host State, bringing it to firmer adherence with the rule of law.[14] With 'unreliable' countries *Schultz* and *Dupont* refer to countries that are in less than full adherence with the principle of legality. In this context, they quote *Kingsbury* and *Schill*, who see investment arbitration as a potential instrument serviceable for promotion of democratic accountability, participation and of good and orderly State administration, and the protection of rights and other deserving interests.[15] In other words, by ruling on the compatibility of the exercise of public powers with treaty or contract obligations under domestic or international law, investment arbitration contributes to preventing undue interferences with investments in breach of the rule of law.[16]

As put by *Calamita* and *Berman*, the assumption is that because of a desire to avoid liability for breaches of investment treaties, developing States will internalise considerations of their international legal obligations into their governmental decision-making, reform their decision-making processes, and thereby, over time, improve the rule of law not just for foreign investors but also for all those within

[9] Council of Europe (2011), p. 6.

[10] Jacob and Schill (2015), p. 719.

[11] Echandi (2019), p. 50.

[12] Schultz and Dupont (2014), p. 1160.

[13] Ibid, p. 1161.

[14] Ibid.

[15] Kingsbury and Schill (2009), p. 8.

[16] Schultz and Dupont (2014), p. 1161.

their territories.[17] It must be noted however that empirical evidence and studies are not conclusive and do not overwhelmingly support this assumed side effect of the investment arbitration system.[18] Along this line, its impact on the rule of law in the Western Balkans appears insignificant to this date, as will be elaborated in the following section.

3 Limited Impact of Investment Arbitration in the Western Balkans

As noted above, there has so far been little evidence to confirm the theory that investment treaties stimulate the strengthening of the rule of law in domestic legal systems. In general, several reasons have been given in literature to be sceptical as to the power of law to trigger reform, including challenges posed by various historical, economic, political or cultural factors.[19] The factors which have contributed towards the limited role of investment arbitration in policy-making in the Western Balkans are looked into below.

3.1 The Dominant Role of the EU Integration Process

The idea that the investment protection standards imposed in investment treaties would serve as the benchmark of good governance for developing countries is not as practical and feasible in the context of Western Balkan countries. As candidates for EU accession, these countries strive towards the *modus operandi* and the specific standards of governance of EU Member States. Hence, reforms (whether effective or not) in Western Balkan countries are predominantly pushed through different EU-driven and -inspired methods such as transposing EU norms into national law and adopting EU standards in nearly all areas of public regulation. The EU also plays a direct role in overseeing, coordinating, encouraging and financing projects of strengthening the capacity of the judiciary and promoting good governance and accountability.[20]

By virtue of their EU-orientated politics, Western Balkan countries internalize EU rules and standards into their governmental decision-making and reform plans. Therefore, on a practical level, it is the prospects and support offered by the EU, and not investment arbitration that facilitate concrete domestic reforms in Western Balkan countries. While developing countries not pursuing EU membership could be more influenced in their general policy postulates by the goal of meeting investor protection

---

[17] Jansen Calamita and Berman (2022), p. 2.

[18] See Bonnitcha (2017), p. 7; Ginsburg (2005), p. 28.

[19] See Davis and Trebilcock (2008), p. 859.

[20] European Court of Auditors (2022), pp. 12–14.

standards enforced by investment arbitration, EU membership candidates are focused on transposing into national law the more precise and normatively developed EU standards. After all, it is difficult for countries to design reforms suitable to respond and ensure compliance with the still vague FET standard endorsed by investment treaties and such difficulties will stand in the foreseeable future as it is still unclear to which limitations the standard precisely entails for State measures affecting foreign investors.[21]

3.2 Lack of Awareness and Small Number of Cases

The assumption is that developing countries understand potential costs and implications of investment treaties and investment arbitration. However, studies have shown most developing countries' governments do not generally engage in sophisticated cost–benefit calculations but rather fail even to consider the risks of the treaties until they were hit by their first claim. Accordingly, 92% of officials from developing countries participating in a study have provided that stakeholders had not realized before the first claim that treaty obligations were far-reaching and enforceable.[22]

Empirical work has shown it is bad experience that often triggers reflection and learning within government on the implications of participation in the investment treaty regime.[23] Accordingly, an analysis of the publicly available information of the outcomes of concluded investment arbitration cases brought against Western Balkan countries shows that seldom have these countries suffered serious financial consequences arising out of investment claims.

The data from Table 1 shows that Montenegro has been very successful in its position as respondent, rebuttling all investor claims thus far. Kosovo has been subject to very few claims and according to news reports, it has only recently, in 2023, been ordered for the first time to pay a sum to an investor due to a treaty breach.[24] Data shows that Bosnia and Herzegovina has seen very few awards rendered against its interests, while the Macedonian state has also been fairly successful in defending investment claims. Albania come out as a winner in most investment arbitration cases it has participated in, although it has been noted that the few unfavourable outcomes have imposed significant financial burden on the Albanian state.[25] At first sight, the statistics in Table 1 indicate that Serbia has been an exception to the perception that Western Balkan states have fared fairly positive in investment arbitration. However, a more in-depth analysis of the eventual effects and financial results of cases against Serbia show a different picture. Practitioners and commentators in Serbia note that

---

[21] Jacob and Schill (2015), pp. 703–704.

[22] See Skovgaard Poulsen and Aisbett (2013), p. 284.

[23] Ibid.

[24] See https://balkangreenenergynews.com/kosovo-ordered-to-compensate-contractor-over-scrapped-thermal-power-plant-project-kosova-e-re/.

[25] See Musabelliu (2023), p. 5.

Table 1 Participation in the investment treaty regime

Country	In favour of state	In favour of investor	Settled
Albania	5	1	2
Bosnia and Herzegovina	1	1	1
Kosovo	1	1	No data
Macedonia	3	1	1
Montenegro	5	0	0
Serbia	4	5	1

Source United Nations Conference on Trade and Development (UNCTAD) Investment Policy Hub[31] and International Centre for Settlement of Investment Disputes (ICSID) Case Database[32]

that the compensation that Serbia has ultimately been ordered to pay is relatively minor.[26] For instance, Serbia's Arbitration Association reports that in *Mytilineos v. Serbia (II)*,[27] the claimant ultimately did not receive any compensation,[28] and also states that Serbia has practically won all other investment disputes, some of great value (for instance, a dispute initiated by Lithuanian companies where from a claim of around 52 million Euros, Serbia was sentenced to pay an amount of less than 2%).[29] Finally, Serbia's Arbitration Association reports that Serbia's only investment arbitration case concluded in a settlement, the investor's claim of over 82 million Euros was eventually withdrawn.[30]

It may be concluded that Western Balkan countries have not suffered liability of disastrous and alarming financial consequences as a result of investment arbitration. It is perhaps for this reason that there are no indications that Western Balkan countries have been inclined to consider investment treaty protections as standards on which they would model institutional and judicial reform. As can be seen, investment claims against respondents from the Western Balkans have until a few years ago been only occasional, and countries have not had a chance to accumulate know-how on handling investment treaties and preventing disputes with investors through institutional adjustments. So much so, that it is reasonable to consider that States would regard serious and well-founded investment claims to constitute low-probability events. In their study on investment treaty claims and policy-making, *Skovgaard Poulsen* and *Aisbett* note that per definition, low-probability events are

---

[26] See https://www.international-arbitration-attorney.com/investor-state-arbitrations-against-serbia/.

[27] Mytilineos Holdings SA v. The State Union of Serbia & Montenegro and Republic of Serbia, UNCITRAL.

[28] See https://www.international-arbitration-attorney.com/investor-state-arbitrations-against-serbia/.

[29] Ibid.

[30] Ibid.

[31] UNCTAD, Investment Policy Hub. Investment Dispute Settlement Navigator. Available at: https://investmentpolicy.unctad.org/investment-dispute-settlement.

[32] ICSID, Case Database. Available at: https://icsid.worldbank.org/cases/case-database.

unlikely to greatly influence decision-makers. Therefore, in the absence of highly 'available' information, decision-makers often fail to give low-probability events due consideration until lightning strikes.[33]

Another problematic aspect in this context is the noted criticism of investment arbitration that the lack of predictability of outcomes resulting from a number of conflicting and inconsistent interpretations of investment protection standards by different investment tribunals.[34] Such unpredictability has been held to only endorse an *ex post facto* 'I will know it when I see it' control of host State conduct.[35] This undoubtedly affects the likelihood and possibility that States take into account investment protection standards in their policy-making process. This is particularly accentuated in Western Balkan countries because of the relatively small number of experts in the field of investment arbitration, with relevant education and experience in the area.

3.3 Lack of Transparency in Investment Arbitration

As stated above and noted in official EU reports and studies, democratic processes in the Western Balkans are stagnating and authoritarianism is on the rise, prompting some countries to be branded by the European Commission as 'captured States',[36] a term used to describe a State whose institutions are being undermined and cannot work for the common good.[37] Such setting and unwanted trend hardly provide a promising environment in which government decision-makers push for meaningful reforms and positive changes in administration on their own initiative. Public pressure and accountability are for this reason vital to force concrete steps from officials towards the strengthening of the rule of law.

On this note, the until recent dominant principle of confidentiality in investment arbitration has been a long-standing issue for several reasons, not least because it prevents the public from becoming aware of what challenged measures has its government adopted and what constituted the eventual finding of improper behavior. This has contributed to the noted perception of investment arbitration as a mechanism shrouded in secrecy and lacking legitimacy, which stems from the fact that the public has had limited access to investment arbitral proceedings and to information regarding the existence of a specific dispute.[38] Public interest in investor-State arbitrations arises from several sources according to *Magraw* and *Amerasinghe*.[39]

---

[33] Skovgaard Poulsen and Aisbett (2013), p. 278.

[34] Reinisch (2023), p. 222.

[35] Kingsbury and Schill (2009), p. 19.

[36] See SWD (2016) 362 final. Available at: https://neighbourhood-enlargement.ec.europa.eu/system/files/2018-12/20161109_report_the_former_yugoslav_republic_of_macedonia.pdf.

[37] Bieber (2020), p. 110.

[38] See Moneke (2020), p. 1.

[39] Magraw and Amerasinghe (2009), p. 339.

First, investor-State arbitrations involve the State in a sovereign capacity, the public has a clear interest in such actions. Second, claimants in investor-State arbitration alleges wrongful behavior by a State, which, again, raises public interest. Additionally, investor-State arbitrations often involve either important natural resources, such as oil and gas, hard rock minerals, forests, fresh water, and fisheries, or major built infrastructure such as facilities regarding water, sanitation, roads and other means of transport, power generation, and dams. The latter, in turn, often implicate the delivery of important domestic services, such as drinking water, sanitation, or electricity. Investor-State arbitrations may also involve challenges to regulatory or other decisions that penetrate deeply into traditionally domestic sovereign prerogatives (e.g., regulations protecting health, safety, or the environment), or activities that similarly have deep roots in domestic institutions. The public interest in maintaining the integrity and effectiveness of these domestic policies and governmental actions they note, is obvious.[40] *Magraw* and *Amerasinghe* also rightly point out that the amount of money at stake in an investor-State arbitration can be very large and would ultimately be borne by the State budget.[41] Therefore, if media, non-governmental organizations and the general public gains access to information on the alleged wrongdoings of officials, public scrutiny and pressure would motivate politicians in the Western Balkans, as in most countries, to take decisive actions against improper and illegal acts of State bodies and alleviate criticism by undertaking proper reforms.

The lack of transparency in investment arbitration has for these reasons been recognized as a legitimate concern and actions have been taken to rectify this predicament on a global and systematic level. Accordingly, amendments have been adopted to the ICSID Arbitration Rules which improve transparency in ICSID arbitration. As a result, ICSID awards are now more regularly and promptly published online and a number of recordings of hearings have more recently been made available. Furthermore, in 2013 the United Nations Commission on International Trade Law (UNCITRAL) prepared and adopted the Rules on Transparency in Treaty-based Investor-State Arbitration (Rules on Transparency), which are considered to transpose the principle of open justice to the conduct of investment arbitration.[42] The Rules on Transparency provide transparency-benefits such as the publication of information at the commencement of arbitral proceedings, the publication of documents and public access to hearings, subject to certain exceptions (business secrets, security interests etc.). Predominantly because the Rules on Transparency do not apply to investor-state arbitrations initiated under the UNCITRAL Arbitration Rules pursuant to a treaty concluded before 1 April 2014,[43] UNCITRAL has adopted the United Nations Convention on Transparency in Treaty-based Investor-State Arbitration (Mauritius Convention on Transparency), which provides for the application of the Rules on Transparency to arbitrations arising out of investment treaties concluded before April 2014. Hence, the Mauritius Convention on Transparency allows the

40 Ibid.

41 Ibid.

42 Ribeiro and Douglas (2015), p. 59.

43 Article 1(2) of the Rules on Transparency.

Rules on Transparency to apply to arbitrations arising under around 3,000 investment treaties.[44] At the time of writing, the Mauritius Convention on Transparency has been signed by 23 countries,[45] none of which are from the Western Balkans. Moreover, there are also no transparency clauses in any of the publicly available model bilateral investment treaties of Western Balkan countries.

Therefore, until investment arbitration proceedings against Western Balkan countries are not subject to transparency obligations and the watchful eye of the public, the confidentiality of the arbitration would ensure that politicians are less likely to be held politically and legally accountable for their potentially damaging and illegal actions affecting investors. This inevitably decreases the potential of investment treaties to promote the rule of law and good governance. In fact, complete confidentiality in investment arbitration has the potential to produce the opposite effect. In case investors pursue the protection of their legal rights through a secretive mechanism, and not through national courts where hearings are generally held publicly and judgments are published in full, it may be argued that in this way investment arbitration stimulates corruption and deceitful acts from officials who are not overly concerned with the potential liability such actions may cause to the public finances and State budget.

On a more theoretical level, enhanced transparency of investment arbitration and their legal reasoning and thought process of arbitrators in deciding on cases, may help States gain more information on the investment arbitration system and awareness as to what is required to ensure compliance with its international obligations. Enhancing transparency in international arbitration would therefore certainly add to overall positive effects on administration reform and the rule of law in the Western Balkans.

3.4 Less Incentive to Invest in Independent and Effective National Courts

Another factor potentially contributing to the limited impact of investment treaties on the rule of law in Western Balkan countries is a point raised by *Ginsburg* in his study on the use of bilateral investment treaties, international arbitration, and multilateral trade commitments by developing countries in their efforts of promoting good governance.[46] *Ginsburg* notes that international institutions can serve as complements to domestic institutions, meaning that a country with both credible domestic institutions and credible international options would be even more attractive as an investment venue. He acknowledges however that international institutions might also serve as substitutes for weak domestic institutions. If, for example, local courts are weak, a country may wish to commit to international enforcement mechanisms for contracts,

[44] Ribeiro and Douglas (2015) p. 62.

[45] See https://treaties.un.org/Pages/ViewDetails.aspx?src=IND&mtdsg_no=XXII-3&chapter=22&clang=_en.

[46] Ginsburg (2005), p. 1.

such an investment arbitration. In this case, the presence of international alternatives can help a country to overcome defects in the domestic institutional environment.[47] The issue here is that the decision to bypass domestic courts may reduce courts' improvement of performance by depriving key political actors from the need and incentive to invest in institutional improvement.[48] It is not unreasonable to think that point is of relevance in the decision-making of politicians in the Western Balkans. Considering the vital importance of foreign investments to the economic and overall development of the countries assessed in this chapter, it is expected that policy-makers would allocate budget funds and determine policy priorities with the aim of attracting as much foreign investors as possible. In this regard, if the decisions of high-profile foreign companies to invest in a Western Balkan country are not affected by a low quality and corrupt domestic judicial system, due to the existence of investment arbitration as a viable alternative, then it is reasonable to assume that political factors would be less inclined to prioritize the promotion of the rule of law through judicial reforms.

While this theory may not be conclusively proven by any measurements and studies, it does shed light on one of the many factors contributing to the limited progress of Western Balkan states noted in the European Commission's annual reports. Even though the substantial flow of new foreign investment in the Western Balkan region in recent years has been noted,[49] the EU continuously reports that the relevant countries' judicial systems are "moderately prepared",[50] or that "no progress was achieved in justice reform, the most challenging area of the rule of law to date." and that the "the judiciary's effective independence, integrity, accountability and professionalism need to be further strengthened."[51] This is despite the continued support of the EU and its Member States for judicial reforms, indicating that there could, indeed, be a lack of political will by stakeholders to invest in judicial reforms as long as domestic shortcoming do not significantly hinder foreign investment flows.

---

[47] Ibid, p. 21.

[48] Ibid, p. 23.

[49] Krasniqi, Ahmetbasić and Barnett (2022), p. 2.

[50] See SWD (2023) 693 final. Available at: https://neighbourhood-enlargement.ec.europa.eu/north-macedonia-report-2023_en.

[51] SWD (2022) 335 final. Available via: https://neighbourhood-enlargement.ec.europa.eu/montenegro-report-2022_en.

4 Increased Number of Arbitration Claims Prompting a Response

As economic integration and cooperation of Western Balkan countries with developed capital exporting economies is increasing and foreign investment has risen drastically in the last few decades, so have the number of investment claims threatening these countries' limited State budgets. The increase in the number of investment arbitration cases brought against Western Balkan countries is not surprising, considering the many foreign investors operating in the region now and the still inexperienced institutions regularly interacting with these investors. *Echandi* points out that, in practice, it is not easy for governments to articulate a coherent, transparent and coordinated implementation of their investment policies and regulations in a context in which a multiplicity and multilayered web of regulatory bodies interacts with investors on an everyday basis. Ensuring efficient and coherent government action can be a challenge even for advanced economies with sophisticated institutions.[52]

This development has in the last few years triggered the interest of institutions in certain Western Balkan countries in pursuing a more coordinated State response to the threat of investment arbitration and to even consider reforms whose purpose is of a more preventive nature, handling investor grievances and ensuring State compliance with investment protection treaty standards.

Macedonia serves as such an example, as it has established a more organized mechanism of handling investment arbitration and a permanent government body which specialized in understanding the gravity of the risks and financial implications arising out of investment arbitration. The country has faced a growing number of investment claims against it, as there are currently six pending investment arbitration cases in which the country is involved in, compared to the five total previous cases since its independence.[53] This has prompted institutional response. In 2017, the Macedonian Government founded the coordination body for monitoring arbitration proceedings arising from international treaties,[54] a body comprised of State officials and experts and responsible for monitoring all arbitration proceedings where the country appears as respondent. The body is predominantly tasked with coordinating *ex post* State response and handling the defence in the already initiated arbitration proceedings. In its annual report published in 2023, the Macedonian State Audit Office cites an analysis of the coordinating body, which has determined that the State stands to lose 945 million Euros and 420 million US Dollars if the tribunals were to uphold all currently pending claims.[55] In light of these potentially devastating financial implications, a different, more preventive approach is now being developed. The Government's 2024 working program envisions the establishment

[52] Echandi (2019), p. 17.

[53] See https://investmentpolicy.unctad.org/investment-dispute-settlement/country/124/north-macedonia.

[54] Decision no. 44-8454/1 adopted by the Government of the Republic of North Macedonia on 19 December 2017.

[55] State Audit Office of the Republic of North Macedonia (2023).

of a coordinating body responsible for early prevention and mediation of investment disputes. As provided in the 2024 working program, the purpose of this body would be to collect and disseminate relevant information on potential investment requests to the competent institutions, but also recommend measures to avoid and resolve investment disputes. Such a body would include representatives from several institutions such as government ministers and representatives of other State administration bodies involved in attracting foreign investments, as well as academics with expertise in the area of IIL and investment arbitration.[56]

Bosnia and Herzegovina has taken similar actions. The country's Council of Ministers in 2017 established the negotiating body of Bosnia and Herzegovina for the amicable settlement of international investment disputes,[57] which aims to ensure timely, coordinated and efficient action of the relevant institutions in representing and protecting the interests of Bosnia and Herzegovina in the process of amicable settlement of international investment disputes and providing support to the State Attorney of Bosnia and Herzegovina as the country's legal representative in such disputes. In its 2021 annual report, the negotiating body in Bosnia and Herzegovina describes the various activities it has undertaken with the aim of determining relevant facts, coordinating activities of all entities associated with the proceedings for amicable settlement of investment disputes, as well as the activities undertaken by the relevant ministries relating to investment policies of Bosnia and Herzegovina and their affect on investment treaties. It ultimately concludes that institutional awareness must be raised as to investment treaties, and the obligations undertaken therein, together with possible implications, with the aim of promoting timely detection and settling disputes before their escalation. It advises institutions to consistently adhere to international treaties and domestic legislation in relation to foreign investors and their investments, in order to avoid investment arbitration claims and possible negative consequences.[58]

Other Western Balkan countries have likely seen the need to set up a spacialized body for this specific purpose and their efforts have thus far been confined to the policy of encouraging public officials and employees within the relevant ministries and public agencies to take active participation in trainings and projects supported by EU countries aimed as strengthening administrative capacities and gaining awareness of experiences in the development of preventive mechanisms for settlement of investment disputes between States and investors.[59]

There is also a recent example of a public backlash by a Western Balkan government against the international investment arbitration system. After an ICSID tribunal ordered Albania to pay more than 110 million Euros in damages, costs, and accrued interest estimated at around 10 million Euros, and Albania failed in an attempt to

[56] Government of the Republic of North Macedonia (2024), p. 112.

[57] Decision no. 329/17 adopted by the Council of Ministers of Bosnia and Herzegovina on 24 November 2017.

[58] See https://ekonsultacije.gov.ba/legislativeactivities/details/120249-.

[59] See Government of Montenegro, Ministry of European Affairs (2024); See Academy of Justice, Republic of Kosovo (2023).

revise such award, the Albanian Prime Minister threatened with the withdrawal of Albania from the ICSID.[60] Although these threats have not materialized at the time of writing, such a reaction suggests that Albania's government is not convinced with the international investment arbitration system and is open to promoting viable alternatives for dispute resolution it may offer to foreign investors. However, only a few months after this public outcry against the ICSID, the Albanian parliament adopted Law no. 52/2023 on Arbitration in the Republic of Albania,[61] signaling that the country is ready to invest in and promote alternative resolution methods, as a means of providing effective legal protection and certainty for foreign investors.

It follows that the established (or planned) Macedonian and Bosnian government bodies are two concrete examples of organized institutional efforts of improving governance and regulatory interaction with investors. Similarly, countries such as Peru, Colombia and South Korea have instituted different types of internal systems to manage disputes with foreign investors and to ensure compliance with investment treaties.[62] However, scholars have found no direct evidence of the extent to which such institutions trigger wider administrative reforms in practice. *Bonnitcha* states that it is possible that such institutions are important mechanisms via which investment treaties induce change in domestic administration, but it is also possible that such institutions primarily address investors' grievances *ex post* and do not trigger significant administrative reform.[63] Nevertheless, the institutional coordination these bodies strive to provide could prove nothing but beneficial for governments. *Echandi*'s findings on the policy implications of investment arbitration supports this statement. He argues that the evidence suggests that the tendency of developing States of losing investment arbitration cases does not often originate from the deliberate intention of public officials to disregard regulatory governance principles, but from the challenge that many governments have in ensuring in practice a coordinated implementation of their policies.[64]

5 Conclusion

It can be concluded that after the previous insignificant impact of investment arbitration, Western Balkan countries are now becoming increasingly aware of the challenges of complying with IIL and the benefits of preventing costly investment arbitration proceedings. It is to be expected that concentrated institutional efforts of preventing disputes with investors will, as *Schill* and *Djanic* put it, have a lasting positive effect on strengthening the rule of law and even help legal systems to overcome domestic obstacles and to adapt their governance structures to the needs of

[60] See Djanic (2023), Musabelliu (2023).

[61] Halili and Turšič (2023).

[62] Bonnitcha (2017), p. 6.

[63] Ibid.

[64] Echandi (2019), p. 17.

increasingly global markets and the concomitant international legal disciplines that accompany them.[65] The extent to which such efforts will actually produce these desired effects, remains to be seen.

References

Academy of Justice, Republic of Kosovo (2023) Trainings program for 2024. https://ad.rks-gov.net/media/Programi%20i%20Pun%C3%ABs%20Trajnimeve/PP2024Srb_.pdf

Bieber F (2020) The rise of authoritarianism in the western Balkans. In: Featherstone K, Economides S, Monastiriotis V (eds) New perspectives on South-East Europe. Palgrave Macmillan, pp 1–150

Bonnitcha J (2017) Assessing the impacts of investment treaties: overview of the evidence. International Institute for Sustainable Development (IISD). https://www.iisd.org/system/files/publications/assessing-impacts-investment-treaties.pdf

Council of Europe (2011) European commission for democracy through law (venice commission), Venice, 25–26 March 2011, Report on the Rule of Law. CDL-AD(2011)003rev

Dabrowski M, Myachenkova Y (2018) The Western Balkans on the road to the European Union. Bruegel Policy Contributions Issue, No.2018/04 https://www.econstor.eu/bitstream/10419/208011/1/1014693047.pdf

Davis KE, Trebilcock MJ (2008) The relationship between law and development: optimists versus skeptics. Am J Comp Law 56(4):885–946

Djanic V (2023) Albania's Prime Minister threatens withdrawal from ICSID following unsuccessful request for revision of Hydro v. Albania award, 7/4/2023, IA reporter. https://www.iareporter.com/articles/albanias-prime-minister-threatens-withdrawal-from-icsid-following-unsuccessful-request-for-revision-of-hydro-v-albania-award/

Echandi R (2019) The debate on treaty-based investor–state dispute settlement: empirical evidence (1987–2017) and policy implications. ICSID Rev – Foreign Invest Law J (Kinnear M, McLachlan C (eds)) 34(1):32–61

European Commission (2018) Communication from the Commission to the European Parliament, the Council, the European Economic and Social Committee and the Committee of the Regions, a credible enlargement perspective for and enhanced EU engagement with the Western Balkans, 6/2/2018, COM (2018) 65 final

European Court of Auditors (2022) Special report: EU support for the rule of law in the Western Balkans: despite efforts, fundamental problems persist. Publications Office of the European Union. https://www.eca.europa.eu/en/publications?did=60343

Ginsburg T (2005) International substitutes for domestic institutions: bilateral investment treaties and governance. Int Rev Law Econ 25(1):107–123

Government of Montenegro, Ministry of European Affairs (2024) Platform for the participation of the Montenegrin delegation at the XIII meeting of the Council for stabilization and association held in Podgorica, 21.II.2024. https://wapi.gov.me/download-preview/77564963-afe5-440e-8bcc-6fa563f41b6b?version=1.0

Government of the Republic of North Macedonia (2024) Program on the work of the Government of the Republic of North Macedonia for 2024. https://vlada.mk/sites/default/files/dokumenti/strategii/programa_za_rabota_na_vrsm_za_2024_godina.pdf

Halili E, Turšič D (2023) New era begins in Albania: parliament passes arbitration law. Kluwer Arbitration Blog. https://arbitrationblog.kluwerarbitration.com/2023/08/19/new-era-begins-in-albania-parliament-passes-arbitration-law/

Jacob M, Schill SW (2015) Fair and equitable treatment: content, practice, method. In: Bungenberg M et al (eds) International investment law: a handbook. Nomos/CH Beck/Hart, pp 700–763

[65] Schill and Djanic (2018), p. 37.

Jansen Calamita N, Berman A (2022) The internalisation of investment treaties and the rule of law promise. In: Berman A, Jansen Calamita N (eds) Investment treaties and the rule of law promise: an examination of the internalisation of international commitments in Asia. Cambridge University Press, Cambridge, pp 1–37
Kingsbury B, Schill SW (2009) Investor-state arbitration as governance: fair and equitable treatment, proportionality, and the emerging global administrative law. In: IILJ working paper 2009/6, global administrative law series. https://iilj.org/wp-content/uploads/2016/08/Kingsbury-Schill-Investor-State-Arbitration-as-Governance-IILJ-WP-2009_6-GAL.pdf
Krasniqi B, Ahmetbasić J, Barnett W (2022) Foreign direct investment and backward spillovers in the western balkans the context, opportunities and barriers to the development of regional supply chains. Southeast Eur 46(1):1–22
Magraw DB, Amerasinghe NM (2009) Transparency and public participation in investor-state arbitration. ILSA J Int & Compar Law 15(2):337–360
Moneke E (2020) The quest for transparency in investor-state arbitration: are the transparency rules and the mauritius convention effective instruments of reform? Arbitr: Int J Arbitr Mediat Disput Manag 86(2):157–186
Musabelliu M (2023) Albania economy briefing: it is time for Albania to pay! The costs of an international legal battle, China-CEE Institute, Weekly Briefing 61(2) (AI). https://china-cee.eu/wp-content/uploads/2023/04/2023e04_Albania-1.pdf
Reinisch A (2023) Investment arbitration and the rule of law. In: Kröll S, Bjorklund AK, Ferrari F (eds) Cambridge compendium of investment commercial and investment arbitration. Cambridge University Press, Cambridge, pp 211–243
Ribeiro J, Douglas M (2015) Transparency in investor-state arbitration: the way forward. Asian Int Arbitr J 11(1):49–67
Schill SW, Djanic V (2018) Wherefore art thou? Towards a public interest-based justification of international investment law. ICSID Rev – Foreign Investment Law J 33(1):29–55
Schultz T, Dupont C (2014) Investment arbitration: promoting the rule of law or over-empowering investors? A quantative empirical study. Eur J Int Law 25(4):1147–1168
Skovgaard Poulsen LN, Aisbett E (2013) When the claim hits: bilateral investment treaties and bounded rational learning. World Polit 65(2):273–313
State Audit Office of the Republic of North Macedonia (2023) Annual report for 2022 of performed audits and the work of the state audit office. https://dzr.mk/sites/default/files/2023-08/DZR_Godisen_izvestaj_2022_mkd_0.pdf
Transparency International (2020) Captured States in the Western Balkans and Turkey. https://www.transparency.org/en/news/captured-states-western-balkans-turkey

Decentral Implementation of EU International Investment Protection Policy and Its Implications for Countries in the Western Balkans

Bianca Böhme

Abstract This chapter examines the decentralized implementation of EU international investment protection policy and its implications for Western Balkan countries. With the Treaty of Lisbon granting the EU exclusive competence over foreign direct investment, a new centralized approach was adopted. However, due to the stagnation of EU-level agreements, investment protection increasingly relies on Member States' BITs, overseen by the European Commission. The chapter explores how this shift affects Western Balkan countries, especially those aspiring EU accession. It discusses the necessary alignment of BITs with evolving EU standards, including substantive and procedural changes, and the broader implications for investment treaty practices in the region. The analysis highlights the challenges faced by these countries in harmonizing their agreements with EU policies and the potential impact on their accession processes.

1 Introduction

For over a decade, the European Union (EU) has been crafting its own international investment policy in relation to third countries. This policy signifies a clear shift from the traditional European gold standard that defined the Bilateral Investment Treaties (BITs) of EU Member States for many years. The new EU approach has prompted a "paradigm change",[1] moving away from solely focusing on high investment protection to more balanced standards and the international rule of law.[2] These new standards of a common EU international investment policy are also expected to be implemented by EU Member States in their own BITs. In fact, due to the stagnation

[1] Bungenberg and Reinisch (2021), p. 440.

[2] On the promotion of the rule of law in the Western Balkans through investment arbitration, see Tokarev (2024) in this book.

B. Böhme (✉)
Foreign Associate at Busse Disputes, Frankfurt Am Main, Germany
e-mail: boehme@busse-disputes.com

M. Bungenberg et al. (eds.), *Alternative Dispute Resolution in the Western Balkans*, European Union and its Neighbours in a Globalized World 20,
https://doi.org/10.1007/978-3-031-76345-8_8

of EU investment protection agreements, the EU's international investment policy is increasingly being implemented through Member States' BITs at the decentral level.

This chapter explores the implications of the EU's move towards a decentralised investment protection policy for countries of the Western Balkans, which are directly or indirectly affected, depending on their status as either EU Member State (in the case of Croatia), or an accession candidate. In both scenarios, they are expected to align their BITs with the EU standards of investment protection. After explaining the shift towards a decentralized EU investment policy (2.), this contribution will provide an overview of key substantive and procedural standards of EU international investment protection (3.). The subsequent section will outline further implications for Western Balkan countries with regard to their BITs with EU Member States (4.). The final section concludes (5.).

2 Decentral Implementation of EU Investment Protection Policy

With the Treaty of Lisbon's entry into force in December 2009, foreign direct investment became an exclusive competence of the EU. Article 207(1) of the Treaty on the Functioning of the European Union (TFEU) now includes foreign direct investment under the EU's Common Commercial Policy, allowing the EU to negotiate international investment agreements on behalf of its Member States. The EU has used its competence under Article 207 TFEU to negotiate with key trading partners such as Canada, Chile, China, India, Japan, Mexico, Singapore, Vietnam, and the UK,[3] resulting *inter alia* in the EU-Singapore[4] and EU-Vietnam[5] Investment Protection Agreements (IPAs), as well as the EU-Canada Comprehensive Economic and Trade Agreement (CETA).[6] However, none of these investment protection agreements have yet entered into force.

This stagnation is largely owed to the European Court of Justice's (ECJ) decision in its *Singapore Opinion*, which stated that non-direct foreign investment and investor-State dispute settlement are shared competences of the EU and its Member States.[7] As

[3] An overview of the EU's investment protection agreements and free trade agreements, which have been concluded or are currently being negotiated, can be found at: https://policy.trade.ec.europa.eu/eu-trade-relationships-country-and-region/negotiations-and-agreements_en.

[4] Council Decision (EU) 2018/1676 of 15 October 2019 on the signing on behalf of the EU of the Investment Protection Agreement between the EU and its Member States, of the one part, and the Republic of Singapore, of the other part, OJ L 279/1.

[5] Council Decision (EU) 2019/1096 of 25 June 2018 on the signing on behalf of the EU of the Investment Protection Agreement between the EU and its Member States, of the one part, and the Socialist Republic of Viet Nam, of the other part, OJ L 175/1.

[6] Comprehensive Economic and Trade Agreement (CETA) between Canada, of the one part, and the European Union and its Member States, of the other part, OJ L 11/1.

[7] ECJ, Opinion 2/15 of 16 May 2017, ECLI:EU:C:2017:376, paras. 238, 292 et seq. See also Cremona (2018), pp. 235 et seqq.

a result of this decision, the Council of the EU categorised EU investment agreements covering these aspects as "mixed agreements", requiring approval both at the EU and national levels. Accordingly, any Member State can block EU investment agreements by delaying or refusing ratification.[8] And this is what has happened in practice. Although the CETA was signed in October 2016, it has been ratified by only 17 Member States so far—nearly eight years later.[9] Certain delays are typical, as mixed agreements take an average of 1,143 days for full ratification, compared to just 348 days for EU-only agreements.[10] However, due to several national hurdles in some Member States, it remains uncertain whether these mixed investment agreements will ever be fully ratified.

In response to these challenges, the EU has increasingly supported a decentralized implementation of its investment policy via the BITs of its Member States. Regulation 1219/2012[11] still allows Member States to negotiate new BITs and amend existing ones, albeit under strict Commission oversight.[12] According to Article 8(1) of Regulation 1219/2012, Member States must notify the Commission before entering BIT negotiations. Subsequently, they require the Commission's approval to start negotiations (Article 9) and to conclude a BIT (Article 11). In addition, they must keep the Commission informed throughout the entire process (Article 10).

This authorization mechanism under Regulation 1219/2012 has been widely used by EU Member States. According to a report by the Commission, there were 442 requests by Member States to authorize the opening of negotiations or conclusion of BITs between 2013 and 2019.[13] Since March 2019, the Commission issued over 100 additional implementing decisions with further authorizations to negotiate or conclude BITs. These implementing decisions are significant, not only because they demonstrate the active engagement of EU Member States in external investment negotiations, but also because they highlight how the Commission shapes these negotiations by imposing numerous requirements emanating from the EU's international investment policy.[14]

In a move to directly influence the language used in these treaties, the Commission recently published a set of annotated Model Clauses to be integrated in Member States' BITs.[15] These are intended to guide the Member States in crafting their BITs to align with overarching EU policies. Although the Model Clauses do not constitute an official EU Model BIT, they effectively mirror the EU's currently stalled

---

[8] Council of the European Union (2018a, b); See also Bungenberg and Böhme (2022), p. 630.

[9] See https://www.consilium.europa.eu/de/documents-publications/treaties-agreements/agreement/?id=2016017.

[10] Freudlsperger (2021), p. 1657.

[11] Regulation (EU) No 1219/2012 of the European Parliament and of the Council of 12 December 2012 establishing transitional arrangements for bilateral investment agreements between Member States and third countries, OJ L 251/40.

[12] Schacherer (2016).

[13] European Commission (2023a, b, c).

[14] Bungenberg, Böhme and Ruf (2023), p. 33.

[15] European Commission (2023b).

external investment policy, which continues to expand through the treaty practice of its Member States. As will be discussed in the ensuing section, this new development has significant implications for the Western Balkans, potentially affecting their investment treaty practice.

3 Implications for Countries in the Western Balkans

The EU has established a policy aimed at the gradual integration of Western Balkan countries into the Union. Croatia became the first of these countries to join on 1 July 2013. Albania, Bosnia and Herzegovina, Montenegro, North Macedonia, and Serbia currently hold candidate country status, with accession negotiations actively underway with Montenegro and Serbia. Additionally, Albania and North Macedonia began negotiations in July 2022, and Kosovo submitted its EU membership application in December 2022.[16] Hence, all these Western Balkan countries have either already become an EU Member State or are on their way towards EU accession.

As the only full EU Member State, Croatia is obligated under Article 4(3) of the Treaty on the European Union (TEU), which provides a duty of sincere cooperation among EU Member States. This provision asserts that "the Union and the Member States shall, in full mutual respect, assist each other in carrying out the tasks which flow from the Treaties". Foreign direct investment policy, detailed under Article 207 TFEU as part of the EU's Common Commercial Policy, is included among these tasks. As a result, the principle of sincere cooperation requires unified actions and appearances by the EU and its Member States on the external scene, when it comes to their policies of investment protection.[17] In fact, Regulation 1219/2012 lays down the EU's interest in harmonized investment standards in treaties with third countries. Consequently, Article 9(2) allows the Commission to direct Member States to adjust their prospective BITs to ensure consistency with the EU's external investment policy.

The other Western Balkan countries, which have not yet become EU Member States, are similarly expected to revise their investment treaty practices supporting their accession ambitions. In fact, the Commission advised the Republic of North Macedonia that it should analyse its BITs "with regard to the need for their harmonisation with EU law".[18] Similarly, the 2023 report for Serbia mandated developing a strategy "for amending or terminating existing treaties that fall short of EU standards and expose the country to risks due to the broad and open language used".[19] Consequently, all Western Balkan countries should harmonise their investment treaties with EU standards as part of their accession process or their obligation as an EU Member State (in the case of Croatia). The ensuing subsections will discuss the main

[16] See https://www.europarl.europa.eu/factsheets/en/sheet/168/the-western-balkans.

[17] Klamert (2014), p. 190.

[18] European Commission (2018).

[19] European Commission (2023b).

adjustments required regarding both substantive (I.) and procedural (II.) standards that these countries should make in their investment agreements with third countries.

3.1 Substantive Changes

EU investment policy is marked by several substantive requirements that both EU and Member States' investment agreements must satisfy. Some of these requirements directly stem from EU primary law, as determined by the ECJ. Accordingly, the ECJ found that the autonomy of the EU legal order would be adversely affected, if investment tribunals could call into question the level of protection of a public interest that led to the introduction of a particular State measure.[20] To avoid this, EU investment agreements must include certain substantive safeguards aimed at establishing a balance between investment protection and the pursuit of public policy objections.[21] Two key aspects to achieve the desired balance are narrowly defined investment protection standards (1.) and sustainable development provisions (2.).

3.1.1 Narrowly Defined Investment Protection Standards

In its implementing decisions, the Commission asks EU Member States to include the following investment protection standards in their BITs[22]:

(a) **Fair and Equitable Treatment (FET)**: This should include a provision against unreasonable, arbitrary, or discriminatory measures.
(b) **National Treatment**
(c) **Most-Favoured Nation (MFN) Treatment**: The clause should be drafted in a manner that prevents the importation of standards of treatment and procedural rights from other investment agreements.
(d) **Protection against Direct and Indirect Expropriation**: Including the right to prompt, adequate and effective compensation.
(e) **Full Protection and Security**: This should safeguard both investors and investments.

If read together with the Commission's annotated Model Clauses, it becomes clear that it would not suffice for Member States to merely include these standards in

[20] ECJ, Opinion 1/17 of 30 April 2019, ECLI:EU:C:2019:341, para. 148.

[21] The Commission, the European Parliament and the Council have all expressed that this constitutes a key aspect of EU international investment policy. See European Commission (2010), p. 9; European Parliament (2022), paras. 23–26; Council of the EU (2010), para. 17. Most importantly, the ECJ noted this requirement in Opinion 1/17 of 30 April 2019, ECLI:EU:C:2019:341, para. 149.

[22] See Commission Implementing Decision of 4 September 2023 authorising Hungary to open formal negotiations to conclude a bilateral investment agreement with the Democratic Republic of Congo.

their BITs. Instead of including unqualified investment protection standards, Member States must restrict their scope in line with current EU policies.

For the FET standard, the annotated Model Clauses foresee a "closed list" approach, which is typical in EU investment protection agreements. In accordance with this approach, the FET standard is defined by reference to a list, enumerating situations that are considered unfair and inequitable treatment, such as denial of justice, a fundamental breach of due process, manifest arbitrariness, targeted discrimination, or harassment. The ECJ was satisfied that the CETA would not adversely affect the autonomy of EU law because its Article 8.10 restricts the scope of the FET standard by specifically circumscribing and exhaustively listing possible infringements.[23] However, since the Commission's implementing decisions merely require Member States to include "unreasonable, arbitrary or discriminatory measures" as breach of the FET standard, it remains uncertain if the "closed list" approach is mandatory for Member States' BITs.

Croatia, which has not entered into new investment agreements since 2008,[24] continues to adhere to the "European gold standard" in its BITs. This traditional approach aims to provide the highest level of investment protection possible, without incorporating the nuanced requirements that characterize contemporary EU policies.[25] With regard to the FET standard, Croatia's BITs include provisions against "unreasonable, arbitrary or discriminatory measures", but do not follow a "closed list" approach.[26] While this policy option may be accepted by the Commission in line with its implementing decisions, other substantive provisions appear to be incompatible with EU investment policy. The current formulation of the MFN clause in the most recent Croatian BIT does not prevent the importation of treatment standards and procedural rights from other investment agreements,[27] as mandated in both the Commission's implementing decisions and annotated Model Clauses. This lack of restriction is a significant departure from a key EU investment policy aim: to prevent undesired treaty shopping that could lead to a significant departure from EU standards. Therefore, it is probable that the Commission will require Croatia to revise the MFN clauses in its BITs, as to align them with EU investment policy.

The BITs from other Western Balkan countries also largely follow the old European gold standard. Regarding the FET standard, there is only one BIT—concluded in 2022 between Serbia and Turkey—that follows the "closed list" approach.[28] With regard to the MFN clause, the Serbia-Turkey BIT clarifies that the provision is not applicable in respect of dispute settlement provisions, but does not explicitly prohibit the importation of substantive standards from other investment agreements.[29] Since

[23] ECJ, Opinion 1/17 of 30 April 2019, ECLI:EU:C:2019:341, paras. 152 et seqq.

[24] In accordance with the database provided by UNCTAD, the last BIT negotiated by Croatia was with Lithuania. The BIT was signed on 15 April 2008 and entered into force on 30 January 2009.

[25] Titi (2015), pp. 640 et seq.

[26] See e.g. Article 3(1) of the Croatia-Lithuania BIT (2009).

[27] See e.g. Article 3(2) of the Croatia-Lithuania BIT (2009).

[28] See Article 3(3) of the Serbia-Turkey BIT (2022).

[29] See Article 4(5) of the Serbia-Turkey BIT (2022).

the Commission's implementing decisions require the prohibition of importation of *both* substantive and procedural standards, Serbia might be required to amend these provisions upon EU accession.

In the other Western Balkan BITs, we mostly find unqualified FET[30] and MFN[31] standards. Besides the Serbia-Turkey BIT, none follow a "closed list" approach regarding the FET standard, even though some explicitly mention unreasonable, arbitrary, or discriminatory measures as possible violations.[32] As discussed above, it remains unclear whether EU Member States are required or only encouraged to include a closed list of possible FET violations, or whether the inclusion of unreasonable, arbitrary, or discriminatory measures is deemed sufficient. Some Western Balkan BITs equally exclude the importation of procedural standards from the MFN clause, but—just like the Serbia-Turkey BIT—fall short of extending this exclusion to the importation of substantive standards.[33]

3.1.2 Sustainable Development Provisions

One of the pillars of EU investment policy is the protection of certain non-investment interests that might become relevant in an investment arbitration, such as the protection of the environment, health, labour standards and human rights.[34] These objectives are often summarized under the term "sustainable development", which seeks to balance social, environmental, and economic interests. Since 2008, the EU has increasingly embedded obligations to uphold labour and environmental standards in its trade and investment agreements.[35] In accordance with this policy, EU Member States are now expected to include specific sustainable development provisions in their BITs. These provisions should cover[36]:

(a) **Climate Action and Energy Transition**: Aligning with the Paris Agreement, BIT provisions should support the transition to clear energy and reflect the EU's positions in ongoing international negotiations.

[30] See e.g. Art. 3 Serbia-Morocco BIT (2013); Montenegro-Moldova BIT (2015); Montenegro-Turkey BIT (2020).

[31] See e.g. Art. 4 Serbia-Qatar BIT (2017); Art. 4 North Macedonia-Vietnam BIT (2016); Art. 4 Albania-Cyprus BIT (2011); Art. 3 Albania-Bosnia and Herzegovina BIT; Montenegro-Moldova BIT (2015); Art. 3(1) Albania-Malta BIT (2011).

[32] See e.g. Art. 2(3) Montenegro-Azerbaijan BIT (2012); Art. 3(4) Serbia-Qatar BIT (2017); Art. 3(2) North Macedonia-Vietnam BIT (2016); Art. 2(2) Albania-Malta BIT (2011).

[33] See e.g. Art. 5(3) Montenegro-United Arab Emirates BIT (2013); Montenegro-Turkey BIT (2020).

[34] Schacherer (2019), p. 208.

[35] Bartels (2017), p. 2.

[36] See e.g. Commission Implementing Decision of 4 September 2023 authorising Hungary to open formal negotiations to conclude a bilateral investment agreement with the Democratic Republic of Congo, p. 3.

(b) **Prohibition of Regulatory Dilution**: Member States are to ensure that investments do not promote the lowering or relaxation of domestic environmental or labour laws, nor should there be a failure to enforce such standards effectively.
(c) **Promotion of Human Rights and Labour Standards**: BITs should include commitments to uphold human rights and international labour standards, alongside globally recognized frameworks for responsible business conduct. Notable examples include the OECD Guidelines for Multinational Enterprises, the UN Guiding Principles on Business and Human Rights and the International Labour Organisation Tripartite Declaration of Principles concerning Multinational Enterprises and Social Policy.

What is notable is that the requirements recommended for Member States' BITs appear to be more extensive than those included in existing EU investment protection agreements.[37] The CETA, the EU-Vietnam IPA and EU-Singapore IPA primarily acknowledge non-investment policy objectives in their preambles and assert the contracting parties' right to regulate in their operative parts, without incorporating detailed sustainable development provisions.[38] In Opinion 1/17, the ECJ considered this to be sufficient in the case of the CETA.[39] In contrast, the Commission's non-paper proposes a comprehensive Model Clause for each non-investment policy area. Hence, the Model Clauses include detailed provisions on "Corporate Social Responsibility and Responsible Business Conduct", "Investment and Environment", "Investment and Climate Change", and "Investment and Labour". Unlike the more general references in EU investment protection agreements, a provision based on these Model Clauses would be included in the operative part of Member States' BITs, thus imposing direct obligations on the contracting parties.[40]

None of the Western Balkan countries include such comprehensive provisions on sustainable development in their BITs. Montenegro's most recent BIT with the Republic of Moldova concluded in 2015[41] does not incorporate any sustainable development clauses in its operative text and the preamble merely acknowledges economic policy objectives. This trend is consistent across other BITs from Montenegro,[42] as well as those from North Macedonia, Bosnia and Herzegovina, Albania, and Croatia, which similarly do not include any reference to sustainable development.[43] A few of

[37] Bungenberg, Böhme and Ruf (2023), pp. 43 et seqq.

[38] See Art. 2.2(1) EU Singapore IPA; Art. 2.2(1) EU-Vietnam IPA; Art. 8(9) CETA.

[39] ECJ, Opinion 1/17 of 30 April 2019, ECLI:EU:C:2019:341, paras. 152 et seqq.

[40] While the EU-Singapore and EU-Vietnam IPAs merely refer to these subject matters in their preamble, the CETA contains a chapter on "Trade and Labour" and "Trade and Environment" outside of the chapter on investment protection. These chapters may be used for interpretative purposes in an investment dispute, but do not create direct legal obligations.

[41] Agreement between the Government of Montenegro and the Government of the Republic of Moldova on Promotion and Reciprocal Protection of Investments, entered into force on 23 June 2015.

[42] See e.g. Montenegro-Moldova BIT (2015), Montenegro-UAE BIT (2013), Montenegro-Macedonia BIT (2011), Montenegro-Malta BIT (2011), Montenegro-Qatar BIT (2009).

[43] See e.g. Bosnia and Herzegovina-Albania BIT (2008); North Macedonia-Viet Nam BIT (2014); Croatia-Lithuania BIT (2008).

these BITs include a provision on the host State's right to regulate,[44] or mention non-investment goals in the preamble.[45] However, such references constitute an exception and are in any case not comparable to the extensive sustainable development provisions included in the Commission's Model Clauses.

Once more, Serbia stands out by (partially) aligning with EU investment policies in the context of non-investment policy goals. The recent Serbia-Turkey BIT (2022) not only includes references to non-investment objectives in its preamble but also integrates these considerations extensively throughout the operative part of the treaty. This includes a General Exception Clause (Article 5) aimed at the protection of health and the environment, and two autonomous treaty provisions on "Health Safety and Environmental Measures" (Article 10) and "Corporate Social Responsibility" (Article 11).

In conclusion, the BIT practices of Western Balkan countries generally do not yet reflect the contemporary standards emphasized in EU investment policy. Among the reviewed treaties, the Serbia-Turkey BIT (2022) stands out as the most aligned with EU standards. However, all countries from the Western Balkans, including Serbia, have concluded numerous BITs based on the old European gold standard in the past.[46] Hence, concluding a handful of new BITs that (partially) align with EU investment policy will not suffice. To fully adhere to current EU investment policy, Western Balkan countries would equally need to undertake extensive renegotiations of their existing BITs with non-EU countries, ideally incorporating the Commission's Model Clauses.

3.2 *Procedural Changes*

The Commission's implementing decisions and Model Clauses also foresee certain procedural provisions that Member States are required to incorporate in their BITs. Many of these provisions constitute elements of procedural modernisation aimed at higher rule of law standards (1.). In addition, Member States are expected to include a provision limiting the law applicable by investment tribunals (2.).

3.2.1 Elements of Procedural Modernisation

The Commission's implementing decisions mandate that Member States include specific elements of procedural modernisation in their BITs to ensure effective

[44] See e.g. Art. 4 of the Montenegro-Turkey BIT (2012).

[45] See e.g. Montenegro-Azerbaijan BIT (2012); Albania-Azerbaijan BIT (2012).

[46] In accordance with the database provided by UNCTAD, Serbia has 46 BITs, Albania has 40 BITs, North Macedonia has 39 BITs, Bosnia and Herzegovina has 37 BITs, Montenegro has 25 BITs, and Croatia has 27 BITs in force.

investor-State dispute settlement. These elements reflect broader trends in investor-State dispute settlement as discussed in Working Group III of the United Nations Commission on International Trade Law (UNCITRAL) and include:

- **Multilateral Investment Court (MIC)**: Member States' BITs must include a provision committing to the establishment of an MIC with an appellate structure. All disputes under the BIT would fall under the jurisdiction of the proposed MIC as soon as established.
- **Transparency**: Member States' BITs should reference the UNCITRAL Rules on Transparency for Investor-State Arbitration or rules ensuring a comparable level of transparency.
- **Code of Conduct**: A binding code of conduct for tribunal members is required, with compliance overseen by an independent external party.
- **Early Dismissal of Manifestly Unfounded Claims**: Member States' BITs should allow for the quick dismissal of claims that are clearly unfounded.
- **Multiple Proceedings**: Provisions to prevent multiple concurrent proceedings on the same issue across different dispute resolution forums should be included.

The push for these procedural innovations is part of the EU's broader strategy to reform the global investment protection regime. The concept of an MIC, which includes an appellate body, has been a central element of EU investment policy for several years.[47] This policy option has equally been taken up in UNCITRAL Working Group III, which has been discussing a possible reform of investor-State dispute settlement since 2017.[48] Following extensive discussions, UNCITRAL Working Group III's Secretariat has recently drafted a statute for a multilateral standing body to resolve international investment disputes.[49] Although it remains uncertain whether a global consensus will be reached, the EU continues to promote this policy goal in its own investment agreements and those of its Member States. Accordingly, while Member States are still permitted to negotiate BITs that provide for traditional investor-State arbitration, they are also required to include a provision that defers to the jurisdiction of an MIC, should it be established.[50] This way, the EU may significantly influence the future procedural framework of the international regime for investment protection, persuading third countries in bilateral negotiations with EU Member States to support the establishment of an MIC.

---

[47] In March 2018, the Council of the EU gave the Commission the mandate to negotiate an MIC. See Council of the EU (2018a).

[48] UNCITRAL (2017) Possible future work in the field of dispute settlement reforms of investor-State dispute settlement (ISDS)—Note by the Secretariat, A/CN.9/917, 20 April 2017.

[49] UNCITRAL (2024).

[50] See e.g. Art. 9(10) of the Hungary-San Marino BIT (2022): "The Contracting Parties shall pursue with each other and other trading partners the establishment of a multilateral investment tribunal and appellate mechanism for the resolution of investment disputes. Upon entry into force between the Contracting Parties of an international agreement providing for a multilateral investment tribunal and/or a multilateral appellate mechanism applicable to disputes under this Agreement, the relevant parts of this Agreement shall cease to apply.".

Even though EU Member States may still negotiate traditional investor-State arbitration for the time being, they must include several elements of procedural modernisation. All these elements are equally being discussed at UNCITRAL Working Group III. They are generally not as controversial as the establishment of an MIC, which would lead to a far-reaching reform of the current investment protection regime. In fact, some BITs of the latest generation of numerous countries worldwide already incorporate certain elements of procedural modernisation for the respective dispute settlement mechanism. However, since most BITs by Western Balkan countries were negotiated several years (if not decades) ago, they generally do not include any of these elements, following again the old European gold standard.[51]

For example, Article 9 of the North Macedonia-Denmark BIT (2015) merely contains a dispute resolution clause, providing for a cooling-off period, the available dispute resolution fora,[52] and the applicable law. No references are made to transparency rules, a code of conduct for the arbitrators, early dismissal of frivolous claims, or multiple proceedings.[53] Even the Serbia-Turkey BIT (2022), which comes close to EU policies with regard to substantive standards of investment protection, does not include any elements of procedural modernisation. Arguably, this deficit could be partially remedied in cases where the investor chooses to submit the relevant dispute to the International Centre for Settlement of Investment Disputes (ICSID). All Western Balkan countries have ratified the ICSID Convention,[54] and their BITs generally name the ICSID as possible venue for investor-State arbitration.

In cases where the investor chooses the ICSID as venue, the ICSID Rules of Arbitration become applicable. These Rules, which were reformed in 2022, contain several elements of procedural modernisation that align with EU investment policy. For instance, Chapter X of the ICSID Rules of Arbitration provides for a rather high level of procedural transparency if compared with other institutional rules primarily aimed at governing commercial arbitration.[55] Accordingly, Rule 62(1) provides that with the consent of the parties, every award, supplementary decision on the award, rectification, interpretation and revision of an award, and decision on annulment will be published. In fact, in accordance with Rule 62(3), the referred documents will be automatically published within 60 days after their dispatch if the parties do not object in writing. Even in case of lacking consent, certain excerpts of the documents will be published. Hence, under those Western Balkan BITs that were negotiated following the old European gold standard, a sufficient level of transparency is nevertheless guaranteed if the investor opts for an ICSID arbitration.

---

[51] Even the Serbia-Turkey BIT (2022), which contains certain substantive elements that align with EU investment policy, does not cover elements of procedural modernization.

[52] The International Centre for Settlement of Investment Disputes, ad hoc arbitration pursuant to the UNCITRAL Arbitration Rules, and the Rules of Arbitration of the International Chamber of Commerce.

[53] Further examples include the Montenegro-Moldova BIT (2015); Croatia-Lithuania BIT (2009); North-Macedonia-Denmark BIT (2015); Albania-Bosnia and Herzegovina BIT (2008).

[54] Albania ratified the ICSID Convention in 1991, followed by Bosnia and Herzegovina in 1997, Croatia and North Macedonia in 1998, Serbia in 2007, and Montenegro in 2013.

[55] On Chapter X of the ICSID Arbitration Rules (2022) see Kalnina/Godbole, pp. 618 et seqq.

Similarly, Rule 41 of the ICSID Arbitration Rules allows a party to object to a claim that is deemed manifestly without legal merit, mirroring another of the procedural concerns expressed by the Commission in its implementing decisions. And in case of multiple proceedings, Rule 46 provides the disputing parties with a procedural opportunity to consolidate or coordinate their arbitrations. A code of conduct for arbitrators is not yet adopted but has been discussed for numerous years jointly by the Secretariats of the ICSID and UNCITRAL. The latest draft of such a joint code of conduct is from February 2024.[56]

Hence, if an investor opts for ICSID arbitration under one of the BITs of the Western Balkan countries, the procedural requirements imposed by the Commission on EU Member States would be partially met. However, the ICSID is just one of several venues for investor-State dispute settlement that are typically provided in BITs and its choice comes within the discretion of the claimant investor. Consequently, the lack of procedural modernisation of the dispute settlement mechanism included in Western Balkan BITs cannot be remedied without amendment of the relevant treaties.

3.2.2 Applicable Law

Another concern of EU investment policy is the delimitation of the law applicable to the relevant investment dispute. This concern is equally addressed in the Commission's implementing decisions, which require EU Member States to specify in their BITs that domestic laws, including EU law, do not constitute part of the applicable law under these agreements. Instead, EU investment protection agreements and recent Member States' BITs provide that domestic law must be treated as a "matter of fact".[57] The EU's aim behind the factual treatment of domestic (and EU law) is to protect the autonomy of the EU legal order.[58] The ECJ uses the principle of autonomy to safeguard the EU legal order from external influences that could undermine its essential characteristics.[59] A major concern in this regard is the potential encroachment of external dispute settlement mechanisms, such as investment tribunals, on the ECJ's sole authority to conclusively interpret and apply EU law.[60] To counter this

[56] See UNCITRAL Code of Conduct for Arbitrators in International Investment Dispute Resolution, available at: https://uncitral.un.org/sites/uncitral.un.org/files/media-documents/uncitral/en/2318944_coc_arbitrators_e-book_eng.pdf.

[57] See e.g. Article 8.31(2) CETA; Article 1.2(p) EU-Vietnam IPA; Article 9(8) Hungary-San Marino BIT (2022); Article 26(2) Colombia-Spain BIT (2021); Article 18(2) Portugal-Côte d'Ivoire BIT (2019).

[58] Böhme (2024), p. 2.

[59] ECJ, Opinion 1/91 [1991] ECR I-06079, para. 21; ECJ, Opinion 1/100 [2001] ECR I-09989, para. 12; ECJ, Opinion 1/09 [2011] ECR I-01137, para. 65; ECJ, Opinion 2/13 [2014] ECLI:EU:C:2014:2454, para. 167; ECJ, Case C-284/16 *Achmea* [2018] ECLi:EU:C:2018:158, para. 33; ECJ, Case C-741/19 *Komstroy* [2021] ECLI:EU:C:2021:655, para. 43.

[60] Thies (2020), p. 51; ECJ, Opinion 1/09 [2011] ECLI:EU:C:2011:123, paras. 78, 89; ECJ, Opinion 2/13 [2014] ECLI:EU:C:2014:2454, paras. 170 et seq., 200.

threat, the Commission insists on the factual treatment of domestic law in EU investment protection agreements and Member States' BITs. This approach is thus aimed at preventing external bodies from interpreting and applying EU law, safeguarding the ECJ's exclusive jurisdiction.[61]

The BITs from Western Balkan countries exhibit varied approaches regarding the law applicable to investment disputes. Some of these BITs specify that international law should apply,[62] others combine both international and domestic law, and again others do not include any clause specifying the applicable law.[63] However, according to the requirements imposed by the Commission, which are based on the case law of the ECJ, none of these approaches comply with current EU standards. The Commission's Model Clauses make it clear that Member States' BITs must explicitly state that domestic law, including EU law, is to be treated as a matter of fact. Since the current BITs of Western Balkan countries do not meet this criterion, they will require amendment if they are to align with EU law.

4 Intra-EU Investment

A final issue that Western Balkan countries should consider in their investment protection policies with a view of EU accession is the incompatibility of intra-EU BITs (i.e. BITs between two EU Member States) with EU law. According to the ECJ, Member States' commitment to a set of common values laid down in Article 2 of the Treaty on Europen Union (TEU) presupposes the existence of mutual trust that all of them will respect these values, including the rule of law.[64] Following this rationale, EU Member States have an obligation to trust the functioning of each other's judicial systems and to expect all other Member States to secure the right to an effective remedy before an independent tribunal in their national legal orders.[65] The submission of intra-EU investment disputes to external dispute settlement mechanisms is deemed a sign of mistrust.[66]

---

[61] However, provisions on the factual treatment of domestic law are problematic in investor-State arbitrator, because they deny the inevitable normative value of domestic law, when interpreted and applied to incidental questions. See Brosseau (2024), p. 136; Alvik (2010), p. 94; See also *Enron Corporation and Ponderosa Assets, L.P. v Argentine Republic,* ICSID Case No. ARB/01/3, Award (22 May 2007) para 206 ("The Respondent is right in arguing that domestic law is not confined to the determination of factual questions."); *Total S.A. v The Argentine Republic,* ICSID Case No. ARB/04/01, Decision on Liability (27 December 2010) para 39 ("[T]he tribunal believes that Argentine law has a broader role than that of just determining factual matters.").

[62] See e.g. Art. 14(2) Serbia-Turkey BIT (2022); Article 33(1) Serbia-Canada BIT.

[63] See e.g. the Serbia-Malta BIT (2010).

[64] ECJ, Opinion 2/13 [2014] ECLI:EU:C:2014:2454, paras. 168, 191; ECJ, Case C-284/16 *Achmea* [2018] ECLI:EU:C:2018:158, para. 34.

[65] ECJ, Opinion 1/17 [2019], ECLI:EU:C:2019:341, para. 128.

[66] Hildebrand Pohl (2018), pp. 767, 788.

In its *Achmea* judgment in 2018, the ECJ found that the intra-EU BIT between the Netherlands and the Slovak Republic would call into question the principle of mutual trust.[67] Following this judgment, 23 EU Member States concluded a "Termination Agreement" of their intra-EU BITs in 2020.[68] Subsequently, EU Member States proceeded to terminate their intra-EU BITs to ensure compatibility with EU law. Croatia fulfilled its obligations arising out of this agreement, terminating its BITs with Portugal, Belgium-Luxembourg Economic Union (BLEU), Romania, Finland, Czech Republic, Austria, Greece, Sweden, Lithuania, France, Germany, Netherlands, Slovenia, Latvia, Bulgaria, Malta, Denmark, Hungary, Slovakia, and Spain.[69]

The other Western Balkan countries will also be required to terminate their intra-EU BITs upon EU accession. North Macedonia has 19 intra-EU BITs in force, Bosnia and Herzegovina has 18, Albania has 22, Serbia has 20, and Montenegro has 15. All these BITs would have to be terminated in the future without any options of re-negotiation. However, it is not advisable for Western Balkan countries to terminate these BITs before their EU accession, since their investors would be left without international investment protection on EU territory after their accession. Even without the protection of intra-EU BITs, Western Balkan investors could use EU judicial remedies, which according to the Commission "provide investors with a high level of protection".[70] In fact, in order to enforce their rights, investors established in the EU could call upon Member States' national courts instead of bringing treaty-based claims before international arbitral bodies. However, investors generally prefer international arbitration and the (arguably higher) standards of protection provided under investment treaties.[71] Therefore, the protection currently afforded at the international level should be kept as long as possible.

5 Conclusion

This contribution discussed key aspects of the decentralised implementation of EU investment protection policy and its implications for the Western Balkans. Countries in this region have a strong interest in aligning their investment treaty practices with EU policies. This interest stems either from their obligations under EU law, as in the case of Croatia, or from their aspirations to join the EU, as with Albania, Bosnia and Herzegovina, Montenegro, North Macedonia, and Serbia. As demonstrated, the BITs of these countries currently do not conform to EU investment protection standards

---

[67] ECJ, Case C-284/16 *Achmea* [2018] ECLI:EU:C:2018:158, para. 34.

[68] Agreement for the Termination of Bilateral Investment Treaties between the Member States of the European Union, OJ L 169, 29 May 2020.

[69] These 20 BITs were all terminated between October 2020 and October 2022. Croatia's BITs with Poland (2019) and Italy (2013) were already terminated before the Termination Agreement was concluded.

[70] European Commission (2018b), pp. 1, 20 et seqq.

[71] Hindelang (2015), pp. 68, 78.

and should be amended accordingly. While this recommendation applies to their BITs with third countries, those with other EU Member States should be maintained until EU accession but must be terminated thereafter (when becoming intra-EU BITs).

EU investment protection policy encompasses more substantive and procedural aspects than those discussed in this contribution, which highlighted several key aspects for an overview. However, the discussion of these selected aspects was sufficient to confirm that the Western Balkan BITs are largely outdated, adhering to an old-fashioned approach to international investment protection and dispute settlement. The Western Balkan countries are not unique in this regard, as their BITs reflect the investment treaty practices common to the majority of countries worldwide. While newer BITs often adopt modern approaches, most countries still maintain a significant number of outdated BITs, which strongly deviate from recent innovations in treaty practices. Even EU Member States, bound by their duty of sincere cooperation under EU law, have not systematically renegotiated their BITs to align with current EU investment protection policy.[72] Western Balkan countries should not be swayed by these poor examples and instead consider the requirements imposed by the Commission for the decentralised implementation of EU investment policy in preparation for their EU accession.

References

Alvik I (2010) The hybrid nature of investment treaty arbitration – straddling the national/international divide. In: Eriksen C, Emberland M (eds) The new international law: an anthology. Brill, Leiden, pp 89–97

Bartels L (2017) Human rights, labour standards and environmental standards in CETA. Legal studies research paper series no. 13/2017

Böhme B (2024) EU law as a Matter of Fact – The implementation of domestic law clauses in EU investment protection agreements. Available at SSRN: https://ssrn.com/abstract=4941180(24/10/2024)

Brosseau J (2024) The jurisdiction of investment tribunals to adjudicate claims and incidental questions grounded in domestic law. Law Pract Int Courts Trib 23:104–137

Bungenberg M, Böhme B (2022) Under the radar – the return of member states in EU investment policy. J Int Econ Law 25(4):627–642

Bungenberg M, Böhme B, Ruf L (2023) Decentral implementation of EU investment policy: convergence, divergence and EU-Plus. In: Bungenberg M, Reinisch A (eds) New frontiers for EU investment policy. External and internal dimensions. Springer, Berlin, pp 31–52

Bungenberg M, Reinisch A (2021) A paradigm change: the CETA investment chapter. Z Für Europarechtliche Studien (ZEuS) 24(3):437–484

Council of the EU (2010) Conclusions on a comprehensive European international investment policy, 3041st foreign affairs council meeting

Council of the EU (2018a) Conclusions on the negotiation and conclusion of EU trade agreements, 9120/18, 22 May 2018

---

[72] Germany can be taken as an example to illustrate this point. As the largest EU Member State and the State with most BITs concluded worldwide, Germany has still 114 BITs in force, which all follow the old European gold standard.

Council of the EU (2018b) Negotiating directives for a convention establishing a multilateral court for the settlement of investment disputes, 12981/17 ADD 1 DCL 1, 20/3/2018
Cremona M (2018) Shaping EU trade policy post-Lisbon: opinion 2/15 of 16 May 2017. Eur Const Law Rev 14(1):231–259
European Commission (2010) Towards a comprehensive European international investment policy, COM (2010) 343 final
European Commission (2018a) The former Yugoslav Republic of Macedonia 2018 report (Chap. 30: External relations)
European Commission (2018b) Communication from the commission to the European Parliament and the council of 19 July 2018, protection of intra-EU investment, COM(2018) 547
European Commission (2023a) Report from the commission to the European Parliament and the council on the application of regulation (EU) No 1219/2012, COM(2020) 132 final
European Commission (2023b) Annotations to the model clauses for negotiation or re-negotiation of member states' bilateral investment agreements with third countries
European Commission (2023c) Serbia 2023 report (Chap. 30: External relations)
European Parliament (2011) Report on the future European international investment policy (2010/2203(INI))
Freudlsperger C (2021) Failing forward in the common commercial policy? Deep trade and the perennial question of EU competence. J Eur Publ Policy 28(10):1650–1668
Hindelang S (2015) Repellent forces: the CJEU and investor-state dispute settlement. Arch Des Völkerrechts 53(1):68–89
Kalnina E, Godbole A (2022), Chapter X. Publication, Access to Proceedings and Non-Disputing Party Submissions, in: Happ R and Wilske S (eds) ICSID Rules and Regulations 2022. Article-by-Article Commentary, Hart/Beck/Nomos, pp. 617–626
Klamert M (2014) The principle of loyality in EU law. OUP, Oxford
Hillebrand Pohl J (2018) Intra-EU investment arbitration after the Achmea case: legal autonomy bounded by mutual trust. Eur Const Law Rev 14(4):767–791
Schacherer S (2016) Can EU member states still negotiate BITs with third countries? Investment Treaty News 7
Schacherer S (2019) The CETA investment chapter and sustainable development: interpretative issues. In: Mbengue M, Schacherer S (eds) Foreign investment under the Comprehensive Economic and Trade Agreements (CETA). Springer, Cham, pp 207–238
Thies A (2020) Principles of EU external action. In: Wessel R, Larik J (eds) EU external relations law. OUP, Oxford, pp 29–60
Titi C (2015) International investment law and the European Union: towards a new generation of international investment agreements. Eur J Int Law 26(3):639–661
Tokarev V (2024) Promotion of rule of law in the western balkans: the impact of investment arbitration. In: Bungenberg M, Koevski G, Böhme B, Fröhlich M, Kocev L, Zraveva N (eds) Alternative dispute resolution in the western balkans: trends and challenges. Springer, Cham
UNCITRAL (2024) Working group III, draft statute of a standing mechanism for the resolution of international investment disputes, Note by the Secretariat, A/CN.9/WG.III/WP.239

The Illegality Defence: Lessons from Investment Arbitrations Involving the Western Balkans

Ilija Mitrev Penushliski

Abstract In recent years, foreign investors have increasingly resorted to international arbitration against the Western Balkan States. In a number of such arbitrations, the respondent States have raised an illegality defence, arguing that the applicable treaties bar access to arbitration to investors who have obtained their investments illegally. This defence strategy has generally proven unsuccessful. This chapter aims to distill the lessons from publicly available awards in which the Western Balkan States have raised an illegality defence. It surveys the approaches taken by tribunals in those disputes and considers the types of illegalities that have been deemed to deprive an investor of access to arbitration, when such illegality must have occurred, and what State conduct may weaken the State's illegality defence.

1 Introduction

There are various commonalities to Albania, Bosnia and Herzegovina, Croatia, Kosovo, Montenegro, North Macedonia, and Serbia, including shared histories and EU-accession aspirations (now realized for Croatia),[1] that have led to these States being referred to as the Western Balkans. Another commonality that the Western Balkan States share (including with other non-Balkan countries) is the battle

[1] Brussels Declaration, 13 December 2023, p 1, available at: https://www.consilium.europa.eu/fr/press/press-releases/2023/12/13/brussels-declaration-13-december-2023/.

I wish to thank Ms Lucie Perrier, Associate at Three Crowns LLP, for her valuable research assistance.

I. M. Penushliski (✉)
Three Crowns LLP, Paris, France
e-mail: ilija.mitrev-penushliski@threecrownsllp.com

M. Bungenberg et al. (eds.), *Alternative Dispute Resolution in the Western Balkans*, European Union and its Neighbours in a Globalized World 20,
https://doi.org/10.1007/978-3-031-76345-8_9

with corruption,[2] an area in which the candidates must make significant progress before joining the EU club.[3]

The Western Balkan States have also increasingly found themselves sued by foreign investors in arbitrations under treaties for the protection and promotion of foreign investments. Many of those treaties require that, to benefit from international legal protection, the investor make its investment in accordance with the law of the host State.[4] Accordingly, as is well established in arbitral jurisprudence, if an investor has breached domestic law when obtaining its investment, it may be deemed not to hold a protected investment and a tribunal may not have jurisdiction to hear the investor's claim under the treaty. In this context, like many other respondents, the Western Balkan States have relied on this treaty language to argue that the foreign investor has obtained its investment illegally, notably via corruption, and that the case should be dismissed for lack of jurisdiction.

This contribution examines the cases in which the Western Balkan States have raised illegality defences and why those have been by and large unsuccessful. To this end, this chapter examines the approaches taken by arbitral tribunals in arbitrations involving these States and focuses on three separate issues: what breach of domestic law renders an investment illegal (**2.**), when must the illegality have occurred (**3.**), and what State conduct may undermine the illegality defence (**4.**). The final section concludes (**5.**).

---

[2] See SELDI (2022); CMI Anti-Corruption Resource Centre (2021); European Parliamentary Research Service (2017).

[3] Brussels Declaration, 13 December 2023, p 2, available at: https://www.consilium.europa.eu/fr/press/press-releases/2023/12/13/brussels-declaration-13-december-2023/.

[4] See e.g. Albania-Azerbaijan BIT (Baku, 9 February 2012, in force on 13 July 2012), Article 1.1; Bosnia and Herzegovina-Turkey BIT (Ankara, 21 January 1998, in force on 10 February 2009), Article 1(2); Croatia-Kuwait BIT (Kuwait, 8 March 1997, in force on 2 July 1998), Article 1.1; Kosovo- Switzerland BIT (Pristina, 27 October 2011, in force on 13 June 2012), Article 2; Montenegro-United Arab Emirates BIT (Abu Dhabi, 26 March 2012, in force on 1 March 2013), Article 1.1(a); North Macedonia-Viet Nam BIT (Skopje, 15 October 2014, in force on 11 January 2016), Article 1.1; Serbia-Qatar BIT (Doha, 7 November 2016, in force on 20 June 2017), Article 1.2.

2 What Breach of Domestic Law Renders an Investment Illegal?

The investments in the Western Balkans that have led to disputes concerned a wide range of industries such as energy,[5] hospitality,[6] agriculture,[7] food production,[8] media,[9] banking[10] and postal services.[11] The investments themselves have also taken a range of forms, including shares, loans[12] or contractual rights, such as licenses to explore and produce oil,[13] and agreements for mineral extraction and metallurgy.[14]

Given the broad industry and legal context in which these investments are made, the question that arises is whether a breach of any law relevant to such investments would mean that access to arbitration should be barred. Indeed, the States of the Western Balkans have raised a variety of illegality allegations including corruption,[15] fraud,[16] misrepresentation,[17] violation of the tender process,[18] and failure to register

[5] See e.g. *MOL Hungarian Oil and Gas Company Plc v Republic of Croatia (I)* (ICSID Case No ARB/13/32) Award, 5 July 2022 (*MOL,* ICSID Award), paras. 352, 354–355, and 360–362.

[6] See e.g. *Mabco Constructions SA v Republic of Kosovo* (ICSID Case No ARB/17/25) Decision on Jurisdiction, 30 October 2020 (*Mabco,* Decision on Jurisdiction), paras. 139, and 160–166.

[7] See e.g. *Rand Investments Ltd, William Archibald Rand, Kathleen Elizabeth Rand, Allison Ruth Rand, Robert Harry Leander Rand and Sembi Investment Limited v Republic of Serbia* (ICSID Case No ARB/18/8) Award, 29 June 2023 (*Rand,* Award), paras. 16–17.

[8] See e.g. *Swisslion DOO Skopje v The Former Yugoslav Republic of Macedonia* (ICSID Case No ARB/09/16) Award, 6 July 2012 (*Swisslion,* Award), para. 53; *Georg Gavrilović and Gavrilović doo v Republic of Croatia* (ICSID Case No ARB/12/39) Award, 26 July 2018 (*Gavrilović,* Award), para. 182.

[9] See e.g. *Hydro Srl, Costruzioni Srl, Francesco Becchetti, Mauro De Renzis, Stefania Grigolon, Liliana Condomitti v Republic of Albania* (ICSID Case No ARB/15/28) Award, 24 April 2019 (*Hydro,* Award), para. 10.

[10] See e.g. *Raiffeisen Bank International AG and Raiffeisenbank Austria dd v Republic of Croatia (I)* (ICSID Case No ARB/17/34) Decision on the Respondent's Jurisdictional Objections, 30 September 2020 (*Raiffeisen,* Decision on the Respondent's Jurisdictional Objections), para. 4.

[11] See e.g. *B3 Croatian Courier Coöperatief U.A. v Republic of Croatia* (ICSID Case No. ARB/15/5) Award, 5 April 2019, para. 584.

[12] See e.g. *MNSS BV and Recupero Credito Acciaio NV v Montenegro* (ICSID Case No ARB(AF)/12/8) Award, 4 May 2016 (*MNSS, Award*), para. 5; *Anglo-Adriatic Group Limited v Republic of Albania* (ICSID Case No ARB/17/6) Award, 29 December 2016 (*AAG,* Award), para. 158.

[13] See e.g. *GBC Oil v the Ministry of Infrastructure and Energy and the National Agency of Natural Resources* (ICC Case No 22676/GR) Final Award, 6 July 2020 (*GBC Oil,* Final Award), paras. 279–285.

[14] See e.g. *Mytilineos Holdings SA v The State Union of Serbia & Montenegro and Republic of Serbia (I)* (PCA) Partial Award on Jurisdiction, 8 September 2006 (*Mytilineos,* Partial Award on Jurisdiction), para 6.

[15] See e.g. *GBC Oil*, Final Award, paras. 330–331; *MOL*, ICSID Award, paras. 364–366.

[16] See e.g. *Rand*, Award, paras. 357 and 368.

[17] See e.g. *Swisslion*, Award, para. 123; *MNSS*, Award, para. 102.

[18] See e.g. *Mabco*, Decision on Jurisdiction, paras. 397–399.

the investment and obtain governmental approval.[19] Laws that have been alleged to have been breached include a building code,[20] securities regulations,[21] criminal provisions,[22] company law,[23] tender rules,[24]and laws on foreign investments.[25]

In that context, States seek to defeat treaty claims by arguing that any investor violation of domestic law carried out in the course of the making of the investment, whatever the law at question and whether *de minimis* or not, would serve to deny access to international arbitration. In contrast, investors have taken the position that only those violations of fundamental rules of domestic law, that have the effect of nullifying the property right as a matter of its proper law, can justify a tribunal declining jurisdiction.

The jurisprudence highlights a spectrum of approaches taken by tribunals, from strict interpretations requiring complete adherence to host State laws to more nuanced perspectives that consider the nature and gravity of the legal breach. In *Phoenix Action v Czech Republic,* the tribunal held there was an implicit requirement that investments must comply with the host State's laws, which implies that the legality of the investment is to be examined under the full breadth of domestic laws.[26] In *Saba Fakes v Turkey*, the tribunal took a more restrictive view. The tribunal reasoned that it would be inconsistent with the object and purpose of investment protection treaties to deny protection to investments based on violations of laws unrelated to the nature of investment regulation. Therefore, the tribunal held that only breaches of fundamental rules related to the admission of investments could be a basis to deny jurisdiction.[27] Other tribunals have taken a similar view that the illegality must be serious to justify a denial of jurisdiction,[28] that what is required are nontrivial violations, investment regime violations, and fraud,[29] and that illegality should offend the host State's legal order.[30]

---

[19] See e.g. *Mytilineos*, Partial Award on Jurisdiction, paras. 50–53.

[20] See e.g. *Mamidoil Jetoil Greek Petroleum Products SA v Republic of Albania* (ICSID Case No ARB/11/24) Award, 30 March 2015 (*Mamidoil,* Award), para. 328.

[21] See e.g. *Rand*, Award, paras. 348 and 353–354.

[22] See e.g. *MOL*, ICSID Award, para 521; *Gavrilović*, Award, para 263; *GBC Oil*, Final Award, para 358.

[23] See e.g. *MNSS*, Award, para. 103.

[24] See e.g. *Mabco*, Decision on Jurisdiction, para. 399.

[25] See e.g. *Mytilineos*, Partial Award on Jurisdiction, para. 53; *Bedri Selmani v Republic of Kosovo* (ICC Case No 24443/MHM/HBH) Award, 1 August 2022 (*Selmani,* Award), para. 306.

[26] *Phoenix Action, Ltd v The Czech Republic* (ICSID Case No ARB/06/5) Award, 15 April 2009, para. 101.

[27] *Saba Fakes v Republic of Turkey* (ICSID Case No ARB/07/20) Award, 14 July 2010, paras. 119–120.

[28] See e.g. *Alpha Projektholding GmbH v Ukraine* (ICSID Case No ARB/07/16) Award, 8 November 2010, paras. 294–297.

[29] See e.g. *Quiborax S.A., Non Metallic Minerals S.A. and Allan Fosk Kaplún v Plurinational State of Bolivia* (ICSID Case No ARB/06/2) Decision on Jurisdiction, 27 September 2012, para. 266.

[30] See e.g. *SAUR International SA v Republic of Argentina* (ICSID Case No ARB/04/4) Decision on Jurisdiction and Liability, 6 June 2012, paras. 308–311; *Flughafen Zürich A.G. and Gestión e*

The decisions of the tribunals involving the States of the Western Balkans largely fall within this spectrum.

In *Mamidoil v Albania*, Albania alleged that the investor breached domestic law in two ways: by failing to perform due diligence before it built a petroleum reservoir and by failing to obtain permits that were required for the construction and exploitation of the petrol tank farm.[31] In assessing the allegations, the tribunal held that an investment can be illegal where it contravenes substantive or procedural rules of domestic law.[32] As to substantive rules, the tribunal considered this to mean not complying with "*material norms regulating investments*", such as prohibitions of certain business activities or norms that reserve certain sectors to national entities or protect certain sectorial or geographical areas.[33] The tribunal then identified the second source of illegality as a contravention of procedural rules, which it defined as follows[34]:

> In the Tribunal's view, an investment can be found illegal for procedural reasons when the investor does not respect the norms regulating the process of investment. The investment may be legal in substance but still tainted by illegality when the investor violates procedural norms and regulations for setting up its investment.

In assessing whether these rules were violated, the *Mamidoil* tribunal sought to strike a balance between the State's clear intent not to arbitrate disputes regarding illegal investment and the State's potential reliance on *de minimis* violations of domestic law to avoid arbitration.[35]

On this basis, the majority found that the investor had failed to apply for a construction site permit or construction permit, which made the tank farm illegal under Albania's Law on Urban Planning.[36] It also held that the investor's failure to obtain the related exploitation permit also constituted a violation of Albania's Law on Control and Regulation of the Construction Works.[37] The tribunal majority thus concluded that Mamidoil "*ha*[d] *not built and ha*[d] *not started operating the tank farm in accordance with Albanian legislation*".[38]

The dissenting arbitrator took the view that an investor should not be subjected to "*a forfeiture of any right to FET protection*" because of a failure to comply fully with domestic permitting and licensing law.[39] He noted that the investor's violations were not related to Albania's laws on foreign investment and that the investor was allowed

---

Ingenería IDC S.A. v Bolivarian Republic of Venezuela (ICSID Case No ARB/10/19) Award, 18 November 2014, para. 132.

[31] *Mamidoil*, Award, paras. 358 and 370.

[32] *Mamidoil*, Award, para. 371.

[33] *Mamidoil*, Award, paras. 370–372.

[34] *Mamidoil*, Award, paras. 372 and 378.

[35] *Mamidoil*, Award, para. 483.

[36] *Mamidoil*, Award, paras. 429–430, and 479.

[37] *Mamidoil*, Award, paras. 445, 457, and 479.

[38] *Mamidoil*, Award, para. 479. The tribunal eventually upheld jurisdiction for other reasons.

[39] *Mamidoil Jetoil Greek Petroleum Products SA v Republic of Albania* (ICSID Case No ARB/11/24) Dissenting Opinion of Steven A Hammond, 30 March 2015 (*Mamidoil*, Dissenting Opinion), para. 125.

to continue exploiting its investment for years after its failure to respect domestic permitting and licensing laws was known to Albania.[40] Citing the *Saba Fakes v Turkey* award, he argued that as a matter of public policy, "*it is inappropriate to subordinate those* [substantive] *protections* [of investment treaties] *to domestic legal requirements*".[41] In his view, the illegality defence can only succeed "*when it goes to the very nature of the investment itself and the domestic rule in issue has the effect of making the investment inherently illegal*", that is, only in cases of contraventions of the host State's substantive laws which regulate investments.[42]

A similar issue arose in *Mytilineos v Serbia.* The dispute concerned seven contracts between Mytilineos and RTB-BOR, a socially-owned company organised under the laws of the (then) Federal Republic of Yugoslavia, for cooperation in the mineral extraction and metallurgy business. Under the contracts, Mytilineos provided financing and spare parts to RTB-BOR, in exchange for the sale of copper.[43] However, this "*strategic alliance*",[44] which was intended to lead to equity participation of the claimant in RTB-BOR in the event it was privatised, failed when RTB-BOR fell into insolvency and a row erupted as to sums allegedly owed by the firm to Mytilineos.[45] In the arbitration, Serbia claimed that its legislation required that Mytilineos' investment be approved by the federal government.[46] Since such approval had not been procured by Mytilineos, the investment could not be protected under the treaty.[47] The majority rejected this argument based on the view that a BIT's legality requirement meant that investments must not be of an illegal nature—it did not mean that investments must be approved by the State.[48]

Serbia's appointee to the *Mytilineos v Serbia* tribunal, Professor Mitrović, deemed the "*in accordance with*" language of the BIT "*by its nature a mandatory rule*",[49] which "*clearly and unequivocally*" required the absence of any violation of domestic law.[50] He further observed that the legality requirement concerned the question of compliance with the domestic laws governing investments in the host State.[51] Serbia's

---

[40] *Mamidoil*, Dissenting Opinion, para. 126.

[41] *Mamidoil*, Dissenting Opinion, para. 130.

[42] *Mamidoil*, Dissenting Opinion, para. 130; *Mamidoil*, Award, para. 377.

[43] *Mytilineos*, Partial Award on Jurisdiction, para. 27.

[44] *Mytilineos*, Partial Award on Jurisdiction, para. 26.

[45] *Mytilineos*, Partial Award on Jurisdiction, para. 27.

[46] *Mytilineos*, Partial Award on Jurisdiction, para. 53.

[47] *Mytilineos*, Partial Award on Jurisdiction, para. 137.

[48] *Mytilineos*, Partial Award on Jurisdiction, paras. 146–151.

[49] *Mytilineos Holdings SA v The State Union of Serbia & Montenegro and Republic of Serbia (I)* (PCA) Dissenting Opinion of Professor Dobrosav Mitrović, 6 September 2006 (*Mytilineos*, Dissenting Opinion), para. 7.3.

[50] *Mytilineos*, Dissenting Opinion, para. 5.

[51] *Mytilineos*, Dissenting Opinion, para. 7.3.1. For a similar limitation of the defence's material scope but in the context of a differently phrased definition of 'investment', see *Selmani*, Award, para. 340 ("*the reference to assets being 'lawfully held'* [...] *refers to the validity of the 'holding,' whether that occurs by lease, concession, license, contract or other mechanism. It does not require that the foreign person be in perfect compliance with all conditions of the operative instrument or*

Foreign Investment Act required the foreign investment contract to be approved and registered by the competent state authority, which was lacking.[52] As such, Professor Mitrović considered that the contracts between Mytilineos and RTB-BOR did not constitute an "investment" under the BIT.[53]

More recently, in *Rand v Serbia*, the tribunal majority similarly rejected Serbia's illegality defences. The majority held that "*only violations of fundamental rules would deprive a tribunal of its jurisdiction*".[54] The majority found that Serbia had not established that the alleged illegalities affected a fundamental principle of Serbian law.[55] Conversely, only acts that "*affect the validity*" of the investment, or its "*ownership*" would qualify as an actionable illegality.[56] Professor Marcelo Kohen dissented on this point, taking the view that foreign investors be "*required to abide by the entire legal system*", or it would otherwise "*create*[] *an undue advantage against other investors.*"[57]

In *Anglo-Adriatic Group v Albania*, the tribunal found that if the claimant had successfully proven that it held a loan as a second investment (which it had not), such an investment would have, in any event, been illegal.[58] Albania's Law on Investment Funds barred investment funds from borrowing money or taking loans of any kind.[59] The tribunal considered it relevant that this domestic law had a "*compelling public purpose*", such that denying investment protection was proportionate to the investor's breach.[60] The tribunal further underscored the public interest underlying the Law on Investment Funds, namely to "*protect*[] *the general public from being deprived of their investments*" in investment funds.[61]

There appears to be no basis in the text of most BITs to limit the illegality inquiry to whether certain types of host State laws have been breached. It may also be unduly narrow to restrict the examination to whether the breach of domestic law leads to a loss of the property right—without any application of the "*in accordance with the law of the host State*" provision, on one school of thought the investor would be

---

with applicable provisions of Kosovar law. Non-compliance with the terms of a lease, concession, license, or contract—such as a failure to pay required rent—might be relevant to merits issues [...] *but it would not strip the investment of its status as such, for purposes of arbitral jurisdiction. The status of being an 'investment' is granted* [...] *so long as the mechanism authorizing the holding* [...] *remains validly in effect, in the sense that it has not been revoked, terminated, or otherwise invalidated as a matter of law.*") (emphasis added).

52 *Mytilineos*, Dissenting Opinion, para. 7.3.1.

53 *Mytilineos*, Dissenting Opinion, para. 8.

54 *Rand*, Award, para. 390.

55 *Rand*, Award, paras. 390 and 393.

56 *Rand*, Award, paras. 390 and 393.

57 *Rand Investments Ltd, William Archibald Rand, Kathleen Elizabeth Rand, Allison Ruth Rand, Robert Harry Leander Rand and Sembi Investment Limited v Republic of Serbia* (ICSID Case No ARB/18/8) Dissenting Opinion of Professor Marcelo G Kohen, 29 June 2023, para. 5.

58 *AAG*, Award, para. 293.

59 *AAG*, Award, para. 187.

60 *AAG*, Award, para. 288.

61 *AAG*, Award, para. 291.

deemed not to hold an investment as it would not have a right *in rem* under the proper law.[62] At the same time, it may be held contrary to the purpose of investment treaties to deprive investors of access to international arbitration for *de minimis* breaches of domestic law, such as minor labour law or company law violations carried out in the course of the making of the investment.

In this context, in recent years, some tribunals have adopted a proportionality analysis, which examines the severity and nature of the breach against the treaty goal of investment protection. The principal case applying the proportionality approach is *Kim v Uzbekistan.*[63] The tribunal established a three-step test to determine whether a claim should be rejected on account of the illegality of the investment: (1) assessing the significance of the obligation under domestic law and how the State has viewed that obligation contemporaneously (including whether it has taken steps to enforce the obligation); (2) assessing the investor's conduct in breaching domestic law (e.g. presence of intent or gross negligence, misunderstanding of the law, and subsequent conduct); and (3) determining whether items (1) and (2) are of such importance that denying access to arbitration under the BIT is warranted.[64] In this way, the *Kim* test attempts to take into account both the investor's and the State's conduct, seeking to ensure fairness and prevent abuse.[65] It has been cited with approval by some other investor-State tribunals.[66]

3 When Must the Illegality Have Occurred?

It is now a matter of *jurisprudence constante* that for an illegality committed by the investor to lead to a finding of no jurisdiction, it must have occurred at the time of the making of the investment.[67] The jurisprudence involving the Western Balkan States is consistent with this view.

For instance, the tribunal in *MNSS v Montenegro* concluded that Montenegro's jurisdictional objection which concerned events taking place during the operation of

---

[62] Douglas (2014), pp. 173–174.

[63] *Vladislav Kim, Pavel Borissov, Aibar Burkitbayev, Almas Chukin, Lyazzat Daurenbekova, Adal Issabekov, Damir Karassayev, Aidan Karibzhanov, Aigul Nurmakhanova, Kairat Omarov, Nikolay Varenko and Gulzhamash Zaitbekova v Republic of Uzbekistan* (ICSID Case No ARB/13/6) Decision on Jurisdiction, 8 March 2017 (*Kim,* Decision on Jurisdiction).

[64] *Kim,* Decision on Jurisdiction, paras. 406–408.

[65] *Kim,* Decision on Jurisdiction, para. 396.

[66] The influence of the *Kim* precedent is growing in international investment arbitration. See *Cortec Mining Kenya Limited, Cortec (Pty) Limited and Stirling Capital Limited v Republic of Kenya* (ICSID Case No ARB/15/29) Final Award, 22 October 2018, para. 320; and *Mr Cornelis Willem van Noordenne, Mr Bartus van Noordenne, Stichting Administratiekantoor Anbadi, Estudios Tributarios AP S.A. and Álvarez y Marín Corporación S.A. v Republic of Panama* (ICSID Case No ARB/15/14) Award, 12 October 2018, para. 153.

[67] *Rand*, Award, para. 390; *Mamidoil*, Award, para. 375.

the claimant's investment was without merit.[68] Likewise, in *Swisslion v Macedonia*, the tribunal referred to the award in *Hamester v Ghana*, and held that "*on the wording of this BIT, the legality of the creation of the investment is a jurisdictional issue; the legality of the investor's conduct during the life of the investment is a merits issue*".[69]

In *Mabco v Kosovo*, the tribunal similarly rejected the investor's argument that the lawfulness of an investment is a merits issue and held that "[a]*ccording to well-established jurisprudence, unless an investment is lawful, it cannot constitute an investment within the meaning of an investment protection instrument, particularly when the instrument specifically requires that an investment be lawful. The Tribunal's jurisdiction* […] *thus depends on the alleged investment being a lawful one*".[70]

Some tribunals had to consider whether an illegality allegation was a jurisdictional, an admissibility, or a merits issue.[71] In *MOL v Croatia*, for instance, because of the complexity of the bribery allegations, and "*the way they related in different ways both to issues of jurisdiction and admissibility and in addition to issues more closely associated with the merits of the investor's claims*", the tribunal deferred its assessment thereof to the merits stage.[72]

In *Selmani v Kosovo*, the question was whether the investment that had already been lawfully obtained by a foreign investor before Kosovo's declaration of independence became illegal once Kosovo was no longer under UN governance. The case was brought under the Kosovo Law on Foreign Investment (2014 LFI), which defines investment as "*any asset owned or otherwise lawfully held by a Foreign Person in the Republic of Kosovo for the purpose of conducting lawful commercial activities*".[73] In analysing this clause, the tribunal held that it extended protection solely to investments that were "*lawfully held* […] *in the Republic of Kosovo*", which the tribunal characterised as "*an implicit temporal requirement*".[74] In the tribunal's

---

[68] *MNSS*, Award, paras. 214–215 ("*The Respondent has also claimed that the Claimants broke Montenegrin law in the operation of their investment. Whether they did or did not and to the extent that it has any relevance, this is a matter to be determined as part of the consideration of the merits of this case should the Tribunal reject all the objections to its jurisdiction*").

[69] See *Swisslion*, Award, para. 125; *Gustav F W Hamester GmbH & Co KG v Republic of Ghana* (ICSID Case No ARB/06/5) Award, 18 June 2010, para. 127. See also *GBC Oil*, Final Award, paras. 438–439 ("[…] *the Tribunal finds that if these allegations were established, they would only concern the performance of the License and Petroleum Agreements, as opposed to suspicions of corruption at the time of their conclusion. Therefore, if established, as in the case of the fourth red flag, the illegality would lead to the termination of the agreements but would not affect their validity ab initio. This is all the more true that Respondents invoke substantially the same facts to allege that Claimant materially breached the Petroleum Agreements*").

[70] *Mabco*, Decision on Jurisdiction, paras. 402 and 407. The tribunal in *Swisslion v Macedonia* stated the complete opposite. See *Swisslion*, Award, para. 125 ("*in most cases, ICSID tribunals have examined arguments that investments were made illegally or in bad faith only at the merits stage. It is only in exceptional circumstances that, for reason of judicial economy, ICSID tribunals have considered the question in a decision on jurisdiction.*").

[71] For further developments on this point, see Brower and Ahmad (2018), paras. 18.14–18.18.

[72] *MOL*, ICSID Award, para. 436.

[73] *Selmani*, Award, para. 335.

[74] *Selmani*, Award, para. 337.

view, this excluded from coverage pre-independence investments that were no longer recognised as valid after independence.[75] On that basis, the tribunal held that, while in 2000 Mr Selmani had obtained from the UN Mission in Kosovo (UNMIK) the right to operate previously State-owned petrol stations, this was not the case after Kosovo's independence.[76] It found that UNMIK had terminated the authorisation in late 2001, which made the investment invalid at the time of the declaration of independence, in 2008.[77] The tribunal did not consider Mr Selmani's continued de facto operation of the petrol stations sufficient to meet the legality requirement.[78] It therefore dismissed the claim for lack of jurisdiction.[79]

4 What State Conduct May Undermine the Illegality Defence?

Within the Western Balkans, there is often State involvement and oversight at the time an investment is made, partially in the context of the States' privatisation efforts starting in the 1990s.[80] State participation can range from administering the auctioning off of public assets,[81] to signing contracts directly with investors,[82] or participating in joint ownership of a newly privatised entity.[83] Organs of the State involved at this stage of the investment lifecycle have included privatisation agencies,[84] courts,[85] ministries,[86] State-owned entities,[87] and heads of State.[88]

As a result, at least some organs of the State may be or ought to be aware of potential illegalities, or may note red flags in the transaction, and/or may have indications that the investment and the process for obtaining it was such that it required closer scrutiny or due diligence on the part of the State. Moreover, the fact that many of these processes for the making of the investment involve the State (sometimes three

[75] *Selmani*, Award, paras. 337–339.

[76] *Selmani*, Award, paras. 80, 344, and 359.

[77] *Selmani*, Award, para. 344.

[78] *Selmani*, Award, para. 348 (emphasis in the original).

[79] *Selmani*, Award, para. 644(b) and (c).

[80] See *AAG*, Award, para. 73; *MOL*, ICSID Award, para. 352; *Gavrilović*, Award, paras. 93–96; *MNSS*, Award, para. 46; *Mabco*, Decision on Jurisdiction, para. 142; *Rand*, Award, para. 8.

[81] *Gavrilović*, Award, paras. 96–99; *Mamidoil*, Award, para. 81; *Mabco*, Decision on Jurisdiction, paras. 160–162; *Rand*, Award, para. 10.

[82] *Mytilineos*, Partial Award on Jurisdiction, para. 25.

[83] *MOL*, ICSID Award, para. 352.

[84] *Mamidoil*, Award, para. 81; *Mabco*, Decision on Jurisdiction, para. 142; *Rand*, Award, para. 8.

[85] *Gavrilović*, Award, para. 96.

[86] *Hydro*, Award, para. 175; *GBC Oil*, Final Award, para. 47; *Swisslion*, Award, para. 56.

[87] *MOL*, ICSID Award, para. 352; *Swisslion*, Award, para. 52; *Mytilineos*, Partial Award on Jurisdiction, para. 25.

[88] *Mamidoil*, Award, para. 70; *MOL*, ICSID Award, para. 365.

or more State organs or entities participating[89]) means an increased opportunity and risk of corruption.

Tribunals have dealt with the question of whether a State should be entitled to defeat a claim based on illegality where the State itself has not investigated or prosecuted the illegal conduct, or was itself involved in it. For instance, in *Wena Hotels v Egypt*, Egypt submitted that the investor's claims should fail, because it had bribed a senior public Egyptian official to obtain the hotel leases.[90] The tribunal dismissed this claim because, although Egypt had been made aware of the illegal conduct, there was no evidence before the tribunal of the actions the State took in respect of the illegality, and whether it had concluded there had been no illegality.[91] In *Fraport v Philippines I*, the tribunal applied the principle of estoppel to find that the State could not object to the legality of the investment where it knowingly overlooked it and "*endorsed an investment which was not in compliance with its law*".[92] In *Arif v Moldova* and *Aven v Costa Rica*, the tribunals similarly appeared to apply the principle of acquiescence to reject the illegality defence.[93] Similar issues arise in the case law involving the Western Balkans.

4.1 State Participation in the Alleged Illegality

In *Gavrilović v Croatia*, the State raised illegality allegations as one of its objections to jurisdiction in three main respects. Croatia argued that the bankruptcy proceedings through which Mr. Gavrilović had acquired five companies in the early 1990s had not been carried out in conformity with its bankruptcy legislation.[94] As to the financing of the investment, Croatia argued that Mr Gavrilović had violated Croatian law because in part it paid the purchase price with public money, through a loan granted by the Croatian Minister of Finance.[95] In addition, Croatia alleged that the investor had acted in violation of international rules when he "*knowingly and illegally transported*

[89] *See Gavrilović*, Award, paras. 94–96; *Swisslion*, Award, paras 52–56; *Mamidoil*, Award, paras. 70, and 81–82; *Hydro*, Award, paras. 171–175; *AAG*, Award, paras. 78–80, and 95.

[90] *Wena Hotels Limited v Arab Republic of Egypt* (ICSID Case No ARB/98/4) Award, 8 December 2000 (*Wena Hotels*, Award), para. 76.

[91] *Wena Hotels*, Award, para. 116.

[92] *Fraport AG Frankfurt Airport Services Worldwide v Republic of the Philippines (I)* (ICSID Case No ARB/03/25) Award, 16 August 2007, para. 346. See also *Bernhard von Pezold and others v Republic of Zimbabwe* (ICSID Case No ARB/10/15) Award, 28 July 2015, para. 416; *Karkey Karadeniz Elektrik Uretim A.S. v Islamic Republic of Pakistan* (ICSID Case No ARB/13/1) Award, 22 August 2017, para. 628.

[93] See *Mr Franck Charles Arif v Republic of Moldova* (ICSID Case No ARB/11/23) Award, 8 April 2013, paras. 374–376; *David R. Aven, Samuel D Aven, Carolyn J Park, Eric A Park, Jeffrey S Shioleno, Giacomo A Buscemi, David A Janney and Roger Raguso v The Republic of Costa Rica* (ICSID Case No UNCT/15/3) Final Award, 18 September 2018, paras. 324–325.

[94] *Gavrilović*, Award, paras. 235–237, 241–242, 246, 250–252, 257–259, and 261–263.

[95] *Gavrilović*, Award, paras. 268–271.

millions of German marks [from Croatia] *into foreign accounts*" to circumvent EU and UN embargos on arms purchases by Croatia during the Balkan wars in the 1990s.[96]

The tribunal found that there was "a *quid pro quo*" between Croatia and the investor: the former was "*fighting a war and needed* [...] *foreign currency, to purchase weaponry* [...] [and] *employed Mr. Gavrilović to assist it in that scheme by smuggling money out of the country and depositing it in foreign bank accounts*"; the latter then "*asked the Government for help in return for his contribution to the war effort*".[97] According to the tribunal, "*the problem for the Respondent in advancing the illegality objections against Mr. Gavrilović is that* [...] *it was the State that orchestrated* [the] *scheme*".[98] It therefore concluded that "*in the absence of evidence that the scheme was initiated or orchestrated by Mr. Gavrilović* [...] *the Tribunal has difficulty accepting that the illegality is opposable to* [him] *under international law*".[99]

4.2 Ratification and Waiver

As explained above, the tribunal majority in *Mamidoil v Albania* found that Mamidoil had violated Albanian law by failing to obtain construction and exploitation permits for the tank farm. It rejected the claimant's estoppel argument based on the fact that the Albanian authorities had consistently insisted that the applications and permits were missing.[100] The majority nonetheless held that the State "*ha*[d]*, by its conduct, declarations, and requests, conveyed to Claimant that it was ready to consider curing the illegalities*" rather than terminate the investment.[101] The majority interpreted the "[State's] *proposals as indications that it was ready to disregard the illegality for the past, to suspend it for the present and to repair it for the future*" and concluded that the legal significance of the lack of permits should be determined on the merits.[102]

In *Mabco v Kosovo*, the investor argued that Kosovo had waived any claim of unlawfulness as it had actively solicited the claimant's participation in the privatisation of the Grand Hotel in Pristina.[103] The investor also argued that "*no public authority* [...] *ever questioned that* [its] *payment* [...] *was made or was legal, nor did it ever raise any breach of either the Tender Rules or the Purchase Agreement.*"[104] The tribunal held that Kosovo had waived the illegality defence, since the record indicated

[96] *Gavrilović*, Award, para. 286.

[97] *Gavrilović*, Award, para. 325.

[98] *Gavrilović*, Award, para. 325.

[99] *Gavrilović*, Award, paras. 325, and 347–349. See also paras. 383–384, and 398.

[100] *Mamidoil*, Award, paras. 315–320, and 491.

[101] *Mamidoil*, Award, para. 492.

[102] *Mamidoil*, Award, paras. 493–494.

[103] *Mabco*, Decision on jurisdiction, para. 405.

[104] *Mabco*, Decision on jurisdiction, para. 405.

that its privatisation agency had engaged in "*substantial negotiations*" regarding the claimant's acquisition of the shares, without ever questioning the legality thereof.[105] It concluded that "*an illegality in an investment that might otherwise disqualify the investment from protection cannot be raised as a jurisdictional defense if the State was aware of the illegality and expressed no objection on that basis*".[106]

4.3 Lack of Witnesses or Lack of Credibility of Witnesses

In the MOL dispute, Croatia vigorously argued that corruption had taken place. But two tribunals that ruled on the matter dismissed the argument for lack of evidence, despite the Croatian courts having convicted the Croatian prime minister of corruption exactly in respect of the MOL affair.[107] MOL is a corporation partly owned by the Hungarian government. In the 2000s, it acquired shares in INA, the largest oil company in Croatia. The dispute concerned subsequent transactions and governance arrangements that allowed MOL to obtain a controlling stake in INA. MOL's stake rose to 47% in 2008 effectively giving MOL management rights over the company.[108] In that context, former Croatian Prime Minister Ivo Sanader was convicted by the Croatian courts for, *inter alia*, agreeing to ensure, in return for a bribe, that MOL would obtain a predominant influence over INA.[109]

The dispute was examined in two separate arbitration proceedings: a commercial arbitration commenced by Croatia, and an investment-treaty arbitration triggered by MOL. The main witness evidence in both cases was from Mr Robert Jezic, a Croatian businessman who was involved in the alleged bribery scheme.[110] Both arbitral tribunals dismissed Croatia's defence on the basis that this witness was "evasive", tendered evidence that was inconsistent with other testimony, and told a story replete with "implausibilities".[111] Both tribunals also noted that several witnesses central to the allegations had not been made available to them.[112] Accordingly, where the evidence before the tribunal is not convincing, an illegality defence may not succeed, even if such an allegation had been accepted by the domestic courts.

---

[105] *Mabco*, Decision on jurisdiction, para. 409.

[106] *Mabco*, Decision on jurisdiction, para. 409.

[107] *Republic of Croatia v MOL Hungarian Oil and Gas Company Plc* (PCA Case No 2014–15) Final Award, 23 December 2016 (*MOL*, PCA Final Award), para. 333; *MOL*, ICSID Award, para. 543.

[108] *MOL*, PCA Final Award, paras. 30 and 336; *MOL*, ICSID Award, paras. 362 and 576.

[109] For a more detailed outline of the developments before Crotian courts, see *MOL*, PCA Final Award, paras. 15–16, 69, and 73–75; *MOL*, ICSID Award, paras. 410, 417, 424, 430, and 431.

[110] *MOL*, PCA Final Award, paras. 24 and 31; *MOL*, ICSID Award, para. 365.

[111] *MOL*, PCA Final Award, paras. 215–217, 222, 249–250, 304–306, and 329; *MOL*, ICSID Award, paras. 537–542.

[112] *MOL*, PCA Final Award, para. 133; *MOL*, ICSID Award, para. 512.

4.4 Failure to Prosecute

In *Rand v Serbia*, the tribunal majority emphasised Serbia's failure to investigate and prosecute one of the four illegality allegations it raised. Serbia argued that a person affiliated with claimants misappropriated funds from the publicly owned company that was undergoing privatisation.[113] It contended that this misappropriation amounted to fraud under Serbian law.[114] The tribunal found the allegations admissible even though they were filed belatedly, but dismissed them on their merits.[115] The tribunal dismissed the misappropriation allegation, largely because at the time of the award, no criminal proceedings had been initiated against that individual, "*despite similar allegations being made against him*" 14 years prior.[116] The tribunal found this "*surprising*" since, at the time the allegations had been made, Serbia was in control of the company from which the funds were allegedly siphoned.[117]

At the same time, when the State does commence criminal investigations, an investor may be tempted to go on the attack and characterise the investigation as a violation of international law. This occurred in *MOL*, where MOL argued that the very initiation of the corruption investigation and ensuing prosecution were a deliberate and *mala fide* act designed to harm it as an investor in INA and amounted to a breach of the Energy Charter Treaty.[118] The tribunal was unconvinced by MOL's allegations, holding that it would be "*very loth indeed*" to stand in the way of a sovereign State's prerogatives to pursue and punish a serious crime.[119] Other tribunals have dismissed similar investor claims of harassment.[120]

4.5 Lateness in Raising the Defence

In *Hydro v Albania*, in an award of 2019, the tribunal held that Albania had expropriated the claimant's media venture, Agonset, through a politically motivated campaign, and awarded EUR 100 million in damages to Hydro.[121] Albania had not

[113] *Rand*, Award, paras. 357–359.

[114] *Rand*, Award, paras. 357–359, and 398.

[115] *Rand*, Award, paras. 385, 389, and 400.

[116] *Rand*, Award, paras. 399–400.

[117] *Rand*, Award, para. 399.

[118] *MOL*, ICSID Award, paras. 563–564.

[119] *MOL*, ICSID Award, para. 564.

[120] See e.g. *Scholz Holding GmbH v Kingdom of Morocco* (ICSID Case No ARB/19/2) Award, 1 August 2022, para 265; *Teinver S.A., Transportes de Cercanías S.A. and Autobuses Urbanos del Sur SA v Argentine Republic* (ICSID Case No ARB/09/1) Decision on Provisional Measures, 8 April 2016, para. 190.

[121] *Hydro*, Award, paras. 681–697, and 914.

alleged illegality on the part of the investor in the arbitration. However, in its application for revision of the award in 2022, Albania argued that certain claimants had been convicted of fraud, forgery, tax evasion, smuggling, and money laundering by a Tirana court in 2022 and that they had used certain companies including Agonset to launder the proceeds of crimes.[122] The State therefore submitted that, by virtue of this decision, it discovered the claimants' "*Illegal Activities*" related to Agonset after the award was rendered.[123] Albania further argued that these newly discovered activities were capable of decisively influencing the award, had the tribunal known about them.[124] The tribunal would have been deprived of its jurisdiction since "*the Tirana Judgment reveals that the Claimants' entire purported investment in Albania was a fraud from start to finish*".[125]

The revision tribunal examined the "*facts*" that Albania asserted it "*discovered*".[126] It noted that Albania had in fact put on record in the original arbitration the indictment against one of the claimants in 2015.[127] It highlighted that the award had dedicated a substantial section of its award to the criminal investigations.[128] Accordingly, it was "*obvious*" that both Albania and the original tribunal had knowledge of the criminal allegations.[129] The revision tribunal therefore decided that "*a domestic court's post-award legal characterization of a pre-award fact*" cannot, in itself, constitute a new fact for the purposes of a revision application, and that such "*fact*" would, in any event, not pre-date the award.[130] Accordingly, it was "*clear, certain and obvious*" that Albania had not discovered a fact capable of warranting a revision of the award, and that the revision application manifestly lacked legal merit.[131]

---

[122] *Hydro S.r.l., Costruzioni S.r.l., Francesco Becchetti, Mauro De Renzis, Stefania Grigolon, Liliana Condomitti v Republic of Albania* (ICSID Case No ARB/15/28) Decision on Claimants' Application to Dismiss the Revision Application Under ICSID Arbitration Rule 41(5), Claimants' Request for Allocation of Advance Payments, Claimants' Requests for Security, and Respondent's Proposal for the Establishment of an Escrow Mechanism, 29 March 2023 (*Hydro,* Decision on Claimants' Application to Dismiss the Revision Application), paras. 54–55.

[123] *Hydro,* Decision on Claimants' Application to Dismiss the Revision Application, paras. 59 and 87.

[124] *Hydro,* Decision on Claimants' Application to Dismiss the Revision Application, para. 99.

[125] *Hydro,* Decision on Claimants' Application to Dismiss the Revision Application, para. 101.

[126] *Hydro,* Decision on Claimants' Application to Dismiss the Revision Application, para. 117.

[127] *Hydro,* Decision on Claimants' Application to Dismiss the Revision Application, para. 120, and fn. 114.

[128] *Hydro,* Decision on Claimants' Application to Dismiss the Revision Application, paras. 121–122.

[129] *Hydro,* Decision on Claimants' Application to Dismiss the Revision Application, paras. 129–130.

[130] *Hydro,* Decision on Claimants' Application to Dismiss the Revision Application, para. 131.

[131] *Hydro,* Decision on Claimants' Application to Dismiss the Revision Application, para. 134.

4.6 Thoughts on the Plea of Illegality and State Conduct

The foregoing shows that, in its assessment of an illegality defence, an arbitral tribunal will consider whether the State participated in the alleged illegal transaction, whether it should have been aware of it, and whether it took legal actions in respect of the illegality. In some cases, the absence of State prosecution has been underscored by tribunals when they have dismissed the illegality objection.

Still, it is for the arbitral tribunal to ascertain whether it has jurisdiction over an investment and, therefore, to assess whether such investment has been obtained illegally under the law of the host State based on the evidence before it. The State's non-prosecution is one of many facts to be examined by tribunals when reaching their decision. Moreover, when illegality concerns corruption, money laundering, or other offences contrary to international public policy, the tribunal is duty-bound to investigate whether such an offence has taken place, regardless of the State's policing of the illegality.[132] More generally, there may be reasons for which a State has failed to prosecute illegality that do not imply the absence of illegality, including lack of or incomplete information, poor assessment of the basis for indictment, human error, corruption on the part of the prosecution, etc.

At the same time, domestic court judgments in which illegality is ascertained are surely relevant for the tribunal's analysis. A tribunal may be wary that a court judgment has been procured with a view to defeating international jurisdiction. But any such decision would in any event have to be examined in detail, including under the lens of *res judicata*. In contrast, in the MOL cases, the tribunals made only limited references to the conviction of the Prime Minister by the Croatian courts.[133]

5 Conclusion

The illegality defences raised by the Western Balkans in treaty arbitrations have mostly failed. Three groups of main reasons can be identified for this: (1) failure on the part of the State to fully, timely, or convincingly raise the objection, and/or marshal evidence; (2) the tribunals largely having restricted the illegality inquiry to breaches of fundamental norms of domestic law and rules related to foreign investment; and (3) tribunals having ascribed important weight to how the State has acted contemporaneously in respect of the illegality at issue, including whether it has ratified or prosecuted it. A common thread in most of these decisions appears to be

[132] Cass Civ 1, 7 September 2022, pourvoi no 20–22,118; Cass Civ 1, 23 March 2022, pourvoi no 17–17,981; CA Paris, 21 February 2017, *Valeriy Belokon v Kyrgyz Republic*, RG no 15/01650; Gaillard (2017), pp. 809–811.

[133] *MOL*, PCA Final Award, para. 333; *MOL*, ICSID Award, para. 543. In the PCA arbitration, the tribunal found that the Croatian judge had "*an obvious bias at the trial*". *MOL*, PCA Final Award, para. 138.

that the illegality defence has been an afterthought, conceived of for the purposes of arbitration.

References

Brower CN, Ahmad J (2018) The state's corruption defence, prosecutorial efforts, and anti-corruption norms in investment treaty arbitration. In: Yannaca-Small K (ed) Arbitration under international investment agreements: a guide to the key issues. OUP, Oxford, pp 455–481

CMI Anti-Corruption Resource Centre (2021) The Western Balkans and Turkey: overview of corruption in the environment and climate sector. https://www.u4.no/publications/western-balkans-and-turkey-overview-of-corruption-in-the-environment-and-climate-sector.pdf

Douglas Z (2014) The plea of illegality in investment treaty arbitration. ICSID Rev 29(1):155–186

European Parliamentary Research Service (2017) Anti-corruption efforts in the Western Balkans. https://www.europarl.europa.eu/cmsdata/226463/EPRS_BRI(2017)599417_EN_The_Anti-corruption_efforts_in_the_Western_Balkans.pdf

Gaillard E (2017) La corruption saisie par les arbitres du commerce international. Revue De L'arbitrage 3:805–838

Mediation of Investment Disputes Under the ICSID Mediation Rules: An Overview

Catharine Titi

Abstract The criticisms that have been voiced against investment arbitration have led to a growing interest in alternative means of dispute settlement, especially mediation. In 2022, as part of an overhaul of its Rules and Regulations, the International Centre for Settlement of Investment Disputes (ICSID) adopted a set of mediation rules, which are the first institutional mediation rules developed specifically for investment disputes. These rules are the focus of this chapter. The chapter reviews the context of the adoption of the ICSID Mediation Rules, before considering the reasons that may have encouraged ICSID to establish them, given that, even before 2022, the Centre provided a framework for the conciliation of investment disputes. The chapter further examines the mediation procedure under the ICSID Mediation Rules, from the initiation of proceedings to their conduct and termination, and considers remaining challenges, which it argues will need to be addressed, if mediation is to become a more mainstream means of settling investment disputes.

1 Introduction

The criticisms that have been voiced against investment arbitration[1] have led to a growing interest in alternative means of dispute settlement.[2] In Working Group III of the United Nations Commission on International Trade Law (UNCITRAL), where

[1] E.g. Waibel et al. (2010), Weber and Titi (2015), UNCITRAL (2018), pp. 3–5.

[2] Titi and Fach Gómez (2019).

The author would like to thank Aurélia Antonietti, Meg Kinnear and Frauke Nitschke for sharing material on the adoption of the ICSID Mediation Rules and for their useful comments on an earlier version of this chapter.

C. Titi (✉)
French National Centre for Scientific Research (CNRS) and CERSA, University Paris-Panthéon-Assas, Paris, France
e-mail: cathy_titi@hotmail.com

M. Bungenberg et al. (eds.), *Alternative Dispute Resolution in the Western Balkans*, European Union and its Neighbours in a Globalized World 20,
https://doi.org/10.1007/978-3-031-76345-8_10

negotiations on the reform of Investor-State Dispute Settlement (ISDS) are ongoing,[3] states have expressed an interest in alternative dispute resolution, including, especially, mediation.[4] The working group has taken the view that mediation could be useful in investor-state disputes, and it continues to explore ways in which to encourage mediation as a dispute settlement option for these disputes.[5] As of the time of writing, UNCITRAL has adopted model provisions on mediation for investor-state disputes and mediation guidelines.[6]

Besides UNCITRAL, an institution that has lent a sympathetic ear to states' growing interest in mediation is the International Centre for Settlement of Investment Disputes (ICSID). Like other institutions, ICSID participates as an observer in the negotiations in Working Group III and has followed closely developments in that context. In 2022, as part of an overhaul of its Rules and Regulations, ICSID adopted a set of mediation rules, which are the first institutional, as opposed to ad hoc, rules developed specifically for the mediation of investment disputes.[7] These rules are the focus of this chapter.

The remainder of this chapter is structured as follows. The chapter starts by examining the context of the adoption of the ICSID Mediation Rules, before considering the reasons that may have led ICSID to establish the rules, given that the Convention on the Settlement of Investment Disputes between States and Nationals of Other States (ICSID Convention) provides for conciliation anyway. That part of the chapter aims to answer the question: What differences between ICSID mediation and conciliation justify the adoption of standalone mediation rules? The next part of the chapter focuses on the mediation procedure under the ICSID Mediation Rules, from the initiation of proceedings to their conduct and termination. Finally, the chapter takes into account remaining challenges that investment mediation faces, and which will need to be addressed, if mediation is to become a more mainstream means of settling investment disputes.

---

[3] See UNCITRAL, Working Group III: investor-state dispute settlement reform, https://uncitral.un.org/en/working_groups/3/investor-state.

[4] See UNCITRAL, Investment mediation and dispute prevention, https://uncitral.un.org/en/investmentmediationanddisputeprevention. See further Böhme and Braun (2023), p. 10.

[5] Knieper and Haddad (2023), p. 240.

[6] UNCITRAL (2023), paras. 35–40.

[7] See ICSID, Rules and Regulations: mediation, https://icsid.worldbank.org/rules-regulations/mediation.

2 The Context of the Adoption of the ICSID Mediation Rules

This is not the first time that ICSID has revised its Rules and Regulations, nor is it the first time that it adopts rules on the settlement of investment disputes by alternative dispute resolution (understood here as alternative to, especially, arbitration).[8] ICSID's Rules and Regulations have evolved on a number of occasions over the nearly sixty years of ICSID's existence.[9] In contrast with the ICSID Convention, a treaty binding on almost 160 states,[10] and whose amendment is generally considered to present insurmountable challenges,[11] the revision of the ICSID Rules and Regulations is a lot simpler.[12] While amendments to the ICSID Arbitration and Conciliation Rules and the Administrative and Financial Regulations and Institution Rules require a two-thirds approval by the Administrative Council, a majority of the votes cast suffices for the adoption of the amended Additional Facility Rules for Arbitration and Conciliation Proceedings and the standalone Mediation Rules.[13] The amendment of the ICSID Rules and Regulations and the adoption of the new set of Mediation Rules are important developments, given ICSID's popularity in the settlement of international investment disputes.[14] The most recent revision is the fourth and "most extensive amendment to date", whose purpose has been to "modernize, simplify, and streamline the rules".[15] The amended rules and regulations, and the new ICSID Mediation Rules, were approved by the majority of states and entered into force on 1 July 2022.[16]

[8] See text to nn. 19 ff.

[9] ICSID, A brief history of amendment to the ICSID Rules and Regulations, 10 March 2020, https://icsid.worldbank.org/news-and-events/speeches-articles/brief-history-amendment-icsid-rules-and-regulations.

[10] ICSID, Database of ICSID member states, https://icsid.worldbank.org/about/member-states/database-of-member-states (information correct as of 1 March 2024).

[11] According to Article 66(1) of the ICSID Convention, an amendment of the Convention would require "ratification, acceptance or approval" by all member states.

[12] Titi (2023a).

[13] ICSID, Press release: ICSID submits amended Rules to the Administrative Council for a vote, 20 January 2022, https://icsid.worldbank.org/news-and-events/news-releases/icsid-submits-amended-rules-administrative-council-vote. See also Parra (2007), p. 57.

[14] Kinnear (2022).

[15] ICSID, ICSID Rules and Regulations Amendment, https://icsid.worldbank.org/resources/rules-amendments (17/5/2024).

[16] ICSID, Press release: ICSID releases 2022 versions of its Rules and Regulations, 22 June 2022, https://icsid.worldbank.org/news-and-events/news-releases/icsid-releases-2022-versions-its-rules-and-regulations.

3 Mediation or Conciliation?

Both mediation and conciliation are negotiations facilitated by a third-party neutral, the mediator or conciliator.[17] In contrast with negotiations, where the disputing parties need to confront each other directly, the presence of the third party neutral in mediation and conciliation has the advantage of removing a layer of tension, where parties find it difficult to establish a productive dialogue.[18] Even before the 2022 introduction of the new Mediation Rules, ICSID proposed a set of Conciliation Rules. In fact, conciliation is provided for in the ICSID Convention itself.[19] Since therefore ICSID already gave disputing parties the opportunity to use conciliation as a means of settling their investment disputes, it is worth briefly considering the differences between conciliation and mediation that may have pushed ICSID to adopt the new mediation rules.

Unlike conciliation, which by comparison is a relatively formal dispute settlement process, mediation is relatively informal and flexible, although both mediation and conciliation allow the parties to retain control over the outcome of their dispute.[20] Despite this difference of degree between the two types of dispute settlement, conciliation and mediation are very similar, and the distinction between them is not always drawn in the literature.[21] What matters more in terms of understanding the need for or interest in adopting a set of mediation rules may have to do less with the formal distinction between conciliation and mediation and more with perceived limitations of ICSID conciliation. It is also worth keeping in mind that, since ICSID conciliation is laid down in the ICSID Convention, a radical amendment was not envisageable, while mediation was unchartered territory.

For ICSID Convention conciliation, the threshold for establishing jurisdiction is relatively high, as will be discussed later.[22] By contrast, ICSID mediation is open to disputing parties with no limitation as regards nationality and no need for ICSID membership of the investor's host or home states.[23] Unlike a request for conciliation, a request for mediation does not need the parties' prior consent, although such consent must ultimately be established.[24] ICSID conciliation tends to be more formal than mediation in other respects too. This is obvious, for example, in the role of the conciliator, who, unlike mediators, is encouraged to make non-binding recommendations

---

[17] UNCTAD (2010), p. xix, Alberstein (2007), p. 334.

[18] Collier and Lowe (1999), p. 27, Tomuschat (2012), p. 125.

[19] For an overview of ICSID conciliation, see Nitschke (2019).

[20] UNCTAD (2010), pp. xiii, xix. See also Salacuse (2007), p. 154. For a comparison between conciliation and mediation, see Sudborough (2023), pp. 69–73.

[21] E.g. in Titi and Fach Gómez (2019) a conscious choice was made not to distinguish between the two dispute settlement systems, due to the important similarity between them. See also Stipanowich (2015), p. 1222.

[22] See text to nn. 35 ff.

[23] See text to nn. 35 ff.

[24] See text to nn. 40–41.

for dispute resolution.[25] Under the ICSID conciliation framework, a conciliation commission, whose purpose is to "clarify the issues in dispute between the parties and to endeavour to bring about agreement between them upon mutually acceptable terms", "may at any stage of the proceedings and from time to time recommend terms of settlement to the parties".[26] As we shall see, the mediator's role is more "modest": to assist the parties in resolving their dispute.[27] The disputing parties are expected to "cooperate in good faith" with the conciliation commission and "give their most serious consideration to its recommendations".[28] The commission is also required to draw up a report noting the parties' agreement or failure to reach an agreement, as the case may be.[29] The mediator, by contrast, is not expected to draw up a report at the end of the proceeding or make recommendations to the parties.[30]

In short, the formal nature and strict jurisdictional criteria of ICSID conciliation, in addition to the fact that this method of dispute settlement has not been very popular over the years, probably explain the interest ICSID and states have shown in adopting new rules for investment mediation.

4 Mediation Under the ICSID Mediation Rules

4.1 ICSID Mediation in General and Institution of Proceedings

ICSID explains that the newly-adopted Mediation Rules complement its existing arbitration, conciliation, and fact-finding rules and can "be used either independently of, or in conjunction with, arbitration proceedings".[31] An author has suggested that the mediation could not only coincide with an arbitral proceeding but may even continue after the tribunal has rendered its award and become functus officio.[32] That the conduct of an arbitration does not prevent the conduct of a mediation, and vice versa, is compatible with the idea that mediation is a means of dispute settlement complementary to arbitration but one that cannot replace arbitration.[33]

The ICSID Mediation Rules have a wide scope of application: they are designed to be able to be used by the broadest categories of parties, so long as the parties

[25] Shane (1995), Sudborough (2023), p. 71. Cf. text to n. 44.

[26] Article 34(1) of the ICSID Convention; Rules 24 and 29(4) of the ICSID Conciliation Rules.

[27] See text to n. 44.

[28] Article 34(1) of the ICSID Convention.

[29] Article 34(2) of the ICSID Convention. See also Nitschke (2019).

[30] See text to n. 85.

[31] ICSID, Rules and Regulations: mediation, https://icsid.worldbank.org/rules-regulations/mediation. See also ICSID (2021), p. 4.

[32] Coe (2019), pp. 62–63.

[33] Titi (2019), pp. 33–34, Coe (2019). See also Coe (2005), discussing specifically conciliation.

consent in writing to submit their dispute to ICSID mediation. ICSID can administer mediations that "relate to an investment, involve a State or [a regional economic integration organisation]", such as the European Union.[34] This contrasts with conciliation under the ICSID Convention, which imposes a relatively high threshold for establishing jurisdiction, requiring that a dispute must be legal, "arising directly out of an investment", and that it must involve a contracting state and a national of another contracting state.[35] It is notable that by not imposing a foreign nationality requirement, the ICSID Mediation Rules allow for an ICSID mediation to take place not only between host states and foreign investors but also between host states and their national investors.[36] This is an interesting development and may encourage states and scholars to consider the desirability of extending other procedural investment protections, notably ISDS, to national investors. Although there is certainly a political cost to such a decision, the idea of guaranteeing protection of one's own nationals at the international level is not unprecedented—for example, this is the case with human rights covenants and regional human rights courts.

ICSID mediation is also broader in coverage than conciliation under the ICSID Additional Facility Rules. The latter still require the existence of a "legal" dispute "arising out of an investment", involving, on the one hand, a state or a regional economic integration organisation, and, on the other, a national of another state, assuming that either the home state of the investor or the respondent state or both states are not a contracting state, or that a regional economic integration organization is a party to the dispute.[37] It is interesting that the ICSID Mediation Rules do not require a "legal dispute"—in fact even the word "dispute" is not mentioned. This is in line with the fact that mediation does not necessarily require the existence of an escalated dispute but is instead sometimes seen as akin to dispute mitigation or dispute prevention.[38] In addition, as a diplomatic means of dispute settlement, mediation may be an attempt to solve the dispute without application of the strict law, either because the parties prefer to achieve a balancing of their interests rather than rely on the existing legal framework or because the legal framework applicable to their dispute is not yet definitely settled.[39]

If the parties have not given their prior written consent to ICSID mediation, a party wishing to institute a mediation may still file a request with the Secretary-General

---

[34] Rule 2(1) of the ICSID Mediation Rules. See also Rule 3(1) of the ICSID Mediation Rules.

[35] Article 25 of the ICSID Convention. The ICSID Convention does not indicate the form that the conciliation commission's finding on jurisdiction must take. However, the Conciliation Rules establish that, if lack of jurisdiction has been raised as a preliminary objection and the commission upholds jurisdiction, it must record its jurisdictional finding in "a reasoned decision", while, in the opposite case, it must render a reasoned report, see Rule 33(5) of the ICSID Conciliation Rules. In practice, conciliation commissions have incorporated their decision on jurisdiction in their final report, see Nitschke (2019), p. 136.

[36] ICSID, Key differences between mediation and conciliation at ICSID, https://icsid.worldbank.org/rules-regulations/mediation/key-differences-between-mediation-and-conciliation.

[37] Article 2(1) of the ICSID Additional Facility Rules.

[38] Titi (2019), pp. 29–31, Sudborough (2023), p. 86.

[39] Titi (2021), pp. 156–157.

inviting the other party to mediate their dispute.[40] This request must be accompanied by the payment of a non-refundable lodging fee to ICSID.[41] Currently, the lodging fee for the institution of proceedings under the ICSID Mediation Rules is US$1,000.[42] ICSID also levies an administrative charge of US$200 per hour for "staff services" in relation to mediation proceedings.[43]

4.2 The Mediator

The role of an ICSID mediator is to "assist the parties in reaching a mutually acceptable resolution of all or part of the issues in dispute".[44] Since mediation, like conciliation, is a soft dispute settlement process, the mediator cannot "impose a resolution of the dispute on the parties".[45] The parties remain in control of their dispute, and they can agree to disagree.

ICSID mediation involves one mediator or two co-mediators, appointed by agreement of the parties.[46] The default rule is one mediator.[47] The parties may request ICSID's assistance to appoint a mediator.[48] The mediator or mediators must be independent and impartial, while the parties may decide to appoint persons who possess specific qualifications or expertise.[49] The parties may also jointly decide that a mediator must resign.[50] Trust in the mediator is vital for the success of the dispute settlement process, and it is for this reason that some limitations that apply to the appointment of arbitrators under the ICSID Convention are not relevant to ICSID mediation (or conciliation).[51] For example, under the ICSID Convention, the majority of the arbitrators cannot have the nationality of the disputing parties, unless the parties agree on all appointed arbitrators.[52] The stated purpose of this provision was to "avoid a situation in which the third arbitrator, as the only one appointed by a neutral party, might find himself in the position of a sole arbitrator in having to maintain a balance between two other arbitrators who were more inclined to act as advocates for the parties appointing them".[53] These considerations do not apply to

---

[40] Rule 6(1)–(2) of the ICSID Mediation Rules.

[41] Rule 6(1) of the ICSID Mediation Rules. See also Point I.3 of ICSID's Schedule of Fees (2023).

[42] Point I.3 of ICSID's Schedule of Fees (2023).

[43] Point II.5 of ICSID's Schedule of Fees (2023).

[44] Rule 17(1) of the ICSID Mediation Rules.

[45] Rule 17(1) of the ICSID Mediation Rules.

[46] Rule 13(1) of the ICSID Mediation Rules.

[47] Rule 13(2) of the ICSID Mediation Rules.

[48] Rule 13(3)–(4) of the ICSID Mediation Rules.

[49] Rule 12 of the ICSID Mediation Rules.

[50] Rule 16(2) of the ICSID Mediation Rules.

[51] Titi (2020), pp. 46–47.

[52] Article 39 of the ICSID Convention.

[53] ICSID (1968), p. 983.

mediation (or, for that matter, conciliation), where no decision is made by the third-party neutral.[54] Accordingly, in ICSID mediation and conciliation, it is possible to appoint a mediator or conciliator of the nationality of the other party.[55] In any event, the fact that mediators are appointed with the agreement of the parties should dispel any doubts about the appropriateness of appointing a mediator with the nationality of one of the parties.[56] That said, independence and impartiality may play a different role in mediation than in arbitration. It has been suggested, for instance, that disputing parties should consider the appointment of mediators proposed by the other disputing party, including when such appointments concern mediators who are nationals of or have the same nationality as the other disputing party.[57] The idea is that this could have the double effect of ensuring that the other party commits to the process and increasing their trust in the third-party neutral.[58]

4.3 Conduct of the Mediation and Procedural Principles

The mediator must conduct the dispute settlement proceeding "in good faith and in an expeditious and cost-effective manner".[59] Cost-effectiveness is an important consideration, since the attractiveness of mediation for investment disputes lies in good part in the fact that mediation is considerably less costly than arbitration; investment arbitration's high cost has encouraged states to explore alternative means of dispute settlement in the first place.[60] The principle of the disputing parties' equality of arms[61] also applies to mediation: the mediator must not only treat the parties equally but must also provide each one of them "with a reasonable opportunity to participate in the mediation".[62] In contrast with arbitration, where ex parte communications are not allowed, the ICSID Mediation Rules make it clear that the mediator is at liberty to "meet and communicate with the parties jointly or separately" no matter whether in person, in writing, or by other means.[63] It has been even suggested that the parties may actually expect to have ex parte meetings.[64] These meetings are known as "caucuses".[65] Caucuses provide opportunities for the parties to express themselves on

---

[54] Titi (2020), pp. 46–47.

[55] See Chap. IV of the ICSID Mediation Rules; Articles 29–31 of the ICSID Convention.

[56] See text to n. 46.

[57] Brower II (2019), pp. 301, 306–307.

[58] Brower II (2019), pp. 306–307.

[59] Rule 17(2) of the ICSID Mediation Rules.

[60] Bottini et al. (2020).

[61] For a discussion of the principle in investment arbitration, see Vanhonnaeker (2024).

[62] Rule 17(3) of the ICSID Mediation Rules.

[63] Rule 17(4) of the ICSID Mediation Rules.

[64] Brower II (2019), p. 317.

[65] Coe (2019), p. 76.

sensitive issues and to appreciate, if relevant, the eventual weakness of their position.[66] In addition, caucuses may increase the probability that the parties are honest and that the mediator can ask questions more freely, without worrying about whether his or her questions will be interpreted by the other party as giving preference to one party or another.[67] Ultimately, caucuses can contribute to the success of the mediation.[68]

In contrast with arbitration, where transparency has become the norm, confidentiality is still important in investment mediation.[69] In principle, all information and all documents related to the mediation are to be kept confidential.[70] The Mediation Rules provide exceptions to the principle, notably if the parties agree to release the information or documents, when the information or documents are independently available, or when disclosure is required by law.[71] The fact that the parties are mediating or have mediated is to be kept confidential, unless the parties agree otherwise.[72] Information given confidentially by one of the disputing parties to the mediator (in a caucus) cannot be disclosed to the other party.[73] In addition, unless the parties agree otherwise, a party may not rely in the course of other dispute settlement proceedings on "any positions taken, admissions or offers of settlement made, or views expressed by the other party or the mediator during the mediation".[74] This is again customary in mediation and the idea behind it is that such confidentiality will encourage the parties to participate in the mediation "with a comfort level that enables them to be forthright in terms of their position regarding the dispute".[75]

Pursuant to the ICSID Mediation Rules, the disputing parties have the duty to cooperate with the mediator or mediators and with one another and, as is the case for the mediator, they too must "conduct the mediation in good faith and in an expeditious and cost-effective manner".[76] At the beginning of the mediation, each party must file with ICSID a brief written statement describing the issues in dispute, and its position on these issues and on the procedure to be followed in the mediation.[77] These statements are then to be transmitted by the ICSID Secretary-General to the mediator and to the other disputing party.[78] Within thirty days after the transmittal of the mediation request, unless the parties agree on a different timeline, the mediator

---

[66] Welsh and Kupfer Schneider (2012), p. 93; Sudborough (2023), p. 90.

[67] Abramson (2004), p. 91.

[68] Brower II (2019), p. 317.

[69] Brown and Winch (2019), Sudborough (2023), p. 108.

[70] Rule 10(1) of the ICSID Mediation Rules.

[71] Rule 10(1) of the ICSID Mediation Rules.

[72] Rule 10(2) of the ICSID Mediation Rules.

[73] Rule 17(4) of the ICSID Mediation Rules.

[74] Rule 11 of the ICSID Mediation Rules.

[75] Tuchmann et al. (2019), p. 111.

[76] Rule 18 of the ICSID Mediation Rules. See also text to n. 59.

[77] Rule 19(1) of the ICSID Mediation Rules.

[78] Rule 19(2) of the ICSID Mediation Rules.

or mediators hold a first session with the parties.[79] After consulting with the parties, the mediator determines the protocol for the conduct of the mediation, including the language of the proceedings, the method of communication, the place of the meetings including whether they will be held in person or remotely,[80] the issue of confidentiality, and the eventual agreement of the parties not to pursue other proceedings for the topics that are being mediated.[81]

The Rules require the mediator to conduct the procedure in accordance with the protocol and to consider the positions of the parties.[82] With the parties' agreement, the mediator may ask for expert advice.[83] In contrast with conciliation, where the conciliation commission may "at any stage of the proceedings and from time to time" make recommendations for the resolution of the dispute to the parties,[84] the mediator can only make such recommendations, whether written or oral, if requested to do so "by all parties".[85]

The mediator (or ICSID, if no mediator has been appointed) terminates the mediation when he or she receives the parties' notice that they have either signed a settlement agreement, that they have agreed to terminate the mediation proceeding, that a party has withdrawn from the mediation (unless the remaining parties wish to continue), or if the mediator determines that the dispute is unlikely to be resolved through the mediation proceeding.[86] The Secretary-General of ICSID will terminate the dispute if the parties have failed to appoint a mediator within 120 consecutive days after the registration of the mediation, or after another period that the parties may have agreed upon.[87]

In the event that the mediation proceeding takes place in parallel with an ICSID Convention arbitration, to the extent that the arbitral tribunal has not yet rendered its award, the arbitral tribunal upon successful conclusion of the mediation must take note of the discontinuance of the arbitral proceeding, if requested to do so by the parties.[88] The parties may also file the mediated settlement agreement and request of the tribunal to include it into the award.[89] In that case, the award rendered by the

---

79 Rule 20(1) of the ICSID Mediation Rules.

80 Since the COVID-19 pandemic, virtual hearings have become more common in arbitration, see Fach Gómez (2023), pp. 111–121. There is every reason to assume that this trend will be reflected in investment mediation too.

81 Rule 20(3) of the ICSID Mediation Rules.

82 Rule 21(1) of the ICSID Mediation Rules.

83 Rule 21(3) of the ICSID Mediation Rules.

84 Article 34(1) of the ICSID Convention. For a discussion, see Nitschke (2019), *passim*; Reif (1990)

85 Rule 21(4) of the ICSID Mediation Rules.

86 Rule 22(1) of the ICSID Mediation Rules.

87 Rules 13(5) and 22(1) of the ICSID Mediation Rules.

88 Rule 55(2) of the ICSID Arbitration Rules.

89 Rule 55(2) of the ICSID Arbitration Rules.

tribunal will be described as a consent or settlement award.[90] The advantage of incorporating the settlement in an ICSID award in such a case is that the settlement agreement will then benefit from the strong enforcement regime of the ICSID Convention.[91] It must however be borne in mind that, strictly speaking, this enforcement regime only concerns pecuniary obligations and not specific performance.[92]

Finally, when it comes to costs, the default rule under the ICSID Mediation Rules is that, unless the parties agree otherwise, the fees and expenses of the mediator and the administrative charges and costs of ICSID are borne equally by the disputing parties.[93] Any other costs, such as legal representation costs, will in principle be borne by the party that has incurred them.[94]

5 Challenges of Mediation

Although mediation is a relatively popular dispute settlement method for some types of disputes, such as cultural heritage repatriation disputes,[95] and some cultures attach particular value to it,[96] it remains a relatively unexplored means of settling investor-state disputes, although its desirability has often been invoked.[97]

There are several reasons for this reluctance to mediate investment disputes.[98] The first is directly related to the involvement of the state and the politics behind settlements. It has been suggested that "active political oppositions" may be "waiting for an opportunity to pounce on the incumbents for having 'betrayed' the national patrimony by settling with an investor"[99] and that the decision to willingly compensate investors for public interest measures will be hard to "sell to constituents".[100] This unease with mediation can also prove to be true in the case of directly negotiated settlement agreements, and, possibly for that reason, such settlements are often kept confidential. In *SPP v. Egypt* (the Pyramids case),[101] the Egyptian Prime Minister had rejected a tentative settlement agreement of 10 million US dollars in favour of arbitration, since he considered that such a settlement "would open him to attack by

[90] Bottini (2024).

[91] See Bungenberg et al.(2024).

[92] Article 54(1) of the ICSID Convention. See also Bungenberg et al. (2024).

[93] Rule 9 of the ICSID Mediation Rules.

[94] Rule 9 of the ICSID Mediation Rules.

[95] For an overview, see Titi (2023), pp. 195–198.

[96] E.g. McFadden (2019).

[97] See Bottini and Lavista (2009), making a similar case for conciliation.

[98] See Titi (2019), pp. 35–38. That said, it has been informally reported to this author that there have been at least 30 investment mediations.

[99] Reisman (2010), p. 26.

[100] Welsh and Kupfer Schneider (2013), pp. 86–87.

[101] *Southern Pacific Properties (SPP) v. Egypt*, ICSID Case No. ARB/84/3.

opponents and the media".[102] This dispute was ultimately settled after arbitration for 17.5 million US dollars.[103]

A probably even more important obstacle to investment mediation is that public officials may not be habilitated to settle with foreign investors or that, if they are, they may bear legal and financial liability and face prosecution, such as on allegations of corruption or for having incurred losses for the state.[104] Moreover, while usually there is authorisation for compensation to be paid to an investor on the basis of an arbitral award, a special authorisation may be necessary for a settlement agreement.[105] This can make a decision imposed by a third party, an arbitrator, preferable and, by the same token, reduce the attractiveness of mediation. Therefore, enabling public officials to reach settlement agreements is key for the success of investment mediation.

A further complication concerns communication inefficiencies between state agencies. Public officials may be uninformed about the facts that have given rise to the investment dispute, and the legal defence of the state often does not start before the state receives the actual arbitration request.[106] The state agency that has adopted the contested measures is typically not the agency responsible for defending the state against legal claims,[107] and it may be weeks or even months before officials in the latter identify their counterparts in the agency at the origin of the dispute.[108] It can take even longer before the legal defence agency can make a first assessment of the merits of the dispute.[109] Such assessment is crucial for the state, since the strength of its legal case can have an impact on its preferred method of dispute settlement.[110]

A final challenge concerns the enforcement of mediated settlement agreements, although the Singapore Mediation Convention is likely to change this. While its applicability to investment disputes still needs to be formally confirmed,[111] the better argument seems to be that it is indeed applicable to at least some investment mediated settlement agreements. According to the *travaux préparatoires* of the Convention, if "a settlement agreement between a government entity and an investor was considered to be of a commercial nature under the applicable law, such an agreement should fall under the scope of the [Convention]".[112] ICSID too has stressed the compatibility of future ICSID mediated settlement agreements with the requirements of the Singapore Convention on Mediation.[113]

---

[102] Salacuse (2007), p. 150.

[103] Salacuse (2007), p. 150.

[104] Valderrama (2021), p. 129, Constain (2014), p. 34.

[105] Legum (2006), p. 2.

[106] Legum and Crevon (2014), p. 3, Sharpe (2014), pp. 43–45.

[107] Legum (2006), p. 1.

[108] Legum (2006), p. 2.

[109] Legum (2006), p. 2. See also Coe (2005), p. 41.

[110] Titi (2023b), pp. 27, 190.

[111] Abramson (2019), Sudborough (2023), pp. 109–115.

[112] UNCITRAL (2016), para. 110.

[113] ICSID, Termination of the mediation—ICSID mediation (2022), https://icsid.worldbank.org/procedures/mediation/termination-of-mediation/2022.

6 Conclusion

ICSID conciliation proceedings have not proved very popular, although ICSID conciliation has been an available dispute settlement option for as long as ICSID Convention arbitration has been available. Will ICSID mediation be more popular? Probably. It is certainly designed to be easier to access and its flexibility should help make it attractive. After all, if one decides against arbitration and in favour of a flexible means of dispute settlement, mediation is a more obvious choice than conciliation, the latter resembling arbitration in its formality.

This does not mean that mediation is going to compete with arbitration for popularity, since mediation and arbitration tend to be appropriate in different circumstances. Arbitration will certainly continue to be more widely used, but just as some disputes are resolved through direct negotiations, from now on some other disputes are likely to be resolved through ICSID mediation. The confidentiality of proceedings may well mean that we know little about it, as we know little about negotiated settlement agreements. However, the fact remains that the new Mediation Rules offer an additional means of settling investment disputes, and this in itself makes their adoption a very welcome development.

References

Abramson H (2004) Mediation representation: advocating in a problem-solving process. National Institute for Trial Advocacy

Abramson H (2019) New Singapore Convention on cross-border mediated settlements: key choices. In: Titi C, Fach Gómez K (eds) Mediation in international commercial and investment disputes. Oxford University Press, Oxford

Alberstein M (2007) Forms of mediation and law: cultures of dispute resolution. Ohio State J Disput Resolut 22(2):321–376

Böhme B, Braun J (2023) The UNCITRAL reform process: improving procedural efficiency through the dismissal of frivolous claims and investor-state mediation. Jean Monnet Paper 02/2023

Bottini G (2024) Consent awards. In: Fach Gómez K, Titi C (eds) The award in international investment arbitration. Oxford University Press, Oxford

Bottini G, Lavista V (2009) Conciliation and BITs. In: Rovine A (ed) Contemporary issues in international arbitration and mediation: the Fordham Papers. Brill, Leiden

Bottini G et al (2020) Excessive costs and recoverability of costs awards in investment arbitration. J World Invest & Trade 21(2–3):251–299

Brower II CH (2019) Selection of mediators. In: Titi C, Fach Gómez K (eds) Mediation in international commercial and investment disputes. Oxford University Press, Oxford

Brown C, Winch P (2019) The confidentiality and transparency debate in commercial and investment mediation. In: Titi C, Fach Gómez K (eds) Mediation in international commercial and investment disputes. Oxford University Press, Oxford

Bungenberg M, Alvarado Garzón AE, Böhme B (2024), Recognition and enforcement of ICSID convention awards. In: Fach Gómez K, Titi C (eds) The award in international investment arbitration. Oxford University Press, Oxford

Coe JJ Jr (2005) Toward a complementary use of conciliation in investor-state disputes: a preliminary sketch. Univ Calif Davis J Int Law Policy 12:7–46

Coe JJ Jr (2019) Concurrent co-mediation: toward a more collaborative centre of gravity in investor-state dispute resolution. In: Titi C, Fach Gómez K (eds) Mediation in international commercial and investment disputes. Oxford University Press, Oxford
Collier JG, Lowe V (1999) The settlement of disputes in international law. Oxford University Press, Oxford
Constain S (2014) Mediation in investor-state dispute settlement: government policy and the changing landscape. ICSID Rev 29(1):25
Fach Gómez K (2023) The technological competence of arbitrators. Springer, Cham
International Centre for Settlement of Investment Disputes (ICSID) (1968) History of the ICSID convention, vol 2, part 2. ICSID, Washington DC
International Centre for Settlement of Investment Disputes (ICSID) (2021) Background paper on investment mediation. ICSID, Washington DC
Kinnear M (2022) The launch of a new generation of the ICSID rules. Columbia FDI Perspectives No. 326, 7 March 2022
Knieper J, Haddad J (2023) The history, evolution, and future of the UNCITRAL mediation framework. In: Gulati R, John T, Köhler B (eds) The Elgar companion to UNCITRAL. Elgar Publishing, Cheltenham and Massachusetts
Legum B (2006) The difficulties of conciliation in investment treaty cases: a comment on professor Jack C Coe's 'toward a complementary use of conciliation in investor-state disputes – a preliminary sketch. Mealey's Int Arbitr Rep 21(4):1
Legum B, Crevon A (2014) An outline of procedure in an investment treaty arbitration: strategy and choices. In: Giorgetti C (ed) Litigating international investment disputes – a practitioner's guide. Brill, Leiden
McFadden D (2019) The growing importance of regional mediation centres in Asia. In: Titi C, Fach Gómez K (eds) Mediation in international commercial and investment disputes. Oxford University Press, Oxford
Nitschke F (2019) The ICSID conciliation rules in practice. In: Titi C, Fach Gómez K (eds) Mediation in international commercial and investment disputes. Oxford University Press, Oxford
Parra A (2007) The development of the regulations and rules of the international centre for settlement of investment disputes. ICSID Rev 22(1):55–68
Reif LC (1990) Conciliation as a mechanism for the resolution of international economic and business disputes. Fordham Int Law J 14(3):578–638
Reisman WM (2010) International investment arbitration and ADR: married but best Living Apart. In: UNCTAD, Investor-state disputes: prevention and alternatives to arbitration II. United Nations
Salacuse JW (2007) Is there a better way? Alternative methods of treaty-based, investor-state dispute resolution. Fordham Int Law J 31(1):138–185
Shane MB (1995) The difference between mediation and conciliation. Disput Resolut J 50(3):31
Sharpe JK (2014) Representing a respondent state in investment arbitration. In: Giorgetti C (ed) Litigating international investment disputes – a practitioner's guide. Brill Nijhoff
Stipanowich TJ (2015) The international evolution of mediation: a call for dialogue and deliberation. Vic Univ Wellingt Law Rev 46(4):1191
Sudborough CM (2023) Mediating sovereign debt disputes. Springer, Cham
Titi C (2019) Mediation and the settlement of international investment disputes: between utopia and realism. In: Titi C, Fach Gómez K (eds) Mediation in international commercial and investment disputes. Oxford University Press, Oxford
Titi C (2020) Nationality and representation in the composition of the international bench: lessons from the practice of international courts and tribunals and policy options for the Multilateral Investment Court. In: CERSA working papers on law and political science 1/2020, pp 1–78. https://papers.ssrn.com/sol3/papers.cfm?abstract_id=3519863
Titi C (2023a) La révision des règlements du CIRDI. Annuaire Français de Droit International 2022 68:777–791
Titi C (2023b) The Parthenon marbles and international law. Springer, Cham

Titi C, Fach Gómez K (eds) (2019) Mediation in international commercial and investment disputes. Oxford University Press, Oxford
Tomuschat C (2012) Article 33 UN charter. In: Zimmermann A et al (eds) The Statute of the International Court of Justice: a commentary, 2nd edn. Oxford University Press, Oxford
Tuchmann EP et al (2019) The International Centre for Dispute Resolution's Mediation practice and experience. In: Titi C, Fach Gómez K (eds) Mediation in international commercial and investment disputes. Oxford University Press, Oxford
United Nations Commission on International Trade Law (UNCITRAL) (2016) Report of working group II (arbitration and conciliation) on the work of its sixty-fourth session, UN Doc No A/CN.9/867
United Nations Commission on International Trade Law (UNCITRAL) (2018) Possible reform of investor-state dispute settlement (ISDS): note by the Secretariat, UN Doc No A/CN.9/WG.III/WP.149
United Nations Commission on International Trade Law (UNCITRAL) (2023) Official records of the general assembly, seventy-eighth session, Supp. No 17, UN Doc No A/78/17
United Nations Conference on Trade and Development (UNCTAD) (2010) Investor–state disputes: prevention and alternatives to arbitration. United Nations, New York and Geneva
Valderrama CJ (2021) Investor-state dispute prevention: the perspective of Peru. In: Titi C (ed) Public actors in international investment law. Springer, Cham
Vanhonnaeker L (2024) Equality of arms. In: Fach Gómez K, Titi C (eds) The award in international investment arbitration. Oxford University Press, Oxford
Waibel M et al (2010) The backlash against investment arbitration: perceptions and reality. Kluwer Law International, Alphen aan den Rijn
Weber J, Titi C (2015) UNCTAD's roadmap for reform of investment dispute settlement. N Z Bus Law Q 21(4):319–327
Welsh N, Kupfer Schneider A (2012) Becoming 'investor-state mediation.' Penn State J Law & Int Affairs 1(1):86–96
Welsh N, Kupfer Schneider A (2013) The thoughtful integration of mediation into bilateral investment treaty arbitration. Harv Negot Law Rev 18:71–144

Expanding the Dispute Resolution Toolbox for Investment Disputes: Opportunities for Dispute Prevention and Mediation in the Western Balkans

Fahira Brodlija

Abstract The multiple ongoing reform processes of investment law and investor-State dispute settlement (ISDS) opened the space to reconsider the default reliance on investment arbitration and to reimagine the role of dispute prevention and amicable settlement mechanisms in this space. Such mechanisms entail several benefits for States, including cost and time efficiency, more leverage and control in the course and outcome of disputes, and the restoration of trust in ISDS more broadly. Dispute prevention mechanisms and mediation have emerged as viable reform options, gaining growing support from States (including the EU and its Member States), investors, and international organizations (UNCITRAL, the World Bank Group, etc.) alike. While dispute prevention mechanisms take different shapes and forms in different countries, amicable settlement (including negotiations, conciliation and mediation) has been available in international investment treaties for decades, in the so-called "cooling-off" period. Nevertheless, it has not been effectively used in ISDS, due to a variety of factors, ranging from the preference for third-party adjudication, motivated by the desire of the competent authorities to avoid personal liability resulting from settlements with foreign investors, and/or a lack of capacities. The Western Balkans governments, navigating the ISDS reform process, while progressing on their path to EU accession, are a good case study for the challenges and opportunities of integrating dispute prevention and mediation into the State toolbox for investment dispute resolution. This chapter will address the regional and international, as well as legal and institutional frameworks for dispute prevention and mediation, the obstacles and challenges in the Western Balkans, and the emerging new structures and best practices, which establish a promising model for the region, with tailored solutions for each State. The chapter will offer perspectives for dispute prevention and mediation as staples of the investment protection frameworks in the Western Balkans on their path to the EU, and as future EU Member States.

F. Brodlija (✉)
GIZ, Sarajevo, Bosnia and Herzegovina
e-mail: fahira.brodlija@giz.de

M. Bungenberg et al. (eds.), *Alternative Dispute Resolution in the Western Balkans*, European Union and its Neighbours in a Globalized World 20,
https://doi.org/10.1007/978-3-031-76345-8_11

1 Introduction

Dispute prevention mechanisms and mediation are increasingly on the radar of States seeking to effectively reform their dispute resolution mechanisms and investment treaties. Mediation, as a tool for facilitated negotiations between disputing parties, is known and practiced as an alternative to, or precondition to litigation or arbitration in international disputes.[1] In investor-State disputes, however, it appears to be under-utilized, even though it is at least implicitly possible under international investment treaties (primarily Bilateral Investment Treaties, BITs).[2] At the same time, existing and prospective foreign investors are concerned with the predictability and availability of a stable legal framework and remedies protecting their investments as an indicator of political risk in a home State.[3] A negative assessment of this factor can lead to a decision not to invest or to withdraw existing investments. Such outcomes can, at times, be more economically harmful for the State than damages awards in investment arbitrations.

For governments in the Western Balkans and the broader South-East Europe region, the effective use of dispute prevention in the pre-dispute phase and mediation in the cooling-off period would be of special benefit as it would allow them to maintain control of the process and prevent disputes or at least reduce their financial exposure. Furthermore, mediation can be a reliable process for the coordination bodies already established in some governments in the region, thus protecting the negotiators from any personal liability or political scrutiny. Finally, as the EU has already included mediation in its recent trade and investment agreements, and endorsed it in the ISDS reform process internationally, aspiring EU Member States in the region can already take advantage of its benefits in pending and new disputes, while remaining in compliance with EU law.

This chapter will capture the current experiences and practices of the Western Balkans' governments in investor-State disputes, and their potential for building up frameworks for dispute prevention and amicable settlement through mediation. This analysis will include an overview of previous cases, challenges and obstacles the region has faced to date, the international, EU and regional perspectives on dispute prevention and investment mediation, and the enabling frameworks that could propel long-term reforms and benefits of such practices in the future.

[1] Mary and Masons (2022), pp. 27, 33, Kings College London (2009), p. 47, Howard (2021), pp. 11–46.

[2] Morek (2024); ICSID Caseload Statistics (2024), p. 14.

[3] Kher et al. (2022), p. 6.

2 Amicable Settlement Provisions in Investment Treaties: Past, Present and Western Balkans Perspectives

While investment conciliation has been available in investment treaties since the conclusion of the ICSID Convention in 1965, direct references to investment conciliation or mediation as an alternative to arbitration has only been notable since the 2000s.[4] This can be attributed to the impact of the adoption of the ICSID framework into BITs, or the evolving language of international investment treaties over time.

A study of all known investment treaties referencing conciliation and mediation in the dispute resolution clauses found that the number of treaties referencing mediation expressly has been on the rise each year since 2000, but still represents a drop in the sea of the investment treaty universe.[5] At the same time, the annual number of treaties referencing conciliation has decreased since the 1990s.[6]

In the midst of the global efforts to reform investment treaties, the existing treaty network combines old-generation treaties, which largely do not reference mediation expressly, and modernized bilateral investment treaties and free trade agreements, which include such references.[7] A recent ICSID study analyzed and categorized investment treaty cooling-off provisions, highlighting the increasing trend towards more concrete and detailed references to mediation over the past decade.[8] This study identified five categories of such clauses:

1. Clauses defining an amicable settlement period and, potentially, a bare direction to seek "amicable settlement" prior to the institution of arbitration[9];
2. Clauses that expressly permit mediation or other specified amicable dispute resolution mechanisms prior to arbitration[10];

[4] Weeramantry et al. (2023), pp. 205–6.

[5] Ibid.

[6] Ibid., p. 209.

[7] The data was derived from the most recent updates to the UNCTAD database entries. See UNCTAD Investment Policy Hub, https://investmentpolicy.unctad.org/.

[8] ICSID Overview of Investment Treaty Clauses on Mediation (2021c), p. 2. The dataset included 900 dispute resolution provisions, which were narrowed down to 350, which were concluded in different periods and in different geographical areas. Another comprehensive study of dispute resolution clauses identified 11 categories of conciliation clauses, and 7 types of mediation clauses in the existing treaties. See Weeramantry et al. (2023), pp. 209–217.

[9] For example, the Bolivia-US BIT (1998) which provides in Article IX (2) that "a ... party to an investment dispute may submit the dispute for resolution" to binding arbitration, provided "that three months have elapsed from the date on which the dispute arose." Other examples include the Peru-UK BIT (1993) Article 10, the Hungary-UK BIT (1987), Article 8, the Indonesia-Netherlands BIT (1994), Article 9, etc.

[10] The China-New Zealand FTA (2008) references in Chapter 11, Article 152, optional third-party procedures during the six-month cooling-off period, and similar provisions appear in the US Model BIT (2012), Article 23, the Argentina-UAE BIT (2018), Article 20, etc. Treaties expressly referencing mediation include Article 10.15 of the CAFTA-DR (2006), providing that "... the claimant and the respondent should initially seek to resolve the dispute through consultation and negotiation, which may include the use of non-binding, third-party procedures such as conciliation

3. Clauses affirmatively encouraging the use of mediation or other amicable dispute resolution mechanisms in the amicable settlement/"cooling-off" period[11];
4. Clauses mandating mediation or other amicable dispute resolution mechanisms prior to arbitration[12];
5. Clauses permitting mediation at any point in time (i.e., stand-alone mediation).[13]

Although the proposition of mandatory mediation may seem at odds with the core notion of continued consent to such amicable settlement, it may be a good solution for States negotiating investment treaties to leverage investment mediation in their favor.[14] Primarily, this would enable States to control the timing of the mediation and improve its predictability, which is not the case in current disputes when investors have the advantage of preparing for the case before sending the notice of dispute.[15] In such a scenario, the State would be mandating the parties to attempt to reach an amicable settlement with the assistance of an objective third party and not the mandatory resolution of the dispute through mediation.

Most dispute resolution clauses in Western Balkans investment treaties fall into the first category, requiring the parties to attempt to settle any dispute amicably (mostly for 6 months), without any procedural steps, identify applicable default rules or a threshold for the conclusion of the amicable settlement process, other than the

and mediation", Kazakhstan-UAE BIT (2018), Article 10, the CPTPP (2018) Article 9.18, the Australia-Hong-Kong Investment Agreement (2019), Article 23, etc.

[11] For example, Article 31 of the ASEAN Comprehensive Investment Agreement (2009), the Canada-Moldova BIT (2018), CETA (2017), Japan-Morocco BIT (2020), etc.

[12] Mediation is provided as a precondition to arbitration in the EU-Vietnam IPA (2019), Article 3.15, which is identical to the provision in the EU-Singapore IPA (2018). The Australia-Indonesia CEPA (2019), Chapter 14, Article 14.23 provides for mandatory conciliation after the initial direct consultations of the parties is provided in the Australia-Indonesia CEPA (2019), Chapter 14, Article 14.23 for consultations in the initial phase, followed by a mandatory conciliation phase. It stipulates that "[i]f the dispute cannot be resolved within 180 days [of consultations] ... the [Respondent State] may initiate a conciliation process, which shall be mandatory for the disputing investor, with a view towards reaching an amicable settlement"; similar provisions are provided in the Mauritius-UAE BIT (2015), Article 10.3, and the Armenia-UAE BIT (2016).

[13] The EU-Singapore and EU-Viet Nam IPAs are examples of treaties with stand-alone mediation options, providing that "[t]he disputing parties may at any time, including prior to the delivery of a notice of intent, agree to have recourse to mediation". These provisions have not yet entered into force pending their ratification by each EU Member State. Other examples include the Burkina Faso-Canada BIT (2015), which provides "[t]he disputing parties may at any time, be it after notice of intent to submit a claim to arbitration has been given or after a claim has been submitted to arbitration, agree to mediation in Article 23." Similar provisions can be found in CETA (2016), Article 8.20, and the Thailand Model BIT (2012), Article 10.

[14] The Western Balkans Governments also recongnized this potential and supported mandatory ediation in their Joint Submisson to the UNCITRAL WGIII. Western Balkans Joint Submission (2020) p. 2.

[15] Article 14(4) of the Costa Rica-United Arab Emirates BIT (2017) provides for consultations and negotiation, followed by third-party procedure such as conciliation or mediation at a domestic institution of the host State, as mandatory preconditions to investment arbitration.

determined timeframe.[16] Therefore, even if no concrete steps are taken towards an amicable settlement in the cooling-off period, the investor can proceed to initiate arbitration against the host State.

None of the applicable old generation treaties address the early grievance and pre-dispute phases, a focal point to which the investor could turn to communicate their grievances at the earliest stages, or a coordination body that could convene and pursue amicable settlement in a timely manner. Without this guidance and internal coordination between the competent institutions, in practice the cooling-off period is usually wasted, while the notice of dispute circulates through government cabinets. Thus, the competent institutions often learn about the incoming dispute with the arrival of the request for arbitration.

This prevents the governments from using a valuable opportunity to prevent or at least mitigate the dispute and collect the necessary information and documents that will be needed for the settlement or eventual arbitration. A textual analysis of the ISDS clauses in Western Balkans investment treaties indicates that they were not a result of detailed negotiations, but were largely similar in different periods, reflecting the international trends of the time, and the model treaties of their European counterparts.[17] However, in the new era of investment disputes, governments will be best served by calibrating their investment treaty dispute resolution provisions and institutional frameworks for the future.

3 Mapping Out the Investment Disputes Against the Western Balkans Governments and Experiences with Amicable Settlement

According to the available data and the information shared in direct communication with the competent institutions, most investment claims raised against the Western Balkans governments relate to government measures and alleged interference, denial or termination of concessions, licenses or permits, contrary to contractual obligations or direct representations by the government.[18] Unlike claims challenging broader

---

[16] For example, Article 11 of the Montenegro-Spain BIT (2004) provides in the relevant part: "2. If these disputes cannot be settled amicably within six (6) months from the date of the written notification mentioned in paragraph 1, the dispute may be submitted for settlement, at the choice of the investor, to the competent court of the host State, ad hoc UNCITRAL arbitration or ICSID arbitration." Similar provisions can be found in Article 11 of the Serbia-Albania BIT (2014), Article 8 of the Denmark-Bosnia and Herzegovina BIT (2008), etc.

[17] The data was derived and analyzed by the author from the most recent updates to the UNCTAD database entries for Albania, Bosnia and Herzegovina, Kosovo, Montenegro, North Macedonia and Serbia. UNCTAD Investment Policy Hub (2024).

[18] These findings are consistent with ICSID data on global disputes. According to ICSID case statistics, 36% of ICSID cases have been settled to date, mostly those arising out of contracts (46%), 11% of which were concluded with a settlement agreement embodied in a tribunal award. 82% of concluded conciliation proceedings resulted in a commission report. The highest rate of

policy or regulatory measures, such disputes may be more susceptible to prevention or mitigation through direct negotiations and amicable settlement.

The most recent data on the outcomes of investment disputes against the Western Balkans governments show that States prevailed in 41% of the concluded cases (whether on jurisdiction or the merits), 19% were decided in favor of the investor, while 19% of cases were settled and 11% otherwise discontinued.[19] It appears that the Western Balkans governments not only have a good track record in defending investment claims, but also that they have already successfully settled investment claims, although there is little to no information about the governments directly negotiated with the foreign investors, or included neutral third persons to conciliate or mediate the dispute.[20]

Due to the lack of internal capacities and coordination between the competent institutions, there were no streamlined mechanisms for the flow of such information across the institutional framework, and to assess the methods and outcomes of such settlements over time. It also prevented the development of standard procedures for broader application, which would allow the governments to fully harness the potential of the practices which previously resulted in favorable outcomes for the State.

3.1 Common Obstacles for State Engagement in Alternative Dispute Resolution

Despite the well-known benefits of mediation, and its use in both domestic and international commercial disputes, respondent States facing investment claims must consider different factors when deciding whether mediation is the appropriate mechanism for amicable settlement in specific dispute. In addition, there are special challenges and factors that may limit their ability or willingness to mediate with foreign investors.

Some general elements for the assessment of the appropriateness of mediation include the desire of the parties to maintain their relationship, the complexity of the dispute, efficiency, any hostility between the parties, or the desire of the parties to reach a tailored solution in the context of their specific case.[21] All of these considerations do not have to be relevant for each dispute, depending on the specific case,

---

settlement is recorded in the construction sector (52%), followed by oil, gas, mining and finances (44% each), while the lowest rate is in tourism (12%). Geographically, by respondent State, the highest rate of settlement is recorded in the Middle East and the North African region (49%) and the lowest in North America (17%) and Western Europe (19%). ICSID Caseload Statistics (2024), pp. 12–13.

[19] The statistics were provided for an ongoing project and are on file with the author. Some government representatives noted that certain settlements were reached without the inclusion of all the competent institutions for investment policy and dispute resolution.

[20] The number of settlements may be higher since it is possible that some of the discontinued cases were also settled between the parties.

[21] ICSID, Background Paper on Investment Mediation (2021a, b), p. 6.

and the parties may consider different factors, including the stage at which mediation may be appropriate and whether it is suitable for all or some of the issues in dispute.[22]

The assessment of the appropriate mechanisms for the prevention, mitigation or settlement of investment disputes requires the understanding of the full spectrum of the investor-State relationship and the most appropriate methods for each (for example, at the stage when the investor is notifying the institutions about a problem or grievance which can be resolved through direct and technical assistance, or at the point when the investor has notified the State of the intent to initiate an investment claim under a BIT, which opens the cooling-off period. This assessment will allow the competent institutions to make informed decisions and engage in dispute prevention or amicable settlement at the right time.[23]

3.2 Obstacles to the Effective Use of Mediation in Investment Disputes in the Western Balkans

As a general matter, researchers and scholars have noted several recurring issues, which prevent governments from engaging more openly and consistently in amicable settlement with foreign investors, which include political risk, unwillingness to take responsibility for the settlement, fear of political backlash, or the internal organizational structure.[24] These factors combine objective limitations in human and institutional capacity, and the desire of government officials directly involved in the negotiations to protect themselves from liability, political or public exposure or pressure.

The Western Balkans governments are no exception to these challenges, as they often start preparing for the arbitral process without any real engagement at the early stages of the dispute. Only in recent years Western Balkans governments have taken a more comprehensive view of the stages of investor-State relations and the types of mechanisms that could apply for each one. As a result, they have started developing the treaty and institutional frameworks for the prevention, mitigation and resolution of investment disputes, including mediation as an option for the settlement of the dispute any time before, during and even after the conclusion of investment arbitration proceedings.[25]

---

[22] UNCITRAL Guidelines (2023a, b, c), p. 3.

[23] The investor-State dispute chronology provided in the ICSID Background Paper on investment mediation is a good illustration of the stages of an investment life-cycle, the various levels of conflicts that may emerge at different stages, and the adequate dispute prevention, amicable settlement and resolution methods and procedures. ICSID Background Paper on Investment Mediation (2021a, b), p. 4.

[24] Reed et al. (2018), pp. 11–20; Kessedjian et al. (2020); de la Rasilla (2023); Ubilava (2022).

[25] Sulejmanovic (2024), p. 168.

From direct exchange with the competent institutions, and as observed from the publicly available information, Western Balkans governments face a number of obstacles stemming from objective limitations as well as previous negative experiences (whether direct or observed). Several recurring issues which emerged over time include[26]:

(a) Terminological misconceptions as consultation, negotiation, conciliation and mediation are used interchangeably[27];
(b) Uncertainty about the existence of a legal basis for dispute prevention and mediation;
(c) The perception of settlements and compromise with private entities as a sign of weakness[28];
(d) Misconceptions about the nature of mediation in general, as well as its availability, procedure, and the role of the State in mediation;
(e) Undefined authority to negotiate and approve settlement agreements in investment disputes;
(f) Previous negative experiences and fear of public scrutiny, political pressure and personal prosecution and liability for government representatives negotiating or approving settlements with foreign investors;
(g) Lack of communication and coordination within the government in the cooling-off period, and with investors in the pre-dispute phase. The competent institutions are often unaware of investor grievances or notices of intent to arbitrate as the communications are sent to the wrong institutions, or such institutions do not consider themselves competent for such matters. Thus, the early opportunities to prevent the dispute, and the cooling-off period are wasted, while the relevant notices circulate through the government structure;
(h) Lack of human resources, institutional knowledge and capacities to engage in dispute prevention and amicable settlement/mediation procedures;
(i) Early engagement of foreign legal counsel, which prevents the governments from considering and assessing the opportunities for amicable settlement.

---

[26] The summary is based on a regional survey of the competent institutions conducted by the author in the GIZ project, and its findings are not publicly available. The survey results and analysis are on file with the author.

[27] This is consistent with the findings of an empirical study about the use of mediation in cross-border EU commercial disputes. The study reported that most respondent companies preferred to attempt direct negotiations, combined with mediation before moving on to adversarial proceedings. They also treated negotiations as an integral part of mediation, or at least as closely related. See Howard (2021), pp. 118–121. Considering the interchangeable use of the ADR terminology in BITs and government discourse (particularly for negotiation and mediation), it is possible that the instances of mediated settlements are underreported in ISDS as well.

[28] This is particularly relevant in the ICSID context, where conciliation and mediation entail different preliminary conditions, and differ significantly in nature, scope and legal effect. See ICSID Background Paper on Investment Mediation (2021a, b).

The fear of public scrutiny and exposure to domestic investigations and prosecution are often an unspoken, but lingering factor preventing Western Balkans governments from taking more concrete action in the amicable settlement stage of an investment dispute. The confidential nature of amicable settlement procedures, combined with the lack of public understanding of their nature and functions, the authority of persons who lead the negotiations and conclude monetary settlements makes them easy political or media targets.

ČEZ v. Albania,[29] an ad hoc arbitration under the UNCITRAL Arbitration Rules, which resulted in a 100 EUR mediated settlement by the Albanian government, remains a cautionary tale in the region about possible negative consequences of the settlement of investment disputes. Although the government reached a successful settlement, it was followed by a number of investigations and prosecutions of the negotiators and other government officials. The case related to the government's revocation of the investor's concession, and its placement under administration, which led to a 190 million investment claim in 2013 under the Energy Charter Treaty (ECT) and the Czech Republic-Albania BIT.[30] Soon after the UNCITRAL arbitration commenced, the parties agreed to suspend the proceedings to attempt to settle through mediation, facilitated by the then Deputy Secretary General of the Energy Community.

The case ultimately settled without any liability attributed to either party in the dispute,[31] against objections from the opposition party.[32] However, the successful mediation was followed by several investigations against the Minister of Energy and State Attorney who participated in the negotiations with ČEZ for alleged abuses of power, as well as the prosecutor who investigated the relevant officials.[33] In the aftermath of this case, the governments in the region have been particularly careful and reluctant to consider investment mediation as a viable alternative to investment arbitration, preferring to leave the decision-making to the tribunals themselves.[34]

Such challenges are an indicator of a need for broader legal and institutional reform to enable the effective use of dispute prevention and mediation within the investment protection framework, including streamlined communication, a transparent structure and process, developed capacities and coordination.[35]

---

[29] *ČEZ v. The Republic of Albania*, UNCITRAL (2014).

[30] Ibid.; Hovet (2014); Agreement between the Czech Republic and the Republic of Albania for the Promotion and Reciprocal Protection of Investments (1995); Energy Charter Treaty (1998). The relevant investment was a 76% share ČEZ held in the sole electro-distribution company in Albania, ČEZ Shpërndrje. See Ener Data (2014).

[31] Mejdini (2015).

[32] Ibid.

[33] Exit News (2018).

[34] Other governments in the region, in previous workshops and direct exchanges have expressed a general skepticism to amicable settlement in investment disputes, mostly with reference to the profile of investors who had previously raised claims against them, including persons escaping domestic criminal proceedings and dual nationals holding the nationality of the home State.

[35] The discussions and direct feedback about the concerns and obstacles faced by the Western Balkans governments were collected through the author's work on regional technical assistance

4 EU Perspective on Dispute Prevention and Alternative Dispute Resolution: Reform Proposals and Treaty Practice

The EU has consistently expressed support for mediation and other forms of alternative dispute resolution as a viable and preferable alternative to litigation of investment disputes.[36] It is recognized as such in recent EU treaties, and it is already contemplated as a likely feature in the framework of a possible multilateral investment court.[37] Recent EU treaties like the Comprehensive Economic and Trade Agreement (CETA) differentiate between investor problems and disputes, which allows the use of mediation as a dispute prevention tool. The Sustainable Investment Facilitation Agreement between the EU and Angola (SIFA) provides some insights into the possible contours of a future EU model for investment dispute prevention.[38] This includes the designation of lead agencies for investment facilitation and coordination,[39] and the establishment of problem-solving mechanisms for existing and potential investors, who may need assistance related to the application of the relevant domestic regulation.[40] The provision explicitly notes the importance of making such mechanisms available and accessible to small and medium-sized enterprises, in line with the broader objectives of the treaty.[41]

At UNCITRAL Working Group III, the EU and its Member States have supported the inclusion of express mediation clauses in investment treaties,[42] as well as the mandatory commencement of mediation as a preliminary step in the dispute resolution process.[43] However, recent EU investment treaties do not provide advance consent to mediation, and only require the requested party to "give sympathetic

---

and capacity development, through a regional GIZ project dedicated to ISDS reform. The relevant reports, minutes and proposals are on file with the author. Information about the objectives of the Legal Reform for Economic Development in the Western Balkans project is available on the GIZ website.

36 Comments of the EU and its Member States to the UNCITRAL Draft Provisions on Mediation (2021a, b), p. 4.

37 Ibid., p. 9.

38 The text of the EU-Angola Sustainable Investment Facilitation Agreement (SIFA) is publicly available, but it is yet to be approved for signature by the EU Council, following which it will require the consent of the EU Parliament to enter into force. European Commission (2013).

39 SIFA text, Article 22.

40 Ibid., Article 23. The provisions on dispute resolution between the treaty parties also refer to the avoidance of disputes, through consultations, mediation and arbitration. The dispute resolution mechanisms do not provide for detailed rules, leaving them to be agreed between the parties, or the arbitrators in case the parties opt to resolve their dispute through arbitration. SIFA text, Chapter VI Dispute Avoidance and Settlement.

41 SIFA text, Article 23.2.

42 EU Submission to the UNCITRAL WGIII (2021), pp. 11–12.

43 Ibid. EU Submission (2021), p. 13.

consideration to the request".[44] It remains to be seen if the EU will turn to mandatory mediation in future treaties. In the broader context of ISDS reform, the EU and its Member States have not proposed any dispute prevention mechanisms in the narrow sense, but they have commented on the Draft Guidelines for the Prevention and Mitigation of Investor-State Disputes, providing constructive feedback, and endorsing such measures as a valuable component of ISDS reform.[45]

Despite the uneven and multi-track ISDS reform efforts unfolding at the international, regional and national levels, it appears that investment mediation is a stabilizing factor, which will be a viable reform option in any context, including the EU.[46] Although there is still room for more clarity on the rules and dynamics for investment mediation within the EU framework, it will likely find its place as a tool for dispute prevention and amicable settlement in the future. This means that the Western Balkans States aspiring to EU membership can continue to pursue their reform efforts in this area, while remaining compliant to EU policies.

5 Enabling Frameworks: Case Study of Bosnia and Herzegovina (BiH)

5.1 New Framework for Treaty-Based and Institutional Dispute Prevention, Mitigation and Resolution for BiH

Bosnia and Herzegovina is currently undertaking a series of comprehensive and cohesive reform measures to create a framework for dispute prevention, management and resolution spanning through the entire investment conflict continuum.[47] This framework includes a robust institutional coordination mechanism, connecting the network of investment protection agencies and a government coordination body. The measures are aligned with international best practices,[48] but tailored to the BiH experiences and interests, and include transition provisions to the EU regime upon its accession to the EU. The Council of Ministers of BiH is deliberating a proposal for the establishment of an early grievance mechanism, which will include an online form through which foreign investors can report their grievances and problems, which

[44] CETA Mediation Rules, Article 3(3).

[45] UNCITRAL Guidelines on Dispute Prevention and Mitigation, EU Comments (2023), p. 11.

[46] EU Commission, Access to Markets Portal, available at: Welcome to Access2Markets to Market Access Database users|Access2Markets (europa.eu).

[47] Ministry of Foreign Trade and Economic Relations BiH, Public Consultations (2024).

[48] Agenda of the 47th Session of the UNCITRAL WG III, available at: https://undocs.org/en/A/CN.9/WG.III/WP.234; UNCITRAL Draft Guidelines for the Prevention and Mitigation of International Investment Disputes (2023); UNCITRAL Compilation (2023); UNCITRAL Forum on dispute prevention (2023), BiH best practice.

should enable an early intervention by the competent institutions, before any further escalation of the issues.[49]

Such a comprehensive framework will not only facilitate the desired dispute prevention process, but also help to streamline the timely flow of information through the government, which may be necessary at the amicable settlement and dispute resolution phases.[50] Importantly, the new BiH Model BIT (discussed below) outlines the available mechanisms in its dispute resolution clause, which will not only improve transparency and give foreign investors a roadmap through the domestic pre-dispute mechanisms, but also promote the predictable and streamlined investment protection framework in the country.[51]

5.2 Enabling Treaty Framework: New BiH Model BIT

The Model BIT for Bosnia and Herzegovina, adopted in August 2023, provides a unique and detailed ISDS clause which expands across the dispute resolution spectrum ranging from dispute prevention, amicable settlement and investment arbitration. Each stage is defined in detail and represents a precondition or trigger for the next stage in the process. Importantly, the BiH Model BIT refers the investors to the competent authorities, which should intervene in the early stages of a dispute,[52] thus putting into motion the available institutional mechanisms in BiH (and potentially the other treaty party) established to possibly prevent the escalation of disputes to international arbitration.

These provisions are a direct response to the recognized challenges and obstacles, which prevent the effective use of dispute prevention mechanisms and cooling-off periods. They also tie into the existing and developing institutional framework in Bosnia and Herzegovina, which aims to facilitate and harmonize the operation of the investment protection framework in the country (as analyzed further in the sections below).

The parties are encouraged to seek to resolve any dispute through amicable settlement (negotiations, conciliation or mediation) without prejudice to any other rights under the treaty.[53] Amicable settlement is available at any time before or after the initiation of arbitration, and the receiving party should give favorable consideration of the request to mediate.[54] Unlike the CETA model,[55] the BiH Model BIT does not

[49] Proposed by the Ministry of Foreign Trade and Economic Relations of BiH. See Tavilovic (2024).

[50] Sulejmanovic (2024), pp. 176–183.

[51] Montenegro and North Macedonia are currently working on similar mechanisms, tailored to their government structures, economic and investment priorities and experiences with investment disputes.

[52] BiH Model BIT (2023), Article 20(2).

[53] BiH Model BIT (2023), Article 19.

[54] Ibid.

[55] CETA (2016), Annex 29-C.

provide detailed procedural rules for mediation, but it allows the parties to select the applicable rules at their discretion.[56] In phase I, the network of foreign investment protection agencies (FIPAs) would act as an early grievance mechanism, transmitting the relevant information about potential disputes to the competent institutions from the earliest stage, seeking a rapid resolution of the issues.

The foreign investor must submit a detailed request for consultations, including information about their identity, status as a foreign investor, a detailed summary of their complaint (factual basis), the measure which allegedly triggered the complaints, the legal basis of the potential claim (provisions of the applicable treaty, investment contract or domestic law), and administrative, judicial or other proceedings which may have been initiated in relation to the relevant claim.[57] If the phase I measures do not resolve the relevant issues, and the investor submits a notice of dispute, the intra-governmental coordination body for the amicable settlement of investment disputes[58] would take over in the phase II mechanism.[59]

The body is composed of representatives of the key competent ministries and agencies, but can also include ad hoc members relevant for a particular case.[60] The body convenes upon notice of a potential dispute to coordinate the strategy and measures in the cooling-off period and to prepare for a potential investment arbitration.[61] The Ministry of Foreign Trade and Economic Relations (MoFTER) of BIH would be a bridge between the two phases and provide the relevant information and guidance on the applicable treaty, and its interpretation.[62]

Finally, if an amicable solution could not be reached in the first two phases, the investor can proceed to arbitration under the ICSID Convention, the UNCITRAL Rules, or other rules selected by the parties. The claims can only relate to issues notified in the request for consultations.[63] This well-rounded mechanism demonstrates the thoughtful design by the competent institutions to enable BiH to take full advantage of the pre-dispute and cooling-off periods to prevent or mitigate the dispute, with mediation as an important tool that can be activated at any time.

---

[56] BiH Model BIT (2023), Article 29; CETA, Article 8.20.

[57] BiH Model BIT (2023), Article 20.

[58] Decision of the Council of Ministers of BiH on the Establishment of the Negotiating Body for the Amicable Settlement of International Investment Disputes (Official Gazette of BiH, no 17/18) (2017); Decision of the Council of Ministers of BIH on the Appointment of the Members of the Permanent Negotiating Team for the Amicable Settlement of International Investment Disputes (Official Gazette BIH, no 58/18) (2017).

[59] Decision of the Council of Ministers of BiH on the Establishment of the Negotiating Body (2017), Article 5.

[60] The permanent members of the Negotiating Body are the Ministry of Justice, Ministry of Foreign Affairs, Ministry of Foreign Trade and Economic Relations, Ministry of Finances, and the State Attorney's Office of BiH. Ad hoc members are determined for each particular case and may include the legal entity, whose actions allegedly caused the dispute, the competent ministry in charge of the relevant sector, as well as the attorney general in the relevant entity, canton or in the District of Brčko in BiH. Council of Ministers of BiH Decision (2017), Article 2.

[61] Council of Ministers of BiH Decision (2017), Article 5.

[62] Information of the Ministry of Foreign Trade and Economic Relations of BiH (2023).

[63] BiH Model BIT (2023), Article 29.

5.3 *Enabling an Institutional Framework: Available Institutional Mediation Rules for Investment Disputes*

States that do not wish to provide detailed procedural rules for investment mediation in their investment treaties can find relief by referencing institutional mediation rules to create the default framework for the process. The mediating parties are free to derogate from such rules or adapt them to each specific case,[64] while starting from a common set of expectations. With the growing interest in investment mediation and the recognition of its potential for States, several institutions have adopted standalone investment mediation rules, complementing their rules for investment arbitration.[65] Most notably, the ICSID adopted standalone mediation rules in 2022, while the VIAC and the SCC did the same in 2021.[66] The UNCITRAL Mediation Rules were revised in 2022 and can be applied in both commercial and investment disputes. Since most investment treaties provide the ICSID or UNCITRAL Rules as options in their dispute resolution clauses, they are particularly relevant for the choice of compatible mediation rules under such treaties.

The ICSID Mediation Rules (ICSID MR) complement the existing dispute resolution framework under the ICSID Convention, which already refers to conciliation and arbitration.[67] The expansion of amicable settlement tools is in line with the objectives of the ICSID Convention, and the historical records of the preliminary discussions and drafting history of the Convention.[68] Aron Broches, the creator of the ICSID Convention, was reportedly motivated to include conciliation provisions in the Convention itself, drawing from direct positive experiences in settling disputes involving sovereign States.[69]

The new ICSID MRs allow a clear distinction between mediation and conciliation, both in terminology, scope and procedure. While conciliation allows for preliminary jurisdictional objections, mediation under the ICSID MRs applies without any nationality requirements, including non-ICSID States and investors, who are nationals of

[64] Provisions on adapting institutional mediation rules, party autonomy, unless the parties otherwise agree (…).

[65] The recent investment mediation rules are contributing to the international reform movements, which emphasize the difference between mediation and other amicable settlement methods, and to promote it as a standalone option in ISDS. For example, UNCITRAL adopted a package of texts dedicated to conciliation, the UNCITRAL Model Law and Rules on Conciliation in 1980 (the Rules were amened in 2002), but has since shifted to mediation with the adoption of the UNCITRAL Model Law on International Commercial Mediation and International Settlement Agreements Resulting from Mediation (2018), The United Nations Convention International Settlement Agreements Resulting from Mediation (2018), and the UNCITRAL Mediation Rules (2021).

[66] There is also a number of soft law instruments and rules that the mediating parties can consider or agree to apply to specific proceedings. Otherwise, they can provide useful guidance, even outside the context of a specific dispute, for example, the Energy Charter Secretariat's Guide on Investment Mediation (2016) and the IBA Rules.

[67] On the ICSID Mediation Rules, see Titi (2024), pp. # et seqq.

[68] Broches (1978), p. 338.

[69] ICSID (1968), para. 5.

the host State. Since mediation requires continued consent by both parties involved, States cannot be forced into mediation without their consent.[70]

The ICSID MRs provide a set of clearly defined procedural steps, from initiation, registration and the appointment of mediator(s), to the separate and joint sessions with the mediators, settlements negotiations, and the conclusion of the mediation either through a successful settlement agreement or its termination.[71] Unlike conciliation, mediation offers more procedural flexibility and the mediator(s) do not issue any decisions or orders,[72] request documents or evidence,[73] nor can they clarify the issues[74] or make recommendations at their initiative (absent a request of the parties).[75] The UNCITRAL Mediation Rules (UNCITRAL MRs), adopted in 2021, provide the procedural structure for mediation in ad hoc disputes under investment treaties, or otherwise before any formal legal claim is raised by the foreign investor. The UNCITRAL MRs are not specifically tailored to investment disputes and are meant to apply regardless of whether the dispute is based on a contract or otherwise (similar to the other UNCITRAL rules and instruments).[76]

The UNCITRAL MRs define mediation as "(...) a process, whether referred to by the term mediation, conciliation or an expression of similar import",[77] which may perpetuate the abovementioned terminological uncertainty, especially for States also looking into the new ICSID MRs. On the other hand, the broad scope of the definition can serve as a catch-all provision enabling the application of the UNCITRAL MRs to the broad ISDS clauses in old generation treaties. However, since the mediating parties can agree to vary or derogate from the UNCITRAL MRs,[78] States can make the necessary adjustments in their BITs to overcome any terminological uncertainty. Therefore, when referring to the UNCITRAL MRs in the dispute resolution clauses of their investment treaties, States can also define the nature and scope of mediation as it should apply in possible disputes with foreign investors applies to disputes arising under the relevant treaty.

Nevertheless, to avoid fragmentation, each State should select and apply the most appropriate investment mediation rules throughout all instruments of consent for investment disputes consistently, i.e. in their investment treaties, legislation and investment contracts.[79]

---

[70] Arbitration and conciliation are dispute resolution mechanisms built into the ICSID Convention and ICSID framework since its inception.

[71] The specific procedural matters covered by the ICSID MRs are outlined further in this section in Table 1, which compares the features of the available mediation rules developed in the context of investor-State disputes.

[72] ICSID Conciliation Rules, Rule 26.

[73] ICSID Conciliation Rules, Rule 24(4).

[74] ICSID Conciliation Rules, Rule 24(1).

[75] Ibid., Rule 24(2).

[76] UNCITRAL MRs (2022), Article 2.

[77] Ibid.

[78] UNCITRAL MRs (2021), Article 1(3).

[79] For example, ECT model instrument (2018), Article 3; UNCITRAL Draft legislative guide (2023).

5.4 *Enabling Reform Instruments: UNCITRAL Working Group III Reform Instruments on Mediation*

In July 2022, the UNCITRAL Commission adopted two instruments developed by the WG III directly addressing mediation on the investor-State context, i.e. the UNCITRAL notes on mediation and UNCITRAL guidelines for mediation in investor-State dispute settlement.[80]

The WG III deliberations on investor-State mediation reflected a generally favorable attitude from all the stakeholders involved, and there was much less friction or resistance to these proposed reform options. In fact, some states proposed the introduction of mandatory mediation during the cooling-off period, as a prerequisite for arbitration[81] While this position did not ultimately prevail, it indicated the desire of some WG III delegations to make mediation a standard feature of investment dispute resolution.

The UNCITRAL Model Provisions on Mediation provide model clauses that States can include in future investment treaties, but which may also be featured in the multilateral instrument for ISDS reform, contemplated by WG III.[82] Mediation is defined broadly, and available at any time before, during or after a dispute.[83] The Model Provisions define the process for the initiation of mediation, the appointment and mandate of mediators and the relationship between mediation and other proceedings.[84] Importantly, there are also provisions on the form and effect of the settlement agreement, to ensure its enforceability.[85] The Model Provisions do not cover all procedural aspects of mediation and refer to existing mediation rules, which States can reference in their treaties.[86]

The UNCITRAL Guidelines on Mediation for International Investment Disputes (Mediation Guidelines) provide a more practical perspective to facilitate the use of mediation in ISDS. As such, they are available for the parties and mediators

[80] The Commission expressly supported and commended the work in this area, thereby acknowledging that alternative dispute resolution methods can be useful and complementary to the broader ISDS reform process. Official Records of the General Assembly No. 17 (A/72/17) (2023), para. 264; the Draft Guidelines on investor-State mediation were also discussed at the 56th session, where the delegations suggested that mediation could be used as a component of the State strategy to prevent and mitigate investment disputes. Dispute prevention was also noted as a key element of ISDS reform. UNCITRAL Secretariat (2023a, b, c, d), pp. 14–15; Comments of the EU and its Member States on the UNCITRAL Secretariat Note (2021).

[81] UNCITRAL, Possible reform of investor-State dispute settlement (ISDS) Dispute prevention and mitigation—Means of alternative dispute resolution (2020a, b); Submission from the Government of Indonesia (2018), p. 4.

[82] UNCITRAL Secretariat, UNCITRAL Model Provisions on Mediation (2023a, b, c, d).

[83] Ibid.

[84] Ibid., Model Provisions 1–4.

[85] Ibid., Draft Provision 5.

[86] Specifically, the Model Provisions on Mediation refer to the UNCITRAL Mediation Rules (2021), the ICSID Mediation Rules (2022), and the IBA Rules for Investor-State Mediation (2012). Ibid., Model Provision 1.

alike, but are not intended to have any binding effect. In substance, the Mediation Guidelines explain the nature and purpose of mediation, its timing and availability, the qualifications and appointment of mediators, and the key stages of the mediation process, including the possibility of online sessions. There is also a list of factors that States can consider as a preliminary matter, when deciding on the suitability of mediation for a particular dispute.[87]

In addition to the UNCITRAL Mediation Rules and UNCITRAL Guidelines on Mediation in Investor-State Dispute Resolution (adopted by the Commission in July 2023), WG III is also working on Draft Guidelines for the Prevention and Mitigation of Investment Disputes, which is likely to be brought to a vote at the Commission's 57th session.[88] At a more structural level, the Advisory Centre for International Investment Law and Dispute Resolution, currently contemplated by WG III, will also likely offer dispute prevention and mediation to its Member States, through its technical and legal assistance services.[89]

6 Outlooks Instead of a Conclusion

After decades of dormancy, dispute prevention and amicable settlement (through conciliation and mediation) are becoming more interesting and viable for States reforming their investor-state dispute settlement frameworks, as they are expanding their toolbox for dispute resolution, and building the relevant capacities. These developments are also boosted by the parallel strengthening and promotion of the normative and institutional frameworks for investment mediation, including the adoption of standalone investment mediation rules and guidelines, the reform instruments adopted in UNCITRAL WG III and the growing number of investment treaties providing for express mediation clauses, some including detailed provisions on the pre-dispute and amicable settlement phase.

Western Balkans governments are fully engaged in these reform efforts, seeking to overcome past challenges with investment disputes, including obstacles to the effective prevention and settlement of investment disputes. Caught at the intersection of the imminent need for foreign investment necessary for their economic development, and pursuing EU membership in the near future, the governments in the region have already managed to develop tailored institutional frameworks to facilitate dispute prevention and amicable settlement procedures, inspired by useful elements of international best practices. This is increasingly reflected in the more recent Model BITs in the region, which capture and give international effects to such frameworks. In light

[87] UNCITRAL (2023a, b, c). Draft Mediation Guidelines, p. 3.

[88] UNCITRAL Report from the 47th Session (2024), p. 20.

[89] Expected to be adopted by the Commission in 2024. The Centre is envisioned as an institution dedicated to providing technical and legal assistance, primarily to developing States, to enable their effective participation in investor-State disputes. Draft Statute of the Advisory Centre (2024), Articles 6 and 7.

of the recent policy direction of the EU and its endorsement of dispute prevention and mediation internally and in UNCITRAL WG III, the Western Balkans governments pursuing this approach can also take advantage of these mechanisms as EU Member States.

In order for these positive movements to come to life, the final piece of the puzzle lies "at home" with the political will to fully endorse and implement a more non-adversarial approach to investment disputes, and a change in the public understanding and attitude towards settlements with foreign investors. Such changes are nothing short of a complete paradigm shift in the Western Balkans, but it appears that the current momentum is an exceptional opportunity to break away from past defaults to suitable solutions for the future.

References

Broches A (1978) The convention on the settlement of investment disputes between states and nationals of other states. In: Recueil des cours: Collected Courses of The Hague Academy of International Law, vol 136

de la Rasilla I (2023) The greatest victory? Challenges and opportunities for mediation in investor-state dispute settlement. ICSID Rev Foreign Invest Law J 38(1):169–200

Ener Data (2014) CEZ settles dispute with Albania over power distribution company. Ener Data Portal. https://www.enerdata.net/publications/daily-energy-news/cez-settles-dispute-albania-over-power-distribution-company.html

Energy Charter Secretariat (2016) Best practices in investment conflict prevention and management. https://www.energycharter.org/what-we-do/publications/best-practices-in-investment-conflict-prevention-and-management/

Energy Charter Secretariat (2018) Energy charter treaty: model instrument on management of investment disputes. https://www.energychartertreaty.org/model-instrument/

EU and its Member States (2021a) Comments on the UNCITRAL secretariat note: possible reform of investor-state dispute settlement (ISDS) – Mediation and other forms of alternative dispute resolution (ADR). https://uncitral.un.org/sites/uncitral.un.org/files/media-documents/uncitral/en/21.12.17_draft_clauses_on_mediation_eu_and_ms_comments.pdf

EU and its Member States (2021b) Comments to the UNCITRAL working group III draft provisions on mediation. https://uncitral.un.org/sites/uncitral.un.org/files/media-documents/uncitral/en/21.12.17_draft_clauses_on_mediation_eu_and_ms_comments.pdf

European Commission (2023) EU-Angola sustainable investment facilitation agreement moves towards approval. https://policy.trade.ec.europa.eu/news/eu-angola-sustainable-investment-facilitation-agreement-moves-towards-approval-2023-06-16_en

Exit News (2018) Public commissioner demands dismissal of prosecutor who closed investigation into minister Gjiknuri. https://exit.al/en/public-commissioner-demands-dismissal-of-prosecutor-who-closed-investigation-into-minister-gjiknuri/.

GIZ (2022) Legal reform for economic development in the Western Balkans. https://www.giz.de/en/downloads/giz2022-en-legal-reform-for-economic-development.pdf

Government of Indonesia (2018) Submission to UNCITRAL working group III (ISDS reform). https://documents.un.org/doc/undoc/ltd/v18/075/93/pdf/v1807593.pdf?token=ZrQIl1G1tqbr18ekAc&fe=true

Howard A (2021) The EU's efforts to promote cross-border mediation. In: Howard A (ed) EU cross-border commercial mediation: listening to disputants – changing the frame, framing the

changes: global trends in dispute resolution. Kluwer Law International, Alphen aan den Rijn, pp 1 –46
ICSID (1968) History of the ICSID convention: documents concerning the origin and the formulation of the convention on the settlement of international disputes between states and nationals of other states, vol 2
ICSID (2021a) Background paper on investment mediation. https://icsid.worldbank.org/resources/publications/background-paper-investment-mediation
ICSID (2021b) Background paper on investment mediation. https://icsid.worldbank.org/sites/default/files/publications/Background_Paper_on_Investment_Mediation_Oct.2021.pdf
ICSID (2021c) Overview of investment treaty clauses on mediation. https://icsid.worldbank.org/sites/default/files/publications/Overview_Mediation_in_Treaties.pdf
ICSID (2024) ICSID caseload statistics (2024-1). https://icsid.worldbank.org/sites/default/files/publications/ENG_The_ICSID_Caseload_Statistics_Issue%202024.pdf
Kessedjian C et al (2020) Mediation in future investor-state dispute settlement. In: Academic Forum (ed) ISDS concept paper 2020/16
Kher, P, Obadia, E, Chun, D (2022) Managing Investor Issues Through Retention Mechanisms. Available at: https://documents1.worldbank.org/curated/en/978811614610086665/pdf/Managing-Investor-Grievances-Through-Retention-Mechanisms.pdf.
Kings College London (2009) Research report, mediating construction disputes. https://www.fenwickelliott.com/sites/default/files/KCL_Mediating_Construction_Part_IV.pdf
Mejdini F (2015) Albanian officials sued for loss-making energy deal. Balkan insight. https://balkaninsight.com/2015/10/15/albania-officials-sued-over-harmful-electricity-agreement-10-15-2015/
Ministry of Foreign Trade and Economic Relations (2022) Information about the status of implementation of bilateral investment treaties and proposals for future measures
Morek R (2024) Investor-state disputes: how arbitration and mediation can intertwine to provide more resonant solutions. Kluwer Arbitration Blog. https://mediationblog.kluwerarbitration.com/2024/02/19/investor-state-disputes-how-arbitration-and-mediation-can-intertwine-to-provide-more-resonant-solutions/
Mary Q, Masons P (2022) Future of international energy arbitration survey report. https://arbitration.qmul.ac.uk/media/arbitration/docs/Future-of-International-Energy-Arbitration-Survey-Report.pdf
Reed L et al (2018) Report: survey on obstacles to settlement of investor-state disputes. National University of Singapore Centre for International Law. Working paper 18/01. https://cil.nus.edu.sg/publication/survey-on-obstacles-to-settlement-of-investor-state-disputes/
Sulejmanovic S (2024) Investor-state dispute prevention and resolution mechanism in Bosnia and Herzegovina. In: Beaumont B, Brodlija F et al (eds) The future of investor-state dispute settlement: reforming law, practice and perspectives for a fast-changing world. Kluwer Law International, Alphen aan den Rijn
Tavilovic D (2024) BiH pokušava odgovoriti investitore od arbitraže. Capital.ba portal. https://www.capital.ba/bih-pokusava-odgovoriti-investitore-od-arbitraze/
Titi C (2024) Mediation of investment disputes under the ICSID mediation rules: an overview. In: Bungenberg M et al (2024) Alternative dispute resolution in the western balkans: trends and challenges. Springer, Cham
Ubilava A (2022) Underutilization of ADR in ISDS: resolving treaty interpretation issues. UCLA J Int Law Foreign Affairs
UNCITRAL (2023a) UNCITRAL guidelines for mediation in investor-state disputes. https://documents.un.org/doc/undoc/gen/v23/027/58/pdf/v2302758.pdf?token=fmVLD3Pm8rG3e1Inx0&fe=true
UNCITRAL (2023b) Forum on dispute prevention. https://uncitral.un.org/sites/uncitral.un.org/files/media-documents/uncitral/en/sulejmanovic_-_ucitral_side_event_-_prevention_of_isds_7-jul-2023.pdf

UNCITRAL (2023c) Model provisions on mediation. https://documents-dds-ny.un.org/doc/UNDOC/GEN/V23/027/46/PDF/V2302746.pdf?OpenElement

UNCITRAL Secretariat (2020a) Dispute prevention and alternative dispute settlement: submission of the Western Balkans. https://uncitral.un.org/sites/uncitral.un.org/files/media-documents/uncitral/uncitral_wg_iii_submission_western_balkans_-_mediation.pdf

UNCITRAL Secretariat (2020b) Possible reform of investor-state dispute settlement (ISDS) Dispute prevention and mitigation – means of alternative dispute resolution. https://documents.un.org/doc/undoc/ltd/v20/002/56/pdf/v2000256.pdf?token=K2sHxiAsmJSGxvYfsv&fe=true

UNCITRAL Secretariat (2023a) Comments on the draft guidelines on prevention and mitigation of international investment disputes. https://uncitral.un.org/sites/uncitral.un.org/files/media-documents/EN/24.02.22_wp235_dpm_eums_comments.pdf

UNCITRAL Secretariat (2023b) Compilation of best practices on investment dispute prevention and mitigation. https://uncitral.un.org/sites/uncitral.un.org/files/media-documents/uncitral/wg_iii_compilation_on_dispute_prevention_and_summary.pdf

UNCITRAL Secretariat (2023c) Draft Legislative Guide on Dispute Prevention Mechanisms in Investor-State Dispute Resolution. Available at: https://documents-dds-ny.un.org/doc/UNDOC/GEN/V23/024/83/PDF/V2302483.pdf?OpenElement.

UNCITRAL Secretariat (2023d) Draft guidelines for the prevention and mitigation of international investment disputes. https://uncitral.un.org/sites/uncitral.un.org/files/media-documents/uncitral/en/2322784e_-_advance_copy_0.pdf

UNCITRAL Secretariat (2024a) Report of working group III (investor-state dispute settlement reform) on the work of its forty-seventh session, Vienna, 22–26 January 2024. https://documents.un.org/doc/undoc/gen/v24/008/72/pdf/v2400872.pdf?token=gGblzxGTAXHApQ0jOB&fe=true

UNCITRAL Secretariat (2024b) Draft statute of the UNCITRAL advisory centre for international investment law and dispute resolution

United Nations (2023) UN Commission on International Trade Law finalizes four legal texts during the first week of its 56th Session in Vienna. https://unis.unvienna.org/unis/en/pressrels/2023/unisl344.html

Weeramantry R et al (2023) Conciliation and mediation in investor-state dispute settlement provisions: a quantitative and qualitative analysis. ICSID Rev – Foreign Invest Law J (Kinnear M, McLachlan C (eds)) 38(1):201–237

Mandatory Initial Mediation Session: Evaluating the Effects of Compulsion in Dispute Resolution—The Case of North Macedonia

Tatjana Zoroska Kamilovska and Milka Rakočević

Abstract Since the adoption of the first Law on Mediation in 2006 until today, various regulatory measures have been undertaken for the promotion and stimulation of mediation in North Macedonia. The mediation model has undergone multiple changes given that the practical experience has consistently indicated that the results of its application are minor. Amendments to the Civil Procedure Act from 2015 introduced a mandatory initial mediation session in commercial disputes up to a certain value as a promising solution in the context of its further promotion. The reasons for this legislative solution were quite poorly explained. The absence of specific indicators for the need of a mandatory initial mediation session in commercial disputes mobilized resistance among many business entities but also among the members of the legal profession. A small number of comparative experiences from EU countries, as well as the initial organizational problems with its implementation in our country, have raised doubts about the perspective of this solution. It seems that several years after the introduction of a certain extent of compulsion in the system of dispute resolution regarding particular commercial disputes is quite a solid time to assess the success of this solution so far, but also to estimate whether such a solution has a long-term potential of reviving mediation in our country and creating a culture of using mediation on a purely voluntary basis.

1 Introduction

For some time now, the promotion of alternative dispute resolution (ADR) has been a political priority of the European Union. ADR has emerged as an essential tool for dispute resolution in Europe gaining significant traction as a mechanism to resolve

T. Z. Kamilovska (✉) · M. Rakočević
Department of Civil Procedural Law, Faculty of Law "Iustinianus Primus", Ss. Cyril and Methodius University, Skopje, North Macedonia
e-mail: t.zoroskakamilovska@pf.ukim.edu.mk

M. Rakočević
e-mail: m.rakocevic@pf.ukim.edu.mk

M. Bungenberg et al. (eds.), *Alternative Dispute Resolution in the Western Balkans*, European Union and its Neighbours in a Globalized World 20,
https://doi.org/10.1007/978-3-031-76345-8_12

disputes outside traditional court proceedings offering parties a more flexible, cost-effective, and often faster route to dispute settlement. Although the extent of its implementation varies from country to country, its integration into national legal systems continues to deepen, indisputably positioning ADR as an integral part of the European legal landscape. Among the variety of different alternative dispute resolution techniques, bearing in mind the achieved results and perspectives, mediation stands out as a synonym for the era of ADR.

Mediation is usually defined as a process of facilitated negotiation, in which a neutral third party, a mediator, helps the parties to the dispute understand the concerns and needs of their opponent and reach a mutual solution, i.e. reach an agreement that resolves their dispute in a manner acceptable to both parties.[1] One of the key features of mediation is that the parties have full control over the process and no one can make a decision on their behalf regarding the manner in which they will resolve their dispute, and if they manage to agree, they conclude a settlement in their mutual interest.

While court proceedings are considered to be authoritative, formalized and oriented to the demands of the parties, mediation offers a flexible and voluntary approach where all aspects of the dispute are considered regardless of their legal significance. Mediation is treated as an informal, cost-effective and fast procedure which makes it preferable to the judicial mechanism of dispute resolution. Mediation is cost-effective both for the participants in the process and for the state. The goals that the state aims to achieve by institutionalizing mediation are unburdening the courts from a considerable number of cases and a significant reduction of the costs of maintaining the court infrastructure through the privatization of dispute resolution methods.[2] In that regard, the considerably high workload of the courts and the need to make serious reforms regarding the costs of civil procedure further strengthened the role of ADR in the civil justice system.[3] Taking into account the unenviable state of civil justice systems globally, in recent years, the promotion of mediation has been intensified through numerous stimulating measures.

At the EU level, efforts are continuously being made to stimulate mediation and ADR techniques in general. Until now, several legal instruments have been adopted regarding the application of ADR techniques.[4] The most relevant among them is the Mediation Directive, given the fact that, unlike other instruments, it provides

---

[1] Assistance of a third neutral (independent) party in the process of identifying the disputed issues, better understanding the disputed situation, and creating mutually acceptable proposals for resolving the dispute between two or more interested parties are the key elements on which the definitions of mediation are built. In that regard, see the definitions in Spencer and Brogan (2006), p. 3, Alfini et al. (2006); Alexander (2006), p. 2.

[2] See Stefflek (2012), pp. 1–2.

[3] Masood (2012), p. 151.

[4] Commission Recommendation 98/257/EC of 30 March 1998 on the principles applicable to the bodies responsible for out-of-court settlement of consumer disputes; Directive 98/10/EC of the European Parliament and of the Council of 26 February 1998 on the application of open network provision (ONP) to voice telephony and on universal service for telecommunications in a competitive environment; Directive 2002/21/EC of the European Parliament and of the Council of 7 March 2002 on a common regulatory framework for electronic communications networks and services

general regulation of mediation at the EU level. This Directive refers to mediation in cross-border disputes but does not prevent Member States from applying it within the domestic legal system. Considering this, the Mediation Directive not only defines the necessary conditions for the use of mediation in cross-border disputes, but also encourages the wider use of mediation within the Member States, as a large part of them transposed the Directive measures to domestic cases.[5]

Regarding North Macedonia, the promotion of mediation is going slowly and with modest results. Since the adoption of the first Mediation Act in 2006[6] until today, various regulatory measures have been undertaken for its stimulation. The latest MA enacted in 2021 is the third novel law concerning this ADR method.[7] The mediation model has undergone multiple changes given that the practical experience has consistently indicated that the results of its application are minor. One of the measures that stands out in that regard is the introduction of mandatory mediation attempt in certain types of disputes prior to initiating a lawsuit before a competent court.

(Framework Directive); Green Paper on Alternative Dispute Resolution in Civil and Commercial Law, Commission of the European Communities, Brussels, 19.4.2002, COM(2002) 196 final); Directive 2008/52/EC of the European Parliament and of the Council of 21 May 2008 on certain aspects of mediation in civil and commercial matters (Mediation Directive); Directive 2013/11/EU of the European Parliament and of the Council of 21 May 2013 on alternative dispute resolution for consumer disputes and amending Regulation (EC) No 2006/2004 and Directive 2009/22/EC (Directive on consumer ADR); Regulation (EU) No 524/2013 of the European Parliament and of the Council of 21 May 2013 on online dispute resolution for consumer disputes and amending Regulation (EC) No 2006/2004 and Directive 2009/22/EC (Regulation on consumer ODR). As for international legal instruments that are valid outside the EU, several recommendations of the Council of Europe are worth mentioning: Recommendation No. R (98) 1 on family mediation (Adopted by the Committee of Ministers on 21 January 1998); Recommendation No. R (99) 19 concerning mediation in penal matters (Adopted by the Committee of Ministers on 15 September 1999); Recommendation Rec (2001) 9 on alternatives to litigation between administrative authorities and private parties (Adopted by the Committee of Ministers on 5 September 2001) и Recommendation Rec (2002)10 on mediation in civil matters (Adopted by the Committee of Ministers on 18 September 2002).

[5] The objective of the Mediation Directive is to facilitate access to alternative dispute resolution and to promote the amicable settlement of disputes by encouraging the use of mediation and by ensuring a balanced relationship between mediation and judicial proceedings. See Art. 1(1) of the Mediation Directive.

[6] Mediation Act 2006, Official Gazette of the Republic of Macedonia, No. 60/2006, 22/2007 and 114/09. The law was drafted in accordance with Strategy for reform of the justice sector for the period 2004–2007.

[7] In the period 2006–2021, at first, several amendments to the MA 2006 were made and then in 2013, in order of further promotion and development of mediation and conception of a functional mediation system, a new Mediation Act was adopted, based on principles that were fully harmonized with the EU Mediation Directive (Official Gazette of the Republic of Macedonia No. 188/2013, 148/15, 192/15 and 55/16). The MA from 2013 was also amended several times but the concept of mediation as provided in the MA from 2013 proved faulty in practice. Adoption of a new MA in 2021 was in accordance with Strategy for reform of the justice sector for the period 2017–2022, where one of the main strategic goals was simplification of access to justice by strengthening mediation. The aim was to improve the legal solutions that will enable setting up conditions for successful application of the law in practice, uniform application of the legal provisions and further promotion of mediation.

2 The Extent of Compulsiveness in the Conceptualization of Mediation Models

Voluntariness is considered to be a fundamental aspect of mediation, serving as the cornerstone of the process, defining the vital notion that participation in mediation should be a choice, not an obligation.

According to the Mediation Directive, mediation is defined as a structured process, however named or referred to, whereby two or more parties to a dispute attempt by themselves, on a voluntary basis, to reach an agreement on the settlement of their dispute with the assistance of a mediator. This process may be initiated by the parties or suggested or ordered by a court or prescribed by the law of a Member State.[8] Considering the given definition, it follows that the Directive accepts only mediation on a voluntary basis. However, the Directive also stipulates that there is no prejudice to national legislation making the use of mediation compulsory or subject to incentives or sanctions, whether before or after judicial proceedings have started, provided that such legislation does not prevent the parties from exercising their right of access to the judicial system.[9] It follows from such provision that EU law accepts the concept of mandatory mediation. In that sense, it can be said that EU law does not consider the conceptualization of mediation via compulsiveness contrary to Art. 6 (1) of the European Convention on Human Rights (ECHR) as long as the parties have the possibility of access to a court.[10]

Given the extent of compulsiveness in the conceptualization of mediation models, four models of mediation have been profiled in the European legal landscape: full voluntary mediation, voluntary mediation with incentives and sanctions, a required initial mediation session,[11] and full mandatory mediation.[12]

The model of voluntary mediation is based exclusively on the spontaneous agreement of the parties to resolve their dispute through mediation. In this model, parties agree, on their own, to opt for mediation as a method of resolving disputes. Such

[8] Art. 3(a) of the Mediation Directive.

[9] Art. 5(2) of the Mediation Directive.

[10] See Radoja (2015), p. 115. In 2014, the European Parliament published an extensive study regarding the implementation of the Mediation Directive with recommendations for increasing the number of mediations at EU level. A comparative analysis of the legal systems of 28 Member States, together with evaluation of the effects of the Directive in relation to the results it produced within EU, showed that only a certain degree of coercion can generate a significant number of mediations. See European Parliament (2014), p. 7. In the report of the European Commission on the implementation of the Mediation Directive published in 2016, it was recommended to the states to promote and encourage the use of mediation in the various ways provided for in the Directive, and in particular to encourage the courts to call on the parties to settle the dispute through mediation. See Report from the Commission to the European Parliament, the Council and the European Economic and Social Committee on the application of Directive 2008/52/EC of the European Parliament and of the Council on certain aspects of mediation in civil and commercial matters, Brussels, 26.8.2016, COM(2016) 542 final, pp. 4, 12.

[11] van Rhee (2021), pp. 7–24, De Pallo (2021), pp. 543–568.

[12] De Pallo and D'Urso (2016), p. 11.

model of mediation existed in most EU Member States even before the Mediation Directive was adopted. Since 2008, most of the EU Member States adopted the model of voluntary mediation with incentives and sanctions in order to encourage the parties to mediate disputes. The nature and type of incentives and sanctions vary but essentially consist of financial relief (such as reimbursement of court costs or fees paid) and financial sanctions (such as an order to pay the court costs of the opposing party, regardless of who won the case if the party did not submit evidence that there was a try of peaceful dispute settlement before going to court). The mandatory initial mediation session model is somewhere between voluntary and fully mandatory mediation. Several essential elements characterize this model: providing an effective start of mediation process through a mandatory initial mediation session with possible sanctions in the eventual court proceedings if the party does not attend this initial session in good faith; ensuring quality of the procedure in a way that the initial session takes place in the presence of a professional qualified/licensed mediator; and providing an opportunity for the parties to easily opt out of the mediation process at the end of the initial mediation session without incurring additional sanctions or other harmful consequences during the court proceedings. The fully mandatory mediation model implies that parties are obliged to attend and pay for the full mediation process as a prerequisite for proceeding to court. The mandatory character refers to the obligation to be a part of the whole process, while the eventual reaching of a settlement always remains voluntary.[13] In relation to the element of compulsiveness, there is also a distinction between so-called opt-in and opt-out models of mediation.[14] In that regard, the mandatory initial session for mediation is considered an opt-in option since the parties are obliged to meet with a mediator and decide whether to commence a regular mediation process. On the other hand, regarding mandatory mediation with an opt-out model, the first meeting is already a part of a regular mediation process, but each party can withdraw at the beginning of the process. Only if the parties agree, the process continues after the first meeting.[15]

According to the Macedonian Mediation Act (hereafter MA),[16] mediation is defined as a procedure for dispute settlement that enables the parties to resolve their dispute in a voluntary, efficient, expeditious and cost-effective manner, through separate or joint meetings with a mediator, that differs from a procedure that is conducted before competent courts.[17] Regarding models of mediation, the MA recognizes three models depending on the manner of commencement of the mediation process: voluntary, contractual and determined by law.[18] This approach also reflects the distinction between types of mediation given the degree of compulsivity. Namely, the latter is a model that induces coerciveness since it stipulates deviation from the principle of

[13] Ibid., pp. 11–17; De Pallo (2018), pp. 6–8.

[14] De Pallo (2021), pp. 543–568.

[15] De Pallo (2018), p. 5.

[16] Law on Mediation 2021 (MA), Official Gazette of the Republic of North Macedonia, No. 294/2021. The MA is harmonized with the EU Mediation Directive.

[17] Art. 3(c) of the MA.

[18] Art. 4(1) of the MA.

voluntariness. According to the MA, legally determined mediation is a mandatory mediation attempt defined by law prior to or after the initiation of a procedure before a court.[19] Although the principle of voluntariness is considered to be fundamental to mediation, the MA stipulates limitations in that sense, providing that an exception to the principle of voluntariness exists when mediation is conducted for a dispute: (1) which results from a previously concluded agreement of the parties; (2) after a referral by a decision of a court or other competent authority and/or (3) for which a mandatory mediation attempt is determined by law.[20]

3 Mandatory Initial Mediation Session in Macedonian Civil Procedure

As already mentioned, numerous legal systems worldwide have shown an eagerness to stimulate the use of mediation and in that sense have introduced certain mandatory aspects.[21] The Macedonian legal system shares the same approach.

In the system of civil procedure, with the Amendments to the Civil Procedure Act (hereafter CPA)[22] from 2010, normative postulations were set for affirming the principle of peaceful resolution of disputes, by institutionalizing the process of mediation during civil procedure, in a manner that an obligation was stipulated for the court, in disputes in which mediation is allowed, at the stage of preparing the main hearing, to indicate to the parties in writing that the dispute can be resolved through mediation. Despite the efforts made, with the 2010 Amendments to the CPA,

---

[19] Art. 4(4) of the MA.

[20] Art. 7(3) of the MA.

[21] In that regard, the mediation scheme that is implemented in Italy is a good example of how the introduction of certain level of coerciveness is a preferable measure in order to stimulate and promote the use of mediation. The experience in Italy throughout the years has shown that introducing mandatory elements, more specifically, mandatory mediation with the ability for parties to opt out has positive results and has increased the number of mediations in the country. Although there were certain turbulences and resistance towards such mediation model when it was firstly introduced, from today's perspective, this model proved to be an effective tool for stimulation of mediation and improvement of the overall efficiency of the civil justice system. In Italy, before 2011, and despite pro-mediation legislation that started in 1993, there were almost no commercial mediations. Things changed significantly in 2011, when a government decree made mediation a prerequisite to initiate a lawsuit in certain cases. In 2012, the Italian Constitutional Court annulled the requirement of mandatory mediation due to over-delegation and a year later, in 2013, the mandatory mediation attempts were reintroduced again. The statistics that are regularly published by the Italian Ministry of Justice for each year regarding civil and commercial mediation show positive results with an increase of mediation proceedings and also mediation settlements. Overall, Italy's mandatory mediation scheme with an easy opt-out possibility has proven to be an effective model that provides benefits of both voluntary and mandatory mediation. On the Italian experience regarding mandatory mediation, see De Pallo (2021), pp. 561–563, Noakes (2020), pp. 426–428; Matteucci (2022).

[22] Official Gazette of the Republic of North Macedonia, No. 79/2005, 110/2008, 83/2009, 116/2010 and 124/2015.

no coercive measures were introduced, but overall, certain attempts were made to stimulate mediation. According to the novelties introduced in 2010, in disputes where mediation is allowed, the court is obliged, together with the summons for preparatory hearing to serve to the parties a written indication that the dispute can be resolved through mediation.[23] The parties are obliged to declare at the preparatory hearing at the latest whether they agree to resolve the dispute through mediation.[24] In small claims procedures, where no preparatory hearing is held, the parties are obliged to give such statement at the latest at the beginning of the main hearing.[25] If the parties agree to mediate the dispute, the litigation procedure is discontinued ex lege. The discontinuance of the litigation procedure in such case lasts for 45 days. If the parties conclude a settlement in the process of mediation, they are obliged to submit it to the court within eight days from the day of its conclusion. The court schedules a hearing where the concluded settlement is noted on a minute attaining the status of a court settlement if the conditions for concluding a court settlement are met in accordance with the provisions regulated by CPA.[26] If the parties failed to reach a settlement through mediation, the proceeding will continue at the request of one of the parties, and if there is no such request, the proceedings will continue at the expiration of 45 days from the date of discontinuance.[27]

In the context of further promoting mediation, five years later, with the 2015 Amendments to the CPA, certain extent of compulsiveness was introduced by stipulating a mandatory attempt for mediation in commercial disputes up to a certain value. This novelty was presented as a promising solution in that regard. Such provision stipulates that in commercial disputes for monetary claims up to the value of 1.000.000 denars (16.000 Euros), where the procedure is initiated by filing a claim before a court, the parties are obliged, before filing the claim, to try to resolve the dispute through mediation.[28] When filing a lawsuit, the plaintiff is obliged to submit written evidence issued by a mediator that the attempt to resolve the dispute through mediation was unsuccessful. The court will dismiss the claim in cases when no such evidence is submitted.[29] The stipulated provisions indicate that the attempt to resolve a dispute through mediation before initiating a lawsuit is considered a procedural prerequisite that determines the admissibility of civil proceedings in certain disputes.

The reasons for such legislative action were barely explained to the public. The absence of particular indicators regarding the introduction of a mandatory attempt for

---

[23] Art. 272(2) of the CPA.

[24] Art. 272(4) of the CPA.

[25] Art. 436(2) of the CPA.

[26] Art. 308(4) of the CPA.

[27] Art. 203(3) of the CPA.

[28] Art. 461(2) of the CPA. Such solution was in accordance with the provisions of the MA of 2013 where it was stipulated that mediation is carried out due to a strict written consent of the parties, except in disputes where the initiation of mediation is provided as a precondition for conducting a court or other proceedings (Art. 6(1) of the MA 2013).

[29] Art. 461(3) and (4) of the CPA.

mediation in this type of dispute led to resistance by many companies, but also by the members of the legal profession. The small number of comparative experiences from European countries, especially the turbulence in maintaining such model in some of them, as well as the initial organizational problems with its practical implementation, raised doubts about the potential of this solution. In that regard, a number of issues have emerged as problematic: the very concept of compulsory elements in mediation; the lack of a sufficient number of qualified mediators to deal with the increasing inflow of cases; the introduction of a mandatory initial mediation session only in certain types of disputes and up to a certain value; increased costs for the parties if the initial mediation session fails; the possible restriction of the right to access to justice, etc. As might be expected, the most questionable among them was the issue whether such regulation contravenes voluntariness as one of the fundamental principles of mediation, and, consequently, whether a mandatory attempt for mediation before litigation intervenes with the right to access to court.

3.1 Mandatory Mediation: An Oxymoron?

The idea of mandatory mediation is contradictory in itself. In mediation, the autonomy of the parties is considered absolute—voluntariness and non-obligation are considered as its immanent characteristics. Hence, the use of the term "mandatory" when referring to mediation usually causes resentment given the fact that mandatory mediation seems to contradict a fundamental principle of this ADR technique, which is voluntariness.[30] As an ADR method, mediation implies self-determination, cooperation, and creative ways of resolving disputes in the interest of both parties. Therefore, any attempt to impose a formal and involuntary procedure can potentially threaten the *raison d'être* of mediation. Introducing any element of coercion in the mediation process is inconsistent, and even incompatible with the fundamental principles of mediation.[31] However, on the other hand, given that practical experiences show that a certain level of compulsion gives encouraging results in terms of promotion and use of mediation, it seems that the concept of mandatory mediation finds its justification. In that sense, in the theory, we will encounter that mandatory mediation is needed as a temporary tool because individuals do not use mediation on a voluntary basis, and therefore, through this concept, they should be given the opportunity to experience its benefits.[32]

Is the concept of mandatory mediation an oxymoron? It seems not. Although we are discussing something that is mandatory, we must not understand that compulsiveness operates in an absolute sense, so it will be considered that parties must mediate and that such process should ultimately result in reaching a settlement. As long as the parties have an opportunity to opt-out of the further course of the process and as

[30] De Pallo and D'Urso (2016), p. 15.

[31] Quek (2010), pp. 481, 484.

[32] Sander et al. (1996), p. 886.

long as there is no coercion regarding the conclusion of a settlement, it is considered that the principle of voluntariness is respected. In other words, the principle of voluntariness is not violated as long as the obligation to commence mediation is imposed on the parties. The parties always maintain the right not to participate in the further course of the process. In that sense, the principle of voluntariness is respected in its entirety.[33] Coercion in the concept of mandatory mediation is only associated with obliging the parties to try to settle the dispute peacefully. That means that parties are not limited in their right to access to justice because mandatory mediation does not imply the exclusion of adjudication. Mandatory mediation is not imposed as the sole method for dispute settlement. In such case, the right of access to court is only postponed to a later moment since the party is not denied the opportunity to initiate a lawsuit if mediation remains unsuccessful.[34]

Given the above, in the context of Macedonian procedural legislation, it can be concluded that the principle of voluntariness is not brought into question. In that regard, it is particularly important to emphasize that the imposed obligation of a mandatory initial mediation session in commercial disputes for monetary claims with a value not exceeding certain amount, does not simultaneously mean an obligation for reaching a settlement. The deviation from the principle of voluntariness is related only to the commencement of mediation, while the continuation of the process always depends on the parties.

3.2 Mandatory Mediation and the Right of Access to Justice

Undoubtedly, one of the most debated questions when a certain degree of coercion is introduced as a stimulating measure for a more intensive use of mediation is whether the concept of mandatory mediation violates the right of access to court. When parties are obliged to try to resolve a dispute peacefully as a precondition for initiating a lawsuit, in such a case they are denied direct access to the court, imposing an additional step in order to obtain the right of access to justice. Such a circumstance may affect their right of access to court as a fundamental procedural guarantee established by Art. 6(1) of the ECHR.

It is apparent that many European countries continuously introduce measures of coercive nature to stimulate mediation. Still, when instituting such measures, clear limits should be set to what extent coercion should be introduced into the system of ADR, taking into account the fundamental procedural guarantees and certain criteria established by the European Court of Human Rights (ECtHR) and the European Court of Justice (ECJ) that must be met in order for the concept of mandatory mediation to be compatible with Art. 6(1) of the ECHR and with EU law.

---

[33] See Vukomir (2016) Prijedlog uvođenja obveznog informativnog sastanka o medijacii u hrvatsko zakonodavstvo, available at: https://medijacija.hr/wp-content/uploads/2020/04/Mladen-Vukmir-Prijedlog-obveznog-informativnog-sastanka-u-medijaciji-1.pdf.

[34] Winston (1996), pp.190–92, Hutchinson (2010) p. 91, cited according to Quek (2010), p. 486.

The rights guaranteed by Art. 6(1) of the ECHR are not absolute and may be subject to limitations in certain cases. In assessing whether the restriction of rights is legal, the ECtHR takes into account the importance of the right of access to justice as a democratic principle.[35] Given the ECtHR case-law, it is considered that the restriction is legal if it has a legitimate purpose, if it is proportional[36] and if the very essence of the right is not threatened or called into question.[37] Proportionality is an essential principle in the case-law of the ECtHR, hence it is considered a key element in determining whether the limitation of the right is legal or not. Proportionality implies establishing a reasonable balance between the legitimate goals of the state (restrictions) and the measures that the state uses to achieve those goals. Proportionality also includes the existence of a reasonable balance between individual rights and the general interest.[38] When the state sets restrictions it should use means that are the least intrusive.[39] Essentially, when restrictions are set, the assessment should focus on whether they are necessary and effective. In the context of mandatory mediation in the Macedonian civil justice system, this approach implies that the state can require the fulfillment of certain prerequisites as a condition for initiating a lawsuit only if a legitimate goal is achieved through such restrictions and if those are proportional and do not threaten the essence of Art. 6(1) of the ECHR.

Likewise, EU law does not diverge from the interpretation established by the ECtHR. According to the ECJ, fundamental rights are not absolute and can be limited, but limitations must be proportionate and not violate the essence of the right.[40] Regarding the use of strong incentive measures to stimulate mediation, the position of the ECJ is that such measures can be used to encourage the parties to use mediation more often.

In the case of *Alessini v. Telecom Spa*,[41] the ECJ ruled that the imposition of a mandatory attempt for mediation before proceeding to a court does not constitute a violation of Art. 6(1) of the ECHR. According to the Court, although the concept of mandatory mediation limits the right to access to justice, the court at the same time stresses that such restrictions have their limits and are directed towards a fast and cost-effective resolution of the dispute and are regulated in favor of the parties. In this case, the restrictions have a justified purpose, which is the general public interest. The principle of proportionality is not violated as long as mediation does not cause unnecessary delays in court proceedings and additional costs to the parties, or if it causes insignificantly small costs. The Court also emphasizes that the following

[35] ECtHR, *Kijewska v. Poland*, No. 73002/01, 6 September 2007, para. 46.

[36] ECtHR, *Ashingdane v. United Kingdom*, No. 8225/78, 28 May 1985.

[37] ECtHR, *Kijewska v. Poland*, No. 73002/01, 6 September 2007.

[38] ECtHR, *Van Mechelen and Others v. the Netherlands*, No. 21363/93, 21364/93, 21427/93 and 22056/93, 23 April 1997, paras. 59–65.

[39] ECtHR, *Saint-Paul Luxembourg S.A. v. Luxembourg*, No. 26419/10, 18 April 2013, para. 44.

[40] Handbook on European Law Relating to Access to Justice (2016) European Union Agency for Fundamental Rights and Council of Europe, p. 115.

[41] CJEU, Joined cases C-317/08 to C-320/08, *Rosalba Alasania v. Telecom Italia Spar, Filomena Califano v. Wind span, Lucia Anna Giorgia Iacono v. Telecom Italia spa* and *Multiservice Srl v. Telecom Italia SpA*, Judgement of 18 March 2010.

postulations must be respected so that the concept of mandatory mediation is considered compatible with the principle of effective judicial protection: mediation should not result in a binding decision for the parties; it should not cause a substantial delay for the purposes of bringing legal proceedings; it should suspend the period for the time-barring of claims; it should not give rise to costs—or gives rise to very low costs—for the parties; electronic means should not be the only means by which the settlement procedure may be accessed; and interim measures should be allowed in exceptional cases where the urgency of the situation so requires. The ECJ has taken an identical position in the case of *Menini and another v. Banco Popolare Societa Cooperativa*, where it pointed out that parties must act in accordance with national law even in cases where domestic rules stipulate a mandatory attempt to settle a dispute through mediation before initiating court proceedings. The ECJ has stressed that it is important to maintain the right to access to the judicial system.[42]

Given the views of the ECtHR and the ECJ, it can be concluded that the concept of a mandatory attempt for mediation does not in itself mean a violation of the right of access to justice, despite the fact that an additional obstacle is imposed on the parties in exercising their right of direct access to justice in a way that the admissibility of judicial protection depends on whether the parties tried to resolve the dispute amicably. The right of access to court guaranteed by Art. 6(1) of the ECHR will not be violated as long as the earlier stage of trying to settle the dispute peacefully does not cause an unnecessary delay in bringing legal proceedings and if it causes only insignificant costs for the parties. What is essential is that the measures applied do not limit the right of access to court in a way that would jeopardize the very essence of such right. Hence, the imposed restrictions will be treated as a violation of Art. 6(1) of the ECHR only if such measures do not achieve a legitimate goal and if there is an imbalance between the means used and the goal to be achieved.

3.3 The Practical Context of the Mandatory Initial Mediation Session—Evaluating the Effects of Compulsion

The practical implementation of a certain degree of compulsion in the Macedonian mediation model and the relevant numbers in that context are not very encouraging and stimulating. The obtained data from the Ministry of Justice regarding the number of initiated mediations and their outcome in commercial disputes does not show satisfactory results.

In the period from 2016 till the end of 2023, in the Registry for records of mediation procedures at the Ministry of Justice, mediators have entered a total of 4952

[42] CJEU, C-75/16, *Livio Menini and Maria Antonia Rampanelli v. Banco Popolare Societa Cooperativa*, Judgment of 14 June 2017.

Table 1 Mediation procedures at the Ministry of Justice, 2016–2023

Year	Total number of mediations in civil disputes	Number of mediations in commercial disputes	Number of settled commercial disputes through mediation	Success rate of mediation in commercial disputes (%)
2016	217	126	40	31.75
2017	1323	198	37	18.69
2018	472	229	40	17.47
2019	362	284	30	10.56
2020	616	353	34	9.63
2021	530	319	26	8.15
2022	935	381	26	6.82
2023	497	341	5	1.46

mediations in civil disputes.[43] In the years following the introduction of the mandatory initial mediation session in commercial disputes till the end of 2023, the available data in Table 1 shows the following.

From the indicated figures, it follows that about 45% of the total number of mediations are in the domain of commercial disputes, and the percentage of successfully completed mediations in this type of disputes is only 10.8%.[44] On the other hand, the total number of lawsuits that are initiated before competent courts of first instance in commercial disputes in the past years is decreasing.[45] But, given the aforementioned numbers, such a decline is not a result of successfully ended mediations if we have in mind the success rate. If we compare the number of initiated lawsuits in the past five years with the number of mediations within the same period for commercial disputes, it turns out that mediation is present in ~41% of such cases. Additionally, given that only commercial disputes that are initiated with a lawsuit fall under the compulsory mediation scheme, the number of total commercial disputes is considerably greater due to the fact that a certain number of commercial disputes fall under the procedure for issuance of a notarial payment order as an out-of-court procedure in the competence of the notary.

Undoubtedly, the number of mediations in commercial disputes in the past years is a result of the introduction of a mandatory initial mediation session in these cases.[46] No information is available on the value of these commercial disputes, nor is there

[43] Mediations are registered in the field of commercial disputes, labor disputes, insurance disputes, property rights disputes, family disputes, consumers disputes and other disputes in civil matters.

[44] As it can be noticed from the indicated numbers, throughout the years, the success rate is in constant decline.

[45] Although we do not operate with the exact number of initiated lawsuits in commercial disputes, their number in the past five years is ~4038. By year: 2019: ~920; 2020: ~996; 2021: ~750; 2022: ~702; and 2023: ~670.

[46] In that regard, it is worth mentioning that the total number of mediations from 2007 to 2016 was exceptionally low, and the number of successfully completed mediations was minor. For example, in

data on the percentage of the total number of mediations in commercial disputes that fall under the concept of a mandatory initial mediation session. Nevertheless, it appears from the analyzed numbers that the introduction of a certain degree of compulsion did not bring positive results and that the model of a mandatory initial mediation session, as it was conceptualized in our legal system, does not represent an effective tool for resolving disputes through ADR techniques and encouragement of their use in that respect. The practice has shown that the mandatory initial mediation session in commercial disputes is an inefficient solution due to the fact that the parties consider the mediation session only as a mere formality for obtaining a written statement from the mediator so they can fulfil the prerequisites for initiating a lawsuit before a competent court. The session where the parties should put effort for the mediation to succeed is treated as a formal act to obtain the necessary statement that the attempt to mediate was unsuccessful without actually discussing the possibilities for resolving the dispute through mediation.

4 Conclusion

Mediation as an ADR technique should be considered an important segment to the system of dispute resolution in general. As such, it should be perceived as complementary to the traditional judicial way of resolving disputes, which does not threaten, but, on the contrary, improves the functioning of the justice system as a whole. The greater presence of mediation in society will imply unburdening the courts, which could lead to a more efficient use of judicial resources. It is obvious that, at least so far, our society does not show an inclination towards "informal" ways of resolving disputes, given that the tradition to litigate is still predominant. It will require serious efforts in terms of raising general awareness of the advantages and benefits of mediation in the society. In that regard, the aim is to create social awareness that ADR methods should be the primary choice for dispute settlement and that the court system should be used in *ultima linea*.

The question of whether mediation should be mandatory or not remains open. Within the EU, there is still no consensus regarding the introduction of the concept of mandatory mediation. Some stakeholders believe that the absence of compulsiveness reflects negatively on the promotion of mediation. Others, on the other hand, believe that mediation should be voluntary in order to be functional and attractive in relation to court proceedings. One way or another, it is indisputable that most stakeholders agree that some form of mandatory mediation is preferable, with the introduction of a soft form of compulsiveness by acceptance of the so-called opt-out model of mediation.[47]

---

the period from 2007 to 2011, the number of initiated mediations was 124, 49 of them in commercial disputes.

[47] European Parliament (2014), pp. 163–164.

In terms of stimulating a greater presence of mediation, the Macedonian legislator introduced a certain degree of compulsion in the mediation process by standardizing an opt-out model of mediation only in commercial disputes up to a certain value. However, the practical implementation of a mandatory initial mediation session, at least for now, has not shown satisfactory results, given that the success rate is considerably low. It seems that the implemented model should be reconsidered and eventually conceptualized in a broader sense by imposing the mandatory element in a wider range of civil disputes (e.g. in all commercial disputes, in family matters, neighbour disputes, disputes over lease and loans, insurance, etc.) with a tendency for the process to be imposed upon the parties as a requirement for initiating a lawsuit, due to the fact that certain degree of compulsion has a potential and is a preferable concept for further stimulating mediation. In that regard, what seems important is for the mandatory scheme to be structured and set up in a way that the compulsory mediation requirement takes place in the earliest stage of dispute settlement (prior to the initiation of a lawsuit) with an easy opt-out option by either of the parties. The concept of early mandatory mediation with an easy opt-out model will likely increase the access to justice, promote cost effectiveness, save time and provide for more effective and efficient dispute settlement. It also seems important to continue developing an atmosphere where stakeholders and practitioners are aware of the benefits of mediation and, consequently, use it where appropriate. Also, the state should consider introducing other measures to stimulate the use of mediation through the system of incentives and sanctions in order to encourage amicable dispute resolution.

References

Alfini JJ, Press SB, Sternlight JR, Stulberg JB (2006) Mediation theory and practice. LexisNexis, Newark, New Yersey

Alexander N (2006) Global trends in mediation: riding the third wave in global trends in mediation. Kluwer Law International, Alphen aan den Rijn

De Pallo G (2018) A ten-year-long "EU mediation paradox" when an EU directive needs to be more … directive. briefing requested by the JURI committee, European Parliament. https://www.europarl.europa.eu/RegData/etudes/BRIE/2018/608847/IPOL_BRI%282018%29608847_EN.pdf

Hutchinson CC (1996) The case for mandatory mediation, 42 Loyola. L Rev

De Pallo G (2021) Mediating mediation itself: the easy opt-out model settles the perennial dispute between voluntary and mandatory mediation. Cardozo J Confl Resolut 22:543–568

De Pallo G, D'Urso L (2016) Achieving a balanced relationship between mediation and judicial proceedings, the implementation of the mediation directive. In: Compilation of in-depth Analyses, pp 4–30

European Parliament (2014) 'Rebooting' the mediation directive: assessing the limited impact of its implementation and proposing measures to increase the number of mediations in the EU

Handbook on European Law Relating to Access to Justice (2016) European Union agency for fundamental rights and council of Europe

Masood A (2012) Implied compulsory mediation. Civ Just Q 31(2):151–175

Matteucci G (2022) Compulsory civil mediation in Italy 2011/ 2021. https://mediate.com/compulsory-civil-mediation-in-italy-2011-2021

Noakes A (2020) Mandatory early mediation: a vision for civil lawsuits worldwide. Ohio St J Disput Resolut 36(3):409–434

Quek D (2010) Mandatory mediation: an oxymoron? Examining the feasibility of implementing a court-mandated mediation program. Cardozo J Confl Resolut 11:479–509

Radoja K (2015) Obvezno mirenje – Osvrt na rješenja iz komparativnog i hrvatskog prava. Pravni Vjesnik 31(2):111–130

Sander FEA, William Allen H, Hensler D (1996) Judicial (mis)use of ADR? A debate. Univ Toledo Law Rev 27

Spencer D, Brogan M (2006) Mediation law and practice. Cambridge University Press, Cambridge

Stefflek F (2012) Mediation in the European Union: an introduction. https://e-justice.europa.eu/fileDownload.do?id=b3e6a432-440d-4105-b9d5-29a8be95408f

van Rhee CH (2021) Mandatory mediation before litigation in civil and commercial matters: a European perspective. Access Just East Europe 4(12):7–24. https://doi.org/10.33327/AJEE-18-4.4-a000082

Vukomir M (2016) Prijedlog uvođenja obveznog informativnog sastanka o medijacii u hrvatsko zakonodavstvo. http://mirenje.hr/wp-content/uploads/2018/06/Mladen-Vukmir-Prijedlog-obveznog-informativnog-sastanka-u-medijaciji-1.pdf.

Winston DS (1996) Participation standards in mandatory mediation statutes: "You can lead a horse to water...,". Ohio St J Disp Resol 11:187–206

The Binding Nature of Mediation Settlements in North Macedonia: Aspects of Validity and Enforcement

Jadranka Dabovikj Anastasovska and Marjana Staninova

Abstract Mediation has emerged as an important tool in contemporary dispute resolution, offering parties a flexible and collaborative approach to resolving conflicts. Unlike traditional litigation, where decisions are imposed by a third party, mediation empowers parties to craft their own solutions, fostering a sense of ownership and satisfaction with the outcome. This autonomy often leads to higher rates of compliance and long-term satisfaction among the parties involved. However, in cases where voluntary compliance with mediated settlements fails, mechanisms for enforcement become paramount. Without a means to ensure compliance with mediated agreements, parties may be hesitant to engage in mediation, fearing that their agreements will not be honored or enforced. This contribution explores the binding nature of mediation settlements in North Macedonia, focusing on aspects of validity and enforcement within the national legal framework. The objective is to emphasize the role that enforcement mechanisms of mediation settlements play in ensuring the success of mediation as a preferred method of dispute resolution.

1 Background

Mediation is now recognized as the principal[1] Alternative Dispute Resolution (ADR) process utilized for legal reform in many common law countries, but many civil law countries have also witnessed an ADR and mediation movement in response to civil litigation problems.[2] North Macedonia is continuously making efforts to promote mediation as an effective and efficient dispute resolution mechanism. On a normative level, the model of mediation has undergone many changes and transformations,

[1] This chapter does not examine the legal framework for mediation settlements in criminal cases.

[2] Brooker (2013), p. 2.

J. D. Anastasovska (✉) · M. Staninova
Faculty of Law "Iustinianus Primus", Ss. Cyril and Methodius University in Skopje, Skopje, North Macedonia
e-mail: j.dabovicanastasovska@pf.ukim.edu.mk

M. Bungenberg et al. (eds.), *Alternative Dispute Resolution in the Western Balkans*, European Union and its Neighbours in a Globalized World 20,
https://doi.org/10.1007/978-3-031-76345-8_13

as the mediation practice showed weak results in the implementation.[3] In 2015, North Macedonia even introduced a mandatory attempt at mediation for commercial disputes with a value of up to 1.000.000 denars.[4]

The act regulating mediation is the Mediation Act (MA)[5] enacted in December 2021, and in force since January 2022. The latest MA is the third novel law regulating mediation aimed at harmonising the national legislation with Directive 2008/52/EC of the European Parliament and of the Council of 21 May 2008 on certain aspects of mediation in civil and commercial matters. The novel MA was enacted with the purpose of improving the legal conditions for the implementation of the law in practice, ensuring equal application of the provisions by the mediators, and providing better solutions for the promotion of mediation as a dispute resolution mechanism and its results.

Under the MA, mediation in North Macedonia is available for disputes in which the parties may freely dispose of their claims unless the law provides for the exclusive jurisdiction of a court or other body.[6] In this sense, mediation is available for a wide range of disputes,[7] including property disputes arising from inheritance proceedings; family disputes; labor disputes; commercial disputes; consumer disputes; insurance disputes; disputes arising from procedures for notary payment orders; disputes related to education; disputes related to health and safety at work; disputes related to the protection of the environment; disputes related to discrimination; disputes related to civil liability for insult and defamation; as well as other types of disputes between domestic and foreign natural persons and/or legal entities in which mediation corresponds to the nature of the dispute and may aid in its resolution.

The effectiveness of mediation lies in the concept of a mediation settlement—it is a voluntary agreement reached by the parties with the assistance of the mediator. As the parties are the "solution-makers", mediation settlements are more likely to be complied with voluntarily. Or, as it has been put in academic literature, "*a settlement agreement freely made between both parties to a dispute ordinarily commands a degree of willing acceptance denied to an order imposed on one party by court decision. A party who settles forgoes the chance of total victory, but avoids the anxiety, risk, uncertainty, and expenditure of time which is inherent in almost any contested action, and escapes the danger of total defeat*".[8] However, the efficiency of such settlements relies heavily on the existence of a robust enforcement mechanism.

An effective enforcement mechanism fosters confidence in the mediation process. Without effective enforcement, parties may be inclined to disregard their agreements, leading to further disputes and undermining the integrity of the mediation process.

---

[3] For a thorough overview, see Zoroska-Kamilovska and Rakocevic (2021), pp. 59–77.

[4] Article 461 of the Civil Procedure Act (Official Gazette of the Republic of North Macedonia no.79/05, 110/08, 83/09, 116/10 and 124/15).

[5] Official Gazette of the Republic of North Macedonia no. 294/2021 on 27 December 2021.

[6] Article 1(1) of the MA.

[7] Article 1(2) of the MA.

[8] Caponi (2015), p. 139.

In commercial contexts, a dependable enforcement mechanism for mediation settlements is essential for fostering business confidence and facilitating international trade. Enforcement of mediation settlements is also important in the international context, as businesses are more likely to engage in cross-border transactions if they have assurance that their mediated agreements will be enforced across jurisdictions.

According to data obtained by the Ministry of Justice of the Republic of North Macedonia in the period of 2016–2021, the case count of conducted mediation procedures is 3497, out of which 1730 mediation procedures ended with a mediation settlement.[9]

2 Mediation Settlements as Contracts: Validity Aspects

When assessing the legal nature of agreements resulting from mediation, it is useful to begin from the assumption that they can normally be defined as settlements of a dispute by mutual concessions.[10] Modern legislation on mediation does not need to thoroughly address topics such as legal effects and avoidance of agreements resulting from mediation.[11] Modern legislation deals only with selected aspects of the validity of the settlements, such as the formal requirements. The MA follows this approach and incorporates provisions that relate to the form and enforcement of a mediation settlement. In this sense, the MA expressly provides that the Law on Obligations governs the conclusion, effect, and termination of the agreement reached in the mediation procedure, as well as the material responsibility of the mediator.[12] In turn, the essential foundation for a legally binding mediation settlement agreement is the ordinary law of contract.[13] The general principlesand rules on contract formation stipulated in the Law on Obligations ("LO")[14] apply to the validity of a mediation settlement.

[9] There is strong inconsistency in statistical data keeping of mediation practice in North Macedonia. This is data obtained from the Ministry of Justice based upon data provided by 32 mediators (14 mediators have not entered any data) in the Registry for reporting mediation cases kept by the Ministry of Justice in accordance with the previous 2013 MA. This number of reported and registered cases does not coincide with the number of cases recorded in the individual registries of the mediators. For this reason, with the 2021 MA, a new E-Registry is formed and an express obligation for the mediators to enter data in the E-Regsitry is stipulated. See more, Bungenberg et al. (2023). Note that different data referencing the Ministry of Justice as a source is presented in Shabani (2021). In addition, different data is presented in a research report by Lazhetikj, Koshevaliska and Nanev (2022).

[10] Caponi (2015), p.129.

[11] Ibid.

[12] Article 29 of the MA.

[13] Cited as Foskett in Caponi (2015), p.130.

[14] Official Gazette of the Republic of Macedonia no. 18/01, 04/02, 05/03, 84/08, 81/09, 161/09 и 123/13 and Official Gazette of the Republic of North Macedonia no. 215/21 and 154/23.

2.1 Principles of Ordinary Contract Law

One of the fundamental dogmas of law is that everyone is free to contract as they wish, as long as no illegality is involved.[15] The general principle on freedom of contract and its limitations are proclaimed in Article 3 of the LO, entitled "Freedom to regulate obligations", which provides that *"[t]he participants in the legal transactions freely regulate the obligations in accordance with the Constitution, laws and good practices"*. Limitations to the freedom of contract are also expressly incorporated in provisions that relate to consideration,[16] basis,[17] and conditions[18] of the contract, as well as the general provision for nullity[19] of the contract. Therefore, the imperative standards for limitation of freedom in "settling" the dispute by a mediation settlement are the Constitution of the Republic of North Macedonia, the laws, and the good practices.[20] Other basic principles incorporated in the LO, such as good faith,[21] equal consideration,[22] and fairness,[23] are also material to the validity of the mediation settlement,[24] as such principles apply to contract formation and the manner of execution of obligations.

It follows that, if the general principles incorporated in the LO are taken into consideration, a more general description of the process of creating a mediation settlement would be the following: "*The parties in the mediation process are free, in good faith, to design a settlement based with equal consideration, that is, a settlement which is in accordance with the Constitution of the Republic of North Macedonia, the laws and the good practices.*"

---

[15] Fridman (1967), p. 1.

[16] See Article 41 and Article 39 of the LO.

[17] SeeArticle 43(2) and Article 44 of the LO.

[18] See Article 67 of the LO.

[19] See Article 95(1) of the LO.

[20] The reference of "good practices" as an imperative standard in the limitation of freedom of contract provides the courts with the right to apply a stretchy criterion in assessing the permissibility and morality of a certain contract. The rationale behind this would be safeguarding the basic moral principles upon which the community system is based. See a similar stance in the comments on Article 10 in Perovich et al. (1995).

[21] See Article 5 of the LO.

[22] See Article 8 of the LO.

[23] The principle of fairness applies in cases expressly stipulated by law, such as for certain aspects related to the liability for damages, general terms and conditions, termination of contracts due to change of circumstances and similar. See Article 10-a from the LO.

[24] See, for example, Article 266-a paragraph 4 of the LO, which provides for nulitty of contracts contrary to the principles of good faith, equal consideration and fairness: (4) The provision agreeing a rate higher than the legal penalty interest rate is null and void in whole or in part if it follows from the circumstances of the case, commercial practices or the nature of the subject of the obligation that the penalty interest rate agreed in this way, contrary to the principles of conscientiousness and honesty, equal value of mutual benefits and equity, as well as provisions for usurious contracts, caused an apparent disproportion between the rights and obligations of the contracting parties.

2.2 *Party Capacity, Mutual Assent, Consideration, and Legality*

Whether a valid contract has been formed depends on the capacity and the mutual assent of the parties, as well as the subject and the legality basis of the agreement.[25] The validity of the contract may also depend on the required contract form.

Concerning the parties and their capacity, the most basic assumption for contract formation is to have at least two parties that have the proper capacity for entering the specific contract.[26] According to the MA, the parties may conclude the mediation settlement themselves, through a legal representative, authorized representative, guardian, or a person authorized by the party.[27]

It can be argued that the description of the representatives in this provision prompts confusion as it mentions "*an authorized representative*" and "*persons authorized by the parties*" as different categories. An authorized representative in mediation is expressly defined in the MA as follows: "*A representative is a natural person who has the legal capacity and who, based upon a notarized power of attorney for representing in mediation, participates in the negotiations in the conduct of the mediation and represents the interests of a participant in the mediation, in accordance with the authorizations specified in the power of attorney*".[28] For the "*persons authorized by the parties*", the MA provides that "*[p]ersons authorized by the parties from paragraph (1) of this Article, participate in the mediation procedure to the extent of the authorizations provided by a power of attorney by the party participant*".[29] A question is imminent: what is the difference between the authorized representative and the persons authorized to represent the party participant?

Notwithstanding the outlined lawmaking uncertainties, it is clear that, unlike litigation,[30] in which a representative of a party may only be an attorney-at-law, a lawyer employed by the party, or a relative, in the mediation process the parties may be represented by any natural person with legal capacity and such person may conclude a valid mediation settlement on behalf of the party. It should be noted that the LO provides an express requirement that the representative must have a special power of attorney for concluding settlements and waive any right without compensation.[31]

Regarding the mutual assent of the parties, while entering the process of mediation is not always voluntary,[32] the conclusion of the mediation settlement is. To establish

[25] Galev and Dabovikj Anastasovska (2012), pp. 327–361.

[26] Article 47-a of the LO.

[27] Article 19 of the MA.

[28] Article 3 (i) of the MA.

[29] Article 29(3) of the MA.

[30] Article 80 of the CPA.

[31] Article 83(4) of the LO.

[32] Article 7(3) of the MA.

a contract, both parties must voluntarily consent to its proposed terms. Undue influence,[33] coercion, or other faults[34] to the consent may render the agreement null or void. Some inspection of the consent obtained in the mediation setting is necessary to ensure a fair result. Imbalanced bargaining power and unequal transaction costs between the parties can threaten the voluntariness of the consent given by the parties. However, it is difficult to create standards that safeguard the fairness of the bargaining process. A fairly bargained-for-agreement, properly supervised by a mediator sensitive to the necessity of obtaining voluntary consent by the parties aware of the option to refuse, yields a valid and enforceable contract.[35] Some authors argue that participation in mediation and execution of a mediation settlement are sufficient evidence of the parties' mutual intent to be bound, even in the absence of the specific language of intent in the agreement.[36]

According to the MA, the mediation settlement is deemed to be concluded on the day that the parties reached consent for the manner of the resolution of the dispute.[37] One might argue that this is not an adequate wording. In this sense, according to the LO, "*[t]he contract is concluded when the contracting parties reached an agreement regarding the substantive elements of the contract*".[38] Hence, rigorous interpretation of the MA's provision would entail that the manner of the resolution of the dispute is the subject of the mediation settlement, which is erroneous. In a mediation procedure, the manner of the resolution of the dispute is the mediation process itself whereas the subject of the settlement would be the solution to the dispute. In this regard, if a more accurate wording of the provision is proposed, it might be: *"The settlement is deemed as concluded on the day the parties reached consent regarding the solution of the dispute"*.

If a mediation settlement is challenged at a later stage on grounds for lack of consent, the court may inspect information and data of the mediation process to assess the consent of the parties, which would be an exemption[39] to the confidentiality principle of mediation.

The subject of the mediation settlement, as in any other contract, might be either to give, to do, to refrain, to tolerate, or any combination of these performances. The subject must be permissible, possible, and determined (or at least, determinable), otherwise the settlement would be null and void.[40] In accordance with the principle of equality in the exchange, the consideration between the parties determined in the subject of the mediation settlement should be equal. The basis of the settlement

---

[33] Article 7 of the LO.

[34] See Articles 52–58 from the LO.

[35] Payne (1986), p.390.

[36] Cited as Burns (1986) in Bruce (1992), p.324.

[37] Article 26(1) of the MA.

[38] Article 18 of the LO.

[39] According to Article 10(7) and (5) of the MA, provides the information will not be of confidential nature in cases where the disclosing of such information is essential for enforcing the mediation settlement.

[40] See Articles 37–42 of the LO.

must be permittable (in accordance with the Constitution of the Republic of North Macedonia, the laws, and the good practices).

Regarding the form of the mediation settlement, the MA prescribes a writing requirement.[41] In addition, the MA expressly prescribes mandatory elements[42] of the content of the settlement. In this sense, it provides that the mediation settlement must entail: the case sign and number; the date of commencement and end of the mediation process; the full name of the mediator and the mediation license number; the type, subject matter, and value of the dispute (if it is determined); the rights and obligations of each of the parties and the time period for their fulfillment; the costs and remuneration for the mediator; and the signature of the natural person, or, signature and stamp[43] of the legal entity and signature and stamp of the mediator.

Considering the general rules on contract formation,[44] the mediation settlement which is not concluded in the prescribed form has no binding effect, unless the purpose of the act by which the form is prescribed indicates otherwise. However, if the parties have executed, fully or in large, the rights and obligations arising out of a settlement concluded in an invalid form, such a settlement is to be considered valid, unless the purpose for which the form is prescribed requires otherwise.[45]

2.3 *Grounds for Challenge*

As already noted, faults in the validity requirements may render a mediation settlement null or void. The general provision[46] for nullity of contracts in the LO provides that a contract that is not in accordance with the Constitution, laws, and good practices shall be null and void, unless the objective of the violated rule indicates another

---

[41] Article 26 of the MA.

[42] Article 27 of the MA. It should be noted that paragraph 2 of the cited Article 27 most likely contains a technical error—by using the wording "and" instead of the wording "additional". In this sense, the wording as it is now, prescribes that the settlement contains the elements prescribed in paragraph 1 of the Article depending on the type of dispute, whereas it is most likely referring to additional elements prescribed by law for certain types of disputes, as additional elements could be prescribed by law for certain types of disputes.

[43] The prescribed requirement of using a stamp of the legal entity might be deemed contrary to the company law of North Macedonia. Namely, in Article 92(5) of the Law on trade companies it is provided that "[*a*]*n official seal shall not be mandatory in the procedure of entry in the trade registry, as well as in the legal transactions. The confirmation of any document with an official seal of the company must not be prescribed by law or another normative act, nor can it be requested by a state body.*" In addition, it is redundant for the legislator to provide such detailed form requirments, as this issue is already covered in other legislation. Furthermore, in cases where the parties are represented by authorized representatives, it cannot be reasonably expected that the authorized representatives would deliver the settlement for signature (and stamp, as the case may be) to the party participant. Such action would diminish the role of the representative.

[44] Article 62(1) of the LO.

[45] Article 65 of the LO.

[46] Article 95 of the LO.

sanction or if the law provides otherwise for the particular case. Furthermore, it provides that if the conclusion of a certain contract is prohibited for only one of the contracting parties, the contract shall remain valid if the law does not provide otherwise for the particular case, while the party in violation of the legal prohibition shall bear the appropriate consequences.

In case of an annulled mediation settlement, each party to the settlement is obliged to give to the other party what it had received based upon the settlement. If restitution is not possible, or if the nature of what was already performed contravenes the restitution, an appropriate monetary compensation is to be made.[47] The party who is at fault for the nullity of the mediation settlement is liable to the other party for the damages it incurred if the other party did not know or, considering the circumstances, did not have to know of the reasons for the nullity of the settlement.[48] Partial nullity of mediation settlement is possible in accordance with the LO.[49]

A mediation settlement is void due to faults regarding party capacity and consent, as well as when such legal consequence is provided by law or other acts of regulation.[50]

Similar to ordinary contracts, challenges to a mediation settlement are also possible in accordance with the rules for the protection of creditors against transactions between the debtor and a third party intended to reduce a debtor's estate. The conditions and procedures for such challenge are prescribed in the general contract law,[51] as well as in other legislation related to enforcing debts.[52]

3 Enforcing Mediation Settlements: National Context

Mediation settlements that are deemed valid hold binding authority over the parties. Given that both parties actively contribute to shaping the resolution during mediation, there tends to be a high level of adherence to the agreed-upon terms. When a judge

[47] Monetary compensation is considered by the prices at the moment the court decision was reached, unless provided otherwise by law. See Article 96(1) of the LO.

[48] Article 96(2) of the LO.

[49] Article 97 of the LO.

[50] Article 103 of the LO.

[51] See Article 269–274 of the LO.

[52] For example, see Article 27 of the Law on Enforcement Procedures, as well as Articles 172–188 of the Bankruptcy Act. For case law regarding the challenge of mediation settlement pursuant to the rules in the bankruptcy law, see Judgement no. TS1-8/17 of the Basic Court in Ohrid dated 24.04.2017, confirmed with Judgement no.TSZ-600/17 of the Appelate Court dated 18.04.2018. In this case, the plaintiff sought annulment of a mediation settlement in accordance the rules for challenge of debtor's transactions in the bankruptcy law. The lawsuit was denied with the reasoning that the plaintiff failed to prove the existence of intent to damage the bankruptcy creditors as well as to prove the fact that at the moment of the conclusion of the settlement, the debtor was insolvent or there was imminent insolvency. This reasoning was also upheld by the Supreme Court of the Republic of Macedonia who rulled upon revision of the case and denied the revision as unfounded by Judgement Rev1.no.90/2018 dated 18.04.2018.

imposes a decision, one party may feel resentful or dissatisfied, which might lead to non-compliance or further disputes. Mediation can increase the likelihood of a lasting resolution that both parties willingly adhere to.[53]

However, in cases where voluntary compliance with mediated settlements fails, mechanisms for enforcement become paramount. Without a means to ensure compliance with mediated agreements, parties may be hesitant to engage in mediation, fearing that their agreements will not be honored or enforced.

The MA distinguishes between two types of mediation settlements based on their enforcement characteristics: those treated as contracts and those regarded as enforcement titles.

3.1 Enforcing Mediation Settlements as Contracts

Mediation settlements treated as contracts may be enforced in courts as binding contracts between parties in accordance with the LO. If a party breaches the mediation settlement, the aggrieved party may use legal remedies[54] to enforce the mediation settlement. Onc of the legal remedies would be claiming performance in court. Hence, the party may seek performance in court proceedings requesting the court to order the breaching party to comply with the agreed-upon terms.[55] Besides the parties, enforcement of the mediation settlement in court may also be requested by a third-party who enjoys a right settled in the mediation settlement. For example, the mediator may seek enforcement of the mediation settlement before the court for the payment of fees.[56] If performance is not claimed by the aggrieved party, the party may also use other remedies, such as contract termination and/or damages against the party in breach. In this regard, the LO provides that, when one contracting party fails to perform its obligation, the other party, unless otherwise determined, is entitled to request the performance of the obligation under the conditions provided in the LO, or, if termination of the contract does not result by law, to terminate the contract with a simple statement; and in any case it has the right to seek damages.

Notwithstanding the voluntary compliance with mediation settlements, in cases of breach of a valid mediation settlement, invoking the remedies requires court proceedings for enforcement of the settlement. Some authors suggest that litigation to enforce mediation settlement is inconsistent with the essence of mediation. In

---

[53] Gavrila and Mohamed (2023).

[54] Article 113 of the LO.

[55] See e.g. Judgement in Case No. MALVP-1636/20 of the Basic Civil Court Skopje dated 26.02.2021. In this case, the plaintiff invoked a mediation settlement with the defendant by which a debt is settled, and requested the court to order the defendant to perform the mediation settlement and pay the debt as agreed in the mediation settlement. The defendant partly accepted the claim, however argued that part of requested debt is owed by a third party. The court admitted the plaintif's claim in its entirety and, without inspecting the relation between the parties prior to the conclusion of the mediation settlement, it found that the basis for the claim is the mediation settlement.

[56] See e.g. Judgement in Case No. MALVP-187/21 of the Basic Court in Ohrid dated 31.12.2021.

this regard, these authors assert that the central quality of mediation is *"its capacity to reorient the parties toward each other, not by imposing rules on them, but by helping them to achieve a new and shared perception of their relationship, a perception that will direct their attitudes and dispositions towards one another"*.[57] For this reason, modern mediation legislation aims to provide mechanisms for direct compulsory enforcement of mediation settlements. Such possibility of enforcing the mediation settlement as an enforcement title is provided in the MA.

3.2 Enforcing Mediation Settlements as Enforcement Titles

The MA establishes special rules regarding mediation settlement agreements that bear the legal effect of an enforcement title. This includes agreements certified by a notary public and those recognized as court settlements.

The types of enforcement titles and the rules on the compulsory enforcement procedure are stipulated in the Law on Enforcement Procedures (LEP).[58] Under the LEP, enforcement titles are: (a) an enforceable court decision and court settlement; (b) an enforceable decision and settlement in administrative procedure, if a payment obligation is stipulated; (c) an enforceable notary title; (d) a notary payment order; and (e) any other title which is stipulated by the law as an enforceable title.[59]

In this regard, the MA provides that, when the parties enter into a mediation procedure before initiating a court procedure, and they want to give the mediation settlement the legal effect of an enforceable document, the content of the settlement, which contains an enforceable clause,[60] is solemnized by a notary.[61] In such case, if parties fail to comply voluntarily with a solemnized mediation settlement, it may be subject to compulsory enforcement procedures as per the rules in the LEP. Before the initiation of the compulsory enforcement procedure, the party-creditor must obtain a certificate of enforcement to the solemnized mediation settlement from the notary.[62]

Mediation settlement agreements may also obtain the status and legal validity of a court settlement and attain an enforceable title in court proceedings. In this regard, the MA provides that, in cases where mediation was successfully conducted upon court referral, the parties are obliged to submit the settlement to the court within 8 days from the date it was concluded.[63] The court schedules a hearing in which the mediation settlement is confirmed in the minutes of the court hearing, by which it

---

[57] Fuller (1971) cited in Parker (1992).

[58] Official Gazette of the Republic of North Macedonia no. 72/16, 142/16 and Official Gazette of the Republic of North Macedonia no. 14/20 ad 154/23.

[59] Article 12(1) of the LEP.

[60] Article 53(1) of the Notary Act.

[61] Article 28(1) and (2) of the MA.

[62] For this, see Article 53(3), (4), (5), (6) and (7) from the Notary Act.

[63] Article 308 paragraph 4 of the CPA.

attains the status of a court settlement if the legal conditions[64] for court settlement are met.

In comparison to the solemnized mediation settlement, the mediation settlement with the status of a court settlement enjoys an additional layer of procedural protection against future challenges. In this sense, if a lawsuit is initiated with a claim that was resolved in a court settlement, such a lawsuit will be dismissed on procedural grounds.[65] This ground is examined by the court *ex officio* and does not have to be invoked or proven by the parties.

The Macedonian legal framework for enforcement provides an open window for enacting provisions that provide for the enforceability of certain types of titles to be attained by law. This means that mediation legislation may incorporate provisions that would give the ordinary mediation settlement an enforcement title, without the solemnization of the notary or the court settlement. Although some might argue that such a legal solution would decrease the costs of the parties, such a solution might be problematic. An opposing argument would be rooted in the voluntary and informal nature of the mediation procedure. The voluntariness aspect predisposes that the parties have a mutual interest in resolving the dispute as well as a mutual interest in complying with the mutually agreed upon solution. Moreover, compulsory enforcement rules require an enforcement title adequate for enforcement, which assumes a significant level of legal expertise among the mediators who facilitate the process. Notably, being a lawyer is not a prerequisite[66] in obtaining a mediator's license in North Macedonia. Hence, such a solution would require certain formalization of the procedure, potentially conflicting with the fundamental principles of mediation.

Current legal solutions provide sufficient mechanisms to make the mediation settlement an enforcement title upon the will of the parties, although enforcing the mediation settlement as an ordinary contract may be time consuming if the other party opposes it. However, many settlement agreements will not require enforcement in the form of an enforcement title. For those situations where compliance may be an issue, making the settlement a judgment is likely to compromise confidentiality to a certain extent, for example, making public the fact that there was a dispute to begin with. However, provided the legislation facilitates the effective enforcement of a settlement agreement, the parties can obtain through mediation a result that has the same value for enforcement purposes as an arbitral award or a judgment, but through a conflict resolution process that is likely to produce more satisfactory results, while preserving confidentiality to a higher degree than ordinary court proceedings.[67]

---

[64] Article 307 of the CPA.

[65] Article 309 of the CPA.

[66] For the prerequisites in obtaining a mediator's license, see Article 54 of the MA.

[67] Fiechter (2005), p. 26.

4 Enforcement of Mediation Settlement: International Context

Mediation plays an important role in settling international disputes. Yet, the recognition and enforcement of mediated agreements often diverges from one jurisdiction to the next. This makes it difficult to predict whether a mediated agreement will be enforced in a particular jurisdiction.[68] The issue of recognition and enforcement of mediated agreements in an international context poses a significant challenge. The lack of uniformity in the recognition and enforcement of mediated agreements across different jurisdictions can indeed create uncertainty for parties involved in international transactions. This inconsistency undermines the effectiveness of mediation as a dispute resolution mechanism, as parties may hesitate to engage in the process if they cannot rely on the enforceability of the resulting agreements.

An effort to address this issue[69] has been made with the United Nations Convention on International Settlement Agreements Resulting from Mediation, also known as the "Singapore Convention on Mediation" (Convention). It is a potential game changer when it comes to the enforceability of international commercial settlement agreements resulting from mediation since it reduces the obstacles for enforcement.[70] The Convention aims to facilitate the enforcement of mediated settlement agreements in cross-border disputes. It was adopted by the United Nations General Assembly in December 2018 and opened for signature in August 2019. Its primary objective is to promote the use of mediation for resolving international commercial disputes by providing a harmonized and efficient mechanism for enforcing mediated settlement agreements across different jurisdictions.

The Convention applies to international settlement agreements resulting from mediation except for settlement agreements concluded to resolve a dispute arising from transactions by a consumer for personal, family, or household purposes, or relating to family, inheritance, or employment law.[71] Also, settlement agreements are enforceable as judgments or arbitral awards fall outside the scope of the Convention.[72]

---

[68] Zeller and Trakman (2019), p.19.

[69] For the forty-seventh session of the United States Commision on International Trade law, the United States proposed that Working Group II develop a multilateral convention on the enforceability of international commercial settlement agreements reached through conciliation, with the goal of encouraging conciliation in the same way that the New York Convention facilitated the growth of arbitration. See A/CN.9/822—Proposal by the Government of the Uited States of America: future work for Working Group II. Available at: https://uncitral.un.org/en/working_groups/2/arbitration. In addition, practitioners and other members of international business and legal communities who participated in a 2014 study to examine the desirability of a multilateral convention establishing a cross-border enforcement mechanism, at a time when the covention was just a proposal: 74% of respondents expressed the belief that such a convention would encourage parties to resort to mediation services more frequently. See Strong (2014), p. 45.

[70] Peters (2019), pp. 13–19.

[71] Article 1(1) of the Singapore Convention on Mediation.

[72] The purpose of this last exclusion is to avoid a possible overlap with existing and future conventions, namely the New York Convention, the Convention on Choice of Court Agreements (2005)

Parties to the Convention may determine their own rules of procedure in relation to enforcement provided they comply with the conditions laid down in the Convention in relation to scope, form, and evidence.[73] If a party seeks to enforce a settlement under the Convention, it is required (1) to produce the mediation settlement signed by the parties and (2) to show evidence that it was procured as a result of a mediation process.[74] Regarding the grounds for refusing to grant relief, the Convention provides an exhaustive list of grounds under which a court may refuse to grant relief.[75] The grounds may be divided into four broad categories: grounds for refusal tied to (a) the law on obligations; (b) mediator (mis)conduct; (c) public policy; and (d) subject matters not amenable to mediation.[76] Certain grounds were inspired by the New York Convention which is the key international instrument for the recognition and enforcement of foreign arbitral awards. These grounds include incapacity of a party to the settlement agreement, a settlement agreement that is null and void, inoperative or incapable of being performed, and if the settlement agreement was not binding.[77]

Although the Singapore Convention might be the solution to the issue of enforcement of international mediation settlements, the adoption of the Convention is limited. Up to now, the Singapore Convention has only 57 signatories and 14 parties. North Macedonia has signed it, but ratification is still pending.

A widespread adoption and implementation of the Singapore Convention are necessary to ensure its effectiveness in promoting the enforceability of mediated agreements globally. In the meantime, parties to international commercial transactions should carefully consider the potential enforcement challenges when choosing mediation as a dispute resolution method and may need to include specific provisions in their agreements to address the recognition and enforcement of mediated settlements in different jurisdictions.

5 Concluding Remarks

In North Macedonia, mediation settlements are treated as contracts and may be enforced as binding agreements. The validity of such settlements is governed by general contract law principles and rules on contract formation, as well as provisions outlined in mediation legislation. Similarly, challenges to mediation settlements include grounds for challenges applicable to ordinary contracts. Oriented towards more effective enforcement, the mediation legislation in North Macedonia also provides options for attaining a mediation settlement with the legal effect of an

---

and the preliminary draft convention on judgments, under preparation by The Hague Conference on Private International Law. See UNCITRAL (2019), p. 2.

[73] Alexander and Chong (2018), pp. 37–56.

[74] Article 4(1)(b) of the Singapore Convention on Mediation.

[75] Article 5 of the Singapore Convention on Mediation.

[76] Chong and Steffek (2019), p. 469.

[77] Bungenberg et al. (2023), p. 20.

enforcement title. In this regard, mediation settlements may be certified by a notary public and be directly enforced, or confirmed in court proceedings to attain the status of a court settlement.

Although Macedonian mediation legislation is not flawless from the law-making aspect, by treating mediated agreements as contracts and providing avenues for enforcement through court proceedings, it ensures that parties can rely on the settlement agreements they reach during mediation.

Despite these mechanisms, challenges persist in the international context, where the recognition and enforcement of mediated agreements across borders lacks uniformity. Efforts such as the Singapore Convention on Mediation aim to address this issue, but a widespread adoption is necessary to ensure the global enforceability of mediation settlements. While North Macedonia has signed the Convention, its ratification is pending, underscoring the ongoing need for cooperation in international mediation enforcement efforts.

References

Alexander N, Chong SY (2018) An introduction to the Singapore convention on mediation: perspectives from Singapore. Nederlands-Vlaams Tijdschrift Voor Mediation En Conflictmanagement 4:37–56

Brooker P (2013) Mediation law: journey through institutionalism to juridification. Routledge, New York

Bungenberg M, Koevski G et al (2023) Legal framework for arbitration and mediation in North Macedonia and Germany. INVESTinADR, Skopje/Saarbrücken. https://www.uni-saarland.de/en/chair/bungenberg/research/investinadr.html

Burns RP (1986) The enforceability of mediated agreements: an essay on legitimation and process integrity. Ohio State J Disput Resolut 2(1):93–116

Caponi R (2015) "Just settlement" or "just about settlement"? Mediated agreements: a comparative overview of the basics. Rabel J Compar Int Priv Law 79(1):117–141

Chong SY, Steffek F (2019) Enforcement of international settlement agreements resulting from mediation under the Singapore convention: private international law issues in perspective. Singap Acad Law J 31(Special Issue):448–486

Feehily R (2013) The legal status and enforceability of mediated settlement agreements. Hibernian Law J 12:1–26

Fiechter WE (2005) Mediation: confidentiality and enforcement issues and solutions. IBA legal practice division mediation committee newsletter 46

Fridman GHL (1967) Freedom of contract. Ottawa Law Rev 2(1):1–22

Galev G, Dabovikj Anastasovska J (2012) Obligaciono pravo. Skopje

Gavrila CA, Mohamed TA (2023) Mediation vs. litigation: the advantages of settling out of court. Kluwer Mediation Blog. https://mediationblog.kluwerarbitration.com/2023/06/14/mediation-vs-litigation-the-advantages-of-settling-out-of-court/

Lazhetikj G, Koshevaliska O, Nanev L (2022) Analysis for the application of mediation in North Macedonia, Skopje. Institute for European Politics. https://epi.org.mk/post/21393

Parker BR (1992) What can be done to enforce mediation agreements. Def Couns J 59(3):322–339

Payne CC (1986) Enforceability of mediated agreements. Ohio State J Disput Resolut 1:385–406

Perovich S et al (1995) Commentary on the law on obligations, savremena administracija, Belgrad

Peters N (2019) The enforcement of mediation agreements and settlement agreements resulting from mediation. Corp Mediat J 1–2:13–19

Shabani F (2021) Mediation – current state of use in the Republic of North Macedonia. Vadyba J Manag 37(1):43–52

Strong SI (2014) Use and perception of international commercial mediation and conciliation: a preliminary report on issues relating to the proposed UNCITRAL convention on international commercial mediation and conciliation. University of Missouri School of Law Legal Studies Research Paper No 28. https://papers.ssrn.com/sol3/papers.cfm?abstract_id=2526302

UNCITRAL (2019) United nations convention on international settlement agreements resulting from mediation "Singapore convention on mediation", information brochure. https://uncitral.un.org/sites/uncitral.un.org/files/media-documents/uncitral/en/accession_kit_october_2019_website.pdf

Zeller B, Trakman L (2019) Mediation and arbitration: the process of enforcement. Unif Law Rev 24(2):449–466

Zoroska-Kamilovska T, Rakocevic M (2021) Obavezni pokušaj medijacije u parničnom postupku Sjeverne Makedonije, Zbornik radova međunarodnog savjetovanja „Aktualnosti građanskog procesnog prava – nacionalna i usporedna pravnoteorijska i praktična dostignuća". In: Pravni fakultet Split, pp 59–77

Mediation Mechanisms in Serbian Intellectual Property Law: A Steady Progression

Dušan V. Popović

Abstract The introduction of mediation mechanisms in Serbian civil law was incited by the accession of the country to the Council of Europe in 2003. The chapter starts by examining the general rules on mediability in Serbian law and applying them to IP-related disputes. As a general rule, mediation may be used as an alternative dispute resolution mechanism: (i) in contentious legal matters in which the parties may freely dispose of their claims; (ii) unless the law stipulates exclusive authority of a court or other relevant entity. This rule sets the objective boundaries of mediation. The subjective boundaries of mediation, related to the criteria that the parties in mediation must meet, are not prescribed in Serbian law. The first criterion is quite extensively defined, given that the parties may freely dispose not only of their property claims but also of non-property claims, as long as this is in accordance with the imperative norms, public order, moral rules and customary rules. The Serbian intellectual property legislation explicitly refers to mediation mechanisms in two cases only. First, the copyright legislation allows for a mediation mechanisms to be employed if a broadcasting organization and a cable operator are unable to reach an agreement on cable retransmission conditions. Second, trademark legislation allows for the parties to trademark opposition proceedings to attempt to resolve the dispute by means of mediation within the time frame of 24 months. Even if an IP dispute is mediable, one should not necessarily conclude that it is always appropriate to resolve it by way of mediation. Accordingly, the chapter examines the advantages and disadvantages of mediation over litigation.

D. V. Popović (✉)
Faculty of Law, University of Belgrade, Belgrade, Serbia
e-mail: dusan.popovic@ius.bg.ac.rs

M. Bungenberg et al. (eds.), *Alternative Dispute Resolution in the Western Balkans*, European Union and its Neighbours in a Globalized World 20,
https://doi.org/10.1007/978-3-031-76345-8_14

1 Introduction

Mediation is a very flexible means of settling certain types of disputes. As other alternative dispute resolution mechanisms (hereinafter, ADR), mediation is a voluntary procedure, which is not focused on determining the parties' legal rights, but on identifying a basis on which the parties may be willing to settle their dispute.[1] At first, the idea of introducing mediation in the Serbian legal system was not warmly welcomed, out of fear that some traditional legal professions, like judges and attorneys, may be jeopardized by it.[2] The introduction of mediation mechanisms in Serbian civil law was incited by the accession of the country to the Council of Europe (hereinafter, the CoE) in 2003. In several occasions, the CoE Committee of Ministers recommended to the Member States to facilitate mediation whenever appropriate, in family matters,[3] penal matters,[4] civil matters,[5] and in disputes between administrative authorities and private parties.[6] In line with the CoE recommendations, the 2004 Act on civil procedure[7] introduced for the first time in Serbian civil law the possibility to resolve a dispute in civil matters by way of mediation. The same approach was maintained by the 2011 Act on civil procedure,[8] which is still in force. Consequently, the court shall direct the parties to mediation or to an informative hearing for mediation or instruct them on the option of pre-trial settlement of the dispute by mediation or in another amicable manner. Moreover, the court shall inform the parties of their right that the procedure can be performed through mediation.[9] The court shall schedule a trial hearing if the parties fail to settle the dispute through mediation within a time limit of 30 days running from the date on which a party informed the court that it renounces of mediation.[10] The 2004 Act on civil procedure laid down some general rules on mediation in civil matters. The specific rules on mediation procedures were prescribed under the 2005 Act on mediation,[11] which was applicable to property disputes of natural and legal persons, commercial, family, labour and other civil law relations, administrative and penal matters, where parties may freely dispose of their

[1] For a more detailed analysis of mediation in business law, see: Wallgren (2006), pp. 3–20; Bühring-Uhle (2006), pp. 176–221.

[2] Milutinović (2006), p. 23.

[3] CoE Committee of Ministers, Recommendation no. R(98)1 on family mediation, 21 January 1998.

[4] CoE Committee of Ministers, Recommendation no. R(99)19 on mediation in penal matters, 15 September 1999.

[5] CoE Committee of Ministers, Recommendation no. REC(2002)10 on mediation in civil matters, 18 September 2002.

[6] CoE Committee of Ministers, Recommendation no. REC(2001)9 on alternatives to litigation between administrative authorities and private parties, 5 September 2001.

[7] Official Journal of the Republic of Serbia, no. 125/2004 and 111/2009.

[8] Official Journal of the Republic of Serbia, no. 72/2011, 49/2013, 74/2013, 55/2014, 87/2018, 18/2020 and 10/2023.

[9] The 2011 Act on civil procedure, Arts. 11 and 305.

[10] The 2011 Act on civil procedure, Art. 341, para. 2.

[11] Official Journal of the Republic of Serbia, no. 18/2005.

claims, unless the law stipulates exclusive authority of a court or other relevant entity. The subsequent Act on civil procedure, adopted in 2011, explicitly prescribed that the general rules on mediation procedure are to be regulated by *lex specialis*.[12] The new Act on mediation,[13] which replaced the 2005 Act, was adopted in 2014, and it further aligned Serbian rules on mediation with the modern comparative legal framework. As an example of types of disputes in which mediation may be appropriate, the 2014 Act on mediation adds onto the existing list the disputes in the field of environmental protection, the consumer disputes, as well as "*(...) all other disputes where mediation corresponds to the nature of the disputes and may help to resolve them*".[14]

The first steps towards the introduction of mediation mechanisms in Serbian intellectual property law were undertaken in line with the National strategy for the reform of the judiciary in the period from 2013 to 2018,[15] and the Instructions on the introduction of mediation,[16] jointly issued by the Minister of Justice and the President of the Supreme Court of Cassation. In accordance with these instructions and with best practices of the World Intellectual Property Organization (hereinafter, WIPO),[17] the Serbian IP Office, the Ministry of Justice and the four courts competent for IP disputes (Commercial Court in Belgrade, Appellate Commercial Court, Higher Court in Belgrade, Appellate Court) signed a cooperation agreement with the aim of introducing mediation mechanisms into Serbian IP law. While there is a global consensus on the efficiency and effectiveness of mediation, one should bear in mind that certain types of IP disputes are not suitable to be settled through mediation. So far, the Serbian legislator explicitly prescribed the possible recourse to mediation only in two situations – one related to trademark matters, the other in the field of copyright law (Sect. 2). Even if an IP dispute is mediable, one should not necessarily conclude that it is always appropriate to resolve it by way of mediation. Accordingly, advantages and disadvantages of mediation should be examined in comparison with the recourse to traditional court dispute resolution (Sect. 3).

2 Mediability of Intellectual Property Disputes

Mediation is a relatively unstructured and informal procedure wherein a neutral mediator helps the parties in reaching an amicable solution. Albeit informal, mediation relies on certain principles. Under the 2014 Act on mediation: (i) a mediation is a

[12] The 2011 Act on civil procedure, Art. 341, para. 1.

[13] Official Journal of the Republic of Serbia, no. 55/2014.

[14] The 2014 Act on mediation, Art. 3, para. 2.

[15] Official Journal of the Republic of Serbia, no. 57/13.

[16] Available at: https://www.mpravde.gov.rs/tekst/16729/uputstvo-za-unapredjenje-medijacije-u-republici-srbiji-po-zakonu-o-posredovanju-u-resavanju-sporova.php.

[17] See for example: Guide to WIPO Mediation, 2018. Available at: wipo.int (Accessed: 18 April 2024).

voluntary procedure; (ii) the parties participating in this ADR procedure are equal; (iii) the parties need to engage personally in mediation; (iv) the procedure is confidential; (v) the mediator must be impartial and neutral; (vi) the procedure is expeditious; and (vii) all discussions and negotiations in mediation must be conducted on a legally privileged basis.[18] Having in mind the principles of mediation, and in particular its voluntary character, one must conclude that not all intellectual property disputes are mediable. Since the Serbian legislator refers to mediation in IP matters in two specific situations only, we shall first examine the general rules on mediability and apply them to IP-related disputes.

2.1 General Rules on Mediability

As a general rule, mediation may be used as an alternative dispute resolution mechanism: (i) in contentious legal matters in which the parties may freely dispose of their claims; (ii) unless the law stipulates exclusive authority of a court or other relevant entity.[19] This rule sets the objective boundaries of mediation. The subjective boundaries of mediation, related to the criteria that the parties in mediation must meet, are not prescribed in Serbian law. The first criterion is quite extensively defined, given that the parties may freely dispose not only of their property claims but also of non-property claims, so as long as this is in accordance with the imperative norms, public order, moral rules and customary rules. The 2014 Act on mediation provides certain examples of mediable disputes, by referring to property-related disputes concerning the fulfilment of the obligation to act, in other property disputes, in family, commercial disputes, administrative matters, disputes relating to environmental protection issues, consumer disputes, and in all other contentious relations where mediation is appropriate to the nature of the contentious relations and can aid in their resolution.[20] Consequently, IP disputes do, in principle, meet this requirement.

Intellectual property rights protect the interests of right owners (pecuniary and/or personal interest) in relation to certain immaterial (intellectual) goods, and they are qualified as private subjective rights. Therefore, an IP right owner is free to dispose of claims related to these rights.[21] For instance, disputes stemming from the execution of contracts on transfer or licencing of IP rights will meet the first criterion of mediability. The same may be concluded in relation to damages claims for IP right infringement. Nevertheless, the mediability of IP disputes should be assessed on a case-by-case basis. For example, certain types of infringement of IP rights may simultaneously be qualified as a civil law delict and a criminal offense. The Serbian Penal Code *inter alia* prescribes that anyone who without permission

[18] The 2014 Act on mediation, Arts. 9–16.

[19] The 2014 Act on mediation, Art. 3.

[20] Ibid.

[21] IP rights, and more generally intangible assets, have become standard assets of business entities that can be disposed of. See: De Werra (2012), p. 57.

publishes, records, copies or otherwise makes publicly available, in part or in its entirety, a copyrighted work, performance, phonogram, videogram or database, shall be punished with imprisonment of up to three years.[22] If that is the case, the recourse to mediation shall be significantly limited in relation to criminal responsibility. The 2014 Act on mediation is applicable to mediation in criminal and misdemeanour proceedings only with respect to property claims and claims for damages.[23]

The industrial property rights are recognized, and may be cancelled, in administrative proceeedings before the IP Office. There are several factors that make the mediability of the subject matter of administrative proceedings a complex issue. First, legal relations established under administrative law rules are traditionally characterized by the inequality of parties that participate in these relations. Second, negotiation after the administrative decision is being made can be legitimate only if the administrative body is authorized by law to amend its earlier decision. Otherwise, it would be contrary to the principle of substantive finality of administrative decisions. Third, many administrative matters affect the legal position of third parties that are not involved in the administrative procedure, which also limits the recourse to mediation. Fourth, even if an administrative authority enjoys discretionary powers in a specific situation, it should exercise its discretion in line with the principle of legitimate expectations. Consequently, all administrative authorities are obliged to act consistently, even when exercising their discretionary power, and to treat the same cases equally.[24]

Bearing in mind these general barriers to the use of mediation in resolving administrative matters, one may conclude that the mediability of the subject matter of administrative proceedings before the IP Office would largely depend on the nature of the subject matter. In case of a single-interest procedure (a relation between an administrative body and a party or parties with the same interest), mediation seems not to be suitable, for reasons of protection of the public interest. On the other hand, the subject-matter of a multi-interest procedure would in principle be mediable. For example, where the legislator makes a distinction between absolute and relative conditions for the recognition of an IP right, as it is the case under trademark and design protection rules, the disputes arising out of the (non-)fulfillment of the absolute conditions for protection would not be mediable. However, the disputes related to the fulfilment of relative conditions for protection could be solved by mediation.[25] The purpose of relative conditions is the protection of the interests of the parties. Indeed, even if during administrative proceedings before the IP Office it is established that a relative condition for protection is not fulfilled, a party may consent to registration. The same approach distinguishing single-interest and multi-interest

[22] Penal Code, Official Journal of the Republic of Serbia, no. 85/2005, 88/2005, 107/2005, 72/2009, 111/2009, 121/2012, 104/2013, 108/2014, 94/2016 i 35/2019, Art. 199. See also Arts. 198, 200–202.

[23] The 2014 Act on mediation, Art. 3.

[24] More on the barriers to the use of mediation in resolving administrative matter: Vučetić (2016), pp. 500–501.

[25] See also: Vujičić (2018), p. 109.

procedure is taken by the Intellectual Property Office of the European Union (hereinafter, the EUIPO). Under the EUIPO Mediation Rules, applicable to EU trademarks and Community designs, mediation may be requested at any time during *inter partes* proceedings before the Office.[26] The previous version of EUIPO Mediation Rules explicitly stated that mediation proceedings were not available in cases of absolute grounds for refusal in the sense of EU trademark rules and Community design rules.[27]

The second criterion for mediability of a dispute is the absence of exclusive authority of a court or other relevant entity. By interpreting this criterion *ratione materiae,* it seems that mediation is not suitable to replace the court proceedings which are initiated with the purpose of establishing the (non-)existence of an IP right. The same can be concluded with a view to administrative proceedings before the IP Office aiming at cancellation of a trademark for non-use of a protected sign, or any other proceedings before the IP Office in which an industrial property right may be recognized or terminated. These conclusions correspond to the views of the EU legislator. As prescribed by Directive 2008/52/EC on certain aspects of mediation in civil and commercial matters,[28] mediation shall apply to civil and commercial matters, except as regards rights and obligations which are not at the parties' disposal under the relevant applicable law.[29]

2.2 *Specific Reference to Mediation in Serbian IP Legislation*

The Serbian intellectual property legislation explicitly refers to mediation mechanisms in two cases only. First, the copyright legislation allows for a mediation mechanism to be employed if a broadcasting organization and a cable operator are unable to reach an agreement on cable retransmission conditions. Second, trademark legislation allows for the parties to trademark opposition proceedings to attempt to resolve the dispute by means of mediation within a time frame of 24 months.

Under the Copyright Act,[30] in case that the broadcasting organization and the cable operator do not reach an agreement on the conditions of cable retransmission of a broadcast, each interested party may call upon the assistance of one or more mediators.[31] If a mediator submits a proposal for resolving the dispute, it shall be assumed that interested parties have accepted the proposal of a mediator, unless within the period of three months from the day of the receipt of the proposal, they express

---

[26] EUIPO, Mediation Rules, Art. 2, para. 1. Available at: https://www.euipo.europa.eu/en/manage-ip/mediation-centre/resources.

[27] OHIM (now: EUIPO), Decision no 2013-3 of the Presidium of the Boards of Appeal of 5 July 2013 on the amicable settlement of disputes, Art. 1, para. 2.

[28] Official Journal of the European Union, L136, 24.5.2008.

[29] Directive on certain aspects of mediation in civil and commercial matters, Art. 1, para. 2.

[30] Official Journal of the Republic of Serbia, no. 104/2009, 99/2011, 119/2012, 29/2016 and 66/2019.

[31] Copyright Act, Art. 29.

its opposition in a written form.[32] Such mediation procedure shall be conducted in accordance with the general mediation rules (i.e. the Act on mediation). These provisions of the Copyright Act are aligned with Directive 93/83/EEC on the coordination of certain rules concerning copyright and rights related to copyright applicable to satellite broadcasting and cable retransmission (hereinafter, the Directive on satellite broadcasting and cable retransmission).[33] The Directive on satellite broadcasting and cable retransmission specifically indicates that the task of the mediators is to provide assistance with negotiation, and that they may submit proposals to the parties.[34] In contrast, the mediators are not authorized to impose binding solutions to the parties. When a mediator submits a proposal for an agreement, the parties have to express their opposition to the proposal within a three-months deadline, if they do not want it to become binding. This motivates the parties to express their negotiation positions clearly, and contributes to the transparency of negotiations.[35] The Directive on satellite broadcasting and cable retransmission permits the inclusion of one or more independent and impartial arbitrators in the process of negotiations between the parties. In case of inclusion of more than one mediator, the literal interpretation of the requirement of independence and impartiality seems to speak in favour of the impartiality of each of the mediators, as opposed to the impartiality of the board of mediators as a whole. However, such interpretation would limit the discretion of the parties to shape the mediation procedure.[36] Typically, the parties would each propose a mediator, and in the second stage the proposed mediators would then appoint an additional one or more mediators. In the report published several years after the entry into force of the Directive, the European Commission noted that this approach is liable to remain little used in the absence of mandatory recourse to a mediation system.[37] In the mediation context, it is the good faith of the parties to the dispute that determines whether the process runs its course satisfactorily and leads, within a reasonable timeframe, to a solution accepted by the two parties.[38] The same conclusion is still valid, both for the European Union and the Republic of Serbia.

The second explicit reference to mediation mechanisms in Serbian IP legislation was made in the Trademark Act,[39] in connection with the opposition procedure. Under the Trademark Act, a trademark applicant and a person lodging the notice of opposition, by means of the request mutually signed, and submitted during the course of the opposition procedure, may require the competent authority to withhold the procedure for 24 months, at the most, in order to attempt to peacefully settle

---

[32] Ibid.

[33] Official Journal of the European Communities, L248, 6.10.1993.

[34] Directive on satellite broadcasting and cable retransmission, Art. 11, para 2.

[35] Walter and Von Lewinski (2010), p. 461.

[36] Ibid.

[37] Report from the European Commission on the application of Council Directive 93/83/EEC on the coordination of certain rules concerning copyright and rights related to copyright applicable to satellite broadcasting and cable retransmission, COM(2002) 430 final, Sect. 3.1.3.

[38] Ibid.

[39] Official Journal of the Republic of Serbia, no. 6/2020.

the dispute. If, within the time limit of 24 months, the trademark applicant and the person filing the opposition, inform the competent authority on the peaceful dispute resolution, and on the fact that the party has withdrawn the opposition request, the competent authority shall suspend the opposition proceedings.[40] The possibility for the parties to opposition proceedings to recourse to mediation is introduced into the Serbian Trademark Act in order to align its provisions with Art. 43 of Directive 2015/2436 to approximate the laws of the Member States relating to trade marks.[41]

3 Factors Influencing the Choice of Mediation Over Litigation in IP Matters

As an alternative dispute resolution mechanism, mediation is a voluntary process from which both the parties and the mediator are always free to withdraw. The parties must recognize their interest in resolving the dispute by means of mediation. Therefore, they must correctly assess the advantages and disadvantages of this alternative dispute resolution mechanism. The parties must take into consideration the characteristics of the mediation procedure they are considering of choosing. Indeed, there are different mediation "styles" – facilitative mediation, evaluative mediation and transformative mediation.[42] The facilitative mediation style focuses on the mediator's role as a mere facilitator of the parties' negotiations by, *inter alia*, re-opening blocked communication chanells and structuring the parties' negotiations. The evaluative mediation style consists in a more "substance-oriented approach" – the mediator evaluates the validity of each party's position, and provides his/her opinion and advice to the parties. Finally, the transformative mediation style consists in a "relationship-oriented approach". The mediator aims not only at resolving the current dispute, but also at improving the future relationship between the parties.

The parties are more inclined to choose mediation as a dispute resolution mechanism if they are involved in a long-term commercial relationship. Also, the mediation is most likely to succeed in such a situation, since the parties will make additional efforts to preserve their business ties. Intellectual property disputes are particularly illustrative in this respect: the parties are typically present in markets with a limited number of participants (publishers, producers, etc.); therefore, they will prioritize dispute resolution over dispute escalation. However, if a dispute has already escalated, this may exclude any possibility of mediation. Also, one of the parties in dispute may wish to initate court proceedings in order to demonstrate to third parties that the behaviour of its collaborator is unacceptable. In such a situation, a complainant may choose litigation over mediation, as a dissuasive strategy.

---

[40] Trademark Act, Art. 37.

[41] Official Journal of the European Union, L336, 23.12.2015.

[42] Berger (2009), pp. 248–251.

The type of IP dispute may significantly influence the parties' choice of mediation over litigation. The legal doctrine[43] differentiates between three basic types of intellectual property disputes. The first category consists of disputes in which the complainant requires to assert their ownership of an intellectual property right and wishes to benefit economically from that right. The second category relates to a situation where one or both parties wish to settle a point of law. The third category consists of disputes where the parties consider some form of shared rights to be an acceptable result. In disputes belonging to the first and the second category, the complainant is not interested in licensing arrangements. For example, disputes regarding the alleged illegal downloading of material from the Internet are unlikely to be suitable for mediation. In this type of dispute, the music industry is not interested in entering into any kind of agreement with the infringer. Instead, it wishes to assert its ownership of the intellectual property and to stop the alleged infringement.[44] The second category of disputes, which concern the validity of an industrial property right or the existence of a copyrighted work, is also unsuitable for mediation. It is a predominant view that only the IP disputes belonging to the third category, where the parties consider some form of shared rights to be an acceptable result, are suitable for mediation.

The complexity of a dispute may contribute to the party's preference for mediation over litigation. Indeed, IP disputes may typically include several interested parties, several (interconnected) rights and obligations in relation to one or more subject matters of protection, or involve several jurisdictions (e.g. a franchising agreement). Complex disputes lead to lengthy court proceedings involving high cost for the parties, which is why they may try to resolve the contention through mediation instead. It is also worth noting that the mediation process is more likely to succeed should the parties be of equal or similar strength. This relates not only to the economic strength of the parties, but also to the absence of any subordinate relations. In case of significant imbalance between the parties, it may not be useful to opt for mediation procedure, since the interests of the "weaker" party may be jeopardized. In such a situation, mediation would not be appropriate from the public interest perspective, either. For example, a dispute between two parties of "equal arms" – a musician and an individual who is alleged to have illegally downloaded the musician's copyright work is more suitable for mediation than a dispute between a music publishing company and an individual.[45]

The main advantage of mediation over "traditional" court proceedings may be found in its voluntary and informal character. The mediation procedure is based on the express consent of the parties, apart from disputes wherein instituting mediation proceedings is envisaged by a separate law as a condition for conducting court or other proceedings. The parties may freely reach an agreement on the manner of conducting mediation, still within the framework set by the imperative provisions of the 2014 Act on mediation and other acts. As prescribed under the 2014 Act on

[43] See for example: Corbet (2011), pp. 65–67.

[44] Ibid.

[45] Corbet (2011), p. 66.

mediation, a mediator shall conduct the procedure in a manner he/she finds appropriate, taking into account the proposals of the parties, circumstances of the case and the need for prompt dispute resolution.[46] The parties may choose the timeframe and rules for initiating mediation proceedings, the procedural phases, the termination of proceedings, or the criteria which the mediator must satisfy. Typically, a mediation would consist of a preparatory phase, opening of proceedings, investigatory phase, negotiations, and termination of mediation. Since the mediation has voluntary character, any party can renounce from it, at any procedural phase, and opt for another type of dispute resolution mechanism.[47] Given the complexity of intellectual property disputes, which may involve more than one disputed issue (e.g. disputes stemming from a licensing agreement), the parties may give preference to mediation over litigation, as this would allow them to resolve all disputed issues within one single proceeding. Moreover, the informal and voluntary character of mediation facilitates the resolution of disputes with a foreign element: (i) disputes where the parties at the time of reaching an agreement for mediation have a domicile or corporate headquarters in different states; or (ii) disputes in which the state wherein the parties have domicile or corporate headquarters is not the state wherein significant part of the obligations from the commercial relationship needs to be performed.[48] Also, the characteristics of mediation facilitate the process of presenting the evidence. As a rule, in a mediation proceeding the presentation of evidence may be allowed only to a limited extent, while the focus of this ADR mechanism remains on negotiations between the parties. Finally, the voluntary character of mediation leads to a consensual outcome, which is accepted by all parties. This is why the outcome of a mediation is frequently described as a "win–win situation"' Contrary to mediation, court proceedings end with a decision which cannot be influenced by the parties and which would typically be to the detriment of one of them. Indeed, court proceedings would typically aggravate the relationship between the parties, while mediation would, given its consensual character, improve the quality of relations or, at least, leave it intact.

From the parties' perspective, mediation is a time-saving mechanism given that it is conducted in an expedited procedure. The Serbian legislator explicitly prescribes that the mediation is conducted without delay, in the shortest time possible.[49] The mediation is terminated upon expiry of 60 days from the date of conclusion of the agreement to undertake mediation, unless otherwise agreed by the parties.[50] However, court proceedings for infringement of intellectual property rights are also conducted in an expedited procedure.[51] Still, the court proceedings tend to last longer than envisaged by the legislator, due to judges' work overload and the complexities of evidence presentation. Moreover, first instance court decisions are frequently being

[46] The 2014 Act on mediation, Art. 9, para. 5.

[47] The 2014 Act on mediation, Art. 23, para. 4.

[48] The 2014 Act on mediation, Art. 5.

[49] The 2014 Act on mediation, Art. 15.

[50] The 2014 Act on mediation, Art. 24, para. 1.

[51] For copyright infringements, see: Copyright Act, Art. 207, para. 2.

appealed before the higher court. The length of procedure is particularly important when deciding on intellectual property disputes, since most IP rights, with the exception of trademarks and designations of geographical origin, have limited duration.[52] Also, intellectual property rights are typically related to innovative products and services, so there is a clear right owner's interest to be able to commercialize them as soon as possible. Further to being time efficient, mediation is a cost-saving procedure. Under the 2014 Act on mediation, each party bears its own costs, and common costs shall be borne in equal shares, unless agreed otherwise. The common mediation costs include a reward for work of the mediator and reimbursement of costs that the mediator has incurred in relation to the mediation procedure. The amount of the reward for work and the amount of costs to be reimbursed are determined according to the pricelist on rewards and reimbursements in mediation procedure, adopted by the Minister of Justice, unless otherwise agreed by the parties.[53] On the other hand, in court proceedings the costs are typically borne by one of the parties, and may include the court fee, cost of representation, cost of expert opinions, etc.

Resolving intellectual property disputes may require specialized knowledge. If the dispute pertains to copyright, the judge may need to have specialized "industry knowledge" on book publishing, music or film industry, for example. In case of a patent dispute, the judge would need to understand the complex nature of a patented invention, for example in the biotechnology sector. Typically, the judges would need to rely on expert opinions in order to properly understand the disputed matter and reach a correct decision. Contrary to court proceedings, in mediation the parties are able to directly appoint as mediator a person already possessing specialized knowledge in relation to the disputed issue. This would not only guarantee substantial quality of the mediation procedure but also decrease related costs. However, the Serbian legislator does not leave complete latitude to the parties when selecting the mediator. In order to carry out tasks of a mediator, a person must fulfil the following requirements: (i) possess legal capacity; (ii) be a citizen of the Republic of Serbia; (iii) have completed basic training for a mediator; (iv) have a university degree; (v) not have been sentenced to unconditional imprisonment for a criminal offence deeming him/her unworthy to conduct the tasks of mediation; (vi) have a permit for mediation; (vii) be enlisted in the Register of mediators.[54] It is regretful that the legislator prescribed these additional requirements, given that no such conditions are imposed onto arbitrators in arbitration proceedings. It may happen that the parties have selected a person possessing specialized knowledge in the disputed matter, but are unable to appoint him/her as mediator merely because of the fact that he/she is not listed in the Register of mediators. In international mediation and mediation in cross-border disputes, a foreign citizen may also be appointed as a mediator, provided that he/she is authorized to conduct mediation in another state, under the condition

---

[52] This is particularly relevant for industrial property rights.

[53] The 2014 Act on mediation, Art. 29.

[54] The 2014 Act on mediation, Art. 33.

of reciprocity. A citizen of the European Union may also be a mediator, provided that he/she is authorized to conduct mediation in an EU Member State.[55]

Finally, one of the substantial advantages of mediation over litigation consists in its confidential character. All information, proposals and statements made during the mediation procedure or related to mediation are confidential, unless otherwise agreed by the parties, except for those that must be communicated pursuant to law, for reasons of protection of public order, particularly where this is necessary to ensure protection of the best interests of a child or to prevent harm to a person's physical or psychological integrity, as well as in the event that it is necessary for implementation of the agreement of the parties.[56] The parties, their legal representatives and proxies, mediator, third parties attending the mediation procedure, as well as persons performing administrative tasks for the purposes of mediation, are obliged to keep secret all information, proposals and statements related to the mediation proceedings.[57] These persons are also liable for the damage resulting from a breach of the confidentiality obligation. The confidential character of mediation may incite the parties to freely state their respective positions, as the proposals made during mediation proceedings cannot be subsequently referred to in other proceedings before the court or arbitration tribunal, nor be made public in any manner whatsoever. This is particularly important for the parties involved in intellectual property disputes, since the mediation rules would allow them to shield themselves from (potential) negative publicity, as well as to protect their business secrets.

4 Concluding Remarks

Although the mediation mechanisms were introduced in Serbian law, and more specifically Serbian IP law, with strong support from all relevant stakeholders, the actual use of these alternative dispute resolution mechanisms in practice remains exceptional. It seems that the parties refrain from using this new and not well known dispute resolution mechanism from fear of abuse, which may be facilitated by the informal and confidential character of mediation. The potential abuse could be the act of a mediator or of one of the parties. The mediator could violate the principle of impartiality and act in the interest of one of the parties.[58] A party, on the other hand, could engage in the mediation only for reasons of delaying the upcoming court proceedings and/or learning about the weaknesses of the other party. The legislator did set a framework for preventing and sanctioning of such behaviour, by prescribing that: (i) the mediator shall be recused from a mediation procedure wherein he/she

[55] Ibid.

[56] The 2014 Act on mediation, Art. 13.

[57] Ibid.

[58] The use of AI-based technologies could potentially help us overcome this risk, provided that we resolve the problem of bias stemming from training of AI systems. For a more detailed analysis on the use of AI-based technologies in ADR mechanisms, see: Menkel-Meadow (2018), pp. 1–20.

has personal interest or if for any other reason he/she is unable to act impartially; (ii) a judge or a person deciding in an administrative proceeding cannot be appointed as mediator in relation to the same dispute; (iii) the mediator is liable for any damage caused to the parties by acting contrary to the Code of ethics, by his/her unlawful conduct, intentionally or through gross negligence; (iv) a mediation permit is revoked if it is established that the mediator failed to comply with the rules of procedure.[59] Still, we are of the view that the risk of abuse does not prevail over the advantages of mediation, as presented in this chapter. Nevertheless, mediation will only be successful if the parties correctly assess the probability of resolving a dispute through this type of dispute resolution mechanism.

References

Berger KP (2009) Private dispute resolution in international business. Kluwer Law International, Alphen aan den Rijn

Bühring-Uhle C (2006) Arbitration and mediation in international business. Kluwer Law International, Alphen aan den Rijn

Corbet SF (2011) Mediation of intellectual property disputes: a critical analysis. N Z Bus Law Q 17(1):51–67

De Werra J (2012) Can alternative dispute resolution mechanisms become the default method for solving international intellectual property disputes? Calif West Int Law J 43(1):39–45

Menkel-Meadow C (2018) Mediation 3.0: merging the old and the new. Asian J Mediat 1–20

Milutinović L (2006) Sud ili medijacija (court or mediation). International Finance Corporation Private Enterprise Partnership Southeast Europe, Belgrade

Vujičić N (2018) Medijacija kao metod rešavanja sporova iz oblasti intelektualne svojine: (ne)realna očekivanja (Mediation as a method for resolution of intellectual property disputes: (un)realistic expectations). Pravo i Privreda 7–9:103–124

Vučetić D (2016) Is mediation viable in administrative matters? Facta Univ 4(14):495–504

Wallgren C (2006) ADR and business. In: Goldsmith JC, Ingen-Housz A, Pointon GH (eds) ADR in business. Practice and Issues across countries and cultures. Kluwer Law International, Alphen aan den Rijn, pp 3–20

Walter MM, Von Lewinski S (2010) European copyright law: a commentary. Oxford University Press, Oxford

[59] The 2014 Act on mediation, Arts. 21, 22, 35 and 39.

Exploring the New Croatian Mediation Framework: A Leap Forward or a Setback?

Juraj Brozović

Abstract In 2023, Croatia enacted the new Amicable Dispute Resolution Act, aimed at providing a new framework for mediation, negotiation, and similar non-adjudicative amicable dispute resolution methods. Despite its ambitions, the changes were not fully implemented, and the new framework has not been unanimously welcomed by the mediation community. The new legislation causes some concerns, as some of the new inadvertent provisions are unclear, or leave dangerous legal gaps leading to uncertainty, with a negative impact on the further expansion of mediation. This chapter offers a critical overview of these changes.

1 Introduction

Although mediation is often considered an autonomous dispute resolution method that more effectively satisfies clients' interests than any form of adjudication,[1] the development of the mediation framework in Croatia has been predominantly viewed through the lens of judicial efficiency.

The first Mediation Act of 2003 (hereinafter: MA 03')[2] was, along with the Arbitration Act of 2001 and the Civil Procedure Act (hereinafter: CPA)[3] Amendments of 2003, a part of a legislative package addressing court backlogs.[4] Even though it was influenced by early recommendations by the Council of Europe and the European Commission, as well as the UNCITRAL Model Law on International Commercial Conciliation of 2002, it still remained somewhat conservative and sceptical towards

[1] Nolan-Haley (2021), p. 155.

[2] OJ, no. 163/2003, 79/2009.

[3] OJ, no. 53/1991, 91/1992, 112/1999, 129/2000, 88/2001, 117/2003, 88/2005, 2/2007, 96/2008, 84/2008, 123/2008, 57/2011, 25/2013, 89/2014, 70/2019, 80/2022, 114/2022, 155/2023.

[4] Uzelac et al. (2004), p. 34, Šimac (2013), p. 5.

J. Brozović (✉)
Department for Civil Procedure, Faculty of Law, University of Zagreb, Zagreb, Croatia
e-mail: juraj.brozovic@pravo.unizg.hr

M. Bungenberg et al. (eds.), *Alternative Dispute Resolution in the Western Balkans*, European Union and its Neighbours in a Globalized World 20,
https://doi.org/10.1007/978-3-031-76345-8_15

the wider use of mediation.[5] The MA 03' was amended in 2009, as a measure to implement Directive 2008/52/EC of the European Parliament and of the Council of 21 May 2008 on certain aspects of mediation in civil and commercial matters (hereinafter: Directive).[6] Two years later, the completely new Mediation Act (hereinafter: MA 11')[7] made further adjustments to implement the Directive. It widened the types of cases that can be mediated and also served as a basis for mediation proceedings regulated by special laws, including court-annexed mediation, previously introduced to the CPA.[8] The need for such amendment was evident because, within the first decade of the implementation of the MA 03', there were multiple concurrent mediation tracks influencing outlooks for the further development of mediation.[9]

The flexibility of the statutory provisions allowed ample room for the mediation initiative to flourish. However, as the second decade drew to a close, the statistics failed to justify the expectations. The precise information on the number of mediations carried out in private remained unknown,[10] while it was estimated that parties in only 0.6% of cases resort to court-annexed mediation.[11] This led the Government to the conclusion that further adjustments to the mediation framework were necessary, coinciding with the imperative to plan investments and reforms under the Recovery and Resilience Mechanism as the European Union's response to the economic repercussion of the coronavirus outbreak.

In the National Recovery and Resilience Plan (hereinafter: NRRP) of 2021,[12] the Government envisaged the establishment of a new Centre for mediation, which was supposed to be in charge of mediation (most likely instead of courts) and accrediting of private mediation centres and mediators.[13] When the working group was established in January 2022 to draft the amendments, no one in the mediation community actually considered them necessary. However, the mandate of the working group was set in stone by the NRRP, and the Ministry of Justice (hereinafter: Ministry) made it clear from the outset which adjustments were non-negotiable.[14]

In order to make sense out of such a mandated, but simultaneously clearly unrequired reform attempt, an initiative was born on the part of the working group to

---

[5] Uzelac et al. (2004), pp. 34–36.

[6] OJ L 136, 24.5.2008, pp. 3–8.

[7] OJ, no. 18/2011.

[8] Arts 186.d–186.e CPA.

[9] Triva and Dika (2004), p. 923. Many of those were state-run (e.g. family mediation) or quasi-state run (e.g. consumer ADR). Uzelac et al. (2010), pp. 1304–1306.

[10] Šimunović (2023), pp. 109–110.

[11] NRRP (2021), p. 727.

[12] It is accessible at (Croatian only): https://planoporavka.gov.hr/UserDocsImages/dokumenti/Plan%20oporavka%20i%20otpornosti%2C%20srpanj%202021..pdf?vel=13435491.

[13] NRRP (2023), p. 728.

[14] Uzelac and Brozović (2023), p. 2.

use this opportunity to introduce a broader Amicable Dispute Resolution Act (hereinafter: ADRA)[15] which would, similarly to recent Montenegrin counterpart,[16] lay down the rules not only for mediation but also for some new amicable dispute resolution (hereinafter: ADR) methods, such as structured negotiations and early neutral evaluation. Drawing inspiration from the Belgian *Commission fédérale de mediation* (hereinafter: Belgian *Commission*),[17] the national Centre for ADR (hereinafter: CADR) could act as a main promotor and coordinator of ADR activities in Croatia.[18] The suggestions seemed to have been accepted by the Ministry and the ADRA drafting process started. The circumstances of its drafting, however, could at the very least be described as chaotic. Despite the initial rush, the Ministry ceased the drafting activities for months and eventually—when it simply ran out of time—unilaterally intervened in the text, without having any serious debate in the working group about any of the solutions. Ideas about introducing new methods, such as early neutral evaluation, were mostly dropped, the CADR's role was only partially accepted, and there were some not well-thought-out amendments to the existing rules on mediation. Now neither the mediation community nor the persons who drafted the initial draft are satisfied with the end result.[19]

The comprehensive critique of the ADRA and its drafting, also highlighting the lost opportunities, has already been published somewhere else.[20] In contrast, the purpose of this chapter is to critically assess only the most important adaptations made to the mediation framework. After outlining the new features of the mediation legislation, this chapter focuses on three specific sets of amendments intended to facilitate the use of mediation, which, according to the author's view, instead of achieving this goal, result in a complete reversal, maintaining the status quo or even exacerbating existing problems.

2 The Reform in Brief: An Outline of the Changes

While the ADRA was envisioned as a comprehensive framework act governing all forms of ADR, the majority of its provisions are slightly modified versions of those found in the former MA 11' or regulations derived from it. However, the institutional aspect is notably more extensively regulated, and a devoted section regulating the relationship between ADR attempts and court proceedings has been introduced.

Both the MA 03' and the MA 11' entrusted the Ministry of Justice to be in charge of the support and coordination of mediation activities in Croatia. It was assessed,

[15] OJ, no. 67/2003.

[16] Uzelac and Brozović (2023), p. 5.

[17] More information about the Belgian *Commission* is available at: https://www.cfm-fbc.be/fr.

[18] Uzelac and Brozović (2023), p. 3.

[19] Uzelac and Brozović (2023), p. 2.

[20] Uzelac and Brozović (2023).

and rightfully so, that the Ministry did not consistently assume this role,[21] so many of the coordinating and regulatory activities were taken by the new CADR, established by the ADRA. In the final iteration, its responsibilities can be categorized into three distinct groups (Art. 6 ADRA):

- Support and promotion of ADR: coordination of cooperation between different courts, state bodies, and private mediation institutions; publication of the information on available ADR proceedings.
- Regulatory activities: registration and accreditation of mediators, trainers, and private mediation centres; independent training or in collaboration with accredited training centres; issuance of mandatory information and mediation meeting certificates.
- Provision of ADR services: mediation and mandatory informative mediation meetings when other mediation institutions cannot provide such service in a timely and costly manner.

Unlike before, the general standards for the accreditation of mediators, trainers, and mediation centres are now established by law, although they are still elaborated in more detail in the regulation (Art. 7–8 ADRA). These standards directly influence the eligibility for accreditation as a mediator, highlighting the central role of the CADR. This change is not only a matter of pride or a private sense of professional responsibility. Instead, it has significant implications. Now, only accredited individuals are recognized as mediators, a change that also impacts the definition of mediation itself. Only mediation carried out by mediators, as defined in the ADRA, is officially considered mediation (Art. 4 para. 1 ADRA).

Another novelty is the introduction of a new chapter regulating the parties' pre-commencement procedural obligation to attempt ADR (Art. 9–10 ADRA). Initially, it was intended to be an extension of the principle of loyal cooperation of judges, parties, and lawyers, in all types of litigation. The circumstances of ADRA drafting, however, led to considerable limitations of that duty, restricting it solely to employment-unrelated damages claims.[22] The pre-commencement duty entails the obligation to negotiate or conduct mediation if requested by one party, which can be refused only in case of justified reasons (Art. 9 ADRA). Failure to comply results in a brief factual pause in the process and referral to the mediation information meeting (hereinafter: MIM), while further non-compliance is not regulated (Art. 9 ADRA).

The provisions, that regulate mediation proceedings, are almost a verbatim version of the rules contained in the MA 11' with a few departures from the previous regime:

- A new terminology was introduced and used throughout the ADRA: mediation (*'medijacija'*) instead of conciliation (*'mirenje'*) and mediator (*'medijator'*) instead of conciliator (*'izmiritelj'*).
- The possible contents of the mediation agreement and corresponding proposal to mediate are now expressly laid down in the law (Art. 13 ADRA).

---

[21] Šimunović (2023), p. 117. Braut Filipović et al. (2024), p. 171.

[22] Uzelac and Brozović (2023), 9–10.

- The mediator is now explicitly mentioned as the party signing the settlement agreement (Art. 19 para. 1 subpar. 4 ADRA).
- The mediator has to inform the CADR about the outcome and duration of the mediation (Art. 19 para. 2 ADRA).
- Mediation proceedings suspend limitation periods instead of interrupting them (Art. 24 ADRA).
- The costs of the mediation attempt and the participation in the MIM are explicitly included in the costs of subsequent litigation (Art. 26 para. 2 ADRA).
- The definition of the residence for the purpose of defining cross-border mediation was aligned with the definition used in the Brussels I bis Regulation (Art. 27 para. 6 ADRA).
- The enforcement of an international settlement agreement may be refused by the court on the grounds moderately inspired by Art. 19 UNCITRAL Model Law on International Commercial Mediation and International Settlement Agreements Resulting from Mediation[23] and even more closely by Art. 5 Singapore Convention on International Settlement Agreements Resulting from Mediation[24] (Art. 28 ADRA).

From this brief overview, it appears that the main objective of the ADRA was to centralize the system and enable better coordination of different ADR activities, while also aiming to formalize and affirm the mediation profession and encourage the preference for mediation over resorting to courts. In the subsequent chapters, we will explore whether these objectives were indeed achieved.

3 ADR Coordination and Promotion

3.1 All Parallel Mediation Tracks Under One Umbrella?

From the very beginning and the first proposal, the ADRA was conceived as the overarching framework in the field of ADR aimed at bringing order to the fragmented system where multiple parallel mediation tracks exist.[25] The general subsidiarity rule was thus introduced, prescribing that the ADRA would apply *mutatis mutandis* to ADR proceedings regulated by special laws to the extent not provided otherwise (Art. 1 para. 2 ADRA). In theory, this presented an opportunity to establish a comprehensive framework, which could be applied in all mediation tracks: mediation at private centres, court-annexed mediation, family mediation, consumer mediation, and employment mediation. However, the drafting process of the ADRA hindered the

[23] The text is available at: https://uncitral.un.org/sites/uncitral.un.org/files/media-documents/uncitral/en/22-01363_mediation_guide_e_ebook_rev.pdf.

[24] The text is available at: https://uncitral.un.org/sites/uncitral.un.org/files/singapore_convention_eng.pdf.

[25] Uzelac and Brozović (2022), pp. 1–2.

discussion and full implementation of that idea. On top of that, last-minute unilateral changes worsened the lack of coordination among the tracks.

For instance, when mediation institutions were defined in MA 11', they were described as a legal entity, body of a legal entity, or organizational unit of a legal entity that organizes and conducts mediation (Art. 3 MA 11'). However, the last-minute change resulted in a provision, which no longer mentions the organizational units as potential mediation providers (Art. 4 ADRA). Such a fundamental shift raises several issues. Does this revised definition imply that the ADRA is not applicable to court-annexed mediation since it is carried out by organizational units? Does at least the procedural part of the ADRA apply, whereas institutional aspects are reserved for private mediation centres only? If so, what are the qualifications needed to become a mediator who can enter the list of mediators determined by the president of each court (Art. 186.d para. 3 CPA) and carry out court-annexed mediation? So many questions are raised and can be solved only by careful interpretation of the new provisions.

The general subsidiarity rule, mentioned above, offers limited guidance on these matters. However, concluding that court-annexed mediation is not mediation within the meaning of the ADRA seems unacceptable. After all, the possibility of carrying out mediation in courts is implicitly mentioned in other provisions (Art. 3 para. 2 and Art. 4 ADRA). It is truly inconceivable that certain general principles, such as confidentiality, neutrality, or party control (Art. 5 ADRA), would not apply to such mediation.[26] It would also be unreasonable to conclude that the rules regarding the initiation (Art. 13 ADRA), conduct (Art. 16–18 ADRA), and conclusion of proceedings (Art. 19 ADRA) do not equally apply to court-annexed mediation.

There seems to be no compelling reason, on the other hand, to conclude that the rule laying down consequences of a pending mediation (Art. 24 CPA) should also apply here. If the claimant has already submitted its claim, thereby initiating court or arbitral proceedings, it has already interrupted the limitation period and submitted the claim in a timely manner (Art. 241 Obligations Act), so there is no deadline left to be suspended after the mediation has started. Likewise, there is no need to apply the enforceability rules (Art. 20 ADRA), as the settlement agreements reached in court-annexed mediation are concluded in the form of a court settlement (Art. 186.d para. 7 CPA) which is already an enforceable title (Art. 23 Enforcement Act).[27]

Whether the institutional rules of the ADRA will apply to court-annexed mediation is yet to be seen in practice, but from the wording of the provisions and current practice, it would seem that the answer would most likely be negative. The official statistics show that the courts do not inform the CADR about the duration and outcome of proceedings as specifically required from private mediation centres (Art. 7 para 8 and 19 para. 2 ADRA). The fact that all judges and judicial advisors, who

---

[26] This should also apply to the rules derived from those principles, such as the rule on the nomination (Art. 14 ADRA), the removal of mediators (Art. 15 ADRA), the consequences of breach of confidentiality (Art. 21 ADRA) or the admissibility of evidence in other proceedings (Art. 22 ADRA). The rule specifying that the mediator is nominated by the CADR in the absence of a consensual proposal from the parties (Art. 14 para. 3 ADRA) should not be applied, as the case allocation would, just like any other court case, be carried out randomly by the ICMS.

[27] OJ, no. 112/2012, 25/2013, 93/2014, 55/16, 73/2017, 131/2020, 114/2022, 06/2024.

are already registered, are now considered mediators regardless of their previous training,[28] raises concerns about the issue of qualifications for the future. It would certainly be commendable, if not implicitly required, for the new court mediators to also undergo basic training just like anyone else pursuing a mediation career.

A somewhat distinct set of challenges arises in the context of family mediation as another concurrent mediation track. The new definition of mediator and mediator providers (Art. 4 ADRA) appears to have left further exacerbated the longstanding dilemma that emerged with the official introduction of family mediation in the Family Act (hereinafter: FA)[29] back in 2014. According to the FA, family mediation can only be conducted by a mediator listed in the official family mediator registry, who must undergo specific training (Art. 341–342 FA). This training significantly differs from the basic 40-h training with an exam required to enter the CADR's registry. It entails either specialized postgraduate studies or a minimum of 140 h of education, 40 h of supervised practice, and 20 h of supervision after having 2 years of experience working with children. In the literature, it has already been noted that these special provisions apply only to free mediation schemes within social work networks, whereas the same service can be provided by private centres and courts.[30] Once more, the only coherent interpretation appears to be that only the procedural aspects of the ADRA apply to family mediation, to the extent they are not already covered by the FA,[31] while institutional rules are sufficiently regulated by the FA and the corresponding regulations.

Employment mediation partly shares the same issues as family mediation, depending on its type. According to the Labour Act (hereinafter: LA),[32] in collective employment cases, where mediation attempt is mandatory (Art. 205 LA), the mediation is carried out by mediators on the special list published by the Economic-Social Council (Art. 206 LA). The Economic-Social Council is a separate three-partite body consisted of the representatives of the Government, unions, and employers' associations, with the task of promoting labour rights and balanced relationship between employers and employees (Art. 221 LA). It introduced special rules on the appointment of mediators and their remuneration, partly departing from the solutions in the MA 11' and now the ADRA.[33] This would mean that both institutional and procedural rules of the ADRA are not applicable to collective mediation cases, providing there are special rules laid down in the LA and its regulations. When individual employment disputes are in question, they depend solely on the parties agreement (Art. 136 LA), which puts in the arena of general rules.[34] Both institutional and procedural rules of the ADRA equally apply to these disputes.

---

[28] Art 11 Regulation on registry of mediators (OJ, no. 100/2023).

[29] OJ, no. 103/2015, 98/2019, 47/2020, 49/2023, 156/2023.

[30] Aras Kramar (2017), p. 311.

[31] Such is the case with impartiality and confidentiality which do not apply when the interest of children are affected (Art. 335 and 339 FA).

[32] OJ, no. 9320/14, 127/2017, 98/2019, 151/2022, 46/2023, 64/2023.

[33] They are published on the website https://gsv.socijalno-partnerstvo.hr/nacionalni-gsv/mirenje.

[34] Uzelac et al. (2010), p. 1291.

The least coordination was needed in regard to consumer mediation. In its introductory provisions, the ADRA explicitly stated that it represents the measure to implement Directive 2013/11/EU of the European Parliament and of the Council of 21 May 2013 on alternative dispute resolution for consumer disputes and amending Regulation (EC) No 2006/2004 and Directive 2009/22/EC.[35] However, this statement is merely declaratory, as the Directive had already been implemented through the Consumer Alternative Dispute Resolution Act in 2016, which also clarified that it does not affect the applicability of the general mediation framework (Art. 5). Even in the absence of these circular provisions, very few rules in the Consumer Alternative Dispute Resolution Act could be deemed incompatible with the general rules. Therefore, we can confidently conclude that both the institutional and procedural rules of the ADRA are applicable in the case of consumer mediation.

3.2 The CADR as the Facilitator of ADR?

The CADR was established in July 2023 following the issuance of a formal decision by the Ministry of Justice (hereinafter: Decision),[36] as mandated by law (Art. 7 ADRA). Contrary to the initial proposal, which sought to mimic the organizational model of the Belgian *Commission*, ensuring institutional and professional independence from the Ministry through several professional bodies,[37] the Decision outlined a simpler structure for the CADR. This structure includes one director and a board comprising five members, four of whom are representatives of the Ministry (Art. 8–9 Decision). Funding for its activities is primarily planned to come from the state budget, supplemented by a smaller contribution from its own income, which includes fees from training, mediation, and other services (Art. 12 Decision).

This is the main reason why the CADR has not had the opportunity to assume the role entrusted to it by the ADRA. In its initial months, the CADR lacked both premises and equipment to carry out its basic activities. However, in 2024, with improved budget planning, the CADR acquired temporary premises and expanded its personnel, in preparation for its move to new facilities planned for construction in 2026.[38] Alongside the director, it now employs a total of 14 staff members. Budget planning reveals that a significant portion of the modest budget, 87.5%, is allocated to gross salaries and other employee expenses and fees.[39] Despite the management's pro-mediation stance and understanding of the CADR's mission, without adequate support, all these legislative efforts may be in vain.

It is evident that certain activities, such as conducting mediation or organizing basic and advanced training, are not feasible at this moment due to a lack of adequate

[35] OJ L 165, 18.6.2013, p. 63–79.

[36] Decision of 24 July 2023, class 700-03/23-02/39, no. 514-03-02-01/01/01-23-20.

[37] Uzelac and Brozović (2023), p. 8.

[38] NRRP (2021), p. 750.

[39] The budget is published on the CADR's website: https://cmrs.hr/dokumenti2/.

space and personnel. Consequently, mediation is conducted in private centres, five of which are accredited to provide basic training and/or training of trainers. The registry indicates that over the years, most mediators (55.49%) received their basic training at the most active mediation institution, the Croatian Mediation Association (hereinafter: CMA), while the remainder trained through various projects or individual initiatives. In 2023, the CMA accounted for 86.75% of the training, and the Centre for mediation "Mediator" for 8.61%, illustrating that training is currently primarily conducted by these two private centres, with the CADR only providing accreditation.

The registry of mediators, mentioned above, along with the registry of private mediation centres is an example of one modest but positive change brought about by the introduction of the CADR. Previously, those registries were mismanaged by the Ministry, rarely updated, rendering them ineffective. New information seems to be regularly updated on the CADR's website.[40] Another novelty, introduced by the ADRA, seems to be yielding the first results. Although the obligation to report on the number, duration, and outcome of mediations was already present in the Consumer Alternative Dispute Resolution Act, this obligation has never been taken seriously.[41] Opposed to that, the CADR is effectively required to collect data on mediations carried out in all private mediation centres (Art. 6 para. 1 ADRA).

The CADR's statistics[42] for the second half of 2023 reveal that many, albeit not all, private mediation centres submitted data, though the quality of data varies. Some centres provided detailed information on case types, referral sources, and outcomes, while others provided only brief information. For the first time, there is a glimpse into the use of mediation: 290 proposals were made, 61 accepted, and 30 resulted in settlement agreements, indicating a success rate slightly below 50%. In the first quarter of 2024, there have been 100 proposals, 28 accepted, and 13 settlement agreements. With some effort and interpretation, these figures allow for a more precise estimate of consumer mediation trends.[43]

On the other hand, the data about court-annexed mediation has to be gathered separately.[44] The data shows that in 2023 there were 384 mediations in municipal courts and 199 in commercial courts. In municipal courts, the success rate was 40.10%, and in commercial courts 51.76%. The statistics of family mediation are only available in the reports of the Ministry of Labour, Pension System, Family, and Social Policy. Unfortunately, the 2023 report is currently unavailable, but in 2022, 1428 couples were referred to mandatory mediation meetings, resulting in parental plans negotiated in 368 cases. This indicates a considerably larger number of cases, but with a success rate of only 25.77%, a significantly lower percentage compared to court-ordered or

---

40 Both registries are available at: https://cmrs.hr/registri2/.

41 Uzelac (2018), p. 162.

42 We are thankful to the director of the CADR Marin Vuković for providing us with this data.

43 It is difficult to assess the total number of consumer mediations, but it is clear that the number was around 50, which was also the reported number in the European Commission Report 2022, available at: https://op.europa.eu/en/publication-detail/-/publication/bb2564ef-6bd5-11ee-9220-01aa75ed71a1/language-en.

44 We are thankful to Nika Vrcić for giving us permission to publish data she collected for her graduate paper soon expected to be defended and published.

party-agreed mediation.[45] Following the Constitutional Court decision of April 2023, which abolished the provision on mandatory mediation in divorce proceedings due to alleged infringements of the right to access to courts,[46] one can anticipate that the numbers for 2023 will be more modest and basically insignificant. The individual and collective employment mediation cases, administered by the Economic-Social Council, are also reported separately, with the number of mediations ranging from around 50 up to 150 in some years and the success rate ranging from approximately 25–50%.[47]

While one might argue that in 2024, we are closer to obtaining an accurate picture of the number of mediations in Croatia, official statistics of the CADR reveal only approximately 3% of all mediation cases. If the aim was to have one institution systematically gathering data on ADR (Art. 6 para. 1 ADRA), unfortunately, this goal has not been achieved. All in all, it seems that the CADR is modestly and gradually assuming its statutory role of regulator and facilitator, while still being far from the envisioned role of the overall system coordinator.

4 Affirmation of the Mediation Profession?

Unlike earlier, when such an obligation was merely prescribed by regulation, now explicit statutory provisions require mediators to attend basic training and to continuously pursue professional development (Art. 8 paras. 2 and 4 ADRA). The regulation specifies in more detail the contents of such training and also envisages a special exam. Failure to comply renders them ineligible for mediator registration (Art. 8 para. 1 ADRA), which means they cannot be considered mediators within the meaning of that law (Art. 4 para. 1 ADRA). While these rules represent significant strides towards professionalizing mediation, there are reasons that raise concerns and warrant careful consideration before fully embracing this solution.

Starting with the issue of continuous training, elevating it to a statutory requirement is indeed commendable. Notably, this mirrors a strong recommendation in the Directive (Art. 4), with similar lifelong professional development mandated for attorneys, public notaries, and judges. However, the irony lies in the fact that this obligation has become even less stringent. Previously, a failure to undergo advanced training every two years would, at least in theory,[48] lead to removal from the mediator registry. Currently, however, one can only be removed from the registry due to registration errors or death (Art. 8 para. 3 ADRA). Therefore, despite being a breach

---

[45] The statistics are avaiable at (Croatian only): https://mrosp.gov.hr/UserDocsImages/dokumenti/Glavno%20tajni%C5%A1tvo/Godi%C5%A1nje%20izvje%C5%A1%C4%87e%202022/Godi%C5%A1nje%20statisti%C4%8Dko%20o%20primijenjenim%20pravima%20socijalne%20skrbi%202022.pdf.

[46] Decision of 18 April 2023, U-I/3941/2015.

[47] Data available at: https://gsv.socijalno-partnerstvo.hr/nacionalni-gsv/mirenje.

[48] Since the Ministry did not regularly update the registry, many mediators remained in the list despite never undergoing advanced training. See note 21.

of an explicit statutory obligation, the lack of continuous training no longer leads to the same consequence. The amendment got stuck halfway.

Connecting the registration requirement to the very definition of a mediator, on the other hand, represents a serious departure from the previous regime. Narrowly interpreted, it might seem that mediation not carried out by a licensed and registered mediator is not mediation at all. Many mediation centres have quality mediators who have not undergone any professional training, which obviously jeopardizes the possibility for them to continue their otherwise successful work. On top of that, it is not only their interest that is in question. If carried out by an unlicensed mediator, it is questionable whether the settlement agreement reached would be as enforceable as the one reached before a licensed mediator, and whether initiation of such mediation would suspend the limitation and prescription periods. Strictly speaking, it is not mediation in the sense the ADRA defines it, so the answer to that question should be negative.

This kind of inconsiderate and not well-thought-out amendment departs not only from traditional domestic definitions in Croatian legislation but also from international instruments that were used as a model. Neither the UNCITRAL Model Law on International Commercial Mediation, nor the Singapore Convention, nor the Directive defines mediators as necessarily "registered" or "accredited" persons but emphasize two distinctive elements: the mediator is a "third person" who does not hold the "power to impose a solution".[49] The distinction from the definition used in the Directive is especially problematic. The European Commission was aware that many Member States have different qualifications criteria for mediators, so the rules on accreditation were omitted.[50] Instead there is a general rule obliging the Member States to "encourage the initial and further training of mediators in order to ensure that the mediation is conducted in an effective, impartial and competent way in relation to the parties" (Art. 4 para. 2 Directive). The intention to preserve the high standards should not, however, impede the goal of ensuring "the proper functioning of the internal market, in particular as concerns the availability of mediation services" (recital 5 Directive). Some Member States effectively tackled this issue.

For instance, in Austria, cross-border mediation can be carried out by unlicensed mediators with the same effect as domestic mediations with licensed mediators.[51] In Belgium, the parties are free to choose any person to mediate their case, but only the settlement agreement reached before a licensed mediator can be homologized and thus become enforceable.[52] Similarly, in Portugal, settlement agreements have to be homologised in order to be enforceable, but that is not required if mediation is carried out by an accredited mediator.[53] Most importantly, all of these different

[49] Compare Art. 1 UNCITRAL Model Law on International Commercial Mediation, Art. 2 Singapore Convention, and Art. 3 Directive.

[50] Feasley (2011), p. 5.

[51] Risak and Lenz (2017), 40–41.

[52] Nigmatullina and Billiet (2017), p. 75.

[53] Walsh and d'Abreu Miguel (2017), p. 633.

distinctions are clearly stated in the law. In contrast to that, these issues are not at all regulated in the ADRA, creating considerable legal uncertainty.

If the Ministry wanted to insist on the quality standards and registration, it could have followed the Austrian example by insisting on the registration for domestic purposes, while allowing different criteria for cross-border mediation. Currently, this could be possible only by way of a stretched interpretation, as the law clearly states in two provisions that all ADRA's provisions are applicable to cross-border mediation (Art. 1 para. 3 and Art. 27 ADRA). Without these necessary amendments, it could be said that the ADRA implemented the Directive to a lesser extent than the MA 11'. Furthermore, in domestic mediation cases, the principle of legal certainty would require clearly regulating the consequences of a mediation carried out by non-licensed mediators, so that both parties and the mediation community can adapt to these legislative expectations.

Currently, continuous training is a loosely enforced obligation, successfully followed by 955 licensed mediators.[54] The statutory obligation will motivate only a small number of mediators, who actually carry out mediations, as they are likely to consider this part of their professional and ethical duty anyway. In our view, the sole state monopoly over registration and accreditation standards will not, by itself, advance the professionalization of the field. Hopefully, broader participation in fundamental training among various professionals, such as educators working with children, will at least foster the adoption of a culture of ADR in the long term. As mentioned earlier, however, such a beneficial coincidental outcome should not compromise Croatia's adherence to its international commitments.

5 Strengthening Incentives for Using Mediation?

In line with the authority expressly granted by the Directive (Art. 5 para. 2 Directive), many Member States have introduced numerous positive and negative incentives to promote the use of mediation. These incentives range from tax benefits and (partial) court fee waivers or reimbursement to suspension of limitation and prescription periods, and adverse cost sanctions for parties that demonstrate a lack of willingness to attempt settling the case amicably.[55]

The ADRA has only modestly contributed to incentivizing mediation in Croatia by explicitly stating that the costs of attempting mediation and participating in the MIM are included in the total costs of subsequent litigation (Art. 26 para. 2 ADRA). This was previously only an implied rule (Art. 151 para. 1 CPA) that courts almost

[54] This does not include family mediators, as 48 of them are registered separately. See: https://mrosp.gov.hr/UserDocsImages/dokumenti/Socijalna%20politika/Evidencije/Registar%20obiteljskih%20medijatora%2024.08.2023..pdf. There is also a separate list of the Economic and Social Council (OJ, np. 116/2016) with 35 people listed.

[55] Menkel-Meadow (2016), p. 30. See also European Parliament (2016), p. 12.

never applied due to restrictive interpretation.[56] During the ADRA drafting, there was no discussion to introduce tax benefits like those in Italy,[57] so income from mediated settlement agreements is still taxed the same way as the income from judgments.[58] The issue with the ADRA, however, is not that it did not introduce many new incentives for using mediation, but that it most likely hindered the existing ones.

The best example is the rule on the effect of mediation proceedings on limitation and prescription periods. Changing a decade-long provision is another item on the list of last-minute changes that have never been subject to serious debate.[59] It actually reintroduced the same rule that was already in force in the MA 09' and the MA 11', stating that both limitation and prescription periods are suspended during mediation (Art. 24 ADRA).[60] Previous versions of this provision had different solutions for each of these periods.

Initially, limitation periods were not affected by pending mediation, unless the parties agreed otherwise, while it interrupted the prescription period, meaning it would restart after the proposal to mediate was rejected or mediation ended without reaching a settlement agreement (Art. 14 MA 03'). In 2011, a considerably more complex provision was introduced. It started with a verbatim adoption of the general principle proclaimed in the Directive that the parties should not be prevented from initiating judicial or arbitration proceedings because of the expiry of limitation or prescription periods during the mediation (Art. 17 para. 1 MA 11 and Art. 8 para. 1 Directive). In the case of limitation periods, this meant that acceptance of the proposal to mediate would interrupt such periods, conditioned upon the successful outcome of the mediation. If the settlement is not reached, the parties still have an additional 15 days after the end of the mediation to initiate court or arbitration proceedings without losing the initial benefit. In the case of prescription periods, they were suspended by the very proposal to mediate, with the suspension extended for 15 days after the refusal of the proposal or the end of the mediation if the proposal was accepted (Art. 6 para. 5 and Art. 17 paras. 2–4 MA 11').

The dual solutions, not necessarily regulated in the clearest way, seemed to have caused confusion in practice,[61] indicating a need for reconsideration. However, this reassessment should have taken place in a debate in which all implications of different solutions would be addressed. Unlike the previous rule, the current one does not work as a strong incentive to mediate in cases where the expiration of limitation or prescription periods is around the corner. For instance, if such periods are expiring in

---

[56] The costs were recoverable only to the extent the ADR attempt was a procedural requirement to initiate the proceedings (see Supreme Court decision of 10 November 2009, Rev-615/09; and High Commercial Court decision of 26 April 2021, Pž-7826/10).

[57] Indovina (2020), p. 77.

[58] See e.g. Opinion of 26 November 2019, class 410–01/19–01/1558.

[59] Uzelac and Brozović (2023), p. 10.

[60] It justified it as a Directive implementation measure, although the irony is that the Ministry had the same justification in 2009 and 2011.

[61] Uzelac and Brozović (2023), p. 10.

10 days and the suspension only occurs if the proposal to mediate is accepted (Art. 13 para. 2 ADRA), for which consideration the other party regularly has 15 days (Art. 13 para. 3 ADRA), would the potential claimants even undertake such a risk to propose mediation, without knowing whether the other party will positively respond in due time? The issue is even more evident in the case of prescription periods because the proposal to mediate no longer affects their progression on its own.

But the problem goes even further. Should the proposal and its subsequent acceptance be timely, and the parties indeed attempt to mediate, what happens in case the mediation is not successful? The limitation and prescription periods simply continue to run where they left prior to the initiation of the mediation (Art. 238 para. 2 Obligations Act). Again, in situations of time pressure, it makes no sense to mediate and risk the possibility of being prevented from effectively initiating court proceedings.[62] The additional time of 15 days that existed in the MA 11' successfully circumvented that problem and offered parties, who are willing to mediate, sufficient time to prepare for the subsequent court or arbitration proceedings.

Our critical assessment does not imply that the solution in the MA 11' was the only possible solution to address the issue of limitation and prescription periods or even that it is the best possible solution, although there are such examples in pro-mediation Member States.[63] There are alternative ways to achieve the same purpose, for instance, by using interim measures.[64] The use of interruptions or additional deadlines should also not lead to abuse by creditors.[65] All these different implications can and should be taken into account when deciding on this matter.[66]

Another example where the introduction of the ADRA hindered the incentives is the case of adverse cost sanctions. Since 2019, parties who did not participate in the mandatory mediation meeting to which they were referred by the court risked being unable to recover the costs of subsequent litigation, even in the event of complete success (Art. 186.d para. 9 CPA). The introduction of the pre-commencement procedural obligations to attempt ADR, either by negotiating or mediating (Art. 9 para. 2 ADRA), expanded the types of cases in which the court is required to refer the parties to mediation. Initially, such obligations should have existed in basically all types of litigation as an extension of the principle of loyal cooperation (Art. 10 para. 1 CPA), but in the final version, it was limited solely to proceedings initiated upon employment-unrelated damages claims (Art. 9 para. 1 ADRA). At some point, the Ministry also decided to differentiate between the MIM and the first mediation meeting, which would not be an issue in terms of incentives had they not decided

[62] Garner (2020), p. 29.

[63] Nigmatullina and Billiet (2017), p. 74.

[64] Uzelac and Brozović (2023), p. 10.

[65] Morek (2017), p. 620.

[66] Bilić (2008), p. 150.

to completely omit the provision laying down the consequences of parties' non-appearance at the MIM.[67] The solution was seen in the interpretation of the CPA and its announced amendments,[68] but these only made the problem worse.

According to the current text of the CPA, the adverse costs sanction does not apply if the party does not participate in the MIM, making it completely optional. The whole point of the ADRA was to force parties to show a minimum token of goodwill and to seriously consider ADR, without forcing them to mediate or settle the case. Instead, the adverse cost sanction applies only if the parties agree to engage in mediation during the MIM and later fail to appear at the mediation session (Art. 186.d para. 9 CPA). Not only does the introduction of the MIM become meaningless, but it also raises questions of constitutionality. Specifically, one of the reasons the Constitutional Court abolished the provision for mandatory mediation meetings in family matters was its (incorrect) assessment that parties cannot leave mediation if they choose, which contradicts the principle of party autonomy.[69] Leaving aside the Constitutional Court's incorrect interpretation of the FA,[70] sanctioning non-appearance at the mediation meeting after the parties have agreed to mediate indeed violates the principle of autonomy (Art. 5 ADRA), as non-appearance, in practical terms, is no different from appearing and then willingly leaving the mediation. Whether the Constitutional Court will react, or the Ministry will correct the mistake before any interventions, remains to be seen.

6 Concluding Remarks

The new Croatian mediation framework serves as a notable illustration of how well-meaning intentions, when rushed and lacking thorough, comprehensive debate, can lead to unintended consequences. Many of the ADRA's provisions lack the necessary clarity and undermine already functioning mechanisms. In particular, the CADR's role remains limited, and only with enthusiastic leadership and support from the Ministry can we expect it to assume its statutory role. Challenges persist in coordinating parallel mediation tracks, as new provisions introduce additional complexities. The pursuit of professionalizing the mediation profession raises doubts about compliance with international commitments, while certain rule adaptations diminish incentives for mediation use and pose constitutional concerns.

One cannot conclude that the Ministry is not making any efforts to facilitate the use of ADR. However, many of these efforts seem akin to running on a hamster wheel, only accelerating the return to the same starting point, occasionally even resulting in being ejected from the wheel. An alternative approach would be to introduce a more

[67] Uzelac and Brozović (2023), p. 10.

[68] Brozovic and Zeljko (2023), pp. 495–496.

[69] Decision of the Constitutional Court, U-I/3941/2015, para. 41.

[70] There has never been any doubt that the parties only need to attend the first meeting and actively participate in it. Mediation as a whole has always been optional.

flexible set of rules while simultaneously providing logistical support to mediation centres and a wide array of incentives for both users and providers of these services. This is not only in the interest of the judiciary, which will no longer have to handle cases that can be resolved independently, but also in the interest of the parties, who should be the main focus of the judicial system.

References

Aras Kramar S (2017) Obiteljska medijacija. In: Rešetar B et al. (eds.) Suvremeno obiteljsko pravo i postupak, Osijek: Pravni fakultet Sveučilišta Josipa Jurja Strossmayera u Osijeku, pp. 291–328
Bilić V (2008) Alternativno rješavanje sporova i parnični postupak. Doctoral thesis. Pravni fakultet u Zagrebu, Zagreb
Brozović J, Zeljko I (2023) 'Obvezni pretprocesni pokušaj mirnog rješenja spora'. In Šago D et a. (eds.) Zbornik radova IX. međunarodnog savjetovanja Aktualnosti građanskog procesnog prava – nacionalna i usporedna pravnoteorijska i praktična dostignuća, Split: Pravni fakultet, pp. 481-499
Braut Filipović M, Čulinović-Herc E, Šimac S (2024) Rješavanje sporova u obiteljskim trgovačkim društvima medijacijom. Zbornik Pravnog Fakulteta Sveučilišta u Rijeci 45(1):153–176
European Parliament (2016) The implementation of the mediation directive 29 November 2016. In: The implementation of the mediation directive workshop 29 November 2016 (europa.eu)
Feasley A (2011) Regulating mediator qualifications in the 2008 EU mediation directive: the need for a supranational standard. J Disput Resolut 2011(2):333–350
Garner WM (2020) Dispute resolution in the twenty-first century: the challenge to get ADR right. Franchise Law J 40(1):25–42
Indovina V (2020) When mandatory mediation meets the adversarial legal culture of lawyers: an empirical study in Italy. HNLR 26:69–112
Menkel-Meadow C (2016) The future of mediation worldwide: legal and cultural variations in the uptake of or resistance to mediation (Chap. 3). In: Macduff I (ed) Essays on mediation: dealing with disputes in the 21st century, global trends in dispute resolution, vol 6. Kluwer Law International, Alphen aan den Rijn, pp 29–46
Morek R (2017) Poland (Chap. 24). In: Alexander N, Walsh S et al (eds) EU mediation law handbook, global trends in dispute resolution, vol 7. Kluwer Law International, Alphen aan den Rijn, pp 601–622
Nigmatullina D, Billiet, J (2017) Belgium (Chap. 3). In: Alexander N, Walsh S et al (eds) EU mediation law handbook, global trends in dispute resolution, vol 7. Kluwer Law International, Alphen aan den Rijn, pp 59–92
Nolan-Haley JM (2021) Alternative dispute resolution in a nutshell. West Academic Publishing, St. Paul
Risak M, Lenz C (2017) Austria (Chap. 2). In: Alexander N, Walsh S et al (eds) EU Mediation law handbook, global trends in dispute resolution, vol 7. Kluwer Law International, Alphen aan den Rijn, pp 33–58
Šimac S (2013) Mirenje kao generator promjena u pravosuđu i pravnoj profesiji. Doctoral thesis. Zagreb, Pravni fakultet u Zagrebu
Šimunović D (2023) Prijedlog novog Zakona o mirnom rješavanju sporova u svjetlu dosadašnje primjene postupka mirenja. Pravo u Gospodarstvu 62(1):101–132
Triva S, Dika M (2004) Građansko parnično procesno pravo. Narodne novine, Zagreb
Uzelac A (2004) Zakon o mirenju: nastanak, izvori i osnovna načela. In: Uzelac A et al (eds) Mirenje u građanskim, trgovačkim i radnim sporovima. TIM Press, Zagreb, pp 33–44

Uzelac A (2018) Izazovi novog uređenja izvansudskog rješavanja potrošačkih sporova. In: Mihelčić G et al (eds) Liber amicorum Aldo Radolović, Rijeka: Sveučilište u Rijeci, Pravni Fakultet, pp 145–165

Uzelac A, Brozović J (2023) Zakon o mirnom rješavanju sporova: Korak unaprijed ili još jedna propuštena prilika? Portal IUSINFO, 14 June 2023. https://www.iusinfo.hr/strucni-clanci/zakon-o-mirnom-rjesavanju-sporova-korak-unaprijed-ili-jos-jedna-propustena-prilika

Uzelac A, Aras S, Maršić M, Mitrović M, Kauzlarić Ž, Stojčević P (2010) Aktualni trendovi mirnog rješavanja sporova u Hrvatskoj: dosezi i ograničenja. Zbornik Pravnog Fakulteta u Zagrebu 60(3):1265–1308

Walsh S, d'Abreu Miguel C (2017) Portugal (Chap. 25). In: Alexander N, Walsh S et al (eds) EU mediation law handbook, global trends in dispute resolution, vol 7. Kluwer Law International, Alphen aan den Rijn, pp 623–636

ADR for Consumer Disputes in the Consumer Protection Legislation of North Macedonia

Neda Zdraveva

Abstract Alternative Dispute Resolution (ADR) is a mechanism that allows consumers and traders to resolve disputes efficiently and effectively. The European Union (EU) has a comprehensive framework for ADR, which is currently under revision. This revision aims to adapt the ADR framework to digital markets, enhance access to ADR in cross-border disputes through digital tools, and streamline ADR procedures. The Directive on Consumer ADR encompasses all categories of disputes pertaining to EU consumer rights and encourages traders to increase their participation in ADR claims through the duty to respond. In North Macedonia, a new Consumer Protection Law, transposing various EU directives related to consumer protection, came into effect in 2022. This law contributes to establishing a legal framework that ensures a higher level of consumer rights protection. It also provides mechanisms for swiftly resolving disputes between traders and consumers. The law favours alternative dispute resolution mechanisms, but the legal framework for ADR in consumer disputes is yet to be fully established. In summary, both the EU and North Macedonia have robust frameworks for consumer protection. These frameworks aim to safeguard consumer rights, ensure fair trade practices, and provide effective mechanisms for dispute resolution. As the EU legislation and practices in this field are evolving and improving, policymakers and enforcement agencies in North Macedonia are yet to catch up and provide an environment conducive to ADR for consumer disputes.

1 Introduction

Alternative dispute resolution (ADR), as an out-of-court procedure for settling a dispute with the assistance of an impartial dispute resolution body, is seen to have a crucial role in protecting consumer rights and ensuring that consumers have access

N. Zdraveva (✉)
Department of Civil Law, Faculty of Law "Iustinianus Primus", Ss. Cyril and Methodius University, Skopje, North Macedonia
e-mail: n.zdraveva@pf.ukim.edu.mk

M. Bungenberg et al. (eds.), *Alternative Dispute Resolution in the Western Balkans*, European Union and its Neighbours in a Globalized World 20,
https://doi.org/10.1007/978-3-031-76345-8_16

to fair and effective ways to enforce their rights. There is no universal ADR system and the mechanisms depend on the national legal framework. They often include mediation, arbitration, Ombudsperson, and similar. By providing consumers with easy and accessible ways to seek redress, the ADR mechanisms should help promote trust and confidence in the market and contribute to the goal of creating a level playing field for consumers and businesses alike.

The key word here would be the ‘level playing field.’ The position of the consumer and the trader is significantly asymmetric in terms of resources and knowledge about alternative dispute resolution. The trader, due to its resources, previous experiences, and ability to rely on legal counsel, is often well-informed about the different options of dispute resolution. This party will be in a position in the consumer contract to provide for a clause regulating the dispute resolution. The very nature of the consumer contract would mean that the other, less informed/less knowledgeable party—the consumer is only in a position to accept (or decline, for that matter) the contract. When the ADR mechanism offered by the trader (and accepted by the consumer) provides for fair and cost-effective dispute resolution, it could be considered that this mechanism supports access to justice and the exercise of the right by both parties. The asymmetry in the positions of the parties is often seen as a primary reason why arbitration could be a risky mechanism for consumer disputes.[1] In business-to-consumer contracts, the validity of the arbitration clauses is questioned from the perspective of its fairness.[2] The application of the regulation protecting consumers from unfair contract terms[3] indicates that post-dispute arbitration clauses agreed upon in arm’s length negotiations are regarded as fair. Pre-dispute arbitration clauses drafted unilaterally and incorporated in consumer contracts may be regarded as unfair if they meet the “significant imbalance” and the “contrary to good faith” requirements in the said regulation.[4]

2 Legislative Framework for ADR of Consumer Disputes in the EU

The European Union (EU), with marked intensity, is engaged in the promotion and protection of consumer rights, a fundamental tenet underpinning the operation of the internal market, as provided in the Treaties. Article 169(1) and point (a) of Article 169(2) of the Treaty on the Functioning of the European Union (TFEU)[5] provide that the Union is to contribute to the attainment of a high level of consumer protection

[1] Moreira (2020), pp. 73–74.

[2] Amro (2016) p. 268.

[3] Council Directive 93/13/EEC of 5 April 1993 on unfair terms in consumer contracts, OJ L 95, 21.4.1993.

[4] Mechantaf (2012), p. 238.

[5] Treaty on the Functioning of the European Union of 13 December 2007—consolidated version, OJ C 202, 7.6.2016.

through measures adopted pursuant to Article 114 TFEU. Article 38 of the Charter of Fundamental Rights of the European Union ('the Charter') provides that Union policies are to ensure a high level of consumer protection.[6]

The EU and the member states share competence when consumer protection is in question. The EU may enact measures aimed at strengthening the position of the consumer on the internal market. This is usually done through numerous secondary instruments, predominantly directives, binding the member states (and the aspirant countries)[7] through their national legislation to attain a set of objectives. However, the modalities of how these objectives are to be met are left to the decision of the national policy-makers. As a result, the levels of protection of consumers across the EU member states differ.[8] This is also reflected in the procedural aspects of consumer protection, including, or in particular when it comes to alternative dispute resolution.[9,10]

The EU's framework on ADR of consumer disputes aims to provide consumers access to simple, efficient, fast, and low-cost ways of resolving disputes, which is particularly important when consumers shop across borders. It gradually developed from non-binding recommendations to unification via the establishment of specific tools to currently undergoing a new process of improvement.

The Directive 2013/11/EU on alternative dispute resolution for consumer disputes, together with Regulation (EU) No 524/2013 on online dispute resolution for consumer disputes[11] (the 'ODR Regulation'), forms the current horizontal EU-level framework for alternative dispute resolution for consumer disputes. They provide an out-of-court solution and tool for consumers to resolve disputes related to the execution of consumer contracts on goods and services purchased from traders established in the single market. This solution and tool, however, are not considered adequate for the new—digital internal market. The process of reform is underway. How the future of the legislative framework on ADR for consumer disputes stands to the moment is not clear.

---

[6] Meskic (2014), pp. 85–89.

[7] The most important instruments are the Stabilization and Association Agreements where the countries aspirant for joining the EU undertake an obligation to align their legislation (and practices) with the standards of the EU.

[8] Rott (2016), p. 809.

[9] Carvalho and Nemeth (2018), p. 81.

[10] Recitals 21, Directive 2013/11/EU of the European Parliament and of the Council of 21 May 2013 on alternative dispute resolution for consumer disputes and amending Regulation (EC) No 2006/2004 and Directive 2009/22/EC (Directive on consumer ADR), OJ L 165, 18.6.2013 (ADR Directive).

[11] Regulation (EU) No 524/2013 of the European Parliament and of the Council of 21 May 2013 on online dispute resolution for consumer disputes and amending Regulation (EC) No 2006/2004 and Directive 2009/22/EC (Regulation on consumer ODR) OJ L 165, 18.6.2013.

2.1 *Commission Recommendations*

2.1.1 Commission Recommendation on Out-of-Court Settlement of Consumer Disputes

The Commission Recommendation 98/257/EC on the principles applicable to the bodies responsible for out-of-court settlement of consumer disputes[12] applies to bodies responsible for out-of-court consumer dispute resolution procedures to resolve a dispute by bringing the parties together to find a solution by common consent. As per the Recommendation, the member states are expected to ensure that these bodies meet binding quality requirements, ensuring they operate effectively, fairly, independently, and transparently. The Recommendation requires each EU country to designate one or several competent authorities that oversee these bodies and ensure their compliance with the quality requirements. The bodies are expected to maintain high transparency. This Recommendation has established seven minimum guarantees/principles designed to boost consumer confidence and provide efficient, appropriate dispute resolution alternatives to court proceedings.

Principle of Independence: Ensures the impartiality of the decision-making body, whether it's an individual or a group, by establishing measures to guarantee their autonomy and competence.
Principle of Transparency: Requires clear communication about the types of disputes handled, procedural rules, costs, and the legal force of decisions, as well as annual reporting of decisions taken.
Principle of Effectiveness: Aims to facilitate consumer access to justice by making the procedure accessible without legal representation, free or low-cost, timely, and actively managed by the competent body.
Principle of Legality: Ensures that decisions do not deprive consumers of the protection afforded by mandatory legal provisions, particularly in cross-border disputes.

2.1.2 Commission Recommendation on the Principles for Out-of-Court Bodies Involved in the Consensual Resolution of Consumer Disputes

The Commission Recommendation of 4 April 2001 on the principles for out-of-court bodies involved in the consensual resolution of consumer disputes[13] aims to enhance consumer confidence and provide for further development of the framework for fair and efficient out-of-court dispute resolution by establishing basic principles for the

---

[12] Commission Recommendation of 30 March 1998 on the principles applicable to the bodies responsible for out-of-court settlement of consumer disputes, OJ L 115, 17.4.1998.

[13] Commission Recommendation of 4 April 2001 on the principles for out-of-court bodies involved in the consensual resolution of consumer disputes (Text with EEA relevance) (notified under document number C(2001) 1016), OJ L 109, 19.4.2001, pp. 56–61.

bodies involved in the ADR of consumer disputes. The Recommendation sets four principles as a minimum standard for third-party bodies responsible for out-of-court consumer dispute resolution procedures that, no matter what they are called, attempt to resolve a dispute by bringing the parties together to convince them to find a solution by common consent (Art. 1, para. 1). These principles, however, are not applicable to customer complaint mechanisms operated by a business and concluded directly with the consumer or to such mechanisms carrying out such services operated by or on behalf of a business (Art. 1(2)). Further, the Recommendation sets an obligation to create a database with data on bodies for alternative dispute resolution (European Extra Judicial Network - EEJNet).

Principle of Impartiality: Impartiality is ensured by appointing individuals responsible for the procedure for a fixed term, with removal permissible only for just cause. These individuals must not have any perceived or actual conflict of interest with either party. Information regarding their impartiality and competence must be provided to the parties prior to the commencement of the procedure.

Principle of Transparency: The procedure must be transparent - information regarding its operation, the types of disputes it can address, its cost, and its timetable should be readily accessible to the parties involved. The Regulation requires that the agreed solution be documented and made available to both parties. Additionally, information concerning the performance of the procedure should be publicly accessible.

Principle of Effectiveness: This principle mandates that the procedure be effective and easily accessible to both parties, potentially through electronic means. It should be cost-free or entail proportionate and moderate costs for consumers. Parties should have access to the procedure without the necessity of a legal representative, although they should not be precluded from being represented or assisted by a third party. The procedure should be time-efficient, addressing disputes in the shortest possible timeframe. The conduct of the parties should be reviewed to ensure their commitment to seeking a fair and timely resolution.

Principle of Fairness: The procedure must adhere to principles of fairness. All parties must be duly informed of their right to decline participation or withdraw from the procedure at any stage. Parties should be afforded the opportunity to submit any pertinent arguments, information, or evidence confidentially. Before consenting to any proposed resolution, parties should be granted a reasonable period to deliberate. Consumers must be clearly and comprehensively informed about various aspects of the proposed resolution, including the potential for the proposed resolution to be less favourable than a court judgment and their right to seek independent advice and pursue alternative dispute resolution mechanisms.

2.2 *Horizontal EU-Level Framework for Alternative Dispute Resolution for Consumer Disputes*

2.2.1 Directive on Consumer ADR

The primary objective of the Directive on consumer Alternative Dispute Resolution (ADR) is to uphold the European Union's commitment to ensuring a high level of consumer protection within the internal market, achieved through measures adopted under Article 114 of the Treaty on the Functioning of the European Union (TFEU) and Article 38 of the Charter of Fundamental Rights.[14] ADR is designed to provide a simple, fast, and low-cost mechanism for resolving disputes between consumers and traders.[15] Its effectiveness is deemed essential for enhancing consumer confidence in cross-border shopping and ensuring the proper functioning of the internal market.[16]

The Consumer ADR Directive intends to create a legal environment that enables consumers to voluntarily submit complaints against traders to entities that provide independent, impartial, transparent, effective, fast, and fair alternative dispute resolution procedures.

The Directive does not affect national legislation that mandates participation in such procedures, provided that such legislation does not impede the parties' right of access to justice. It applies to procedures for the out-of-court resolution of domestic and cross-border disputes concerning contractual obligations arising from sales or service contracts between a trader established in the Union and a consumer resident in the Union, except those explicitly excluded,[17] facilitated by an ADR entity. The Directive applies to both domestic and cross-border disputes arising from contractual obligations between consumers and traders established within the EU. It relates to transactions conducted both online and offline. Member States are mandated to ensure the availability of ADR entities that comply with the quality requirements delineated in the Directive. These entities must be listed and made publicly accessible.

Consumers are entitled to access ADR procedures for resolving disputes with traders. These procedures should be straightforward, swift, and cost-effective. Traders are encouraged to participate in ADR procedures and are required to inform consumers about the availability of ADR mechanisms.

---

[14] Recital 1, Directive on consumer ADR.

[15] Recital 5, Directive on consumer ADR.

[16] Recital 15, Directive on consumer ADR.

[17] This Directive does not apply to procedures before dispute resolution entities where the natural persons in charge of dispute resolution are employed or remunerated exclusively by the individual trader, unless Member States decide to allow such procedures as ADR procedures under this Directive and the requirements set out in Chapter II, including the specific requirements of independence and transparency set out in Article 6(3), are met. It also does not apply to procedures before consumer complaint-handling systems operated by the trader, non-economic services of general interest, disputes between traders, direct negotiation between the consumer and the trader, attempts made by a judge to settle a dispute in the course of a judicial proceeding concerning that dispute, procedures initiated by a trader against a consumer, and health services.

Member States are obligated to report on the functioning of ADR entities and to enforce penalties for non-compliance with the Directive's provisions.

2.2.2 ODR Regulation

The overarching goal of the ODR Regulation is to bolster consumer confidence in cross-border e-commerce by providing a reliable and efficient mechanism for resolving disputes, thereby contributing to the growth and integration of the digital single market. This Regulation aims to enhance consumer protection and the internal market's functioning by providing a single point of entry for the out-of-court resolution of disputes arising from online transactions.

The Regulation mandates the creation of an ODR platform, which serves as a centralized hub for consumers and traders to resolve disputes through ADR entities linked to the platform. This platform is designed to be user-friendly, ensuring accessibility, efficiency, and transparency in the resolution process.

2.3 Way Forward in the EU Legislation

The 2023 Edition of the Consumer Conditions Scoreboard indicates that consumers within EU member states perceive out-of-court dispute resolution mechanisms as more accessible than judicial proceedings. Specifically, 45% of consumers reported that resolving disputes with retailers and service providers through out-of-court bodies is straightforward, compared to 34% who found court proceedings to be similarly manageable. This trend is observed across all member states, albeit with significant variations (Fig. 1).[18]

The assessment of the impact of the ADR Directive and the ODR Regulation[19] identified three overarching problems at the EU level: (1) The ADR Directive is not fit for digital markets, (2) Low engagement in ADR among businesses and consumers, (3) ADR is not sufficiently used in a cross-border context. The causes of these problems are clustered in two groups:

1. Megatrends and market-related drivers: quick growth and increased concentration of e-commerce and online advertising, increased cross-border shopping, including with traders located outside the EU, consumer disputes in digital markets going beyond contractual issues, significant rate of non-compliance with EU consumer law.

---

[18] Consumer Conditions Scoreboard, 2023 Edition, European Commission, Directorate-General for Justice and Consumers, March, 2023, p. 24.

[19] Commission Staff Working Document, Impact Assessment Report Accompanying the document Proposal for a Directive of The European Parliament and of the Council amending Directive 2013/11/EU on alternative dispute resolution for consumer disputes, as well as Directives (EU) 2015/2302, (EU) 2019/2161 and (EU) 2020/1828.

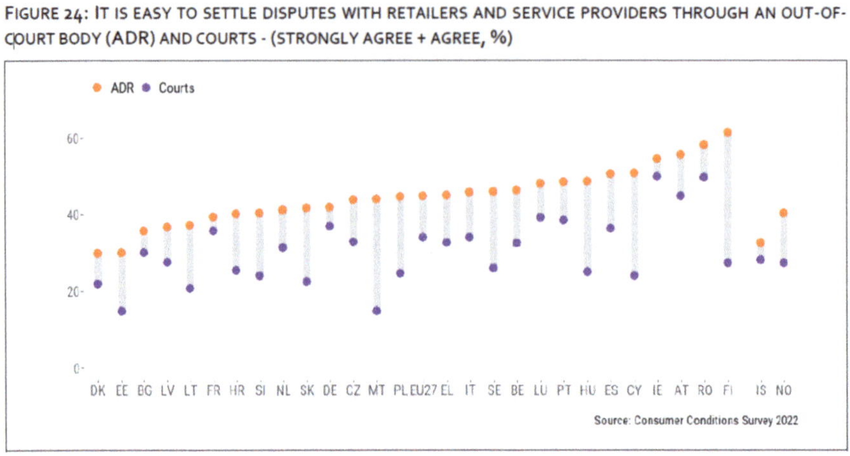

Fig. 1 How easy it is to settle disputes with retailers and service providers through an out-of-court body (ADR) and courts. *Source* Consumer Conditions Scoreboard, Edition 2023, p. 24

2. Enforcement-related drivers: access barriers to ADR (lack of awareness and costs of procedures) and increased use of private online dispute resolution (PODR) systems operated by online marketplaces.

It is estimated that the consequence of these problems for consumers is a total annual detriment of EUR 383 million.

As a result, four policy options were considered: A - Non-regulatory intervention, B - Procedural and geographical scope revision, C - Material scope amendments and new business obligations, and D -Architectural changes and increased harmonization. Policy option C (scope amendments and new business obligations) has been identified as the preferred policy option. It maintains the current minimum harmonization approach of the Directive and does not require Member States to make participation in ADR mandatory for traders. This option is consistent with the principle of subsidiarity governing EU action. As a result proposal Directive on amending Directive 2013/11/EU on alternative dispute resolution for consumer disputes, as well as Directives (EU) 2015/2302, (EU) 2019/2161 and (EU) 2020/1828[20]; as well as a proposal for a Regulation repealing Regulation (EU) No 524/2013 and amending Regulations (EU) 2017/2394 and (EU) 2018/1724 with regards to the discontinuation of the European ODR Platform[21] have been officialized at the end of 2023.

[20] Proposal for a Directive of the European Parliament and of the Council amending Directive 2013/11/EU on alternative dispute resolution for consumer disputes, as well as Directives (EU) 2015/2302, (EU) 2019/2161 and (EU) 2020/1828; COM/2023/649 final.

[21] Proposal for a Regulation of the European Parliament and of the Council repealing Regulation (EU) No 524/2013 and amending Regulations (EU) 2017/2394 and (EU) 2018/1724 with regards to the discontinuation of the European ODR Platform, COM/2023/647 final.

3 The Alternative Resolution of Consumer Disputes in North Macedonia

The national legislation has undergone significant changes in the past years. The dominant reason for the enactment of the (new) Law on Consumer Protection[22] was the alignment of the consumer protection legislation with the *EU Consumer Acquis*.[23]

In the context of consumer disputes, the LCP introduces general provisions on out-of-court dispute resolution mechanisms. However, there are no specific provisions that would provide for transposition of the ADR Directive. Namely, as the issues pertaining to dispute resolution are categorized under procedural law, whereas the primary focus of the LCP is the regulation of consumer rights rather than the enforcement mechanisms thereof.

There is no relevant data on the application of these provisions of consumer protection. The traders, the courts, and the ADR bodies do not keep a statistical record or do not make these data publicly available, although they are obliged by different laws.

3.1 Are the Consumer Disputes Resolved? and How?

The Annual Report (2023) of the Consumer Protection Organisation[24] gives us a glance at the status quo. In 2023, the Consumers' Organization of Macedonia conducted 1,523 consultations with consumers regarding their rights in sales and service contracts, addressing disputes with traders concerning these rights. Over 50% of the complaints pertained to the purchase of goods (822), with the highest number of complaints related to home appliances and IT equipment. Approximately 22% of the complaints involved the provision of services, equally divided between private entities and public services. In the private sector (less than 10%), most complaints concerned tourist services and repairs, while in the public sector (10%), the majority of complaints related to the provision of electricity, telecommunications services, thermal energy, and services offered by public utility companies. A small number of complaints (44) were related to financial services, specifically credit products offered by banks, including issues with high variable interest rates, problems with cards and transactions, and services from financial companies. About 7% of the complaints were related to online shopping, primarily from social media marketplaces, where consumers reported issues with the conformity of goods and the lack of return policies.

The role of the Consumers' Organization in these cases was twofold: (1) to provide information on consumer rights, thereby empowering consumers to resolve disputes

---

[22] Law on Consumer Protection ("Official Gazette of the Republic of North Macedonia no. 236/2020); hereinafter: LCP.

[23] Dabović-Anastasovska (2023), pp. 22–25.

[24] https://opm.org.mk/wp-content/uploads/2010/10/Godishen-izveshtaj-2023.pdf.

directly with traders or enforce their rights through the State Market Inspectorate, relevant regulatory bodies, or courts; and (2) to communicate directly with traders or service providers to facilitate the resolution of disputes with consumers.

3.2 *The Legislation*

LCP provides (Art. 188) that the consumer may exercise the protection of their rights through:

1. Submitting a consumer complaint to traders;
2. Initiating a consumer dispute in civil proceedings; and
3. Out-of-court resolution of consumer disputes.

3.2.1 Consumer Complaints

The consumer complaints mechanism provided in the law is foreseen as a means for peaceful/amicable settlement of the disputes between the consumer and the trader without initiation of a formal ADR or court proceeding.

Traders, including those providing public services (Art. 189), are obliged to facilitate the submission of consumer complaints in instances where consumer rights are infringed upon. Traders are required to address these complaints in accordance with the law, irrespective of the specific terminology used to describe the complaint. Further, the traders (Art. 190) have an obligation to inform consumers about their right to submit complaints. This information must be prominently displayed inside the business premises and, where applicable, on the trader's website. If a trader adheres to a code of conduct, this obligation extends to the code's holder. Additionally, traders providing public services must include this information on issued bills. The traders must (Art. 191) allow complaints to be submitted orally or in writing at their business premises, ensuring the presence of an authorized person to receive complaints during working hours. When it comes to public service providers, they are obliged (Art. 196) to establish a department for handling consumer complaints. Additionally, these traders must publish information about the department's existence and operations on their websites at least biannually, however, in practice, this is not the case.[25]

Complaints can also be submitted via mail, fax, or email. For public services, complaints can be submitted through a basic rate telephone line. Traders may also offer electronic submission via their website.

---

[25] For the purpose of this chapter a brief overview on the content of the web pages of the main public services providers—electricity company, utilities' (water supply and hygiene) public enterprises was carried out. Although they have general information that their pubic relations offices handle consumer complaints no other information on the procedure as provided.

Upon receiving a complaint, traders must promptly issue a receipt, either on paper or a durable medium, depending on the submission method. Importantly, traders are prohibited from charging for the submission and handling of complaints.

Once the trader receives the complaint, as per Art. 192, they are obliged to respond to the consumer within 15 days of receipt. The response must indicate whether the complaint is accepted, provide a brief explanation of the decision, and, where applicable, propose a specific deadline for resolving the complaint. These provisions do not apply if the complaint is resolved in direct communication between the consumer and the trader.

When it comes to the procedure for handling consumer complaints, the trader who proposes a resolution to which the consumer agrees must implement it within a month. Only by exception, the deadline may be prolonged for eight days. The trader, per LCP (Art. 195), must maintain and regularly update a record of submitted consumer complaints. Traders are also required to provide extracts from this record to market surveillance authorities upon request.

LCP (Art. 197) prohibits traders from imposing additional requirements for the submission and handling of consumer complaints through internal rules, general conditions, or other means unless explicitly provided by law. It also forbids traders and third parties from advertising or communicating that consumer complaints can be handled according to provisions different from those established by law.

The LCP is strict on the effect of the consumer complaint. Thus, in Art. 194 provides that the submission and handling of consumer complaints cannot be construed as a waiver of the consumer's available measures and means for fulfilling their rights, nor can it be considered a prerequisite or assumption for such fulfillment.

3.2.2 Out-of-Court Settlement

Out-of-court resolution of consumer disputes, as per Art. 200 of LCP, involves resolving a consumer dispute based on a submitted consumer complaint or a request by the consumer or authorized bodies for the protection of collective consumer interests and rights, before a code of conduct holder, through mediation, arbitration, and other methods of out-of-court resolution of consumer disputes in accordance with specific regulations. This general provision sets the ground for the issue of the ADR of consumer disputes to be regulated by a special law, but also for the application of the relevant laws in the field.

Provisions that provide for the application of ADR also exist in other laws that regulate specific consumer relations. Thus, the Law on Consumer Credits[26] in Art. 33, provides that creditors and consumers will strive to resolve arising disputes through

[26] Law on Consumer Protection in Consumer Credits ("Official Gazette of the Republic of Macedonia" no. 51/11, 145/15, 23/16, 20/19 and "Official Gazette of the Republic of North Macedonia" no. 122/21).

reconciliation, settlement, mediation, or other peaceful means. Provision with almost the same wording (Art. 19) exists in the Law on Distance Financial Services.[27]

3.2.3 Mediation of Consumer Disputes

Mediation is governed by the Law on Mediation.[28] This law defines the principles of mediation, the concept of a mediator, the mediation procedure, and the organization of mediators. The legal framework for mediation in the country began to take shape in 2006 with the adoption of the first Law on Mediation.[29] This law has subsequently been amended several times, resulting in the enactment of a new law in 2013.[30] The development of the legislation aimed at creating an environment that will enable out-of-court settlement of disputes through mediation, facilitating access to mediation and amicable transformation of a dispute to an agreement.[31]

As mediation in North Macedonia is discussed in other chapters of this book, here we will focus on mediation of consumer disputes.

This Law on Mediation regulates mediation in disputes where the parties are free to dispose of their claims unless another law establishes the exclusive jurisdiction of a court or other authority, whether conducted before or after the commencement of judicial or other proceedings. The Law enlists the disputes where mediation may be applied, and consumer disputes are explicitly included (Art. 1 para.2, p.5). The mediation in consumer disputes, having in mind the overall legislative framework, may be a voluntary mediation, as per the choice of the parties prior to or in the course of court proceedings (Art. 4). It is not excluded, but it is yet to be seen the mediation of the consumer disputes to be contractual, in case the consumer contract foresees this mechanism for resolution of the dispute as a prior step to a court settlement. In such cases, as per Art. 4 para. 3, the parties are obliged to attempt to settle the dispute amicably through mediation, and any claim submitted to the court prior to such attempt may be rejected as the court would not have jurisdiction in the case. The mediation may be carried out for the settlement of cross-border consumer disputes as well.

If the principles of mediation of the national law are compared to those set in the EU legislation, including in the ADR Directive, we may conclude that it reflects the positions.

A specific form of mediation are the cases where a Regulatory Body participates as an intermediary in the settlement of consumer disputes for public services.

---

[27] Law on the Provision of Financial Services at a Distance ("Official Gazette of the Republic of Macedonia" No. 158/10 and 153/15 and "Official Gazette of the Republic of North Macedonia" No. 122/21).

[28] Law on Mediation ("Official Gazette" no. 294/2021).

[29] Law on Mediation ("Official Gazette" no. 60/06, 22/07 and 114/09).

[30] Law on Mediation ("Official Gazette" no. 188/13, 148/15, 192/15 and 55/16).

[31] Зороска Камиловска (2007), p. 594.

The Law on Electronic Communications[32] stipulates (Art. 53) that the Agency for Electronic Communications carries out a procedure for settlement of *inter alia* end users (consumers) and electronic communication operators. The procedure is initiated upon request of one of the parties. Before the Agency decides upon the dispute in meritum, it is obliged to propose to the parties a procedure for 'mediation' where the Agency acts as an intermediary. In the case where the parties do not accept such a mediation procedure or there is no settlement reached, the Agency solves the case. What is to be noted is that as per the Law on Electronic Communication in the procedure for deciding upon the case, the Agency applies the Law on General Administrative Procedure.[33] In the dispute, the agency proposes to the parties its settlement by 'mediation,' which is expected to result in an agreement between the parties. The Agency, as an intermediary in this procedure, applies the principles of impartiality, equity, and fairness while ensuring compliance with the objectives and regulatory principles of the Law. The procedure is confidential. The specificities of the procedure are defined by a by-law enacted by the Agency.[34]

3.2.4 Arbitration of Consumer Disputes

There are no general provisions in the national legislation that provide for arbitration as a mechanism for consumer dispute resolution. However, some specific laws that *inter alia* regulate consumer relations in their clauses for dispute resolution forsee the arbitration. The Law on Electronic Commerce in Art. 23 regulates the "Out-of-court Dispute Resolution—Arbitration". It provides that an information society service provider and a user of services may agree on the jurisdiction of arbitration as a dispute resolution *fora*. It also stipulates that for proceedings before arbitration or other out-of-court dispute resolution authority, the regulations governing these areas shall apply. As the national legislation[35] provides that a dispute may be settled by a selected court (arbitration) if the parties have an agreement in writing on the election of that court, it remains unclear to which extent these rules may apply to consumer disputes.

---

[32] Law on Electronic Communications ("Official Gazette of the Republic of Macedonia" No. 39/14, 188/14, 44/15, 193/15, 11/18, 21/18 and "Official Gazette of the Republic of North Macedonia" no. 98/19, 153/19 and 92/21).

[33] Law on General Administrative Procedure ("Official Gazette of the Republic of Macedonia" No. 124/2015 and 65/2018).

[34] Rules on the Manner of Conducting Mediation in the Agency for Electronic Communications ("Official Gazette of the Republic of Macedonia" No. 42/2015).

[35] See further Bungenberg et al. (2023), p. 72.

4 Conclusion

Any policy on alternative dispute resolution (ADR) of consumer disputes necessitates data—data on parties, types of disputes, subject matter, duration of procedures, costs of procedures, etc. The national legislator does not have such data as none of the relevant institutions, organizations, or entities, except for consumer organizations, create and maintain such databases. Any legislative intervention, therefore, would be theoretical—as academics find most adequate (provided they are included in the processes) or very practical—to address the specific needs of interested parties or solely for the purpose of approximating national legislation with EU legislation.

The national legislation on the alternative resolution of consumer disputes comes down to general provisions on the availability of ADR as a mechanism and even its preferability to in-court settlement of consumer disputes. Still, there is a lack of specific legislation regulating the processes and their principles.

Considering the process of approximating national legislation to EU Law, the starting point should be the new EU legislation in the field. However, any solutions to be implemented in the national legal framework should take into consideration the specificities of the local market, consumers' awareness of their rights, and the general (lack of) trust in dispute resolution bodies. It should also consider the position of traders and service providers, their structures, and inherent advantages in the knowledge and information they have compared to consumers.

Only legislation that creates an environment where all parties find the bodies involved in ADR to be fair and impartial and the process to be effective and efficient will fulfill its purpose—making ADR mechanisms for consumer disputes a valuable means of access to justice.

References

Amro I (2016) The resolution of consumer disputes through online arbitration. Int J Arbitr Mediat Disput Manag 82(3):265–280

Bungenberg M, Koveski G et al (2023) Legal framework for arbitration and mediation in North Macedonia and Germany, INVESTinADR. Skopje/Saarbrücken. https://www.uni-saarland.de/en/chair/bungenberg/research/investinadr.html

Carvalho JM, Nemeth K (2018) Implementation of the consumer ADR directive in the EU member states. J Eur Consum Mark Law 7(2):81–82

Dabović-Anastasovska J (2023) Implementacija novina potrošačkog prava Europske unije u potrošačke zakone zemalja regije. Zbornik radova "Aktualnosti građanskog i trgovačkog zakonodavstva i pravne prakse" XX. Međunarodno savjetovanje, pp 7–35

Mechantaf K (2012) Balancing protection and autonomy in consumer arbitrations: an international perspective. Int J Arbitr Mediat Disput Manag 78(3):232–246

Meskic Z (2014) Consumer's right to protection as a fundamental right in accordance with the charter of fundamental rights of the EU. Ann Fac Law Univ Zenica 14:85–112

Moreira JI (2020) The limits to voluntary arbitration in establishing a fair, independent and accessible dispute resolution mechanism outside large contractual disputes. Access to justice in arbitration: concept, context and practice. Kluwer Law International, Alphen aan den Rijn, pp 59–74

Rott P (2016) Improving consumers' enforcement of their rights under EU consumer sales. Common Mark Law Rev 53(2):509–526

Камиловска ТЗ (2007) Медијацијата како алтернатива на судењето-нека спорот стане договор. Зборник на Правниот факултет „Јустинијан Први" – Скопје, Актуелни прашања за државата и правото во Република Македонија и во Руската федерација, Том II, Скопје, pp 592–612

Tech-Driven Justice: Navigating Schemes for the Resolution of Content-Moderation Disputes with Online Platforms

Ivana Kunda

Abstract In today's world where online information flows are constantly rising, the illegality of the content that recipients place on the online platforms is causing profound concern. Forced by the developments in legislation and case-law, the online platforms are putting together architectures of different content-moderation mechanisms. The Digital Services Act is one such legislative instrument aimed at harmonising and solidifying the techno-legal landscape in which online platforms take on the role of quasi-adjudicating authority in moderating illegal or objectionable content. This paper is focused on a segment of this system—the out-of-court dispute settlement mechanism. Explored in detail are the parties and the matter of the proceedings, the bodies certified to carry out the proceedings, and the regulated elements of the procedure with the aim of assessing whether this new addition to the ARD menu in the EU will contribute to the reduction of illegal online content, especially by assuring sufficient human expert verification of the decisions related to a disputed content.

This paper has been written as part of the University of Rijeka project "Transparency and Fairness in the Digital Environment" (uniri-iskusni-drustv-23-101).

I. Kunda (✉)
Faculty of Law, University of Rijeka, Rijeka, Croatia
e-mail: ivana.kunda@uniri.hr

M. Bungenberg et al. (eds.), *Alternative Dispute Resolution in the Western Balkans*, European Union and its Neighbours in a Globalized World 20,
https://doi.org/10.1007/978-3-031-76345-8_17

1 The Alternative Dispute Resolution Landscape in the EU and Croatia

1.1 *State of Affairs Before the DSA*

Increased e-commerce and an overall number of legal relations in the digital environment[1] have brought about the need to facilitate alternative dispute resolution in addition to classical court proceedings. In 2013, the EU dispute resolution landscape was boosted by Directive 2013/11/EU of the European Parliament and of the Council of 21 May 2013 on alternative dispute resolution for consumer disputes and amending Regulation (EC) No 2006/2004 and Directive 2009/22/EC (Directive on consumer ADR)[2] and the Regulation (EU) No 524/2013 of the European Parliament and of the Council of 21 May 2013 on online dispute resolution for consumer disputes and amending Regulation (EC) No 2006/2004 and Directive 2009/22/EC (Regulation on consumer ODR).[3] The Regulation was intended to enable consumers to reach out to online traders and to propose to solve their dispute using a quality ADR entity compliant with the ADR Directive. Envisioned as cornerstones of the legal framework to ensure efficient access to consumer redress in the EU, they failed at many levels mostly due to low level engagement by consumers connected primarily with the low level of traders' engagement. The unattractiveness of the system may be attributed, *inter alia*, to the lack of awareness on the side of consumers[4] and even lower responsiveness of the traders, which in turn discourages even aware and willing consumers.[5]

The situation of ADR in Croatia has evolved since the beginning of this millennium, particularly in response to the challenges and inefficiencies within the judiciary[6] and owing to the accession to the EU and related harmonisation of the national

[1] The market share of e-commerce in the EU-27 where 68% of consumers aged from 16 to 74 years bought or ordered products or services for own consumption at least once in 2022. Eurostat, E-commerce statistics for individuals (2024), https://ec.europa.eu/eurostat/statistics-explained/index.php?title=E-commerce_statistics_for_individuals.

[2] OJ L 165, 18.6.2013, pp. 63–79.

[3] OJ L 165, 18.6.2013, pp. 1–12. Also, the subsequent Commission Implementing Regulation (EU) 2015/1051 of 1 July 2015 on the modalities for the exercise of the functions of the online dispute resolution platform, on the modalities of the electronic complaint form and on the modalities of the cooperation between contact points provided for in Regulation (EU) No 524/2013 of the European Parliament and of the Council on online dispute resolution for consumer disputes, OJ L 171, 2.7.2015, pp. 1–4, complemented the ODR Regulation with modalities for the exercise of the functions, an electronic complaint form and cooperation between contact points of the platform.

[4] Only 6% of consumers who experienced a problem with a trader had reported it to an ADR body. See European Commission Report COM/2023/648 (2023), p. 5.

[5] In between 80 and 85% of complaints go unanswered on the platform and only about of 1% of the complaints (i.e. less than 200 cases) result in an ADR outcome. European Commission Report COM/2023/648 (2023), p. 8.

[6] Uzelac et al. (2010), p. 1266, Kunda (2021), pp. 73–75.

law with the EU law.[7] The benefits of improving, widening, and promoting ADR were also recognised by the Croatian Parliament as part of strategic goals in the development of the national judiciary.[8] The current statistical data concerning the use of the ARD/ODR scheme, however, are truly unsatisfactory in some parts of the EU, including Croatia. Croatia has the lowest absolute number of such disputes, while the numbers adjusted for the population size reveal that this state of affairs is shared throughout South and East Europe. In Croatia, in particular, the factors undermining the success of the ADR/ODR framework relate also to the missed opportunities in the transposition of these instruments in the national legislation. While some advocate for mandatory ADR in consumer disputes,[9] others warn of the inadequacies in the system.[10] Previous research has shown that the manner in which the transposition[11] was made was not fully compliant with the principle of effectiveness in EU law due to the restriction of ADR to purely domestic disputes, thereby excluding disputes between consumers domiciled in Croatia and trader established in another EU Member State. Furthermore, the law failed to create a duty for traders to inform consumers of the ARD bodies and procedures by means of its general terms and conditions. The law also neglected the limitation periods for bringing a lawsuit, which may adversely affect consumers' right to access to justice.[12] Additionally, the selection of the entities to perform this function has been criticised as inappropriate.[13] Thus, an efficient ADR/ODR scheme could have been achieved only by combining EU and national legislative and awareness-raising measures.

The general tendency of consumers not to bring actions against traders,[14] including online platforms, and the particular acuteness of this tendency in the SEE region, including Croatia, has been proven also with regard to the ADR/ODR scheme. This tendency is particularly hard to reconcile with the growing number of disputes related to content management, which does not affect only the private rights of the parties but has a fundamental impact on human rights and freedoms in a democratic society. The development of the content management tools by individual providers of online platforms was a direct result of the pressure exerted by States to protect their citizens' fundamental rights and freedoms, and to maintain the "safe harbour" system

7 Tepeš (2009).

8 Hrvatski Sabor, Strategija razvoja pravosuđa, za razdoblje od 2013. do 2018. godine, NN 144/2012.

9 Primorac and Miletić (2016), p. 418.

10 A comparative overview of consumer dispute resolution in the EU is available in Part II. of the study commissioned by the European Commission: An evaluation study of the impact of national procedural laws and practices on the free circulation of judgements and on the equivalence and effectiveness of the procedural protection of consumers under EU law, JUST/2014/ RCON/PR/CIVI/0082, prepared by the Croatian national reporters Tomljenović V. and Mišćenić E.

11 There was a delay in the Croatian transposition of the Directive on consumer ADR, hence the Alternative Consumer Dispute Resolution Act (Zakon o alternativnom rješavanju potrošačkih sporova, NN 121/16, 32/19) was enacted only in the end of 2016.

12 Mišćenić and Butorac Malnar (2017), pp. 136–137.

13 Uzelac (2018).

14 Rühl (2015), p. 432.

from intermediary liability established under Directive 2000/31/EC of the European Parliament and of the Council of 8 June 2000 on certain legal aspects of information society services, in particular electronic commerce, in the Internal Market (Directive on electronic commerce).[15] This directive was later replaced in that part by the provisions of the Regulation (EU) 2022/2065 of the European Parliament and of the Council of 19 October 2022 on a Single Market for Digital Services, and amending Directive 2000/31/EC (Digital Services Act—DSA).[16]

1.2 New Features Under the DSA

The DSA, which comes as part of the package,[17] is a horizontal legislative instrument aimed at strengthening the regulatory control over the online services sector, in particular providers of intermediary services. In addition to producing a somewhat recalibrated system of "safe harbour" from intermediary liability, it is also intended to provide a new set of due diligence obligations for a transparent and safe online environment applicable to providers of online platforms. This was necessary in view of the behaviour pattern of online service providers, who tend to act for the benefit of recipients of the service only when there is an incentive for them to do so.[18] Many of the obligations under the DSA pertain to the content posted on the platforms, which has exponentially grown ever since the business models based on user-generated content (UGC), a phenomenon that has rapidly expanded since it marked the inception of Web 2.0.[19] The massive increase of UGCs is *pari pasu* followed by the huge increase in illegal and objectional content verified and acted upon by the online platforms.[20] While resorting to courts is reserved for more severe cases related to online content or for more persistent parties,[21] the vast majority of disputes cannot

[15] OJ L 178, 17.7.2000, pp. 1–16.

[16] OJ L 277, 27.10.2022, pp. 1–102.

[17] The other half of the package is the Regulation (EU) 2022/1925 of the European Parliament and of the Council of 14 September 2022 on contestable and fair markets in the digital sector and amending Directives (EU) 2019/1937 and (EU) 2020/1828 (Digital Markets Act—DMA), OJ L 265, 12.10.2022, pp. 1–66. See, e.g., Eifert et al. (2021).

[18] About their tendency to ignore the problems rather than to solve them, see Woods and Perin (2022), p. 93.

[19] O'Reilly (2007).

[20] Quintais et al. (2023), p. 885.

[21] See e.g. ECtHR, *Delfi v Estonia*, No. 64569/09, 16 June 2015; ECtHR, *Magyar Tartalomszolgáltatók Egyesülete and Index.hu Zrt v. Hungary*, No. 22947/13, 2 February 2016; ECtHR, *Magyar Jeti v Hungary*, No. 11257/16, 4 March 2019; Tribunale ordinario di Roma, *Sezione specializzata in materia di Impresa*, 11 dicembre 2019, No. 59264, https://globalfreedomofexpression.columbia.edu/wp-content/uploads/2020/01/sentenzacpifb.pdf; Tribunale ordinario di Roma, *Sezione diritti della persona e immigrazione civile*, 23 febbraio 2020, No. 64894 del 2019, https://globalfreedomofexpression.columbia.edu/wp-content/uploads/2021/06/Tribunale-di-Roma-Measure-February-23-2020-1.pdf; BGH, 29. Juli 2021—III ZR 179/20 und III ZR 192/20, https://www.bundesgerichtshof.de/SharedDocs/Pressemitteilungen/DE/2021/2021149.html.

be expected to ever be handled by the courts if the risk of overburdening them or even blocking them is to be avoided. According to a recent study, the total number of content moderation decisions in the EU by the sampled 8 online platforms was over 2 million in just one day.[22] Similar figures seem to have informed the legislative actions and policies resulting in the DSA, along with the confirmed general persuasion among people (75% in the sample) that sharing harmful content should indeed be prohibited and punished.[23]

Therefore, one of the main focuses of the DSA is on online content management by internet intermediaries, including online platforms. An important novelty is the detailed content and treatment of the notices regarding information that is considered illegal content by a natural or legal person.[24] Although many providers of online platforms have already put in place internal complaint-handling systems for decisions related to alleged illegal or objectionable content that is incompatible with their terms and conditions, these systems are now more standardised and subject to stricter legal requirements.[25] Online platforms are also required to engage with certified out-of-court dispute settlement bodies to resolve disputes with recipients of their services.[26] Connected to this is also the obligation to publish reports on platform activities relating to the removal and disabling of information considered to be illegal or objectionable content.[27] As a consequence, platforms will be forced to enhance these systems—deemed inadequate by governments—by building additional technical, technological, and human capacities. They must also integrate their now-recognised role as co-guardians of public interest to more efficiently deal with problematic content.

In view of the huge amounts of content-moderation requests by recipients, the DSA scheme for dispute resolution is designed to prevent disputes related to content-moderation decisions from reaching the courts, placing them predominantly in the realm of private justice. While private adjudication of online speech currently appears to be the only viable avenue for resolving the numerous disputes related to posted UGC,[28] it raises profound concerns due to its profit-oriented purpose and potential for censorship.[29] It has been suggested that to avoid the risk of "opaque and illegitimate complex systems of co-regulatory speech control", legislators must ensure regulatory independence and implement a holistic approach combining competition,

[22] A total of 2,195,906 was distributed as follows: Facebook (903,183), Pinterest (634,666), TikTok (414,744), YouTube (114,713), Instagram (111,379), Snapchat (11,505), X (5384) and LinkedIn (332). See Dergacheva et al. (2023), p. 5.

[23] Vahed et al. (2024).

[24] See Article 16 of the DSA.

[25] See Article 20 of the DSA.

[26] See Article 21 of the DSA.

[27] See Article 24 of the DSA.

[28] Advocating in favour of this role of online platforms, Gillespie (2018), Suzor (2019).

[29] See e.g. Zuboff (2019), p. 201.

e-commerce, data, and other concerns, as is being initiated by the DSA and DMA package.[30]

On the other hand, the DSA has been heavily criticised for promoting fragmentation rather than approximation and for not recognizing the platform operators' freedom of contract.[31] It was also criticised for not being coordinated with other ADR regimes, which is potentially discouraging because of the variety of schemes and institutions that adds to the complexity of the ADR system as a whole.[32] Indeed, different ADR schemes[33] are still the reality as there are some 430 ADR entities in the European Economic Area (EEA) according to the most recent collection of data.[34] Besides these disadvantages, the DSA is still far detached from the second-generation content-moderation systems, which would be focused on the *ex ante* institutional design choices involved in creating a system of mass administration, and is still mostly based on an individual error correction approach.[35]

The criticism is also addressed from the perspective of the accumulated platform powers in three main areas, which concern content moderation: managing their business (including the code[36]), autonomously designing their rules (by means of terms and conditions), and autonomously enforcing the rules (by means of technical control over the recipients' actions). It has been argued that the accumulated powers are one of the main obstacles to an accountable content-management system, and need to be separated in the administrative structure of the platforms.[37] Some authors would also like to witness the shift of focus from content to platform system, design of the service, the business model, the tools for recipients, and resources allocated to recipients' complaints and safety.[38] Others are concerned with businesses other than Big Tech, which cannot fulfil the DSA requirements, such as for automated systems and data collection for reporting purposes, and do not pose the same threats as the Very Large Online Platforms (VLOPs). Critics fault the legislator for having a narrow focus on only those Big Tech platforms with which regulators are familiar and which use algorithms for content moderation.[39]

Apart from the above-stated comments, this chapter focuses on the issue of whether the bodies offering out-of-court dispute settlement will be able to sustainably operate and deliver intended results regarding the content-moderation decisions, in view of the particular features of the out-of-court dispute settlement scheme. For this reason, the provisions defining the parties and the matter of the proceedings, the

---

[30] Moore and Tambini (2022), pp. 340–341.

[31] Wimmers (2021), p. 389.

[32] Ortolani (2022), p. 562.

[33] See about this issue before the ADR/ODR system in Knudsen (2011).

[34] European Commission Report COM/2023/648 (2023), p. 4.

[35] About the properties of a second-wave content moderation institutional design, see Douek (2022), pp. 584–605.

[36] See Dolata (2021), p. 108, Zuboff (2019), p. 201.

[37] Douek (2022), p. 587.

[38] Woods and Perin (2022), p. 94.

[39] Tushnet (2023), p. 931.

certification of the bodies, and the procedural aspects regulated in the DSA are analysed in detail. This should form the basis for concluding whether this new addition to the ARD menu in the EU can contribute to the reduction of illegal content, especially by means of assuring higher share of human expert verification of the decision related to the disputed content in the overall number of such decisions, which are predominantly machine-generated.

2 Parties to Out-Of-Court Dispute Settlement

One important issue concerns the parties involved in the out-of-court dispute settlement mechanism provided by the DSA. On one side are the recipients of the service, and on the other, the special category of service providers—online platforms. Because the recipients are defined by reference to the online platforms, the latter are addressed first.

2.1 Entities Obliged to Out-Of-Court Dispute Settlement

The obligations under the DSA are intended towards online platforms in particular.[40] The notion of "online platform" has been used in various communications between EU institutions without a clear definition,[41] until its introduction in the DSA. The notion of "online platform" is defined in EU legal sources by reference to higher-ranking notions, ordered from highest to lowest as follows: "service", "information society service",[42] and "intermediary service".[43] Although one might be tempted to include "hosting service" in this list, it may not fit the precise taxonomy.

The term "online platform" is defined as a hosting service that, at the request of a recipient of the service, stores and disseminates information to the public, unless that activity is a minor and purely ancillary feature of another service or a minor

---

[40] This is to some extent also true for the 'online search engines' (Article 3(j) of the DSA), but they are not captured by Article 21 of the DSA. This is in line with the reservations in that sense which were expressed in the course of the legislative procedure leading to the adoption of the DSA. See, e.g. Peukert et al. (2022), 365–366.

[41] See, e.g., Communication from the Commission to the European Parliament, the Council, the European Economic and Social Committee and the Committee of the Regions: A Digital Single Market Strategy for Europe, COM(2015) 192 final; Communication from the Commission to the European Parliament, the Council, the European Economic and Social Committee and the Committee of the Regions: Online Platforms and the Digital Single Market Opportunities and Challenges for Europe, COM/2016/0288 final.

[42] This notion is defined in Article 1(1)(b) of Directive (EU) 2015/1535 of the European Parliament and of the Council of 9 September 2015 laying down a procedure for the provision of information in the field of technical regulations and of rules on Information Society services (codification), OJ L 241, 17.9.2015, pp. 1–15.

[43] Article 3(g) of the DSA.

functionality of the principal service and, for objective and technical reasons, cannot be used without that other service, and the integration of the feature or functionality into the other service is not a means to circumvent the applicability of this DSA.[44]

The definition consists of two parts: the core definition and the exception. The core part of the definition reads: "a hosting service that, at the request of a recipient of the service, stores and disseminates information to the public". Although it may appear that the notion of "hosting service" functions as the *genus proximum* to the notion of "online platform", this needs to be examined more carefully. A "hosting service" is defined as an intermediary service consisting of the storage of information provided by, and at the request of, a recipient of the service.[45] Comparing these two definitions reveals an overlap in the storage of information provided by and at the request of the recipient, while the online platform performs the additional defining activity of "dissemination of information to the public".[46] Thus, the "online platform" cannot be understood as merely a subordinate to "hosting service". Instead, it partially overlaps with and extends beyond the "bare" hosting service. Consequently, it should be considered a direct subordinate of the notion of "intermediary service" and positioned at the same level as "hosting service". It is thus submitted that the inclusion of the term "hosting service" in the definition of "online platform" is not to denote a *genus proximum*, but to link the definition with a notion that is previously known and partially overlapping with the new one.

While the notion of "online platforms" does not encompass "bare" hosting services,[47] since they do not disseminate information to the public, it does include equally single-sided "online platforms" (e.g. streaming services) and two or multiple-sided "online platforms" (e.g. social media and marketplaces). This is also apparent from the list of designated VLOPs.[48] VLOPs are defined as online platforms which have a number of average monthly active recipients of the service in the EU equal to or higher than 45 million, and which are designated as VLOPs pursuant to the Commission decision under Article 33(4).[49] The European Commission, under the DSA, has so far identified 21 VLOPs in its designation decisions. These include Alibaba AliExpress, Amazon Store, Apple AppStore, Booking.com, Facebook, Google Play, Google Maps, Google Shopping, Instagram, LinkedIn, Pinterest, Pornhub, Shein, Snapchat, Stripchat, TikTok, X (formerly Twitter), Wikipedia, XVideos, YouTube, and Zalando.[50] These are just examples of the largest such online platforms, but others

[44] Article 3(i) of the DSA.

[45] Article 3(g)(iii) of the DSA.

[46] See also Buiten (2021), p. 368.

[47] Peukert et al. (2022), p. 12, stating in the context of the intersection of the DSA and copyrights that "mere" hosting service providers are exempted from sharing detailed empirical data on their practices related to automated blocking.

[48] The notion, which is subordinate to the notion of "online platform", is "very large online platform".

[49] Article 33(1) of the DSA.

[50] Decisions of the European Commission of 25 April 2023, C(2023) 2727 final; of 20 December 2023, C(2023) 8842 final; of 26 May 2024, C(2024) 2842 final/2. An annulment of this decision was requested by Zalando and Amazon. See Case T-348/23: Action brought on 27 June 2023—*Zalando*

may also qualify as "online platforms" provided they are not covered by the exclusion specified in Article 3(i), second sentence, of the DSA. This exclusion aims to accommodate business models based on services different from "online platforms", where the content-hosting and content-disseminating are considered a "minor and purely ancillary feature" of the principal service, or "a minor functionality of the principal service", which "for objective and technical reasons, cannot be used without that other service".

There is a special exception provided only for Chapter III, Sect. 3 of the DSA. This Section[51] does not apply to providers of online platforms that qualify as micro or small enterprises.[52] The exception from obligations in Sect. 3 of the DSA concerns providers of online platforms that previously qualified for the status of a micro or small enterprise, during the 12 months following their loss of that status pursuant to Article 4(2) of Recommendation 2003/361/EC, except when they are VLOPs in accordance with Article 33 of the DSA. Thus, this Section applies to VLOPs even if they qualify as micro or small enterprises.[53]

2.2 *Recipients Entitled to Out-Of-Court Dispute Settlement*

Persons entitled to an out-of-court settlement of disputes under Article 21 of the DSA are the "recipients of the service, including individuals or entities that have submitted notices, addressed by the decisions referred to in Article 20(1)".[54] This provision refers to the general notion of "recipient of service" and a special category thereof. The general notion of "recipient of the service" refers to any natural or legal person who uses an intermediary service, in particular for the purposes of seeking

v Commission, OJ C 314, 4.9.2023, pp. 9–11, currently subject to appeal before the CJEU under C-647/23; Case T-367/23: Action brought on 5 July 2023—*Amazon Services Europe v Commission*, OJ C 296, 21.8.2023, pp. 41–42, currently subject to appeal before the CJEU under C-639/23, but Amazon obtained an interim suspension of the EC decision in the part in which it is required to disclose certain customer data. See Order of the President of the General Court, 27 September 2023, Case T-367/23 R, EU:T:2023:589. The annulment of the other decision was also sought by Aylo, a Candan-based company which operated Pornhub, Action brought on 1 March 2024—*Aylo Freesites v Commission*, Case T-138/24, and by Technius LTD, a Cyprus-based company operating the platform Stripchat, Action brought on 29 February 2024—*Technius v Commission*, Case T-134/24, and WebGroup Czech Republic, a.s., a Czech-based company operating the platform XVideos, Action brought on 1 March 2024—*WebGroup Czech Republic v Commission*, Case T-139/24, all three alleging that the Commission erred having inaccurate data about the number of their respective visitors. The list also includes 2 very large online search engines (VLOSEs), which are not subject to the obligations in Chapter III, Section 3 of the DSA.

[51] With the exception of Article 24(3) thereof.

[52] Micro or small enterprises are defined in the Commission Recommendation of 6 May 2003 concerning the definition of micro, small and medium-sized enterprises (Text with EEA relevance) (notified under document number C(2003) 1422), OJ L 124, 20.5.2003, pp. 36–41.

[53] Article 19 of the DSA.

[54] Article 21(1) of the DSA.

information or making it accessible.[55] These may be a variety of persons given the horizontal reach of the DSA, including account holders at social networks, sellers or buyers at online marketplaces, and readers of aggregated newsfeeds.

Thus, the persons who intentionally or not view the content at any of the mentioned types or other online platforms are captured by this notion as well. Some online platform providers offer services that consist of a mere display of information. Therefore, if a person is simply looking at the content on an online platform and considers this content illegal because it is infringing that person's rights, it will be considered a recipient of service. This understanding does not seem to be shared by all without reservations.[56] However, it seems logical to include in the notion of "recipients of the service" also mere viewers of the content on the platform, because content on the internet, in general, is dominantly consumed by simple viewing. This is not only recognised by the broad definition of a "recipient of the service" in the DSA but also by many online platforms, whose terms and conditions provide that whoever browses the information on their webpages submits to their terms and conditions, regardless of the reason for such browsing. Thus, both are recipients of the service: the person who has an account on an online marketplace and posts content showing goods for sale marked with another person's trademark, and the trademark holder who does not have an account but is merely browsing (either directly or through a proxy) the platform in search of content that infringes on his or her trademark (or for any other reason). That is not to say that their legal positions are identical with respect to the online platform and other recipients of the same service; their rights and obligations may differ as they belong to different subcategories of recipients of the service. However, one right they do share is the right to out-of-court dispute settlement under Article 21 of the DSA.

This leads to the mention of a special category of recipients of the service who have the right to use out-of-court settlements to pursue claims against online platforms. Their mention in Article 21(1) of the DSA aims to clarify that those entitled to out-of-court dispute settlement include persons who have submitted a notice pursuant to Article 16 of the DSA, which has been addressed through a decision within an internal complaint-handling system as per Article 20 of the DSA. This notice may inform the service provider of the presence of specific information on their service that the person considers illegal content. The resulting decisions may involve removing or disabling access to or restricting visibility of the information, suspending or terminating the provision of the service or the recipients' accounts, or suspending, terminating, or otherwise restricting the ability to monetize information provided by the recipients. The understanding here proposed regarding the inclusion of a special category of recipients in Article 21(1) of the DSA would affirmatively resolve the doubts discussed about whether the original author of a social media

[55] Article 3(b) of the DSA.

[56] See Ortolani (2022), pp. 535, 563: The author agrees that not only "users at the receiving end of a content-moderation measure" but also "parties that have filed an unsuccessful notice under Article 16" have a right to out-of-court settlement but fails to view such parties as "users". The same author also states that "in many scenarios, a third party (not necessarily a user) will have an interest in the removal of content, in the deactivation of a user's account, or in other moderation measures".

post republished on a different platform could also be deemed entitled to dispute a decision affecting such content.[57] It is submitted here that even without the second part of the provision, which mentions the special category of persons, the original author of a social media post, as described in the hypothetical, would be covered by Article 21(1) of the DSA. By using the service to seek information, he or she would in any case fall under the definition of a "recipient of service", as explained above.

A further question discussed is the rationale behind subjecting trusted flaggers to the same dispute settlement mechanism as other recipients under Article 22 of the DSA, particularly when disputes arise from their notifications. This concern stems from the fact that trusted flaggers operate within their designated area of expertise, and their assessment might be more thorough and informed than those made by less specialised settlement body.[58] However, it is argued that this concern lacks practical relevance. The initiation of the out-of-court dispute settlement procedure pursuant to Article 21 of the DSA is a prerogative reserved only to recipients of the service, including trusted flaggers, with online platforms acting merely as potential defendants. Thus, if a trusted flagger is not satisfied with the available out-of-court dispute settlement bodies under Article 21(3) of the DSA, it cannot be forced into the proceedings before such a body. It is reasonable to assume that a trusted flagger would assess the body's competences prior to initiating any such proceedings.

For the sake of completeness, this analysis also addresses whether a person affected by a decision to restrict content that violates the terms and conditions of an online platform would be entitled to an out-of-court settlement of the dispute. The affirmative answer appears to derive from the provision that makes this type of dispute settlement available to all recipients of the service, and from the understanding that the special category of recipients mentioned in Article 21(1) of the DSA serves the purpose of clarification for cases that might otherwise be seen as far more uncertain than this one.

2.3 *Fixed Procedural Roles of the Parties to Out-Of-Court Dispute Settlement*

Upon ascertaining who may be the parties to the out-of-court dispute settlement mechanism laid down in Sect. 3 of the DSA, further commentary relates to the parties' procedural positions. The relevant part of Article 21(1) of the DSA reads: "recipients of the service […] shall be entitled to select any out-of-court dispute settlement body in order to resolve disputes relating to those decisions, including complaints that have not been resolved by means of the internal complaint-handling system". A literal interpretation does not conclusively determine that the parties' procedural roles are fixed, with the service recipient always as the applicant and the online platform provider as the defendant. Article 21(1) specifically states that a recipient

[57] Barata (2023).

[58] Barata (2023).

is entitled to "select", and Recital 59 mentions that a recipient may "choose" among various options to protect their interests against online platform providers. While the wording per se could suggest a potential reversal of roles, neither teleological nor systemic interpretations[59] support this. The structure of subsequent sentences in Article 21 substantiates this view, such as the one stating the right to out-of-court settlement is "without prejudice to the right of the recipient of the service concerned to initiate, at any stage, proceedings to contest those decisions by the providers of online platforms before a court". Another provision allows "providers of online platforms to refuse to engage with such out-of-court dispute settlement body" only exceptionally, under specific conditions. Apparently, this out-of-court settlement is conceived as an entitlement for the recipient, who decides whether to initiate it, opt for another mechanism, or do nothing, while the online platform provider is expected to "engage, in good faith' and may only refuse if the exact same dispute has already been resolved".

Thus, the out-of-court proceedings under Article 21(1) may be brought by the recipient of a service against the provider of an online platform. Such a constellation of procedural roles also results from the actual situation for which this mechanism is envisaged. It is the provider of an online platform provider which has the sole technical and operational possibility to moderate content on its platform, including making the decisions referred to in Article 20(1)(a)-(d) of the DSA, removing the content, blocking the account, or similar actions. These decisions are the only possible cause of dispute that may be initiated before the out-of-court settlement body. Since these decisions are necessarily rendered by the online platform provider and the content is controlled by it, only the service recipient will ever have reason to contest the decision and hence initiate the proceedings to that effect before the out-of-court settlement body, as outlined in Article 21(1) of the DSA.

3 The Subject of Out-Of-Court Dispute Settlement

3.1 Illegal and Objectional Content

An important question related to the out-of-court dispute settlement mechanism laid down in Sect. 3 of the DSA concerns the types of disputes that may be brought before such bodies. To ascertain this, it is necessary to go back to Article 21(1) of the DSA, which in the relevant part states that the purpose of selecting an out-of-court settlement is "to resolve disputes relating to those decisions [referred to in Article 20(1)], including complaints that have not been resolved by means of the internal complaint-handling system referred to in that Article". Thus, irrespective of whether a notice was submitted pursuant to Article 16 of the DSA or not, the following decisions may be the subject of dispute before the selected out-of-court

[59] These are standard interpretative methods used by the CJEU in interpreting EU law. Lenaerts and Gutiérrez-Fons (2013), pp. 13, 24.

settlement body: decisions on removing or disabling access to or restricting visibility of information, decisions suspending or terminating the provision of the service or the recipients' account, and decisions suspending, terminating or otherwise restricting the ability to monetise information provided by the recipients.[60]

Since the legal ground for content moderation decisions may be State (including EU) law in force or the online platform's terms and conditions (sometimes called community guidelines or content policies), the challenged decision in a particular case may concern illegal content under the law or objectionable content under the contractual terms and conditions.[61] "Illegal content" is defined as "any information that, in itself or in relation to an activity, including the sale of products or the provision of services, is not in compliance with Union law or the law of any Member State which is in compliance with Union law, irrespective of the precise subject matter or nature of that law".[62] Examples include content involving defamation or harassment, intellectual property infringement,[63] discriminatory or hate speech, depictions of violence, riots, terrorist propaganda, or harm to animals and the environment. The reference to the law of EU Member States requires online platforms operating in different EU Member States to observe EU law and potentially 27 other national laws.[64]

A special case is copyright, which has also been extensively regulated in the online environment and appears to largely fall outside Article 21 of the DSA. The DSA is without prejudice to EU law on copyright and related rights, including directives that establish specific rules and procedures that should remain unaffected.[65] Scholarship is not fully in agreement about the scope of the copyright exclusion. While some believe that the provisions on an effective and expeditious complaint and redress mechanism in Article 17(9) of Directive (EU) 2019/790 take precedence over Articles 20 and

[60] Other issues between the recipient and provider, such as proper access to the service, quality of the service and charging of fees, do not fall within this out-of-court settlement mechanism.

[61] See Ortolani (2022), pp. 542, 555, Barata (2023).

[62] Article 3(h) of the DSA.

[63] The special case is the copyright infringement, which occurs if an online content-sharing service provider (OCSSP) gives the public access to copyright-protected works or other protected subject matter uploaded by its users, and this content is infringing. In such a situation, the OCSSP is considered to perform an act of communication to the public or an act of making available to the public and is deemed to be a primary infringer. It is also deprived of the 'safe harbour' under the DSA. See Article 17 of the Directive (EU) 2019/790 of the European Parliament and of the Council of 17 April 2019 on copyright and related rights in the Digital Single Market and amending Directives 96/9/EC and 2001/29/EC, OJ L 130, 17.5.2019, pp. 92–125.

[64] Wimmers (2021), p. 390.

[65] Directive 2001/29/EC of the European Parliament and of the Council of 22 May 2001 on the harmonisation of certain aspects of copyright and related rights in the information society, OJ L 167, 22.6.2001, pp. 10–19; Directive 2004/48/EC of the European Parliament and of the Council of 29 April 2004 on the enforcement of intellectual property rights OJ L 157, 30.4.2004, OJ L 195, 2.6.2004, pp. 16–25 (corrigendum); Directive (EU) 2019/790 of the European Parliament and of the Council of 17 April 2019 on copyright and related rights in the Digital Single Market and amending Directives 96/9/EC and 2001/29/EC, OJ L 130, 17.5.2019, pp. 92–125.

21 of the DSA,[66] others suggest they may complement each other.[67] With regard to audiovisual media services,[68] it is to be noted that specific legislation has priority over the DSA concerning video-sharing platform providers and user-generated content (videos), while the DSA only complements the *lex specialis*.[69] Finally, the overlap between the DSA and P2B legislation[70] has been noted, further complicating the delineation of the scope of DSA content-moderation-related rules.[71]

In addition, the dispute settlement mechanism under Article 21 may also apply to content that the platform itself deems objectionable, but which is not necessarily illegal. The objectionable character is typically defined by a respective rule in the terms and conditions that the provider of the online platform incorporates into contracts with the recipients of its service.[72] There may be overlaps where a single piece of content is both illegal and objectionable, especially in light of indications that providers of online platforms may more effectively combat illegal content if it is also prescribed in the terms and conditions.[73]

3.2 Types of Claims

Regardless of the legal grounds, questions may arise as to the claims that can be brought. Following the list in Article 20(1) of the DSA, it may be concluded that a recipient may request the removal or restoration of content, the enabling or disabling of access, and the removal of restrictions on the visibility of information. The claim depends on whether the recipient is the one whose content is illegal or the one seeking protection against such content. Additionally, the recipient may request that the provision of a suspended or terminated service be reinstated, or that a suspended or terminated account be recovered, provided that the time since termination is not

[66] Wimmers (2021), p. 390.

[67] Spindler (2021), p. 65.

[68] Directive (EU) 2018/1808 of the European Parliament and of the Council of 14 November 2018 amending Directive 2010/13/EU on the coordination of certain provisions laid down by law, regulation or administrative action in Member States concerning the provision of audiovisual media services (Audiovisual Media Services Directive) in view of changing market realities, OJ L 303, 28.11.2018, pp. 69–92.

[69] Recitals 10 and 68 of the DSA.

[70] Regulation (EU) 2019/1150 of the European Parliament and of the Council of 20 June 2019 on promoting fairness and transparency for business users of online intermediation services, OJ L 186, 11.7.2019, pp. 57–79.

[71] Wimmers (2021), p. 391.

[72] See e.g. Apple Website Terms of Use, https://www.apple.com/legal/internet-services/terms/site.html (25/6/2024); Shein Marketplace's General Conditions of Use, https://m.shein.com/eur/Terms-and-Conditions-a-399.html?lang=eur; X Terms of Service, https://x.com/en/tos#intlTerms (25/6/2024); Zalando Standard Terms and Conditions, https://www.zalando.ie/zalando-terms#:~:text=Standard%20Terms%20and%20Conditions%201%201.%20Formation%20of,merchandise%20up%20to%2030%20days%20after%20receipt%20.

[73] Quintais et al. (2023).

excessively long. Finally, the recipient may seek the restoration of the ability to monetise information if it was suspended, terminated, or otherwise restricted. This clearly demonstrates that the EU legislators are moving away from a binary content moderation—limited to simple content removal or non-removal and account suspension or non-suspension—to a more nuanced array of options.[74]

While it is straightforward to deduce the basic claims from the types of decisions that can be challenged under the DSA, other claims are less obvious. For instance, can recipients request compensation for damages caused by the removal of legal content or the failure to remove illegal content (e.g., defamatory or infringing content)? Similarly, can recipients claim compensation for losses (including loss of profit) suffered due to the inability to monetise their content? The notion of "dispute related to decisions" might be construed narrowly to include only actions concerning the upholding or reversing of these decisions, or more broadly to also encompass other claims related to those decisions, including claims for damage compensation.

Although there is no provision in the DSA explicitly prohibiting claims for damage compensation, certain elements suggest a tendency towards a narrow interpretation. One such element is the explicit requirement for the expertise of the settlement body members, which must relate to issues "arising in one or more particular areas of illegal content, or in relation to the application and enforcement of terms and conditions of one or more types of online platform".[75] Awarding damages would require verifying legal grounds for damages, taking evidence, calculating amounts based on that evidence, and in cross-border cases, determining the applicable law and ascertaining its content—tasks necessitating different legal expertise than that envisaged by the DSA. Further supporting a narrow interpretation is the short timeframe within which the body must deliver a decision.[76] In many cases, addressing a claim for damages would prolong the time needed for the resolution of the dispute. Above all, it seems that the purpose of this out-of-court mechanism is primarily to settle disputes related to content moderation decisions rather than any related issues that might arise along the way.

4 The Out-Of-Court Dispute Settlement Body

The out-of-the court dispute settlement may only be commenced and conducted before a certified body. The certification is regulated in Article 21(3) of the DSA. The out-of-court dispute settlement body must be established in an EU Member State. It can be established not only by a private person but also by an EU Member State, or its establishment may be supported by an EU Member State.[77] Once established, it

[74] This shift was noted in the literature, see e.g. Goldman (2021), p. 12, Leerssen (2023).

[75] See Article 21(3)(1)(b) of the DSA.

[76] See Article 21(4)(3) of the DSA.

[77] See Article 21(6) of the DSA.

can make a request to the Digital Services Coordinator (DSC)[78] of the EU Member State in which it is located to certify it. Provided that the body proves that it meets all the requirements in Article 21(3)(1)(a)-(f) of the DSA, the DCS will certify it. The requirements are less intense than those in the Directive on consumer ADR,[79] probably with the intent to ease the certification process in view of the limited scope of the matters to be decided by such bodies and the important advantage in the development and functioning of this means of out-of-court dispute settlement. The certification is issued for a maximum period of five years, and is renewable,[80] but it may also be revoked if the DSC determines that the requirements are no longer met.[81] To facilitate the choice of the out-of-court dispute settlement body, the Commission keeps an updated list of such certified bodies,[82] while the DSC will, where applicable, specify in the certificate the particular issues to which the body's expertise relates, and the official language(s) of the institutions of the EU in which the body is capable of settling disputes.[83] The required expertise relates to areas of illegal content, and the application and enforcement of terms and conditions of online platforms.[84] It is doubtful whether any of the out-of-court settlement bodies will be able to attract sufficient number of experts, given that their profits are limited by the very DSA provisions on the costs of the procedure explained below. The way out of the vicious circle of underfunded bodies is in the support that a body may receive from the EU Member State in which it is established, as allowed under the DSA. Such support may be logistical, financial, or other, which would enable a sustainable operation of the body in question.

5 The Out-Of-Court Dispute Settlement Procedure

5.1 Partial Regulation in the DSA

It has been stated that the DSA adopts the "procedure before substance" approach,[85] and does not create its own substantive user rights regarding the out-of-court dispute settlement mechanism.[86] There are, however, certain rights to information that are established to the benefit of the recipients of the service. One such right is the right to information about the availability of out-of-court dispute settlement, which must

[78] See Article 49 of the DSA.

[79] Ortolani (2022), p. 561.

[80] Upon certification, the out-of-court dispute settlement body has to submit the annual report to the DSC on its functioning. Article 21(5) of the DSA.

[81] Article 21(7) of the DSA.

[82] Article 21(8) of the DSA.

[83] Article 21(3)(2)(a)-(b) of the DSA.

[84] See Article 21(3)(1)(b) of the DSA.

[85] Ortolani (2022), p. 544.

[86] Berberich and Seip (2021), pp. 4–7.

be made easily accessible on the platform's online interface, and be user-friendly.[87] The consequences for non-compliance are specified only for VLOPs.

With respect to the actual manner in which the out-of-court dispute settlement body should operate, the DSA mainly outlines procedural principles, while the body intending to apply for certification is expected to draft its own rules of procedure and submit them to the DSC for evaluation against the criteria set in the DSA. These rules of procedure must be "clear and fair" and "easily and publicly accessible". They also have to "comply with applicable law", including Article 21 of the DSA.[88] The procedural rules in this Article relate to the impartiality and independence, language, means of communication, time limits, costs of proceedings, and the nature of the proceedings and decisions.

5.2 Commencement of the Proceedings

The out-of-court dispute settlement procedure is commenced by a complaint, provided that the respective provider of online platform does not refuse to engage as explained below. The complaint has to be lodged against the platform's decision regarding content, as determined within its internal complaint-handling system, or in response to a complaint that was not resolved through this system.[89] Thus, the out-of-court dispute settlement serves as a kind of facultative appeal against a content-moderation decision taken by the provider of the online platform, or as a facultative instance when no decision is made following the recipient's initial complaint. It seems logical that this dispute settlement is not planned as the first resort, because the solution for the allegedly illegal or objectionable content should first be sought in direct communication between the recipient and the platform provider within the provider's internal systems.

Both the submission of the complaint, whereby the proceedings are commenced, and the submission of any other requisite supporting documents, must be made possible by online means. The procedure must be conducted using electronic communications technology and be easily accessible to the parties.[90] Both parties are obliged to "engage, in good faith, with the selected certified out-of-court dispute settlement body with a view to resolving the dispute". The provider of the online platform may refuse to engage with the body selected by the recipient of the service if a dispute concerning the same information and the same grounds of alleged illegality or incompatibility of content has already been resolved.[91]

[87] Article 21(1)(2) of the DSA.
[88] Article 21(3)(1)(f) of the DSA.
[89] Article 21(1) of the DSA.
[90] Article 21(3)(1)(d) of the DSA.
[91] Article 21(2)(1) and (2) of the DSA.

5.3 Course and Completion of the Proceedings

The certified body must be impartial and independent, including financial independence, from both providers of online platforms and of recipients of the service.[92] The independence of the out-of-court dispute settlement bodies should also be ensured at the level of the natural persons in charge of resolving disputes, including through rules on conflict of interest.[93] These qualities are further guaranteed by the limitation of the ways in which members of the body may be remunerated, which should not be linked to the outcome of the procedure.[94] There is no defined language in which the procedure has to take place, but the requirement that the body operates in at least one of the official languages in EU[95] coupled with the requirement that the body is established in the EU, should ensure a sufficient number of bodies meet the language needs of recipients in different EU Member States.

Essential is also the capability of the body to settle disputes in a swift, efficient, and cost-effective manner.[96] Swiftness and efficiency are to be assured *inter alia* by setting time limits within which the out-of-court procedure must be completed. Certified bodies shall make their decisions available to the parties within a reasonable period of time, and no later than 90 calendar days after the receipt of the complaint. In the case of highly complex disputes, the certified out-of-court dispute settlement body may, at its own discretion, extend the 90 calendar-day period for an additional period that shall not exceed 90 days, resulting in a maximum total duration of 180 days.[97]

The costs of the proceedings are also important for the effectiveness and attractiveness of these settlement bodies, and the exact fees or the way they are calculated must be made known to both parties. The fees differ for different parties and depend on the success of the dispute. If the decision is made in favour of the recipient of the service, including the individual or entity that has submitted a notice, the provider of the online platform will bear all the fees charged by the out-of-court dispute settlement body, and will have to reimburse that recipient for any other reasonable expenses that it has paid in relation to the dispute settlement. The fees charged for the dispute settlement by the out-of-court dispute settlement body to the providers of online platforms have to be reasonable and, in any event, not exceed the costs incurred by the body. For recipients of the service, the dispute settlement must be available free of charge or at a nominal fee. If the decision is rendered in favour of the provider of the online platform, the recipient of the service will not be required to reimburse any fees or other expenses that the provider of the online platform paid or should pay in relation to the dispute settlement, unless the body finds that the recipient manifestly acted in bad faith.[98] These rules on the costs of the procedure

[92] Article 21(3)(1)(a) of the DSA.

[93] Recital 59 of the DSA.

[94] Article 21(3)(1)(c) of the DSA.

[95] Article 21(3)(1)(e) of the DSA.

[96] Article 21(3)(1)(e) of the DSA.

[97] Article 21(4)(3) of the DSA.

[98] Article 21(5) of the DSA.

may incentivise recipients to use this mechanism rather than other available ones, including the judiciary.[99]

The element which may severely jeopardise not only the individual efficiency of the proceedings but also the entire scheme[100] is the lack of power of the body to impose a binding settlement on the parties.[101] Perhaps the transparency obligation may somewhat reverse the balance because the online platform has to report the percentage of decisions they complied with despite their non-binding nature.[102] But the question remains whether this information will actually be accessed by the recipient, given the increasingly larger overall volume of information provided to recipients under different regulatory schemes.

The proceedings are further weakened by the fact that they are without prejudice to the right of the recipient of the service to initiate, at any stage, proceedings to contest those decisions by the providers of online platforms before a court in accordance with the applicable law. Thus, if a recipient of the service needs to react to illegal or objectionable online content, they have options to choose between the internal complaint mechanism, an out-of-court dispute settlement, and, at any time, judicial proceedings. This parallelism is understandable in view of the "lightness" of this out-of-court dispute settlement and the need to retain access to an effective judicial remedy under Article 47 of the Charter of Fundamental Rights of the European Union,[103] as well as judicial control over decisions concerning fundamental rights and freedoms. Similar parallelism is also established in favour of recipients who are consumers, who have the option to always turn to the ADR/ODR body. The rules on the DSA out-of-court dispute settlement are without prejudice to the Directive on consumer ADR, hence, recipient-consumers may opt for that mechanism at any time and withdraw from the DSA out-of-court procedure at any stage if they are dissatisfied with its performance or operation.[104]

6 Conclusion

According to the DSA, a regulatory framework is established which recognises the role of quasi-adjudicating authority to the providers of online platforms for the purpose of moderating illegal or objectionable content. While this may be objectionable on different theoretical bases, it seems practically inevitable given the enormous amounts of content generated and disseminated online by recipients of online services. The processing capacities for content moderation are necessarily based on

[99] Ortolani (2022), p. 565.

[100] See Ortolani (2022), p. 564, making comparisons to the unsatisfactory performance of the ODR system in EU.

[101] Article 21(2)(3) of the DSA.

[102] Article 24(1)(a) of the DSA.

[103] OJ C 326, 26.10.2012, pp. 391–407.

[104] Article 21(9) and Recital 60 of the DSA.

automated systems, while humans play a marginal role. In this context, analysis of the out-of-court dispute settlement mechanism provided for in the DSA seems valuable, especially with regard to the potential for human expert control over decisions related to disputed content.

Upon exploring the regulated features related to the parties, the subject of the proceedings, the certified bodies, and the procedure, it may be concluded that one of the challenges to ensuring human supervision over the outcome of content-related dispute is the strict cost-effectiveness of the mechanism with little fees to be charged. Low fees paid to the experts engaged by the certified body who decide the disputes out of court will surely result in low demand for such engagement and consequently a lower level of expertise. These are poor guarantees for the high-quality decisions rendered by the certified bodies. Eventually, the value of the entire scheme and the initial purpose for its establishment could be frustrated.

To prevent this, the EU Member State in which the body is or should be established could devise a supporting scheme (financial, logistical, or other) for these bodies in the performance of their tasks and thus assure their sustainable operation. The feasibility of this for EU Member States is a completely different question, but alleviating the burden on the State judiciary in the matter of content moderation should not be understood as transferring the related costs entirely to the parties. These are not commercial entities willing to finance arbitration; often the recipient interested in commencing the proceedings is a natural person who would be disincentivised to pursue out-of-court dispute settlement if connected to costs higher than negligible.

References

Barata J (2023) The out-of-court settlement mechanism under the DSA: questions and doubts. https://dsa-observatory.eu/2023/10/26/the-out-of-court-settlement-mechanism-under-the-dsa-questions-and-doubts/

Berberich M, Seip F (2021) Der Entwurf des digital services act, Gewerblicher Rechtsschutz und Urheberrecht. Praxis Im Immaterialgüter- und Wettbewerbsrecht 13(1):4–7

Buiten MC (2021) The digital services act from intermediary liability to platform regulation. J Intellect Prop Inf Technol E-Commerce Law 12(5):361–380

Dergacheva D et al (2023) One day in content moderation: analyzing 24 h of social media platforms' content decisions through the DSA transparency database, lab Platform Governance, Media, and Technology (PGMT). Centre for Media, Communication and Information Research (ZeMKI), University of Bremen. https://doi.org/10.26092/elib/2707

Dolata U (2021) Varieties of internet platforms and their transformative capacity. In: Suter Ch et al (eds) The future of work. Seismo, Zürich and Genève, pp 100–116

Douek E (2022) Content moderation as administration. Harv Law Rev 136(2):526–607

Eifert A et al (2021) Taming the giants: the DMA/DSA package. Common Mark Law Rev 58(4):987–1028

European Commission (2023) Report from the commission to the European Parliament, the Council and the European Economic and Social Committee on the application of Directive 2013/11/EU of the European Parliament and of the Council on alternative dispute resolution for consumer disputes and Regulation (EU) No 524/2013 of the European Parliament and of the Council on online dispute resolution for consumer disputes, COM/2023/648 final

Gillespie T (2018) Custodians of the internet: platforms, content moderation, and the hidden decisions that shape social media. Yale University Press, New Haven

Goldman E (2021) Content moderation remedies. Mich Technol Law Rev 28:1–60

Knudsen LF (2011) Diversity of ADR schemes: does it mean diversity of ADR effectiveness? Curr Issues Econ Manag Sci 350–358

Kunda I (2021) Experiences and challenges of croatia as EU member state. In Kellerhals A, Baumgartner T (eds) Current challenges of European integration: 12th network Europe conference. EIZ Publishing, Zürich, pp 61–80. https://eizpublishing.ch/publikationen/current-challenges-of-european-integration/

Leerssen P (2023) An end to shadow banning? Transparency rights in the digital services act between content moderation and curation. Comput Law Secur Rev 48:105790

Lenaerts K, Gutiérrez-Fons JA (2013) To say what the law of the EU Is: methods of interpretation and the European court of justice. AEL 2013/9, Academy of European Law European University Institute, San Domenico di Fiesole. https://cadmus.eui.eu/bitstream/handle/1814/28339/AEL_2013_09_DL.pdf

Mišćenić E, Butorac Malnar V (2017) Online rješavanje potrošačkih sporova. Godišnjak Akademije Pravnih Znanosti Hrvatske VII I(1):103–142

Moore M, Tambini D (2022) Conclusion: without a holistic vision, democratic media reforms may fail. In: Moore M, Tambini D (eds) Regulating big tech. Oxford University Press, New York, pp 338–347

O'Reilly T (2007) What is web 2.0: design patterns and business models for the next generation of software. Commun & Strat 65(1):17–37

Ortolani P (2022) The resolution of content moderation disputes under the digital services act. Giustizia Consensuale 2(2):533–573

Peukert A et al (2022) European copyright society – comment on copyright, and the digital services act proposal. Int Rev Intellect Prop Compet Law 53(3):358–376

Primorac Ž, Miletić N (2016) Europski pravni kontekst izvansudskog rješavanja sporova. Zbornik Pravnog Fakulteta u Zagrebu 66(2–3):391–420

Quintais JP et al (2023) Using terms and conditions to apply fundamental rights to content moderation. German Law J 24(5):881–911

Rühl G (2015) Alternative and online dispute resolution for cross-border consumer contracts: a critical evaluation of the European legislature's recent efforts to boost competitiveness and growth in the internal market. J Consum Policy 38:431–456

Spindler G (2021) Der Vorschlag für ein neues Haftungsregime für Internetprovider – der EU-Digital Services Act Teil 2: Große und besonders große Plattformen. Gewerblicher Rechtsschutz und Urheberrecht 123(5):653–662

Suzor N (2019) Lawless: the secret rules that govern our digital lives. Cambridge University Press, Cambridge

Tepeš N (2009) Izvansudsko rješavanje potrošačkih sporova u Hrvatskoj. In: Tomljenović V et al (eds) Republika Hrvatska na putu prema Europskom pravosudnom području: Rješavanje trgovačkih i potrošačkih sporova. Pravni fakultet u Rijeci, Rijeka, pp 171–200

Tushnet R (2023) Three sizes fit some: why content regulation needs test suites. Berkeley Technol Law J 38:921–932

Uzelac A (2018) Izazovi novog uređenja izvansudskog rješavanja potrošačkih sporova. In: Slakoper Z et al (eds) Liber amicorum Aldo Radolović. Sveučilište u Rijeci, Pravni fakultet, Rijeka, pp 145–165

Uzelac A et al (2010) Aktualni trendovi mirnog rješavanja sporova u Hrvatskoj: dosezi i ograničenija. Zbornik Pravnog Fakulteta u Zagrebu 60(3):1265–1308

Vahed S et al (2024) Moral judgment of objectionable online content: Reporting decisions and punishment preferences on social media. PLoS ONE 19(3):e0300960. https://journals.plos.org/plosone/article?id=10.1371/journal.pone.0300960

Wimmers J (2021) The out-of-court dispute settlement mechanism in the digital services act: a disservice to its own goals. J Intellect Prop Inf Technol E-Commerce Law 12(5):381–401

Woods L, Perin W (2022) Obliging platforms to accept duty of care. In: Moore M, Tambini D (eds) Regulating big tech. Oxford University Press, New York, pp 93–109
Zuboff S (2019) The age of surveillance capitalism: the fight for a human future at the new frontier of power. Profile Books, London

Plea Bargaining and Guilty Plea as Negotiated Justice Instruments in Macedonian Criminal Trials

Gordana Lažetić and Boban Misoski

Abstract The authors elaborate on the practical implementation of the two newly enacted elements for negotiated justice within the Macedonian criminal procedure. In this occasion, the authors perform research of the practical implementation of the sentence bargaining and guilty plea in front of the courts for the period of seven years. Authors conclude that instead of having a wider use of these negotiated instruments in practice and by that improving the efficiency and efficacy of the Macedonian courts, the contrary situation can be observed, as the number of cases resolved through these instruments are declining. The chapter analyses the reasons for such situation and provides theoretical and practical possible solutions for improvement of the observed trend in the use of these negotiated justice instruments.

1 Introduction

Historically, the introduction of the concepts of mutual dispute resolution and negotiated justice in criminal trials was viewed as an alien und unacceptable form to resolve criminal cases. However, as criminal procedures have become notoriously overburdened with formalism, inflexibility and predominantly ineffective, new solutions for improvement of their efficiency and efficacy were considered as a must. The solution was to search for mechanisms from comparative law that were proven as efficient and less time and resource consuming, thereby enhancing a more efficient, effective, and just resolution of criminal disputes. Examples of such mechanisms include the

This article is based upon a wider research of the efficiency of the guilty plea and sentence bargaining procedure, titled: The Effectiveness of the Adversarial System of Criminal Procedure in Term of Delayed Justice and Use of Plea Bargaining in North Macedonia, performed in 2020 with the grant from the US Embassy in Skopje. Available at: Microsoft Word—Анализа за спогодување (maclc.mk) (21/5/2024).

G. Lažetić · B. Misoski (✉)
Department of Criminal Procedural Law, Faculty of Law "Iustinianus Primus", Ss. Cyril and Methodius University, Skopje, North Macedonia
e-mail: b.misoski@pf.ukim.edu.mk

M. Bungenberg et al. (eds.), *Alternative Dispute Resolution in the Western Balkans*, European Union and its Neighbours in a Globalized World 20,
https://doi.org/10.1007/978-3-031-76345-8_18

introduction of abbreviated criminal trials, plea bargainings, and the extended use of mediation as an out-of-court settlement in criminal trials.[1]

This trend was reinforced by the Council of Europe's (CoE) 1987 Recommendation on the acceleration of criminal trials in,[2] which advocated for the introduction of the mechanisms for negotiated justice in criminal trials to improve their efficiency and effectiveness. In response to these recommendations, and to improve the efficiency of Macedonian criminal trials, the Macedonian legislator enacted a new Criminal Procedure Code (CPC) in 2010. The CPC introduced a series of innovations aimed at increasing the efficiency of the criminal procedure and enhancing procedural guarantees, particularly the defendant's right to a fair trial and to a trial within a reasonable time.[3]The most significant novelties of the 2010 CPC included the introduction of an adversarial main hearing with a passive role for the judge and multiple mechanisms for the acceleration of the criminal procedure.

The main mechanisms introduced for accelerating criminal trials included: (i) allowing a guilty plea during the first hearing of the main trial or during the indictment examination phase; (ii) introducing a sentence bargaining during the investigative phase; (iii) widening the use of mediation to resolve criminal trials; (iv) issuing penal orders as an alternative to commencing a full trial; and (v) broadening the use of abbreviated procedures as a distinct type of criminal procedure.[4]

Recognizing that effective criminal justice can be ensured through procedures that promote decriminalization, depenalization, alternative forms of criminal prosecution, or simplification of criminal procedure, it is necessary to differentiate between guilty pleas, sentence bargaining, and other forms of negotiation within the provisions for accelerated justice in the CPC. Guilty pleas and sentence bargaining alternatives to court proceedings involving the defendant, his/her defense attorney, and the public prosecutor the authorized plaintiff. In contrast, negotiations for compensating damages from crimes, which occur between the defendant and the injured party and are facilitated by an impartial third party (mediator), serve as alternatives to prosecution.

The main goal of this article is to examine the efficiency of the guilty plea and sentence bargaining as tools to accelerate criminal procedures and as alternative to traditional trials. The effectiveness of other negotiated justice instruments will only be partially considered as part of the above-mentioned analysis.[5]

---

[1] See Kambovski et al. (2007).

[2] See Recommendation no. (87) 18 of 17 September 1987, adopted at the 410th session of the Ministers and their deputies from the member states of the Council of Europe. Available at: https://wcd.coe.int/com.instranet.InstraServlet?command=com.instranet.CmdBlobGet&InstranetImage=608011&SecMode=1&DocId=694270&Usage=2.

[3] See Official Gazette of the Republic of Macedonia, No. 150/2010.

[4] See Bužarovska et al. (2008), p. 205.

[5] See Lažetić et al (2021), pp. 10.

2 Theoretical Background of the Guilty Plea and Sentence Bargaining as Concepts of Negotiated Justice in Macedonian Criminal Trials

Negotiated justice, as originally conceived in the United States federal criminal justice system, is divided into two modalities.[6] The first modality is a plea agreement, where the defendant together with his/her defense counsel reach a mutual settlement with the prosecutor concerning guilty pleas and the structure of the indictment, known as charge bargaining. The second modality is a full plea agreement, commonly referred to as sentence bargaining, which involves negotiations between the parties of the criminal procedure on the type and severity of the criminal sanction.[7]

In charge bargaining, as a form of plea bargaining, the parties negotiate and mutually agree on the defendant's guilt through the formulation of charges within the indictment. Hence, this agreement implicitly includes the type and amount of the sanction. This conclusion is evident from the outcome of the charge bargaining procedure, where negotiations between the defendant and the prosecutor undoubtedly influence the determination of the proposed type and severity of the criminal sanction.

On the other hand, sentence bargaining, as a type of plea bargaining, specifically excludes negotiations between the prosecutor and the defendant regarding the composition of the charges stated in the indictment, focussing instead on the determination of the type and severity of the criminal sanction. During sentence bargaining, the prosecutor and the defendant, represented with his/her defense attorney, do not contest the description of the charges in the indictment but negotiate the type and amount of the criminal sanction in the agreement. The agreed-upon sanction should be mutually acceptable and in line with the law.

This division of the original concept of plea bargaining into charge bargaining and sentence bargaining has further theoretical and practical implications, since it offers multiple possibilities for replication in other criminal justice systems.

Considering that the Macedonian criminal justice system adheres strictly to the principle of mandatory prosecution, where the public prosecutor is required to initiate criminal prosecution whenever there is evidence that a crime that is prosecuted *ex officio* has been committed, it is evident that sentence bargaining is the only acceptable possibility for plea bargaining between the prosecutor and the defendant.[8]

The newly established Macedonian concept of sentence bargaining is essentially based on the original US concept of sentence bargaining with regard to several aspects. The first aspect is that the Criminal Code allows the bargaining procedure

---

[6] Regarding the modalities of the settlement procedure, there is another form in the original model—nolo contendere admission of guilt, where the accused only admits the crime, but not the consequences of it. Given the fact that even in the federal system of criminal justice in the United States, this form of confession is considered a relic and more of a problematic and complicated concept, it does not find a wider justification in the countries that introduce the settlement procedure in their criminal justice systems, and that is why we do not pay extra attention to this form on this occasion.

[7] See Fisher (2003), pp. 21 et seqq.

[8] See Bužarovska and Misoski (2010), pp. 3.

for all types of crimes, regardless of the severity of the proscribed sanctions[9] (see Art. 483, para. 1 of the CPC).

Another aspect is that the CPC provides identical guarantees by the court regarding the protection of the defendant's rights from unfounded indictments or vindictiveness by the public prosecutor.[10] These guarantees are provided in the Articles that establish the court's obligation to evaluate whether the proposed draft settlement resulting from the sentence bargaining procedure is made by an informed defendant, ensuring the defendant's awareness of the consequences of accepting the draft settlement, and to evaluate whether this acceptance is voluntary (Art. 488, para. 2).

Finally, although the CPC only recognizes sentence bargaining as negotiation on the type and severity of the criminal sanction, the Macedonian model is somehow similar but also differs from the original model of sentence bargaining. A key similarity is that the extent of sentence mitigation proposed is not mandatory for the courts. However, the Macedonian model differs because its criminal justice system lacks sentencing guidelines that would aid the prosecutor and defendant in framing their agreement and the sanction to propose to the court. The Macedonian CPC only regulates that proposed sanctions can be mitigated to the minimum limits of the penalty prescribed in the Criminal Code.[11]

Considering the phases of the criminal procedure during which sentence bargaining is available, we can conclude that this procedure can be applied both during the investigative phase and during the phase where the legality of the indictment is reviewed.

The specifics of this procedure in relation to the different stages of the criminal procedure primarily concern the defendant's guilty plea. Depending on the stage of the criminal procedure, the requirements differ as to whether a guilty plea is a formal precondition to initiate the sentence bargaining procedure. Specifically, a formally given guilty plea obligates the prosecutor to start the sentence bargaining procedure only if it is given in the phase of the control of the indictment, as outlined in Art. 334 of the CPC. During the investigative phase of the criminal procedure, however, a formal guilty plea is not a prerequisite for initiating the sentence bargaining. In this case, the procedure can be commenced once the defendant expresses his/her readiness to negotiate with the prosecutor. Under these legal provisions, the defendant's willigness to negotiate is considered an implicit guilty plea, acknowledging the indictment by not disputing the facts. In such case, there is no need for an explicit guilty plea from the defendant, since there is no formal indictment to plead guilty to.

On the other hand, in cases where the guilty plea is given during the defendant's first interrogation before the court, the focus shifts to the court's responsibilites. In such cases, the court is obliged to protect the defendants' rights primarily to check

---

[9] See for example the Italian or French system of sentence bargaining, where such procedure is allowed only for the lesser crimes. See Bužarovska et al. (2008), pp. 201–240.

[10] See the remarks of the United States Supreme Court in *Bordenkircher v. Hayes* regarding the protection of an accused person against prosecutorial retaliation in the absence of a plea bargaining. See Supreme Court of the United States, *Bordenkircher v. Hice*, 1978. 434 US 357, 98 S.Ct. 663, 54L.Ed.2d 604.

[11] See Matovski et al. (2011), pp. 71–72.

whether the guilty plea is both voluntary and informed. If the court confirms this, the evidentiary procedure is shortened, and the parties focus only on evaluating the evidence that is important for the court to determine the type and severity of the sanction that will be imposed (Art. 380 and 381 of the Criminal Code).

3 Practical Implementation of the Sentence Bargaining Procedure in Front of the Macedonian Courts

3.1 Data Analysis

In order to analyse the significance of these mechanisms of accelerated justice within the Macedonian criminal courts, a comprehensive longitudinal study was conducted in 2021, analysing data from various courts and public prosecution offices.[12] Considering the available data on the work performance of the Macedonian courts and public prosecution offices, we can conclude that in practice the number of cases resolved through guilty pleas during the main hearing, as well as those settled by sentence bargaining during the investigative phase of the criminal procedure, is in constant fall.

Hence, considering the data on the total number of resolved criminal cases and their correlation with cases resolved upon guilty pleas, it can be concluded that a very small percentage of cases were resolved by defendants' guilty pleas during the main hearing. Furthermore, considering the data obtained from interviews with judges, we can conclude that the number of draft settlements submitted during the investigative phase of the criminal procedure has significantly decreased. During the phase of indictment evaluation, almost no settlements have been submitted.

Considering the data from Fig. 1, we observe a consistent downward trend in the number of cases resolved through sentence bargaining procedures or guilty pleas.

The decision to portray only the data from the Basic Criminal Court in Skopje is based on the fact that it is the largest court in the Republic of North Macedonia in terms of the number of cases. Furthermore, within this court operates a specialized unit with jurisdiction over the entire state, established specifically for adjudicating cases involving defendants indicted for perpetrating organized crimes. Hence, we consider such data to be reliable for drafting general conclusions about the aforementioned trends. Moreover, the conclusions from the Basic Criminal Court in Skopje are in correlation with other available data from other courts, as shown in the Courts' Annual Statistical Reports.[13]

Combining these data with the available data from the Public Prosecution's offices in regard to verdicts delivered upon a submitted draft settlement between the defendant and the public prosecutor as a result of a sentence bargaining procedure, as

[12] See: Lažetić et al (2021), pp. 15.

[13] Ibid.

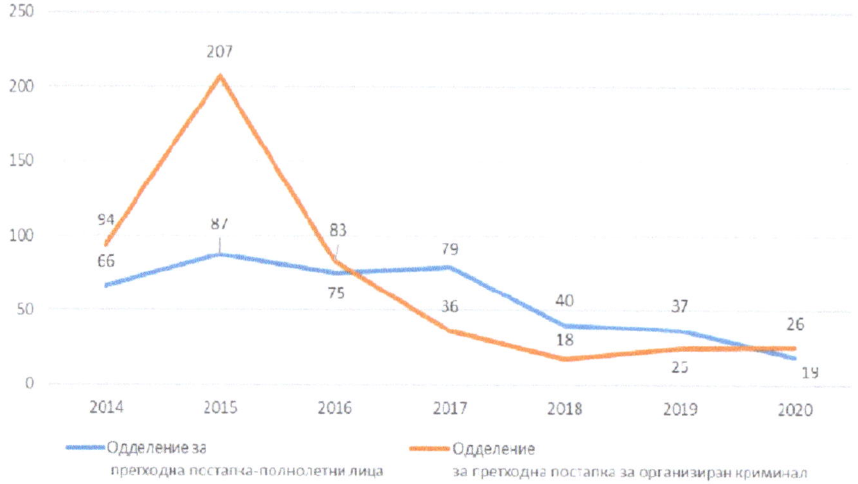

Fig. 1 Data from the Basic Criminal Court Skopje from 2014 to April 2020. Blue line: Department for pretrial procedure—adolescents. Orange line: Department for pretrial procedure—organized crime. *Source* Data received from The basic criminal court Skopje

Table 1 Total number of judgments based on draft settlement proposals

Year	Total number of judgments based on proposed settlements	Trends in relation to previous year
2014	284	/
2015	300	+6%
2016	458	+53%
2017	327	−29%
2018	280	−14%
2019	272	−3%

Source See Lažetić et al (2021), p. 18

observed in the Public Prosecution's Office of the Republic of North Macedonia Annual reports,[14] reveals similar trends.

Hence, taking into account the numbers from Table 1, we can conclude that the annual number of such verdicts is consistently low, with a relative tendency toward a reduction in cases.

To obtain unbiased information, we can also analyse the reports from the independent NGO *Coalition All for Fair Trials*, which annually monitors specific court proceedings. It reported recording 40 verdicts based on a defendant's guilty plea during the analyzed period of 2017. This number decreased to 26 in 2018, and in

[14] Available at: https://jorm.gov.mk/category/dokumenti/izvestai/ (21/5/2024).

2019, observers noted only 7 cases where the courts delivered verdicts based on a defendant's guilty plea.[15]

3.2 Discussion

The reasons for such rare, or almost sporadic, application of the sentence bargaining procedure and guilty plea as novel instruments for negotiated justice within the Macedonian criminal justice system may be owed to several aspects.

A first aspect is the lenient penal policy of the courts in regard to the delivering of criminal sanctions after the regular criminal procedure. The impact of the type and severity of the criminal sanction is treated as one of the main factors that influence the low percentage of application of the procedure for sentence bargaining. In addition, defendants do not see real incentive or motivation to enter into a plea agreement with the public prosecutors, since in any case they would receive a favorable sentence from the courts after the commencement of the regular criminal procedure. Even more, we can conclude that the defendant's incentive for entering into sentence bargaining during the pretrial procedure, usually results in the prosecutor's proposal of a stricter criminal sanction as starting point for negotiation. According to numerous defense attorneys,[16] this stance of the public prosecutors has a demotivating effect, leading to unfavorable views of both defendants and their attorneys on the sentence bargaining procedure.

A second aspect is the absence of sentencing guidelines that would provide stronger predictability of the criminal sanctions after the trials as an incentive for more frequents implementation of the sentence bargaining procedure before or during the main hearing of the trial.[17] The absence of data on the expected sanction, as well as the absence of proper and previously established criteria for determining the type and severity of the criminal sanction in relation to which the public prosecutor and the defendant would negotiate, leads to the impression that the defendants treat this option primarily as a public prosecutor's tool that does not offer them any privileges for an effective and efficient termination of the criminal trial.

In this fashion, we should mention the Law on Determination of the Type and Severity of the Criminal Sanctions,[18] which was briefly in force and then declared as unconstitutional by the Constitutional Court.[19] This law was primarily intended to serve as a tool for judges to determine the type and severity of criminal sanctions. However, this Law was too rigid and did not provide sufficient maneuverable space

[15] See Misoski et al. (2018, 2019, 2020).

[16] See Lažetić et al (2021), pp. 30.

[17] See Gruevska Drakulevski and Misoski (2014).

[18] See Kanevchev (2017), Tupanceski and Deanoska Trendafilova (2017), Lažetic Bužarovska (2014).

[19] Decision of the Constitutional Court of Republic of North Macedonia, U. No. 169/2016-1 of 16.11.2017, available at: http://ustavensud.mk/?p=11736.

for judges, providing rigid mandatory guidelines for determining sanctions. Hence, the law was received as negative impact on judges' free will and individual right to adjudicate the cases in accordance with the observed facts during the criminal trial. To the contrary, judges felt that this law would convert them into mathematicians, who simple calculate aggravating and mitigating factors of the crime and by that simply count the months of the imprisonment that they would impose on the defendants.[20]

Furthermore, the Constitutional Court found that this law directly contradicts the CoE's Recommendation No. R(92)17 of 1992 on Consistency in Sanctioning,[21] according to which previous convictions should not be mechanically used as a factor against the defendant at any stage of the criminal procedure. Despite this, the aforementioned law specifically provided that a previous conviction was automatically considered as aggravating factor in the determination of sanctions in the criminal procedure.[22]

However, we believe that to achieve predictability and certainty of sanctions within criminal trial, and thereby increase the use of negotiated justice mechanisms for acceleration of these trials, judicial independence and autonomy in decision-making should not be compromised. Therefore, we believe that a potential solution might be the introduction of an automated tool that generates the average or most common sanctions for similar crimes under similar circumstances. This tool would use data from a comprehensive database of all pronounced sentences over a specific period of time and could serve as a basis for negotiating sanctions between the public prosecutor, the defendant and his/her defense attorney.[23]

Another aspect is the lack of consistent or harmonized court practices, especially the failure of the Supreme Court of Justice to produce principled positions and legal opinions. This absence hinders the improvement of court practices regarding sentence bargaining procedures and the rewarding of guilty pleas during the main hearing of the criminal trial.

The timeliness of trial is another aspect that influences the implementation of negotiated justice instruments. In situations where criminal trials are notably prolonged, defendants might view the extended duration of the trial as advantageous rather than as a violation of their right to a trial in a reasonable time. This conclusion is based on the fact that in several court proceedings in front of Macedonian courts lengthier trials have not been observed by the defendants as a factor that negatively affects the swift and efficient resolution of their cases, since in most of such cases the statutes of limitation were met, resulting in factual impunity for the defendants.[24]

Legal imperfections and/or systemic principles can also be seen as obstacles to the more frequent use of sentence bargaining procedures and guilty pleas. One of the main reasons for the low number of settlement procedures in practice is the principle

[20] Lažetić–Bužarovska et al. (2016).

[21] Recommendation No. R (92)17 concerning consistency in sentencing, 19.10.1992.

[22] Bužarovska and Nanev (2017).

[23] See the solution for sketching the sanction or the so-called "sentence canvasing" in UK courts. For more details, see Sprack (2005), pp. 92.

[24] As for example the case of the "Trajectory" subject led by SPO. See Petrovska et al. (2020).

of mandatory prosecution of crimes by public prosecutors. This obligation, along with the rigid by-laws that govern these procedures at the Public Prosecutor's Office, also acts as a deterrent to parties to consider these options in practice. However, considering the prevailing legal culture, we believe that it is premature to propose reducing the principle of mandatory prosecution at this time. Any proposals for amending such a fundamental aspect should be based on a more extensive analysis of the potential overall impact of such a change on the entire criminal procedure, and not solely on the need to increase the number of sentence bargains in practice.

A further problematic issue in criminal procedure is the lack of a strict provision in the CPC that would prevent the possibility of resubmitting a draft settlement, initially rejected by a court during a sentence bargaining procedure due to an ill-founded defendant's will or lack of evidence, to another judge who might accept the same draft settlement. We believe this practice, known as "judge shopping", should be eradicated because it de facto contaminates the outcomes of criminal proceedings.

Finally, the absence of a sentencing hearing as a distinct part of the main hearing significantly undermines the public perception of a just and fair process of adjudication in cases involving a guilty plea by the defendant, or a sentence bargaining procedure. Hence, the absence of legal provisions in the CPC for the establishment of such sentence hearing reduces the possibility for public hearings of criminal trials. This reduction may lead to increased distrust in the courts and in public prosecutors as they deliberate cases through such negotiated justice instruments. The absence of a sentence hearing, where the parties could elaborate on the evidence in open court might be observed as deterring the use of sentence bargaining or guilty pleas, since in such situations judges and prosecutors might feel uncomfortable making decisions without the support of public scrutiny and evaluation of the available and submitted evidence.

4 Conclusion

After ten years of implementing the new Criminal Procedure Code, which introduced many novelties, in particular several that specifically address the acceleration of criminal trials, we still cannot conclude that the Macedonian criminal justice system is just, efficient and effective. Even more, the borrowed legal transplants, such as negotiated justice instruments, have failed to significantly impact the reduction of criminal trials that are adjudicated through regular criminal procedures, or to reduce the duration of these trials. Despite research conducted over a significant period, we were not able to find sufficient data from resolved cases through sentence bargaining that would markedly improve the performance of Macedonian courts.

Some of the reasons for the poor implementation of these negotiated justice instruments aimed at accelerating the criminal procedure can be attributed to the absence of additional support mechanisms for the implementation of sentence bargaining and guilty plea procedures. In particular, the absence of a practical tool for sentence canvassing has been identified as a necessary mechanism that might increase the use of the sentence bargaining procedure. For these reasons, it is necessary to upgrade the courts' automated system to provide average sentences for identical crimes committed under similar social conditions. Bearing in mind that every court already has an automated system in place, which contains records of every sanction, we believe that upgrading this system should not be considered "mission impossible".

Another problematic area is the lenient court sanctioning policy, which has proven to be a demotivating factor for the sentence bargaining procedure, since the defendants often do not see any reason for entering into a bargain with the prosecutor, knowing they might receive the same or even a more lenient sanction after a full criminal trial. This issue, coupled with the unpredictability of criminal sanctions and the tendency of public prosecutors to propose more rigid sanctions during sentence bargaining compared to what might be issued after a lengthy trial, results in negotiated justice instruments not being considered a priority in the adjudication of criminal cases.

Hence, we need further reforms in order to reevaluate the sanctioning policy of the Macedonian courts and strengthen the role of the prosecutors during the negotiation procedure. Such reforms would provide stricter legal frameworks for determining criminal sanctions for specific crimes, with greater emphasis on mitigating and aggravating factors. Finally, certain amendments to the CPC should be considered and thoroughly researched, since the current rigid requirement for mandatory prosecution of crimes by public prosecutors has been found to be overly burdensome, hindering their more active involvement in bargaining procedures, which are essential to negotiated justice.

References

Bužarovska G, Misoski B (2010) Plea bargaining in the new law on criminal procedure in the Republic of Macedonia. Macedonian Law J 2:1–16

Bužarovska G, Misoski B, Nanev L (2008) Comparative research of solutions for speeding up and simplifying the criminal procedure. MRKPK 1

Bužarovska G, Nanev L (2017) Analysis of the application of the Law on determining the type and amount of punishment in the basic courts of Tetovo, Veles, Kočani and Kavadarci, May 2017. http://www.merc.org.mk/Files/Write/Documents/04798/mk/Analiza_Primena-na-ZOVOVK_SPPMD-Juni-2017.pdf

Fisher G (2003) Plea bargaining's triumph: a history of plea bargaining in America. Stanford University Press, Stanford

Gruevska Drakulevski A, Misoski B (2014) Comparative analysis of sentencing guidelines mechanisms: the US sentencing guidelines. MRKPK 21(1). http://maclc.mk/Upload/Documents/06.pdf

Kambovski V, Krapac D, Kalajdziev G, Bužarovska G (2007) Strategy for reform of criminal law. Ministry of Justice 2007

Kanevchev M (2017) On some (controversial) decisions from the Law on determining the type and measuring the amount of the penalty. MRKPK 24(1). http://maclc.mk/Upload/Documents/Metodija%20Kanevchev%202.pdf

Lažetic Bužarovska G (2014) Uneven penal policy and its impact on the settlement of criminal sanctions according to the Law on Criminal Procedure. MRKPK 21(1). http://maclc.mk/Upload/Documents/03.pdf

Lažetić Bužarovska G, Tupanceski N, Mujoska E (2016) Mandatory sentencing guidelines: the case of Macedonia. Eur Sci J 12(22):1857–7881. https://eujournal.org/index.php/esj/article/view/7941

Lažetić G, Misoski B, Ilikj Dimovski D (2021) Guilty plea and sentence bargaining procedure, titled: the effectiveness of the adversarial system of criminal procedure in term of delayed justice and use of plea bargaining in North Macedonia, performed in 2020 with the grant from the US Embassy in Skopje. Microsoft Word - Анализа за спогодување (maclc.mk) (21/5/2024)

Matovski N, Bužarovska G, Kalajdziev G (2011) Criminal procedural law. Second amended and supplemented edition, Akademik, Skopje

Misoski B, Avramovski D, Petrovska N (2018) Analysis of the data collected from the court proceeding monitored in 2017. Coalition all for fair trials, Skopje

Misoski B, Avramovski D, Petrovska N (2019) Analysis of the data collected from the court proceeding monitored in 2018. Coalition all for fair trials, Skopje

Misoski B, Avramovski D, Petrovska N (2020) Analysis of the data collected from the court proceeding monitored in 2017. Coalition all for fair trials, Skopje

Petrovska N, Amet S, Hadji Zafirov Z (2020) Effective criminal justice: analysis of cases from SPO, FIOOM. https://all4fairtrials.org.mk/wp-content/uploads/2020/04/BP-TA2020-FK-MKD.pdf

Sprack J (2005) A practical approach to criminal procedure, 10th edn. Oxford University Press, Oxford

Tupanceski N, Deanoska Trendafilova A (2017) One year since the application of the Law on determining the type and measuring the amount of the penalty– problems and challenges, MRKPK 24(1). http://maclc.mk/Upload/Documents/Tupanceski,%20Deanoska.pdf

FSC
www.fsc.org
MIX
Papier aus verantwortungsvollen Quellen
Paper from responsible sources
FSC® C105338

If you have any concerns about our products, you can contact us on
ProductSafety@springernature.com

In case Publisher is established outside the EU, the EU authorized representative is:
Springer Nature Customer Service Center GmbH
Europaplatz 3, 69115 Heidelberg, Germany

Printed by Libri Plureos GmbH
in Hamburg, Germany